THE OFFICIAL® PRICE GUIDE TO DEPRESSION GLASS

**FROM THE EDITORS OF
THE HOUSE OF COLLECTIBLES**

SECOND EDITION

THE HOUSE OF COLLECTIBLES
NEW YORK, NEW YORK 10022

© 1986 The House of Collectibles

All rights reserved under International and
Pan-American Copyright Conventions.

Published by: The House of Collectibles
201 East 50th Street
New York, New York 10022

Distributed by Ballantine Books, a division of Random House, Inc., New York and simultaneously in Canada by Random House of Canada Limited, Toronto.

Manufactured in the United States of America

Library of Congress Catalog Card Number: 86-641371

ISBN: 0–87637–001–6

10 9 8 7 6 5 4 3 2 1

TABLE OF CONTENTS

ACKNOWLEDGMENTS

The House of Collectibles would like to thank the following persons for their invaluable assistance in the preparation of this book: Barbara Wolf of Anchor Hocking Corporation, Lancaster, OH 43132, who supplied the original Hocking and Anchor Hocking materials found reprinted throughout the book; Millie and Bill Downey of Millie's Glass and China Shop, Orlando, FL 32801; and The Central Florida Depression Era Glass Club, Altamonte Springs, FL 32701.

NOTE TO READERS

MARKET REVIEW

Collecting Depression glass is a little bit like going back to school. The days are gone when collectors simply admired their glass for its beauty or for its usefulness. People are now recognizing that Depression glass is a little piece of American history and we all know what goes with history. Studying.

Now more than ever, it's almost necessary for the successful collector to do his or her homework. The leading collectors and dealers do extensive research. They read old trade journals; they visit the various glassware manufacturer's "morgues;" they research old publications for glass advertisements; they interview past and present glassware company employees; and most of all, they maintain a network of contacts that help them keep their finger on the pulse of Depression glass collecting. Of course, not everyone can or wants to be a leading collector, but there is no doubt that understanding Depression era glassware collecting for what it is, a dynamic, changing hobby with a detailed, often unknown past, only adds to one's appreciation of the entire field.

Depression glass, like every collectible, has its "stars." Certain patterns like Miss America, Cameo and Hocking's Mayfair are certainly good examples of what a star pattern is. They are in constant demand and always attract a lot of attention at shows and at shops. Prices on these patterns are always on the rise. For example, a Cameo butter dish in yellow can now be expected to bring anywhere from $700.00 to $1,000.00 and quite possibly even more. That's a considerable jump from even just a few years ago. The price rises will not always be dramatic on star patterns however. Sometimes these patterns are more like blue-chip stocks. They make slow, steady and dependable gains. More often than not, they are good investments.

Other patterns that always do well are Parrot, American Sweetheart, English Hobnail, and Dogwood. Fire-King dinner and kitchenware is also doing well as is Manhattan, a relative newcomer to the upper ranks of collecting, and yet is making quite a name for itself recently.

Some patterns that used to do very well have suffered lately due to reproductions. Indiana's Sandwich is the most dramatic example. Collectors are really staying away from it, especially in crystal, since the new pieces are virtually identical to the old. Cherry Blossom has also been damaged by reproductions, but not as severely. Prices have dropped a bit, but there is still hope of recovery. In Sandwich, there is very little hope.

Reproductions are also a topic of serious concern in elegant patterns. Several original Cambridge molds, most notably Caprice, have found their way onto the open market. Summit Art Glass of Ohio is making some pieces of Cambridge and these will be identical to the originals. Several of the original Candlewick molds are also up for grabs. Viking Glass is making some pieces for Mirror Image of Lansing, Michigan, but as of now will only be producing colored pieces. Crystal remains safe for the time being.

Of course, the big news in preventing reproductions is the Heisey Collectors of America (HCA). They raised $229,150.00 to buy all the original Heisey molds from Lancaster Colony. The HCA took the initiative and now Heisey collectors can reap the benefits. They can collect their glass in the future undisturbed by reproductions.

Elegant patterns is a steady market. Year to year, the same patterns perform well. Heisey and Cambridge have been good investments for years and continue to do well (despite the Cambridge reproductions). There isn't one elegant pattern without a devoted following and continued growth can be expected. Fostoria is doing particularly well lately so one can expect some big price jumps there.

Elsewhere in Depression glass, children's sets are a small but growing hobby. Again, it's difficult to say what manufacturers or what patterns are out-performing the others, but it is possible to say that more and more collectors are entering this field. Children's dishes are at the point that Depression adult sets were at in the early 1970s. They're at shows and they have their following, but it's still a field in its infancy. Whether it will grow or not is up to you, the collectors, but it would seem to be a safe assumption that it's an area on the rise.

All in all, the economic woes of the late 1970s and the early 1980s slowed Depression glass' growth but didn't stop it. The collectors are too devoted for that to happen. New collectors join the ranks every day and their enthusiasm is apparent. The number of Depression glass clubs is high and growing higher. They are the backbone of the hobby. Through them, a collector can find out tremendous amounts of information. If you don't already belong to a Depression glass club, consult the club listings in this book or in *The Depression Glass Daze* and see if there's one in your area. If there is, join it. It will add to your enjoyment of the glass immeasurably. Most of all, it will help you to enjoy your fellow collectors and they're what makes this hobby tick. Happy hunting and good luck!

INTRODUCTION

In the years from 1925 through the 1940s, American glass manufacturers produced inexpensive lines of clear and colored glass dinnerware which has come to be termed as Depression glass. The new glass manufacturing technique of tank molding permitted automatic pressing and pattern etching and tooling using acid. These fancy designs not only added to the attractiveness of this dinnerware, they also served to cover up the many bubbles and flaws caused by the pressing process itself.

The scope of the glass referred to as Depression has been evolving steadily over recent years and now also includes the expensive, high quality glassware made by Cambridge, Fostoria, Hiesey and others during the Depression era and continuing through the 1950s. This glassware was sold in fine jewelry and department stores unlike traditional Depression glass which was given away as a premium at gas stations, theatres, store openings, and in boxes of breakfast cereal and laundry detergent. Old Sears, Roebuck and Company catalogs feature complete sets for $1.99.

Often in reference books you will find that Depression glass is grouped according to motif design. The earliest patterns had etched designs. Other classifications include raised, geometric, cut glass, opaque and pressed pattern. Manufacturers rarely marked the inexpensive wares with more than a pattern label. Some of the primary manufacturers of Depression glass were:

Anchor Hocking Glass Company
Belmont Tumbler Company
Cambridge Glass Company
Diamond Glass Company
Federal Glass Company
Fostoria Glass Company
Hazel Atlas Glass Company
A. H. Heisey and Company
Hocking Glass Company
Imperial Glass Company
Indiana Glass Company

Jeannette Glass Company
L. B. Smith Glass Company
Lancaster Glass Company
Liberty Works
Macbeth Evans Glass Company
McKee Glass Company
New Martinsville Glass Company
Paden City Glass Company
Tiffin Glass Company
U. S. Glass Company
Westmoreland Glass Company

While Depression glass is most often collected by pattern, this is by no means the only approach taken. For example, there are a number of people who specialize in cobalt blue glass and include pieces of Depression glass, art glass, pattern glass, Victorian colored glass, modern glass and bottles in their collections. Many Depression glass enthusiasts have broadened their interest to include kitchenware and ceramic tableware of the 1930s, 1940s and 1950s. In fact, many collectors acquire at least a few pieces of these to round out their collections.

Speaking of Depression glass collectors, you won't find a better informed group of hobbyists anywhere in the collecting world. They are extremely well organized due to the network of dynamic local Depression glass clubs which are found all over the country. It is these local clubs which sponsor the shows and sales which are the very core of the Depression glass world. At these shows a much wider variety of glassware is made available to collectors providing them with access to pieces they might not be able to find in local shops. As a result, prices of Depression glass tend to be more specific and uniform throughout the country. Of course, regional differences in supply and demand do occur, but they have been minimized by mail order dealers who advertise in collector publications like *The Depression Glass Daze*. These classified ads provide collectors with the opportunity to acquire pieces which may be unavailable in their particular area. It is this harmonious blend of shows and mail order business which is undoubtedly responsible for stabilizing prices throughout the country.

We have previously stated that Depression glass collectors are a very knowledgeable, well informed group. They have been educated to a large extent by Hazel Marie Weatherman, Gene Florence and Nora Koch, who is editor of *The Depression Glass Daze*.

The contribution of Hazel Marie Weatherman cannot be overstated. Ms. Weatherman has painstakingly researched Depression glass and is considered to be the foremost authority in the field. It is largely through her efforts that documentation of companies, patterns, colors, and pieces produced has been achieved. Her many books on the subject of Depression glass are listed in the bibliography of this book.

Former teacher Gene Florence of Lexington, Kentucky, is an author and dealer who devotes most of his time to researching and writing Depression glass books. He is perhaps best known for *The Collector's Encyclopedia of Depression Glass* now in its seventh edition. Mr. Florence has also written books on Akro Agate, occupied Japan, Depression era kitchenware, and elegant patterns of the Depression era. His books are listed in the bibliography found in the back of this book.

The Depression glass collector is fortunate indeed because one of the finest of all collector publications is devoted to depression glass. This publication is, of course, *The Depression Glass Daze*, known to its subscribers simply as *The Daze*. It is an indispensable source of information on every aspect of Depression glass and dinnerware. Informative articles, old catalog reprints, club news, reproduction alerts—in short, everything of interest pertaining to Depression glass is covered in detail. The driving force behind *The Daze* is its editor, Nora Koch, who has imprinted this publication with her inimitable warmth and enthusiasm. Of special interest are the classified ads where readers may buy and sell Depression era glass and dinnerware with confidence.

BUYING AND SELLING

In order to buy successfully, you must develop a certain instinct for Depression glass. To acquire this instinct you must study the glass first-hand. There simply is no substitute for seeing Depression glass in person. When viewing it, ask yourself the following questions. Are the colors of the glass true to the pattern? Are there small bubbles and impurities in the glass? Is the surface etching or relief worn with age and are there scratches caused by the use of utensils? Remember that this glass was used every day and should show the normal signs of wear. Does the pattern look too sharp and new? Reissues and reproductions are the main pitfalls in Depression glass. Only a firm knowledge of true Depression glass can help you avoid mistakes.

In addition to seeing as many good specimens of glass as possible, subscribe to periodicals and newspapers on Depression glass. Many of these publications exist for today's glass collector and they are listed in the bibliography of this book. Publications like *The Depression Glass Daze* provide tremendous help to beginning collectors as well as to the more advanced hobbyist. Not only do they contain informative articles and news of glass shows and sales, they usually have an extensive ad section for both buying and selling purposes. Reading the ads will also give you a good idea of the general availability of any particular pattern and piece. This is very helpful since certain patterns are more plentiful in some parts of the country than they might be in others.

Shopping by mail provides you with the opportunity to acquire pieces which may be difficult to find in your immediate area and therefore more expensive when they do appear on the local market. The ads are taken out by reputable sellers with most dealers offering a ten day return privilege. They will often provide complete lists of their inventory if you send them a SASE (self-addressed stamped envelope). Prices are quoted per piece and postage, insurance and handling are extra.

If you are looking for a special piece and have had no success in locating it, you can place an ad stating that you want to purchase that particular item. Response to the "want" ads is generally excellent and the chances are good that you will find the piece you are looking for.

When selling your glass to a dealer you will be offered 40–70% of the retail price depending on many factors. These include condition, popularity of pattern and color, whether it's highly sought by collectors and how much of this particular pattern he has in inventory. Basically, supply and demand will determine the offer.

RARITIES

In this chapter you will find a listing of particularly valuable and expensive pieces of Depression glass. Keep your eyes open for these items at garage sales, flea markets and thrift shops. Most people would never dream that Depression glass could be worth hundreds of dollars and therefore it is possible that you could stumble onto the buy of the century.

Basically, covered butter dishes, salt and pepper sets, pitchers, lamps and covered cookie jars command high prices across the board. Also, certain colors are rare in various patterns. **A word of caution:** Reproductions abound so make sure the glassware is an authentic Depression era piece before you buy it.

Adam

Covered butter dish which has both Adam and Sierra pattern on cover, pink	460.00
Covered butter dish, green	217.50

American Pioneer

Pitcher, 5", green	127.50
Pitcher, 7", crystal	115.00
Pitcher, 7", green	150.00

American Sweetheart

Lampshade, monax	430.00
Plate, 15½", monax	155.00
Pitcher, 60 oz., pink	370.00
Pitcher, 80 oz., pink	350.00
Footed salt and pepper, pink	240.00
Footed salt and pepper, monax	215.00
Covered sugar, monax	150.00
Three tier tidbit, monax	150.00
Bowl, 18", red	630.00
Bowl, 18", blue	700.00
Lampshade, cremax	425.00
Lamp, floor, cremax	600.00
Plate, 12", red	130.00
Plate, 12", blue	155.00

Plate, 15½", red... 230.00
Plate, 15½", blue 290.00
Three tier tidbit, red.. 430.00
Three tier tidbit, blue 550.00

Aunt Polly
Covered butter, green/irridescent......................... 190.00
Covered butter, blue... 150.00
Pitcher, 48 oz., blue 120.00
Salt and pepper, blue 150.00

Avocado #601
Pitcher, 64 oz., pink 300.00
Pitcher, 64 oz., green 500.00
Tumbler, pink 75.00
Tumbler, green.. 100.00

Beaded Block
Pint, crystal, pink, amber, green.......................... 125.00

Block Optic
Vase, 5¾", green... 130.00
Covered butter, blue... 130.00

Butterflies and Roses
Flower Garden with Butterflies, ashtray, all colors ... 160.00
Candy dish, heart, all colors 275.00
Vase, 10", all colors.. 120.00

Cameo
Covered butter, green.. 135.00
Covered butter, yellow 630.00
Bowl, 8¼", pink 110.00
Covered candy jar, 4", pink.................................. 360.00
Cocktail shaker with lid, crystal 350.00
Decanter with stopper, crystal 150.00
Domino sugar cube tray, pink 150.00
Wine goblet, 3½", green 150.00
Wine goblet, 4", pink.. 180.00
Water goblet, 6", pink... 115.00
Ice tub, pink.. 400.00
Ice tub, crystal.. 180.00
Covered jam jar, crystal 100.00
Pitcher, 20 oz. 5¾", green.................................... 140.00
Pitcher, 20 oz., 5¾", yellow 180.00
Pitcher, 56 oz., 8½", crystal................................. 230.00
Footed salt and pepper, pink 500.00
Sandwich server, center handle, green.................. 1400.00
Tumbler, 15 oz., 6⅜", footed, green..................... 155.00

Cherry Blossom
Bowl, 9" with handles, jadite................................ 280.00
Bowl, 10½", tri-footed, jadite 280.00
Mug, pink 145.00
Mug, green 140.00

Platter, 9″, oval, pink... 630.00
Salt and pepper, scalloped edge on base, pink....... 950.00
Salt and pepper, scalloped edge on base, green..... 675.00
Bowl, 8½″, yellow.. 360.00
Bowl, 8½″, red... 380.00
Plate, 9″, green 180.00
Plate, 9″, red 180.00

Cloverleaf
Covered candy dish, yellow 175.00

Colonial
Mug, 4½″, pink.. 150.00
Mug, 4½″, green.. 625.00
Salt and pepper, pink 110.00
Salt and pepper, green 115.00

Coronation
Pitcher, 7¾″, pink 130.00

Cube
Pitcher, 8¾″, pink 140.00
Pitcher, 8¾″, green 150.00

Dogwood
Bowl, 10¼″, pink.. 180.00
Bowl, 10¼″, green.. 100.00
Cake plate, 11″, pink.. 160.00
Cake plate, 13″, monax and cremax 130.00
Pitcher, 8″, decorated, pink 130.00
Pitcher, 8″, decorated, green................................. 460.00
Pitcher, 8″, American Sweetheart style, pink 475.00
Platter, 12″, oval, pink 250.00

Doric
Soup bowl, 5″, green... 130.00
Pitcher, 6″, no base, delphite................................. 380.00
Pitcher, 7½″, footed, pink...................................... 260.00
Pitcher, 7½″, footed, green.................................... 460.00
Pitcher, 7½″, footed, yellow 775.00

Doric and Pansy
Covered butter dish, green, teal 650.00
Creamer, green (ultramarine), teal 170.00
Salt and pepper, green (ultramarine), teal 400.00

English Hobnail
Lamp, base, all colors... 120.00
Lampshade, clear 120.00
Pitcher, all colors, all four sizes . . . depending on
size.. 120.00–160.00

Fire-King Philbe
Covered candy jar, pink, green............................... 130.00
Covered candy jar, blue 160.00
Covered cookie jar, crystal 110.00
Covered cookie jar, pink, green.............................. 210.00

Covered cookie jar, blue......................................	360.00
Pitcher, 6″, crystal	150.00
Pitcher, 6″, pink, green.......................................	300.00
Pitcher, 6″, blue	460.00
Pitcher, 8½″, crystal	260.00
Pitcher, 8½″, pink, green.....................................	360.00
Pitcher, 8½″, blue	500.00

Floral

Cream soup, green...	250.00
Comport, pink..	280.00
Comport, green..	300.00
Dresser set, green..	960.00
Crystal frog for vase	600.00
Ice tub, pink..	380.00
Ice tub, green..	400.00
Hurricane lamp, pink, green.................................	120.00
Pitcher, 8″, cone shaped, footed, green.................	450.00
Pitcher, 10¼″, pink...	170.00
Pitcher, 10¼″, green...	180.00
Tumbler, 4½″, green...	160.00
Rose bowl, tri-footed, green	390.00
Vase, tri-footed, green	390.00
Vase, 6⅞″, green...	390.00

Florentine No. 1

Covered butter dish, all colors.............................	100.00–140.00
Pitcher, 6½″, footed, blue....................................	430.00
Pitcher, 7½″, pink	100.00
Pitcher, 7½″, yellow..	140.00

Florentine No. 2

Covered candy dish, pink	100.00
Covered candy dish, yellow	130.00
Pitcher, 7½″, footed, cone shaped, blue	400.00
Pitcher, 7½″, 48 oz., yellow	130.00
Pitcher, 8″, 76 oz., yellow...................................	180.00
Pitcher, 8″, 76 oz., pink	200.00

Lace Edge

Bowl, 10½″, tri-footed, clear pink	130.00
Candlestick, pair, clear pink.................................	120.00
Comport, 9″, clear pink.......................................	500.00
Vase, 7″, clear pink..	220.00

Lincoln Inn

Salt and pepper, footed, blue and red	130.00

Madrid

Ashtray, crystal, amber	130.00
Gravy boat with underliner, crystal, amber	850.00

Mayfair

Console bowl, 9″, tri-footed, pink..........................	2000.00
Covered vegetable bowl, 10″, yellow......................	230.00

Covered butter dish, 7″, green and yellow 900.00
Covered candy dish, yellow 300.00
Covered candy dish, green................................... 430.00
Celery dish, 9″, green and yellow 100.00
Covered cookie jar, blue..................................... 150.00
Covered cookie jar, green.................................... 460.00
Covered cookie jar, yellow................................... 500.00
Creamer, green 150.00
Creamer, yellow.. 150.00
Cup, green.. 130.00
Cup, yellow... 150.00
Goblet, 3¾″, pink and green 350.00
Goblet, 4″, green.. 260.00
Goblet, 4½″, green.. 260.00
Goblet, 5¼″, pink and green 380.00
Goblet, 5¾″, green.. 260.00
Goblet, 7¼″, pink... 130.00
Pitcher, 6″, green and yellow............................... 360.00
Pitcher, 8″, blue 1000.00
Pitcher, 8″, green and yellow............................... 320.00
Pitcher, 8½″, blue 130.00
Pitcher, 8½″, green and yellow.............................. 360.00
Platter, 12″, oval, open handles, green and yellow .. 120.00
Platter, 12½″, solid handles, green and yellow........ 160.00
Salt and pepper, green and yellow........................ 600.00
Salt and pepper, footed, pink 2000.00
Saucer with cup ring, green and yellow 100.00
Sherbet, footed, green and yellow......................... 130.00
Open sugar, footed, green and yellow 150.00
Covered sugar, pink, green and yellow.................. 860.00–900.00
Tumbler, 4¾″, green and yellow 160.00
Tumbler, 5¼″, footed, yellow............................... 160.00
Tumbler, 6½″, footed, green 180.00
Vase, pink and green... 125.00–150.00

Miss America
Bowl, incurved top, red 300.00
Covered butter dish, crystal 190.00
Covered butter dish, pink 375.00
Creamer, footed, red 130.00
Goblet, 3¾″, red 150.00
Goblet, 4¾″, red 150.00
Goblet 5½″, red.. 150.00
Salt and pepper, green 260.00
Sugar, red 130.00

Moondrops

Covered butter dish, blue and red.........................	360.00
Covered butter dish, all remaining colors	230.00
Pitcher, 6⅞″, blue, red..	125.00
Pitcher, 8⅛″, blue and red....................................	140.00

No. 612—Horseshoe

Covered butter dish, green	500.00
Pitcher, 8½″, green	190.00
Pitcher, 8½″, yellow...	210.00

Parrot-Sylvan

Covered butter dish, green	230.00
Covered butter dish, amber	560.00
Hot plate, green...	360.00
Pitcher, 8½″, green	750.00
Salt and pepper, green	180.00
Sherbet, 4¼″, green	130.00
Covered sugar, amber	120.00

Patrician

Covered butter dish, pink	200.00
Covered cookie jar, green...................................	275.00

Princess

Covered butter dish, topaz and amber..................	425.00
Pitcher, 6″, topaz and amber...............................	500.00
Pitcher, 7⅜″, footed, green and pink.....................	400.00
Covered cookie jar, blue.....................................	400.00

Pyramid

Ice tub, yellow	170.00
Covered ice bucket with wire bail handle, yellow.....	500.00
Pitcher, crystal and pink.....................................	150.00
Pitcher, green..	170.00
Pitcher, yellow	350.00

Rock Crystal

Covered butter dish, crystal	200.00
Centerpiece bowl, footed, red	150.00

Royal Lace

Covered butter dish, green	230.00
Covered butter dish, blue	360.00
Covered cookie jar, blue.....................................	220.00
Salt and pepper, green	115.00
Salt and pepper, blue	200.00

Sandwich–Hocking

Ice pitcher with lip, green	170.00

Sandwich–Indiana

Covered butter dish, pink and green	160.00
Covered butter dish, ultramarine...........................	200.00
Cruet with stopper, ultramarine	130.00

Sharon

Covered cheese dish, amber................................	160.00

Covered cheese dish, pink **600.00**

Strawberry

Covered butter dish, pink and green **130.00**

Pitcher, 7¾", pink and green **140.00**

Pitcher, 7¾", crystal and irridescent...................... **150.00**

Sunflower

Trivet, tri-footed, pink and green........................... **115.00**

Swirl

Covered butter dish, pink **135.00**

Covered butter dish, ultramarine........................... **200.00**

Pitcher, 48 oz., footed, ultramarine **775.00**

Tea Room

Pitcher, 64 oz., footed, amber **250.00**

Thistle

Bowl, 10¼", green.. **105.00**

Bowl, 10¼", pink.. **160.00**

Waterford

Covered butter dish, pink **180.00**

PERIODICALS

Depression Glass Daze, P.O. Box 57, Otisville, MI 48463. A monthly newspaper with articles and ads.

The Glass Collector, P.O. Box 27037, Columbus, OH 43227. A quarterly magazine on late 19th century and 20th century American glassware.

Glass Review, P.O. Box 542, Marietta, OH 45750. A monthly magazine on 20th century glassware with articles, pictures, and ads.

Heisey Glass Newscaster, P.O. Box 102, Plymouth, OH 44865. A quarterly pamphlet on identification and research.

The Paden City Partyline, 13325 Danvers Way, Westminster, CA 92683. A quarterly newsletter about Paden glass on new discoveries and pricing.

CLUB DIRECTORY

The following directory lists local and national glass clubs and organizations. Complete information is included for clubs that were contacted. We were unable to contact those organizations that have only club name and city listed. To have your club included in future editions, please send pertinent information to Depression Glass editor, House of Collectibles, 1904 Premier Row, Orlando, FL 32809.

For further club information, refer to the club news sections of *Depression Glass Daze.*

ALABAMA

City: Fairhope
Name: **Dixie Land Depression Glass Society**

City: Phil Campbell
Name: **Bama Depression Glass Club**
Meeting Time and Place:
2nd Monday, 6 p.m., Northwest Alabama Junior College, SGA Conference Room
Information:
Uni and Keith Marbutt
Rt. 2, Box 167B
Phil Campbell, AL 35581
(205) 993–4397

ARKANSAS

City: Little Rock
Name: **Arkansas Travelers Depression Glass Club**

City: Weiner
Name: **Northeast Arkansas Antique and Depression Glass Club**

ARIZONA

City: Laveen
Name: **Arizona Depression Glass Club**

City: Tucson
Name: **Thunderbird Depression Glass Club**
Meeting Time and Place:
1st Tuesday, 7:30 p.m.
Information:
Mary Bucy
(602) 296–2676
Mary Chatto
(602) 296–4255

CALIFORNIA

City: Bakersfield
Name: **Glass & China Collectors**

City: Humboldt
Name: **Humboldt Area Glass Society**

City: Huntington Beach
Name: **Huntington Beach Depression Glass Club**
Meeting Time and Place:
3rd Wednesday, held at members' homes
Information:
G. Finley
(714) 846–3792

City: Lodi
Name: **Northern California Carnival Glass Club**
Information:
630 North Lower Sacramento Road
Lodi, CA 95240

City: Long Beach
Name: **California Cambridge Collectors**
Information: (213) 433–8437

City: Montclair
Name: **The Montclair Depression Glass Club**

City: Oxnard
Name: **Glass of the Past—Ventura County**

City: Riverside
Name: **Depression Heirz**

City: Sacramento
Name: **International Depression Glass Club**
Meeting Time and Place:
2737 Wissemann Drive
Sacramento, California 95826

City: San Diego
Name: **Greater San Diego Depression Glass Club**

City: San Francisco
Name: **Bay Area Glass Society San Francisco to San Jose**

City: San Jose
Name: **Depression Obsession Glass Society**

City: Torrance
Name: **South Bay Depression Glass Society**

COLORADO

City: Colorado Springs
Name: **Pikes Peak Depression Glass Club**
Meeting Time and Place:
3rd Thursday, 7:30 p.m., Otero Savings and Loan, Highway 115 and Cheyenne Mountain Blvd.
Information:
M. Speirs
814 Clinton Way
Colorado Springs, CO 80907
(303) 473-6368

City: Denver
Name: **Rocky Mountain Depression Glass Society**
Meeting Time and Place:
3rd Tuesday, 7:30 p.m., Brighton Savings & Loan Hospitality Room, Commerce City
Information:
11902 E. Louisiana Ave.
Aurora, CO 80012

City: Springfield
Name: **Yesteryears Glass Collectors**
Meeting Time and Place:
2nd Tuesday, 7:30 p.m.
Information:
N. McElroy
632 W. 8th
Springfield, CO 81073

CONNECTICUT

City: Hartford
Name: **Charter Oak Depression Glass Club—Southeast CT**

City: Southington
Name: **Nutmeg Depression Glass Club of Connecticut, Inc.**
Meeting Time and Place:
3rd Tuesday, September through June, Masonic Hall, Southington, CT
Information:
Tony Bosse, President
230 Hillside Avenue
Naugatuck, CT 06770
(203) 723-2298

FLORIDA

City: Altamonte Springs
Name: **Central Florida Depression Era Glass Club**
Meeting Time and Place:
1st Thursday, 8 p.m., Altamonte Community Chapel, Highway 436
Information:
Millie Downey
5805 Luzon Plc.
Orlando, Fl. 32809

City: Boca Raton
Name: **South Florida Depression Glass Club**

City: Bradenton
Name: **Depression Era Glass & Collectables**
Meeting Time and Place:
1st Tuesday, 7:30 p.m., Florida Power Community Service Room
819 U. S. Highway 301 Blvd. W.
Information:
Lois V. Busick
1801 28th St. W.
Bradenton, FL 33505
(813) 748-5319

City: Clearwater
Name: **Sparkling Clearwater Depression Glass Club**
Meeting Time and Place:
  3rd Monday, 7:30 p.m.,
  Clearwater YWCA Building
  222 S. Lincoln
Information:
  Barbara Flowers
  2444 Timbercrest Circle W.
  Clearwater, FL 33575
  (813) 796–5496

City: Hollywood
Name: **South Florida Depression Glass Club**
Meeting Time and Place:
  2nd Thursday, 7:30 p.m.,
  Hollywood Art and Culture
  Center, 1301 S. Ocean Dr.,
  Hollywood, FL
Information:
  Mrs. Sally Stanton
  (305) 987–7225

City: Jacksonville
Name: **Depression Glass of Northeast Florida**
Meeting Time and Place:
  1745 Flagler Avenue,
  Apartment #1
  Jacksonville, FL 32207

City: Lakeland
Name: **Central Florida Glassaholics**
Meeting Time and Place:
  2nd Monday, 8:00 p.m.,
  Tuesday Music Club
  421 E. Park Street
  Lakeland, FL
Information:
  Joann Graham
  (813) 646–4028

City: Miami
Name: **South Florida Depression Glass Club**

City: Ocala
Name: **Rainbow Glass Collectors Club**

Meeting Time and Place:
  4th Tuesday, 7:30 p.m.
Information:
  A. Tomyn
  (904) 622–3781

City: Pensacola
Name: **City of Five Flags Depression Glass Club**

City: St. Augustine
Name: **Ancient City Glass Collectors**

GEORGIA

City: Athens
Name: **National Candlewick Collectors' Club**

City: Augusta
Name: **CSRA Depression Glass Club**

City: Marietta
Name: **Peach State Depression Glass Club**
Meeting Time and Place:
  East Marietta Library,
  Lower Roswell Road
Information:
  Jimmy McRae
  (404)753–2861
  Nancy Roemer
  (404) 943–6585

ILLINOIS

City: Chicago
Name: **Land of Lincoln Carnival Glass Association**
Information:
  5113 North Nordica
  Chicago, IL 60656

City: Danville
Name: **Kickapoo Valley Depression Glass Club**
Meeting Time and Place:
  2nd Thursday in members'
  homes

Information:
  J. Guymon
  1508 East English St.
  Danville, IL 61832

City: LaGrange
Name: **20-30-40 Society, Inc.**
  Chicagoland

City: Rushville
Name: **Rushville II**

City: Springfield
Name: **Lincolnland**

City: West Central
Name: **Forgottonia Depression**
  Glass Club
Meeting Time and Place:
  1st Thursday, 7:30 p.m.
Information:
  Don Irwin
  1056 N. Scrafford Blvd.
  Bushnell, IL 61422
  (309) 772-2543

INDIANA

City: Indianapolis
Name: **Mid-America Reamer**
  Collectors

City: Kokomo
Name: **National Greentown Glass**
  Association
Information:
  1807 West Madison
  Kokomo, IN 46901

City: Mentone
Name: **International Carnival Glass**
  Association
Information:
  R.R. #1
  Mentone, IN 46539

KANSAS

City: Manhattan
Name: **Heart of America Carnival**
  Glass Association
Information:
  3048 Tamarak Dr.
  Manhattan, KS 66502

City: Shawnee Mission
Name: **National Depression Glass**
  Association, Inc.
Information:
  8337 Santa Fe Lane
  Shawnee Mission, KS 66212

City: Wichita
Name: **Glass Gazers**
Meeting Time and Place:
  4th Thursday, 7:30 p.m.,
  members' homes
Information:
  T. E. Smith
  (316) 685-1620

LOUISIANA

City: Baton Rouge
Name: **Red Stick Depression**
  Glass Society

City: Metairie
Name: **Crescent City Depression**
  Glass Society

City: Shreveport
Name: **American Cut Glass**
  Association
Information:
  P.O. Box 7095
  Shreveport, LA 71107

MARYLAND

City: Bethesda
Name: **DEL-MAR-VA Club**
Meeting Time and Place:
  7420 Westlake Terrace
  Bethesda, MD 20034

City: Bethesda
Name: **Potomac Depression Era**
  Glass Club
Meeting Time and Place:
  3rd Thursday, 8 p.m.
Information:
  Susan Gordon
  2628 Cory Terrace
  Wheaton, MD 20902
  (301) 942-0639

City: Clinton
Name: **Pairpoint Cup Plate Collectors of America, Inc.**
Information:
9308 Brandywine Road
Clinton, MD 20735

City: Forestville
Name: **Del-Mar-Va Depression Glass Club, Inc.**
Meeting Time and Place:
2nd Tuesday, Marlow Heights
Recreation Center, St. Clair Dr.,
Marlow Heights, MD
Information:
Charles W. Smith
P.O. Box 47125
Forestville, MD 20747
(301) 568-8570

City: Oxon Hill
Name: **National Capital Duncan Glass Club**

City: Silver Spring
Name: **Imperial Glass Collector's Society**
Information:
P.O. Box 4012
Silver Spring, MD 20904

City: Westminister, Hampstead, Reisterstown
Name: **Old Line Depression Glass Club**
Meeting Time and Place:
3rd Wednesday, members'
homes
Information:
(301) 833-8822

MASSACHUSETTS

City: Boston
Name: **The National Early American Glass Club**
Information:
S. Pope
9 Commonwealth Ave., Apt. 4A
Boston, MA 02116

City: Georgetown
Name: **Yankee Dee Gee'ers**

City: Ipswich
Name: **Bay Colony Glass Association**

City: New Bedford
Name: **New Bedford Glass Society**
Information:
P.O. Box F655
65 N. Second Street
New Bedford, MA 02740

MICHIGAN

City: Charlotte
Name: **Eaton Co. Depression Glass Society**

City: Dearborn
Name: **Henry Ford Museum Glass Collectors**

City: Dearborn
Name: **Michigan Depression Glass Society**

City: Dowaglac
Name: **Monday Night Depression Glass Club of South Michigan and North Indiana**

City: Grand Rapids
Name: **Glass Grabbers of West Michigan**

City: Livonia
Name: **Michigan D.G. Society**

City: Rochester
Name: **Great Lakes Depression Glass Club—S.E. Michigan**
Meeting Time and Place:
4th Thursday, 7 p.m.,
September–June
Rochester Community Center
816 Ludlowe Ave.,
Rochester, MI
Information:
J. Saeger
1740 Westwood
Troy, MI 48083
(313) 689-1697

City: Sawyer
Name: **The National Toothpick
Holder Collector's Society**
Information:
Membership Chairman
P.O. Box 246-G
Sawyer, MI 49125

MINNESOTA

City: Minneapolis
Name: **Go-Fer Glass Club**

MISSOURI

City: Gladstone
Name: **Happy Rock Pottery &
Glass Circle**
Meeting Time and Place:
Four-five times per year,
members' homes
Information:
Helen Brink
2210 N. Pursell Rd.
Gladstone, MO 64118
or
June Vandiver
6100 N. Wyandotte
Gladstone, MO 64118

City: Kansas City
Name: **American Custard Glass
Collectors**
Information:
P.O. Box 5421
Kansas City, MO 64131

City: Lee's Summit
Name: **Heart of America Glass
Collectors**
Meeting Time and Place:
721 Cambridge Drive
Lee's Summit, MO 64063

City: Kansas City
Name: **Kansas City Depression
Glass Club**

City: St. Louis
Name: **Gateway Depressioneers
Glass Club of Greater St. Louis**
Meeting Time and Place:
1st Monday, Farm & Home

Savings Community Room
11710 Manchester
Information:
Mark Graham
833 Town House Lane
Hazelwood, MO 63042
(314) 895-4255

City: St. Louis
Name: **Stained Glass Association
of America**
Information:
1125 Wilmington Avenue
St. Louis, MO 63111

NEW HAMPSHIRE

City: Salem
Name: **Akro Agate Art Association**

NEW JERSEY

City: Brick Town
Name: **Central Jersey Depression
Glass Club**

City: Butler
Name: **North Jersey D.G.'rs**

City: Point Pleasant
Name: **Central Jersey Depression
Glass Club**
Meeting Time and Place:
301 Maxon Avenue
Point Pleasant, NJ 08742

City: Toms River
Name: **Depression Era Collectors
of Northern Ocean County**

City: Woodbridge
Name: **Garden State Depression
Glass Club**
Meeting Time and Place:
1st Tuesday, 7:30 p.m.,
September-June, Woodbridge
Main Library
Information:
Dorothy Boeddinghaus
54 Roosevelt Blvd.
Edison, NJ 08837
(201) 225-9127

NEW YORK

City: East Islip
Name: **Long Island Depression Glass Society**

City: Elmhurst
Name: **New York, New York Depression Glass & Pottery Club**
Meeting Time and Place:
2nd Tuesday, Italian Charities of America, 83–20 Queens Blvd.
Information:
Georgiana Sanders
(212) 632–8597

City: New Hartford
Name: **Mohawk Valley Glass Club**

City: New York
Name: **The Big Apple Depression Glass Club**
Meeting Time and Place:
2nd Tuesday, 8 p.m.
St. Margaret of Scotland
58–30 193 St.
Fresh Meadows, NY
Information:
Anna Ferrera
4804 28th Ave.
Astonia, NY 11103
(212) 278–6005

City: Rochester
Name: **D.G. Club of Greater Rochester**

City: Syracuse
Name: **Upstate D.G. Club– Syracuse, NY**

City: Walden
Name: **Hudson Valley Depression Glass Club**

City: West Sayville
Name: **Long Island Depression Glass Society Ltd.**
Meeting Time and Place:
P.O. Box 119
West Sayville, NY 11796

NORTH CAROLINA

City: Durham
Name: **Tar Heel Depression Glass Club**

City: Charleston
Name: **Depression Glass Grabbers of Historic Charleston**
Meeting Time and Place:
Rte. 6, Box 529H
Summerville, NC 29483

OHIO

City: Cambridge
Name: **National Cambridge Collectors, Inc.**
Information:
P.O. Box 416
Cambridge, OH 43725

City: Cincinnati
Name: **Greater Cincinnati DG/CP Club**

City: Eastlake
Name: **Classic Glass Collectors of N.E. Ohio**
Meeting Time and Place:
3rd Tuesday, 7:30 p.m.
Reformation Lutheran Church
34730 Lakeshore Blvd., Eastlake
Information:
Virginia T. Houston
107 Keewaydin Dr.
Timberlake, OH 44094
(216) 946–0179

City: Findley
Name: **Hazelnut D.G. Club**

City: Gnadenhutten
Name: **American Carnival Glass Association**
Information:
P.O. Box 273
Gnadenhutten, OH 44629

City: Newark
Name: **Heisey Collectors of America, Inc.**

Information:
P.O. Box 27
Newark, OH 43055

City: Orwell
Name: **Ohio Candlewick Collectors Club**
Meeting Time and Place:
Spring and fall, members'
homes
Information:
Jean Fry
613 S. Patterson St.
Gibsonburg, OH 43431

City: Parma
Name: **Western Reserve Depression Glass Club**

City: Perrysburg
Name: **Fenton Finders—Toledo Area**
Meeting Time and Place:
2nd Tuesday, 7:30 p.m., Troy
Villa Mobile Home Court
Recreation Building, Rt. 280 &
Truman
Information:
Bernadine Ditman
24861 State Route 51
Millbury, OH 43447
(419) 836-1905

City: Sandusky
Name: **Buckeye Dee Gee'ers**

City: Toledo
Name: **Antique and Historical Glass Foundation**
Information:
P.O. Box 7413
Toledo, OH 43615

City: Toledo
Name: **Glass Art Society**
Information:
Tom McGlauchlin
Toledo Museum of Art
Toledo, OH 43609

City: Toledo
Name: **Glass Collectors Club of Toledo**

Meeting Time and Place:
3rd Tuesday, 7:30 p.m.,
September–November;
January–May
Information:
Bonnie Taylor
2235 St. Charles
Toledo, OH 43615
or
Warren Rayman
6855 Queen Anne's Ct.
Toledo, OH 43615

City: Toledo
Name: **Toledo Glass Society**

OKLAHOMA

City: Oklahoma City
Name: **Oklahoma Depression Era Club**

OREGON

City: Eugene
Name: **Eugene Depression Possession Club**

City: Portland
Name: **Portland's Rain of Glass**
Meeting Time and Place:
3rd Tuesday
Information:
W. Dussenberry
28035 S.W. Parkway #227
Wilsonville, OR 97070
(503) 682-1932

City: Santa Clara
Name: **Eugene Depression Era Collectors**
Meeting Time and Place:
2nd Tuesday, 7:30 p.m., Civic
Center, 2615 River Road,
Santa Clara
Information:
N. Dowell
4241 Royal Ave.
Eugene, OR 97402
(503) 689-4931

City: Talent
Name: **Rogue Valley Depression Era Study Club**

PENNSYLVANIA

City: Berwick
Name: **Fly By Night Depression Glass Club of PA**

City: Blakeslee
Name: **Pocono Mountain Depression Glass Club**

City: Indiana
Name: **Rainbow Diamond Glass Club**
Meeting Time and Place:
3rd Wednesday, 7 p.m., Eagles Club, 420 Philadelphia St.
Information:
Ralph Greene
105 Bradley Court
Indiana, PA 15701

City: Philadelphia
Name: **Liberty Bell Depression Glass Club**

City: Pittsburgh
Name: **Three Rivers Depression Era Glass Society**
Meeting Time and Place:
1st Monday, Tonidale Restaurant, Rt. 22 & 30 exit of Parkway West.
Information:
A. Palcic
R.D. #1, Box 287
Bentleyville, PA 15314

City: Washington
Name: **The National Duncan Glass Society**
Information:
P.O. Box 965
Washington, PA 15301

SOUTH CAROLINA

City: Charleston
Name: **Depression Glass Grabbers of Historic Charleston**

City: Easley
Name: **Carolina Depression Glass Club**

City: Greenville
Name: **Sandlapper Depression Glass Club**
Meeting Time and Place:
3rd Tuesday, First Citizens Bank, Wade-Hampton Blvd.
Information:
S. Gray
503 Leyswood Dr.
Greenville, SC 29615
(803) 244-0152

TEXAS

City: Dallas–Ft. Worth
Name: **Metroplex Glass Club— Dallas–Ft. Worth Area**

City: Houston
Name: **Gulf Coast Depression Glass Society**
Meeting Time and Place:
2nd Tuesday, 7:30 p.m., High School for Law Enforcement and Criminal Justice, 4701 Dickson
Information:
L. Rippert
(713) 495-0189
or Carol (713) 664-6500

City: Lubbock
Name: **Top of Texas Depression Era Glass Club**

City: Odessa
Name: **Permian Basin Depression Glass Club**
Meeting Time and Place:
3rd Tuesday, 7:30 p.m., St. Luke's United Methodist Church parlor, 1601 East 42 St.
Information:
Charles or Patsy Terrell
708 Adams Ave.
Odessa, TX 79761
(915) 366-2722 or 332-0851

VIRGINIA

City: Charlottesville
Name: **Paperweight Collectors Association**

City: Chesapeake
Name: **Tidewater Depression Glass Club**
Meeting Time and Place:
 1st Thursday, 7:30 p.m.,
 Pembroke Recreation Center
Information:
 D. Finch
 (804) 547-2451

City: Fairfax
Name: **Old Dominion D.G. Club**

City: Hopewell
Name: **Happy Hunters Carnival Glass Club**
Information:
 B. Allen
 3316 Boston St.
 Hopewell, VA 23860

City: Lynchburg
Name: **The Seven Hills Depression Glass Club**

WASHINGTON

City: Bremerton
Name: **Yesteryear Glass and Collectible Club**

City: Graham
Name: **Green River DG Club**

City: North Bend
Name: **Pacific Northwest Carnival Glass Club**

Information:
 48900 Middle Fork Road
 North Bend, WA 98045

City: Tacoma
Name: **Evergreen Depression Era Glass Collectors**

City: Veradale
Name: **Spokane Falls DG Etc Club**

WEST VIRGINIA

City: Huntington
Name: **The Glass Club of Huntington**

City: Moundsville
Name: **Fostoria Glass Society of America, Inc.**
Information:
 P.O. Box 826
 Moundsville, WV 26041

WISCONSIN

City: Appleton
Name: **Fenton Art Glass Collectors of America, Inc.**
Information:
 P.O. Box 2441
 Appleton, WI 54911

City: Milwaukee
Name: **20-30-40 Society of Wisconsin**
Meeting Time and Place:
 2nd Sunday, 2 p.m., Equitable
 Savings and Loan, 145th St. &
 Capitol Drive
Information:
 S. McKee
 1421 A Josephine St.
 Waukesha, WI 53186

MUSEUMS

Allen Art Museum
Oberlin College, Oberlin OH

Art Institute of Chicago
Chicago, IL 60603

Bennington Museum
Bennington, VT 05201

John Nelson Bergstrom Art Center and Museum
Neenah, WI 54956

Cambridge Glass Museum, The
Cambridge, OH 43725

Carnegie Institute Museum of Art
Pittsburgh, PA 15213

Chryser Museum at Norfolk
Norfolk, VA 23510

Corning Museum of Glass and Glass Center
Corning, NY 14830

Currier Gallery of Art
Manchester, NH 03104

Degenhart Paperweight and Glass Museum, Inc.
Cambridge, OH 43725

Edison Museum
Milan, OH

Fenton Art Glass Company
Williamstown, WV 26187

Greentown Glass Museum, Inc.
Greentown, IN 46936

Henry Ford Museum
Dearborn, MI 48121

Historical Society of Western Pennsylvania
Pittsburgh, PA 15213

Jones Gallery of Glass and Ceramics
Sebago, ME 04075

Judy's Museum
Mountain View, MO

Lightner Museum
St. Augustine, FL 32084

Marathon County Historical Society
Wausa, WI 54401

Metropolitan Museum of Art
New York, NY 10028

Morse Gallery
Winter Park, FL

National Heisey Glass Museum
Newark, OH 43055

New Bedford Glass Museum
New Bedford, MA 12742

New York Historical Society
New York, NY 10024

Oglebay Institute-Mansion Museum
Wheeling, WV 26003

Old Sturbridge Village
Sturbridge, MA 01566

Philadelphia Museum of Art
Philadelphia, PA 19101

Portland Art Museum
Portland, ME

Sandwich Glass Museum
Sandwich, MA 02563

Smithsonian Institution Museum of History and Technology
Washington, D.C. 20560

Study Gallery
A Center for Glass & Ceramics
Douglas Hill, ME 04024

Toledo Museum of Art
Toledo, OH 43697

Wadsworth, Atheneum
Hartford, CT 06103

GLOSSARY

AKRO AGATE. Founded in 1911 in Akron, Ohio, this company manufactured marbles, moving to Clarksburg, West Virginia several years later. In the early 1930s they added a line of novelty items including ashtrays, planters, vases, flowerpots, and children's toy dishes. These items were made in solid and marbleized opaque glass.

AMBER. Yellowish brown color of glass.

AMETHYST. Shades of purple from very light to dark.

AOP. Abbreviation for "all over pattern."

APRICOT. Deep yellow shade.

ART GLASS. Various kinds of late 19th century American decorative glassware in the Victorian style. It was ornamental glass that was made into free-blown, pressed tableware and decorative glassware.

BERRY BOWL. Small round bowl for individual serving of fruit.

BLACK AMETHYST. Dark purple glass that almost looks black.

BLOWN-MOLDED GLASS. A method of glassmaking in which hot glass is blown through a blowpipe into a preformed metal mold. The mold was used for giving shape to a glass vessel and for impressing a design on its surface. It is easily discernible from pressed glass since the pattern is also on the inside of the piece.

BONBON. Small, uncovered candy dish.

BREAD AND BUTTER PLATE. Six-inch plate.

BRIDE'S BASKET. Glass bowls contained by silverplate frames. They were favorite wedding gifts from the 1890s to the 1920s.

CAMBRIDGE GLASS COMPANY. This Cambridge, Ohio company produced fine quality tableware from 1901 to 1954. They are best known for their fine blown and pressed glasswares which featured intricate etching and engraving. Cambridge glass was available in a full array of colors as well as crystal.

CARAFE. A bottle used for serving wine or water, carafes were especially popular late in the Victorian era.

CARNIVAL GLASS. An inexpensive glass produced after World War I and used as prizes at carnivals or fairs consisting of fruit bowls, sugar bowls, pitchers, creamers, etc. Carnival glass has molded decorations in iridescent colored glass.

CHIGGER BITE. Term used by glass dealers, collectors, auctioneers and other experts to describe small chips on glass pieces.

CHOP PLATE. Salver; large serving plate.

CHUNKED. Damaged glass in very poor condition.

CLAMBROTH. Semi-opaque grayish color.

COBALT BLUE. A dark, rich shade of blue produced by mixing cobalt and aluminum oxides.

COMPORT. Usually a small, stemmed, open shallow dish or bowl.

CONSOLE BOWL. Centerpiece bowl, often accompanied by matching candlesticks as a set.

COVERED BUTTER DISH. Round dome shaped glass cover over flat bottom glass dish. Smaller than covered cheese dish.

CREAM SOUP. Small two handled dish for soup.

CRUET. Small decanter, often handled. Two are often used together to serve oil and vinegar.

CUSTARD. A creamy or yellowish color.

CUT GLASS. Glass decorated with faceted designs. The glass was carved or ground into deep sparkling facets by revolving wheels layered with an abrasive. It enjoyed a revival during the Brilliant period of cut glass in America which dated from 1876–1916.

DISPENSERS. Glass container with a spigot for dispensing cold water from the refrigerator. Also includes the juice dispensers found in drugstore soda fountains.

DRESSER SET. Glass accessories with glass tray for a dressing table. A set includes such items as a hair receiver, puff box, glove box, hat pin holder, hairpin tray, perfume and cologne bottles.

EBONY. Black colored glass.

EPERGNE. An ornamental centerpiece for a dining table incorporating a number of small dishes around a central bowl.

FENTON ART GLASS COMPANY. Founded in Martin Ferry, Ohio, this company has been producing fine glassware since 1907. In the early years they made carnival, custard, opalescent and a variety of other pressed and molded wares. Over the years they added hobnail, stretch, slag and overlay pieces to their line. Famous for their hand decoration work, Fenton is still producing quality glassware in Williamsburg, West Virginia today.

FIESTA WARE. This colorful line of dinnerware made by Homer Laughlin was produced from 1936 to 1973 and is characterized by its bright solid colors. These include orange, green, red, yellow, tan, blue, ivory, chartreuse, dark green, navy, turquoise, cobalt and medium green.

FINGERBOWL. Fingerbowls, placed at each tablesetting, were filled with water to cleanse fingers with in between courses.

FLORENCE, GENE. This Lexington, Kentucky dealer and author is one of

America's leading experts on Depression glass and has written a number of books on the subject. These include *The Collector's Encyclopedia of Depression Glass, Kitchen Glassware of the Depression Years, The Collector's Encyclopedia of Akro Agate Glassware, Elegant Glassware of the Depression Era, The Pocket Guide to Depression Glass* and *The Collector's Encyclopedia of Occupied Japan Collectibles.*

FOSTORIA GLASS COMPANY. Founded in Fostoria, Ohio in 1887, Fostoria continues in production at their Moundsville, West Virginia factory today. Many of their lovely glassware lines are considered to be "elegant" Depression era glass and these patterns are avidly sought by collectors today.

FROG. A small, domed object made of heavy glass, a frog has holes in it to hold flowers in place in a vase.

GRILL PLATE. Plate divided into three sections by means of raised ridges.

HALL CHINA COMPANY. Founded in 1903 by Robert Hall, this company produced numerous lines of china dinnerware and kitchenware. The most famous of these patterns is Autumn Leaf which was made for the Jewel T Company and given as a premium to their customers.

HARLEQUIN. This colorful pottery dinnerware was produced from 1938 to 1964 by the Homer Laughlin Company. It is found in solid colors and features concentric rings and angular art deco styling. It was sold exclusively through Woolworth's.

HAZEL ATLAS GLASS COMPANY. This large company produced pressed wares from 1902 to 1956. Factories were located in Pennsylvania, Ohio and West Virginia.

HEISEY GLASS COMPANY. This Newark, Ohio factory produced glassware of the highest quality from 1896 to 1957. Fine crystal tableware, as well as colored glass, Ivorina Verde and opalescent pieces were a specialty. Heisey figurines are avidly collected.

HOCKING GLASS COMPANY—ANCHOR HOCKING CORPORATION. The history of Anchor Hocking Corporation is the story of a company that started small, but grew through initiative and desire on the part of its founders and employees. In the years that have passed since the Hocking Glass Company was founded in 1905 in Lancaster, Ohio by I. J. Collins, it has grown into the Anchor Hocking Corporation worldwide. The company is a leading manufacturer of glass and ceramic tableware, glass and plastic containers, plastic and metal closures, plastic dinnerware, decorative hardware and plastic and glass forming mold equipment. Manufacturing facilities and sales offices are located in the United States, Canada, the Netherlands, and the company has licensing agreements with a number of foreign companies.

HOMER LAUGHLIN CHINA COMPANY. This company, founded in 1871 by brothers Homer and Shakespeare Laughlin is truly one of the giants of the American pottery industry. Two of their most famous lines are Fiesta and

Harlequin which are avidly sought by collectors. This company continues to be one of the largest manufacturers of dinnerware in the world.

ICE LIP. A rim which prevents ice from spilling out of the spout of a pitcher.

IMPERIAL GLASS COMPANY. This Bellaire, Ohio, company has produced fine glassware since 1901. Over the years they have become famous for their clear iridescent and carnival wares.

INDIANA GLASS COMPANY. Founded in Dunkirk, Indiana in 1907, this company is one of the largest glass manufacturers today.

JADEITE. Pale green opaque glass color.

JEANNETTE GLASS COMPANY. This company has been producing glassware in Jeannette, Pennsylvania since around the turn of the century.

JELLY TRAY. Small shallow tray with rim for serving sliced cranberry jelly or jellied consomme.

JENNYWARE. Kitchenware items made by Jeannette are called Jennyware by collectors. The aquamarine pieces are the most sought after and the most common.

KOCH, NORA. An authority on Depression glass, her national publication, *Depression Glass Daze*, is a bible for Depression glass collectors. It focuses on the buying, selling and collecting of colored glassware from the 1920s and 1930s. Nora Koch keeps readers informed with her expertise and insight.

LIBERTY WORKS. This glass company was located in Egg Harbor, New Jersey and produced glassware from 1903 to 1932.

LUNCHEON PLATE. Eight or nine inch plate, smaller than a dinner plate, larger than a salad plate.

MACBETH EVANS GLASS COMPANY. With several locations in Indiana, Macbeth Evans has produced glassware since 1899.

MAYONNAISE. Open compote often with underplate. Used for serving mayonnaise.

McKEE. Involved in United States glassmaking since the 1840s, the McKee Glass Company was organized in the late 1800s in Jeannette, Virginia. In 1961, it was bought by the Jeannette Corporation.

MILK GLASS. An opaque glass, hand blown and decorated like porcelain, in the 17th and 18th century, popular for pressed glass.

MORGANTOWN GLASS WORKS. Located in Morgantown, West Virginia, Morgantown Glass Works produced glassware from the 1800s to 1972.

MUSTARD JAR. Small glass jar with lid, which has indentation for a spoon, used to serve mustard.

NAPPY. Old English term, which refers to a bowl. Often found with one or two handles.

NEW MARTINSVILLE GLASS COMPANY. Starting in 1901, New Martinsville Glass Company produced art glass for many years. The company later produced pressed pattern glass, novelty items and Depression glass. In 1944, New Martinsville was bought by another company and became The Viking Glass Company.

OLD GOLD. Deep amber stain.

OLIVE DISH. Small shallow relish dish.

OLIVE JAR. Glass container with wide mouth and lid used to serve olives.

OPAL GLASS. Milk glass.

OPALESCENT GLASS. Iridescent glass made by adding heat sensitive chemicals to the batch and refiring. Bluish milky color.

OPALINE GLASS. A luxurious variety of glass, employed in the manufacture of pressed and art wares. It seems to have been introduced, or at any rate popularized, by Baccarat in the 1820s, but they in no way held any monopoly on its manufacture.

OPAQUE GLASS. A glass with little or no translucency and highly colored.

OPAQUE-WHITE GLASS. A porcelain-like glass with a milky quality.

OVERLAY GLASS. A glass molding technique of placing one colored glass over another, with designs cut through one layer only.

PADEN CITY GLASS COMPANY. Known primarily for the glass it produced, Paden City also produced pottery. Started in 1916 in Paden City, West Virginia, the company closed in 1951. Many of the Depression glass elegant patterns were made by Paden City.

PARFAIT. Tall, footed ice cream dish in which sundaes are served.

PATTERN GLASS. A kind of pressed glass, popular in the 1830s when it was imitative of the design and appearance of cut glass. In time the patterns became more complex, including circular, oval and elliptical patterns. In the 1860s, the New England Glasshouse developed a way to press soda-lime glass, which was of inferior quality and did not make a bell-like ring when struck, as did the formerly used flint glass. To compensate for such imperfections, the entire surface was covered with more ornate designs. This type of glass was extensively produced in the second half of the 19th century.

PATTERN-MOLDED GLASS. A blown-molded glass in which the pattern is first impressed in a small mold before the glass is blown to full size.

PICKLE CASTOR. Glass jar held in a silver plated metal frame with handle and spoon. Used during the Victorian period for serving pickles.

PICKLE DISH. Oblong tray smaller than a celery dish.

PIDGEON BLOOD. Brown highlighted ruby glass.

PLATONITE. Heat resistant white glass by Hazel Atlas.

PLATTER. Oval shaped or oblong tray.

PONTIL, PUNTEE OR PUNTY ROD. Long iron bar which holds vessel after it has been detached from the blowpipe and while the final touches are being done.

PRESERVE DISH. Footed candy dish.

PRESSED GLASS. An inexpensive substitute for free-blown cut glass, thicker and heavier, and formed in a mold by mechanical pressure rather than by blowing. It was developed in the early 19th century and soon was in general use in American glasshouses.

PUFF BOX. Small lidded box used for powder and powder puff, found on Victorian dressing tables.

PUNCH BOWL. Large deep glass bowl used for serving punch. Often it has a pedestal base.

PUNCH CUP. Glass cup, usually with handle, used for serving punch or lemonade.

PUNCH LADLE. Glass dipper used to serve punch or lemonade from punch bowl.

RANGE SETS. Also called grease sets or drip sets for range tops that include a large salt and pepper and a drippings jar. Other items in a range set could include a flour jar, sugar jar or spice shaker.

RAYED. Design or sunburst cuts on bottom of glassware.

REAMER. Juice extractors, reamers consist of a handled, highsided saucer with a pouring lip. In the center of the saucer is a pointed cone reaming section. The citrus half is seated on the reaming section and turned to produce juice.

REFRIGERATOR CONTAINERS. Refrigerator containers are glass kitchenware items made for use in the refrigerator. Some are made to hold butter, vegetables or leftovers, and some are made for easy stacking in the refrigerator.

RELISH. Pickle dish; oblong tray, sometimes with one or two handles.

RIVIERA. Made by Homer Laughlin from 1938 to 1950, this Depression era dinnerware features squared plates and cups.

ROSE BOWL. Small, round often tri-footed bowl having small opening in center.

SALVER. Large platter, 11 to 12 inches.

SANDWICH GLASS. An American pressed glass, popular in America and Europe, and used as a substitute for cut glass, produced in Massachusetts during the 19th century.

SANDWICH SERVER. Center handled salver.

SASE. Abbreviation for self-addressed stamped envelope. Used in mail order advertisements in glass and antique publications.

SHAWNEE. Formed in the 1930s in Zanesville, Ohio, Shawnee produced inexpensive commercial pottery, kitchenware and dinnerware.

SHERBET. Small, footed dessert dish.

SICK GLASS. Poor quality glass which has either been damaged by external factors or was simply made from inferior materials and with inferior processes.

SPOON HOLDER OR SPOONER. Tall cylindrically shaped holder with or without handles, used to hold dessert spoons.

SUGAR AND LEMON TRAY OR DISH. Two tiered serving dish. Cut lemons were placed on the bottom tier and sugar was held by bowl which made up the top tier.

SUGAR BOWL. Small bowl with or without lid used for serving sugar; usually found with matching creamer.

TEAL. Blue-green glass.

TIDBIT TRAY. Tiered dish for serving hors d'oeuvre. Generally a metal pole runs through the center of each tier which is largest on the bottom, becoming smaller as they go up.

TIFFIN GLASS COMPANY. Based in Tiffin, Ohio, the Tiffin Glass Company was a subsidiary of U. S. Glass Company. It closed in 1980.

TOOTHPICK HOLDER. Small glass container found in novelty shapes and sizes used to hold toothpicks.

TOPAZ. Bright yellow glassware.

TRANSLUCENT. Glass which diffuses light in such a way that objects cannot be clearly seen through it.

TRANSPARENT. Glass which permits light to pass through which makes it easy to see through.

TRIVET. Footed hot plate.

TUMBLE UP. Water bottle and inverted glass set which is intended for a night stand, should its owner wish a glass of water while in bed.

TUMBLER. A glass vessel, not having a stem or handle, resting upon a base rather than a foot or other support. The normal shape is cylindrical, capacity varies.

ULTRAMARINE. Blue-green by Jeannette.

U.S. GLASS COMPANY. U.S. Glass Company had factories in Pennsylvania, Ohio and Indiana. They produced glass from 1891–1966.

WEATHERMAN, HAZEL MARIE. The premier authority on Depression glass,

Hazel Marie Weatherman wrote the first book on Depression glass, *A Guide to Colored Glassware of the 1920s and 1930s*. She has since produced supplements, including the recent *1984 Supplement and Price Trends to Book I*. She has also written *The Decorated Tumbler*, *Fostoria: Its First Fifty Years*, and *Third Fostoria Price Watch*. Her thorough knowledge and extensive research make her books a necessity for the Depression glass collector.

WESTMORELAND GLASS COMPANY. Located in Grapeville, Pennsylvania, Westmoreland has produced glassware since 1890.

WHISKEY TUMBLER. Small flat bottom glass for serving whiskey.

WINE GLASS. Stemmed glass for serving wine.

WINE SET. Decanter and wine glasses usually on a matching tray.

MANUFACTURERS' MARKS

Anchor Hocking Glass Co.

D.C. Jenkins Glass Co.

VITROCK

Hocking Glass Co., Vitrock

Federal Glass Co.

Hazel Atlas Glass Co.

Indiana Glass Co.

Hazel Atlas Glass Co.

Jeannette Glass Co.

Imperial Glass Co.

L.E. Smith Glass Co.

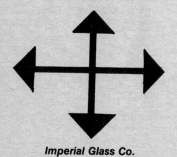

Imperial Glass Co.

Maryland Glass Corporation

McKee Glass Co.

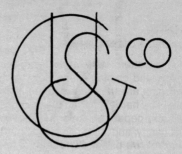

United States Glass Co.

New Martinsville Glass Co.

Westmoreland Specialty Co.

HOW TO USE THIS BOOK

This book is divided into three sections: Depression Glassware, Elegant Glassware and Children's Dishes. Within each section, patterns are listed in alphabetical order, along with pattern pieces and colors. There are three price columns found next to each listing. The first columns create a price range. The range shows the lowest and highest retail selling price for each piece. These prices reflect the geographical differences of the glassware market, as well as the laws of supply and demand. Dealers usually sell at retail price, but buy at wholesale value. Therefore, if a collector sells to a dealer, he should expect a lower price than if he sold at an auction or flea market.

Values were determined by averaging the prices of actual sales across the country and should be used only as a guideline.

The third column is an average of last year's prices for the item. This allows a person to determine which objects have decreased or increased in value over the last year.

DEPRESSION GLASS

ADAM
Jeannette Glass Co.

This pattern was made from 1932 to 1934. The colors are green, pink, yellow and crystal. Some delphite (opaque blue) has been reported. Green and pink are the most commonly found colors. Yellow and crystal are very rare. The hardest to find pieces in this pattern are the cereal bowls, the green salt and pepper shakers and the ice tea tumblers. In case you didn't notice, the candy and sugar lids are interchangeable. An interesting piece is the *Adam/Sierra* butter dish. The top has both the *Adam* and the *Sierra* patterns. The bottom can be either pattern; it's the top that makes the difference. A reproduction of the standard *Adam* butter dish has been on the market since 1981. It is available only in pink and can be told from the original fairly easily. The color is lighter than the real piece and if you inspect the top carefully, you'll find that on the real top, the large veins in the leaves all touch the center vein. On the new top, they don't. The bottom is also different; the pattern has been shifted about 90°. On the real bottom the points go towards the sides; on the new bottom, they point to the corners.

Adam

	Current Price Range		Prior Year Average
Ashtray, square, length 4¼"			
☐ pink	20.00	25.00	22.00
☐ green	15.00	17.50	16.00
Bowl, dessert, 4¾"			
☐ pink	8.00	11.00	9.00
☐ green	9.00	12.00	10.00

	Current Price Range		Prior Year Average
Bowl, cereal, 5¾"			
☐ pink	24.00	30.00	27.00
☐ green	26.00	32.00	29.00
Bowl, 7¾"			
☐ pink	13.00	17.00	15.00
☐ green	14.00	18.50	16.50
Bowl, with lid, 9"			
☐ pink	35.00	42.00	37.00
☐ green	38.00	45.00	40.00
Bowl, no lid, 9"			
☐ pink	18.00	24.00	20.00
☐ green	20.00	26.00	22.00
Bowl, oval, 10"			
☐ pink	13.00	18.00	15.00
☐ green	15.50	21.00	17.00
Butter Dish and Cover, Sierra mold, Adam motif			
☐ pink	65.00	69.00	67.00
☐ green	210.00	222.00	215.00
Cake Stand, footed, diameter 9⅞"			
☐ pink	11.50	15.00	12.50
☐ green	14.00	17.00	15.50
Candlesticks, pair, squared base, with a goblet-shaped body, height 4"			
☐ pink	47.00	55.00	53.00
☐ green	65.00	75.00	70.00
Candy Jar and Cover, diameter 2½"			
☐ pink	50.00	60.00	55.00
☐ green	70.00	80.00	75.00
Cereal Bowl, diameter 5¾"			
☐ pink	20.00	23.00	21.50
☐ green	18.00	22.00	19.50
Coaster, diameter 3¾"			
☐ pink	13.00	16.00	13.50
☐ green	10.50	13.00	11.50
Creamer, paneled sides, with the leaf and flower design on the top border, and a plain handle straight at the top and swooping downwards, height 3¾"			
☐ pink	11.00	15.00	13.00
☐ green	13.00	15.00	14.00

	Current Price Range		Prior Year Average

Cup, rounded, paneled sides, with the leaf and flower design on the top border and a straight topped handle that sweeps downwards

☐ pink	15.50	19.50	17.50
☐ green	13.00	16.50	14.00
☐ yellow	70.00	80.00	75.00

Dessert Bowl, diameter 4¾"

☐ pink	8.50	11.50	9.50
☐ green	8.00	11.00	9.00

Dinner Plate, squared, length 9"

☐ pink	14.00	18.00	16.00
☐ green	13.00	16.00	14.00

Lamp, made from a sherbet dish which is frosted and notched to accommodate a switch

☐ pink	68.00	78.00	74.00
☐ green	80.00	90.00	83.00

Pitcher, with a wide, plain bordered top section, the body of which tapers, with close paneled sides, to a round footed base with concentric rings, 32 oz., height 8"

☐ pink	33.00	39.00	34.50

Plate, sherbet, 6"

☐ pink	3.00	5.00	4.00
☐ green	3.50	5.50	4.50

Plate, square, 7"

☐ pink	6.00	8.50	7.00
☐ green	7.00	8.00	8.00

Platter, length 11⅝"

☐ pink	9.50	12.00	10.00
☐ green	10.00	13.00	11.00

Relish Plate, 8", oblong, 2-part tab handles

☐ pink	7.00	10.00	8.50
☐ green	9.00	12.00	10.50

Salad Plate, squared, length 7½"

☐ pink	5.00	8.00	6.00
☐ green	6.00	9.00	7.00
☐ yellow	90.00	100.00	93.00

Salt and Pepper, pair, with a paneled tapered body on a squared base, height 4"

☐ pink	40.00	44.00	41.00
☐ green	71.00	77.00	72.50

	Current Price Range		Prior Year Average

Saucer, squared, length 6″
□ pink	1.50	4.00	2.50
□ yellow	1.50	4.00	2.50

Sherbet, rounded body tapering to a square footed base, diameter 3″
□ pink	13.00	17.00	14.50
□ green	17.00	21.00	18.00

Sherbet Plate, diameter 6″
□ pink	2.50	4.50	3.00
□ green	2.75	4.75	3.25

Sugar, with cover bearing the Adam motif and a bell-shaped finial, two handles, paneled body
□ pink	7.50	10.50	8.50
□ green	10.00	15.00	11.50

Tumbler, 7 oz., cone shaped, with a top border decorated with the flower and leaf design, paneled sides mounted on a squared foot, height 4½″
□ pink	15.50	18.00	16.00
□ green	14.50	17.00	15.00

Tumbler, iced tea, 9 oz., cone shaped with a top border decorated with the flower and leaf design, paneled sides, mounted on a squared foot, height 5¾″
□ pink	32.00	37.00	34.00
□ green	22.00	27.00	24.00

Vase, with a flange rim at the mouth, a plain top border, and a rounded, wide-paneled body which gradually narrows at the base, height 7½″
□ pink	120.00	130.00	125.00
□ green	27.00	32.00	28.50

AMERICAN PIONEER
Liberty Glass Works

This pattern was made from 1931 to 1934. The colors were green, pink, crystal and amber. Green and pink are the most common and enjoy the greatest following. Amber is very rare. The whiskey and the covered bowls are very hard to find. This is not one of the big patterns in Depression glass but it does have its fans.

	Current Price Range		Prior Year Average

Bowl, handled, diameter 5¼″

☐ pink 6.50 9.00 7.00
☐ green 7.00 9.50 7.50

Bowl, covered, with a finial on the lid, diameter 8½″

☐ pink 52.00 57.00 54.00
☐ green 64.00 69.00 65.00

Bowl, handled, diameter 9″

☐ pink 10.00 14.00 11.50
☐ green 12.00 17.00 13.50

Bowl, covered, diameter 9¼″

☐ pink 68.00 74.00 70.50
☐ green 84.00 90.00 85.50

Bowl, console, diameter 10½″

☐ pink 33.00 37.50 34.00
☐ green 43.00 47.50 44.00

Candlesticks, pair, with a round, beaded base and a plain stem fitted with harp-shaped handles, height 6½″

☐ pink 42.00 46.00 43.50
☐ green 52.00 56.00 53.50

Candy Jar and Cover. tall, with a bottom that projects straight upward at the rim, capacity one pound

☐ pink 54.00 58.00 55.00
☐ green 69.00 74.00 71.00

Candy Jar and Cover, capacity 1½ pounds

☐ pink 57.00 62.00 58.00
☐ green 82.00 90.00 84.00

Cheese and Cracker Set, indented platter and compote

☐ pink 20.00 30.00 23.50
☐ green 28.00 38.00 32.00

Coaster, diameter 3½″

☐ pink 11.50 15.00 12.50
☐ green 12.50 16.00 13.50

Creamer, with a thick, gently curved handle, height 2¾″

☐ pink 10.00 14.00 11.50
☐ green 12.00 16.00 13.00

Cup

☐ pink 4.00 7.00 4.50
☐ green 6.00 9.00 7.00

	Current Price Range		Prior Year Average

Dresser Set, two cologne, powder jar, on indented tray, length 7½"

| ☐ pink | 75.00 | 85.00 | 78.00 |

Goblet, for wine, with a simple column stem on a rounded plain base, 3 oz., height 4"

| ☐ pink | 15.00 | 19.00 | 16.50 |
| ☐ green | 19.00 | 24.00 | 21.00 |

Goblet, 8 oz., height 6"

| ☐ pink | 19.00 | 25.00 | 21.00 |
| ☐ green | 24.00 | 29.00 | 25.00 |

Ice Bucket, overhanging metallic handle, height 6"

| ☐ pink | 25.00 | 30.00 | 26.00 |
| ☐ green | 28.00 | 35.00 | 30.00 |

Lamp, ball-shaped, height 5½"

| ☐ pink | 54.00 | 60.00 | 55.50 |
| ☐ amber | 64.00 | 70.00 | 65.50 |

Lamp, tall, height 8¾"

| ☐ pink | 54.00 | 60.00 | 55.50 |
| ☐ green | 64.00 | 70.00 | 65.50 |

Pitcher, covered urn, with a swoop-curved handle and a flat-topped finial on the lid, height 5½"

☐ pink	90.00	100.00	95.00
☐ green	124.00	134.00	125.00
☐ amber	195.00	207.00	198.00

Pitcher, covered urn, with a swoop-curved handle and a flat-topped finial on the lid, height 7"

☐ pink	110.00	122.00	113.00
☐ green	144.00	155.00	146.00
☐ amber	240.00	255.00	247.00

Plate, diameter 8"

| ☐ pink | 4.50 | 6.50 | 5.00 |
| ☐ green | 5.00 | 7.00 | 5.50 |

Plate, handled, diameter, 11½"

| ☐ pink | 8.00 | 11.00 | 9.00 |
| ☐ green | 10.00 | 14.00 | 11.00 |

Saucer

| ☐ pink | 2.00 | 5.00 | 2.50 |
| ☐ green | 3.00 | 6.00 | 3.50 |

	Current Price Range		Prior Year Average
Sherbet, with a small stem on a round base, height 3½″			
☐ pink	8.00	12.00	9.00
☐ green	10.00	14.00	11.50
Sherbet, with a small stem on a round base, height 4½″			
☐ pink	12.00	17.00	13.50
☐ green	17.00	21.00	18.50
Sugar, with two swoop-curved handles, on a round base, no cover, height 2½″			
☐ pink	10.00	14.00	11.50
☐ green	11.00	17.00	12.50
Sugar, with two swoop-curved handles, on a round base, no cover, height 3½″			
☐ pink	11.00	15.00	12.00
☐ green	13.00	17.00	14.00
Tumbler, for juice, 5 oz.			
☐ pink	11.00	15.00	12.00
☐ green	15.00	20.00	16.50
Tumbler, 8 oz., height 4″			
☐ pink	12.00	17.00	13.50
☐ green	17.00	22.00	18.50
Tumbler, 12 oz., height 5″			
☐ pink	17.00	22.00	18.50
☐ green	27.00	33.00	29.00
Vase, issued in four styles: straight edged, curved outward only slightly; a rolled, wide edge that is sharply flared outward; a curved inward edge; and a scalloped edge, height 6¾″			
☐ pink	47.00	55.00	49.00
☐ green, issued only in the straight edge and the rolled, wide edge	67.00	74.00	68.50
Whiskey, 2 oz., height 2¼″			
☐ pink	27.00	33.00	29.00
☐ green	29.00	35.00	31.00

AMERICAN SWEETHEART
Macbeth Evans Glass Co.

American Sweetheart was manufactured from 1930 through 1936. The colors are pink, monax (transluscent white), blue, red and some crystal. Berry sets and lampshades have also been reported in cremax (transluscent beige). Pink was the first color issued, followed by monax. In 1934, dessert sets were issued in red and blue. The pitchers and tumblers were made in pink only. The rarest pieces in this pattern today are the cream soups, the pitchers, the 10 oz. tumblers and the pink shakers. There is an overabundance of the basic items in *American Sweetheart*. Cups and saucers and plates are very easy to find. This probably accounts for its popularity. It's a great pattern with which to start your collection.

	Current Price Range		Prior Year Average
Berry Bowl, low, flat, diameter 3¾″			
☐ pink	20.00	25.00	21.50
Berry Bowl, round, diameter 9″			
☐ pink	16.50	22.00	17.50
☐ monax...	32.00	34.00	30.50
Bowl, cream soup, 4½″			
☐ pink	24.00	29.00	26.00
☐ monax...	27.00	32.00	28.00
Bowl, flat soup, 9½″			
☐ pink	22.00	28.00	25.00
☐ monax...	37.00	42.00	39.00
Bowl, oval, vegetable, 11″			
☐ pink	28.00	34.00	31.00
☐ monax...	44.00	52.00	48.00
Cereal Bowl, flat, diameter 6″			
☐ pink	7.50	11.00	8.00
☐ monax...	7.50	11.00	8.00
Console Bowl, wide flange rim, diameter 18″			
☐ monax...	274.00	285.00	275.00
Creamer, oval footed			
☐ pink	6.00	8.50	7.00
☐ monax...	5.50	8.00	6.50
Cup			
☐ pink	8.50	11.50	9.00
☐ monax...	6.50	9.50	7.00
Lampshade, sometimes found with orange, green, blue or brown panels down the sides			
☐ monax...	410.00	440.00	420.00
Plate, bread and butter			
☐ pink	2.50	4.50	3.50
☐ monax...	3.00	5.50	4.00
Plate, salad, 8″			
☐ pink	6.00	9.00	7.25
☐ monax...	6.25	9.50	7.50
Plate, luncheon, 9″			
☐ monax...	7.00	10.00	8.50

	Current Price Range		Prior Year Average
Plate, dinner, either 9¾″ or 10¼″			
☐ pink	13.00	16.00	14.50
☐ monax	14.50	17.50	15.50
Plate, chop plate, 11″			
☐ monax	9.00	13.00	11.50
Plate, salver, 12″			
☐ pink	10.00	13.00	11.50
☐ monax	11.00	14.50	12.50
Plate, server, 15½″			
☐ monax	150.00	200.00	175.00
☐ crystal	125.00	175.00	145.00
☐ blue	265.00	315.00	280.00
☐ red	200.00	255.00	230.00
Platter, with a flange rim, oval-shaped, diameter 12½″			
☐ pink	15.50	20.00	16.50
☐ monax	33.00	43.00	36.00
Pitcher, with a swelled shape, ice guard, and swoop-curved, lined handle, 60 oz., height 7″			
☐ pink	350.00	375.00	340.00
Pitcher, with a swelled shape, ice guard, and swoop-curved, lined handle, 80 oz., height 8″			
☐ pink	330.00	360.00	340.00
Salt and Pepper Shakers, with a lean, slightly tapered body, footed on a round base			
☐ pink	220.00	250.00	230.00
☐ monax	195.00	220.00	203.00
Saucer			
☐ pink	2.00	3.00	2.25
☐ monax	1.50	2.00	1.75
☐ blue	24.00	32.00	27.00
Sherbet, low foot, diameter 4″			
☐ pink	10.00	14.00	12.00
Sherbet, low foot, with the motif inside or outside, diameter 4¼″			
☐ pink	9.50	12.50	11.50
☐ monax	16.00	17.00	19.00
Sherbet, with a stub stem and a metal base			
☐ crystal	2.00	4.00	2.50

	Current Price Range		Prior Year Average
Sugar, open, two-handled, on an oval foot			
☐ pink	5.50	8.50	6.50
☐ monax...	4.50	7.50	5.50
Sugar Cover, with two style knobs			
☐ monax...	144.00	154.00	147.00
Tid-bit Set, 3-tier, 8″, 12″ and 15½″ plate, metal center rod, handle			
☐ monax...	175.00	225.00	200.00
Tumbler, for juice, 5 oz., height 3½″			
☐ pink	29.00	35.00	31.00
Tumbler, 8 oz., height 4″			
☐ pink	27.00	33.00	28.00
Tumbler, 10 oz., height 4½″			
☐ pink	37.00	43.00	39.00

ANNIVERSARY
Jeannette Glass Co.

Although this pattern is technically not true Depression era glass, having been introduced in 1947, high collector interest warrants its inclusion here. Pink was the first color made and then later some milk glass. In the early 1970s, Jeannette manufactured the pattern again in crystal and an iridescent amber, which resembles Carnival glass. The most recent name for *Anniversary* was *Diamond Cut,* which suggests the sharp, geometric motif, a series of spiked lines emanating outward from the base of the object with a central medallion of the same lines separated from the outer design by a plain, circular border.

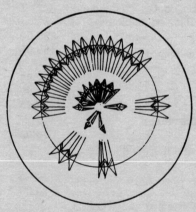

Anniversary

	Current Price Range		Prior Year Average
Berry Bowl, diameter 4⅞″			
☐ pink	2.50	3.50	3.00
☐ crystal	1.25	2.50	1.50
Bowl, 7⅜″			
☐ pink	5.00	8.00	6.00
☐ crystal	3.00	4.00	3.50
Bowl, fruit, 9″			
☐ pink	9.00	11.00	10.00
☐ crystal	7.00	9.00	8.00
Butter Dish and Cover			
☐ pink	36.00	44.00	38.00
☐ crystal	20.00	27.00	23.00
Cake Plate, diameter 12½″			
☐ pink	6.00	10.00	7.50
☐ crystal	3.50	6.00	4.50
Cake Plate and Cover			
☐ pink	11.00	14.00	11.50
☐ crystal	8.00	12.00	9.00
Candlesticks, pair, 4⅞″			
☐ crystal	12.00	15.00	13.50
Candy Jar and Cover, with a pointed finial on the lid			
☐ pink	21.00	29.00	23.00
☐ crystal	15.00	19.00	16.00
Compote, open, 3 legged			
☐ pink	6.00	9.00	7.00
☐ crystal	2.00	4.00	2.75
Creamer, with a handle pointed on the top edge, footed on a round base			
☐ pink	5.00	8.00	6.00
☐ crystal	2.00	4.00	2.50
Cup			
☐ pink	2.50	5.50	3.50
☐ crystal	1.00	3.00	1.50
Pickle Dish, diameter 9″			
☐ pink	4.00	8.00	5.00
☐ crystal	2.00	4.00	2.50
Plate, sherbet, diameter 6¼″			
☐ pink	1.50	2.25	1.75
☐ crystal	1.00	1.75	1.25
Plate, dinner, diameter 9″			
☐ pink	4.00	6.00	5.00
☐ crystal	3.00	5.00	4.00

	Current Price Range		Prior Year Average
Plate, server, 12½"			
☐ pink	6.50	8.50	7.50
☐ crystal	4.00	6.00	5.00
Relish Dish, diameter 8"			
☐ pink	5.00	8.00	5.75
☐ crystal	3.75	5.50	4.00
Saucer			
☐ pink	1.00	2.00	1.25
☐ crystal	.50	1.50	.75
Sherbet, stub stem, footed on a round base			
☐ pink	3.00	5.50	4.00
☐ crystal	1.00	3.50	1.75
Sugar, open, with two handles pointed on the top edge			
☐ pink	4.50	6.50	5.00
☐ crystal	2.25	4.00	2.75
Sugar Covers, with a pointed finial			
☐ pink	3.00	5.00	3.50
☐ crystal	2.00	4.00	2.50
Vase, with a scalloped rim, height 6½"			
☐ pink	8.00	11.00	8.50
☐ crystal	4.50	7.50	5.00
Vase, wall pin-up			
☐ pink	13.00	17.00	14.00
☐ crystal	8.00	12.00	9.00
Wine Glass, footed on a round base, 2¾ oz.			
☐ pink	8.50	11.50	9.50
☐ crystal	5.00	8.00	6.00

AUNT POLLY
U.S. Glass Co.

This pattern was manufactured in the late 1920s. It is available in blue, green and iridescent. This is not an easy pattern to collect. It wasn't made in large quantities so our supply is small today. There are no cups or saucers in *Aunt Polly* so don't bother looking. This can be a drawback to some collectors. There are also some distinct shade variations, so matching *Aunt Polly* pieces, even in the same color, are not always easy to find. The difficult items to find are the pitchers, the sugar lids and the salt and pepper shakers. None of the bowls are easily found and the blue butter dish seems especially good at avoiding collectors. The sugar and candy lid are interchangeable.

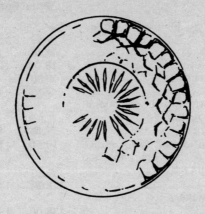

Aunt Polly

	Current Price Range		Prior Year Average
Berry Bowl, diameter 4⅜″			
☐ green	5.00	8.00	6.50
☐ blue	8.00	10.00	8.50
Berry Bowl, diameter 7⅛″			
☐ green	12.00	16.00	14.00
☐ blue	17.00	22.00	18.50
Bowl, height 2″, diameter 4½″			
☐ green	7.00	10.00	7.50
☐ blue	9.00	13.00	10.00
Bowl, oval, length 8⅜″			
☐ green	25.00	31.00	27.00
☐ blue	38.00	43.00	40.00
Butter Dish and Cover			
☐ green	185.00	230.00	200.00
☐ blue	135.00	155.00	145.00
Candy Jar, with a pointed finial on the cover, and two flat, thumbprint topped handles			
☐ green	30.00	40.00	33.00
☐ blue	43.00	55.00	45.00
Comport, handled			
☐ green	7.00	10.00	8.00
☐ blue	12.00	16.00	13.50

	Current Price Range		Prior Year Average

Creamer, with a flat, thumbprint topped handle

☐ green	11.00	16.00	13.00
☐ blue	18.00	24.00	20.00

Luncheon Plate, diameter 8″

☐ blue	7.00	10.00	8.00

Pickle Bowl, oval, with two flat, thumbprint topped handles, diameter 7½″

☐ green	7.50	11.00	8.50
☐ blue	10.50	14.50	11.00

Pitcher, with a scalloped rim and plain handle, 48 oz., height 8″

☐ blue	115.00	130.00	120.00

Salt and Pepper Shakers

☐ blue	138.00	155.00	143.00

Sherbet, smooth stub stem on a plain round base

☐ green	6.00	9.00	7.00
☐ blue	7.00	10.00	8.00

Sherbet Plate, diameter 6″

☐ green	2.00	4.00	2.50
☐ blue	3.00	6.00	3.50

Sugar, with two flat, thumbprint topped handles

☐ green	9.50	13.00	10.25
☐ blue	13.00	18.00	14.50

Sugar Cover, with a pointed finial

☐ green	25.00	32.00	26.50
☐ blue	36.00	44.00	38.00

Tumbler, 8 oz., height 3⅝″

☐ blue	11.00	15.00	12.00

Vase, slightly flared body, footed on a round, decorated base, height 6½″

☐ green	20.00	26.00	21.00
☐ blue	27.00	32.00	29.00

AURORA
Hazel Atlas Glass Co.

This pattern was manufactured in the late 1930s. It is most often found in cobalt blue but has been reported in small amounts in pink. It appears to be a breakfast line since so few items were issued. It was released originally with no name but collectors dubbed it *Aurora*.

Aurora

	Current Price Range		Prior Year Average
Bowl, 4½″			
☐ cobalt...	8.00	11.00	9.00
☐ pink	8.00	11.00	9.00
Cereal Bowl, diameter 5¼″			
☐ cobalt...	3.00	5.00	3.50
Creamer, 4½″			
☐ cobalt...	7.00	10.00	8.00
☐ pink	7.00	10.00	8.00
Cup			
☐ cobalt...	3.50	6.00	4.50
Milk Pitcher, 4″ high			
☐ cobalt...	6.75	9.50	7.50
Plate, diameter 6½″			
☐ cobalt...	2.50	4.50	3.00
☐ pink	2.50	4.50	3.00
Saucer			
☐ cobalt...	1.50	3.50	2.00

	Current Price Range		Prior Year Average
Tumbler, 10 oz., height 4¾″			
☐ cobalt..	9.00	12.00	9.50
☐ pink	9.00	12.00	9.50

AVOCADO, NO. 601
Indiana Glass Co.

This pattern was made from 1923 to 1932. The original colors issued were pink and green. The central motif in this design is two pears surrounded by a profusion of leaves that gather to the outer edge, giving the piece an irregular shape. The pattern was doing very well until 1974 when the Indiana Co. started its Tiara Exclusive Home Products line. They reproduced *Avocado* in many colors including pink. The other colors made were yellow, blue and amethyst. These are obviously easy to spot as reproductions since these colors were not made in the original issues. The reproduced pink is more orange than the original so it, too, can be detected but make sure before buying a piece. Some pieces have turned up with an apple rather than a pear design. Buy them if you like them, but their scarcity probably won't add to their value.

Avocado #601

	Current Price Range		Prior Year Average
Bowl, two-handled, diameter 5¼″			
☐ pink	20.00	24.00	22.00
☐ green	22.00	26.00	23.00

	Current Price Range		Prior Year Average
Bowl, footed relish, diameter 6"			
☐ pink	14.00	19.00	16.00
☐ green	17.00	22.00	19.00
Bowl, one handle, 7"			
☐ pink	12.00	16.00	14.00
☐ green	15.00	18.50	16.50
Bowl, two-handled, with an oval shape, diameter 8"			
☐ pink	12.50	15.00	13.50
☐ green	17.00	21.00	17.50
Bowl, height 3", diameter 9½"			
☐ pink	54.00	61.00	55.75
☐ green	74.00	81.00	76.00
Cake Plate, two-handled, diameter 10¼"			
☐ pink	22.00	29.00	25.00
☐ green	32.00	39.00	35.00
Creamer, footed			
☐ pink	23.00	27.00	24.00
☐ green	27.00	31.00	28.00
Cup, footed, on a round base			
☐ pink	25.00	28.00	25.75
☐ green	26.00	29.00	26.75
Luncheon Plate, diameter 8¼"			
☐ pink	12.50	15.00	14.00
☐ green	14.00	18.00	16.00
Pitcher, cone-shaped, footed on a round, smooth-edged base that contains a single row of leaves, but with the typical pear and leaf design on the body and the ragged top rim, 64 oz.			
☐ pink	280.00	315.00	290.00
☐ green	475.00	520.00	490.00
Saucer			
☐ pink	18.00	22.00	19.00
☐ green	20.50	24.50	21.50
Sherbet			
☐ pink	44.00	49.00	45.50
☐ green	49.00	54.00	51.00
Sherbet Plate, diameter 6¼"			
☐ pink	8.00	11.50	9.00
☐ green	9.00	13.00	10.00
Sugar, two-handled, footed			
☐ pink	23.00	28.00	25.00
☐ green	27.00	32.00	28.25

	Current Price Range		Prior Year Average
Tumbler, cone-shaped, slightly flared rim, on a round base			
☐ pink	70.00	80.00	76.00
☐ green	96.00	104.00	98.00

BANDED RINGS
Hocking Glass Co.

This pattern was made from 1929 through 1932. It is similar to *Circle*, which was also made by Hocking. The main difference is that *Circle* can have anywhere from four to nine rings while *Banded Rings* always has only four. The original colors issued were green, crystal and crystal with a platinum rim. Later issues included many different color rings. Some of the tumblers can also be found in pink.

Berry Bowl, diameter 4⅞″			
☐ crystal	1.00	3.00	1.50
☐ green	2.00	4.00	2.50
☐ decorated	2.00	4.00	2.50
Berry Bowl, diameter 8″			
☐ crystal	3.00	5.00	3.50
☐ green	4.50	7.00	5.00
☐ decorated	4.50	7.00	5.00
Butter Tub, tab handled			
☐ crystal	7.00	11.00	7.75
☐ green	11.00	15.00	12.00
☐ decorated	11.00	15.00	12.00
Cocktail Glass, pedestal foot, height 3″			
☐ crystal	3.00	5.00	3.50
☐ green	3.50	5.75	4.00
☐ decorated	3.50	5.75	4.00
Cocktail Shaker			
☐ crystal	6.00	9.00	6.75
☐ green	11.00	15.00	12.00
☐ decorated	11.00	15.00	12.00
Creamer			
☐ crystal	2.00	4.50	3.00
☐ green	3.00	5.50	4.00
☐ decorated	3.00	5.50	4.00

	Current Price Range		Prior Year Average

Cup
☐ crystal	1.00	3.00	1.50
☐ green	2.25	5.00	3.00
☐ decorated	2.25	5.00	3.00

Decanter, faceted stopper
☐ crystal	12.50	16.00	13.50
☐ green	21.00	28.00	22.50
☐ decorated	21.00	28.00	22.50

Goblet, cocktail, 3½ oz.
☐ crystal	7.00	11.00	9.00
☐ green	7.00	11.00	9.00
☐ decorated	6.00	10.00	8.00

Goblet, stemmed, 9 oz., height 7¼"
☐ crystal	3.00	6.50	4.00
☐ green	8.00	11.50	9.00
☐ decorated	8.00	11.50	9.00

Goblet, 9 oz., height 7¾"
☐ crystal	2.50	3.75	3.25
☐ green	3.50	4.75	4.25
☐ decorated	3.50	4.75	4.25

Ice Bucket
☐ crystal	7.00	10.00	8.00
☐ green	10.00	14.00	11.00
☐ decorated	10.00	14.00	11.00

Iced Tea Glass, pedestal foot, height 6"
☐ crystal	4.00	6.00	4.50
☐ green	7.00	10.00	8.00
☐ decorated	7.00	10.00	8.00

Juice Tumbler, 5 oz., height 3½"
☐ crystal	1.50	4.00	2.25
☐ green	2.50	5.00	3.00
☐ decorated	2.50	5.00	3.00

Pitcher, 60 oz., height 8"
☐ crystal	7.00	10.00	8.00
☐ green	13.00	17.00	14.00
☐ decorated	13.00	17.00	14.00

Pitcher, 80 oz., height 8½"
☐ crystal	8.75	12.00	9.25
☐ green	15.00	19.00	16.00
☐ decorated	15.00	19.00	16.00
☐ pink	17.00	23.00	19.00

Plate, diameter 6"
☐ crystal	.75	2.50	1.00
☐ green	2.50	4.50	3.00
☐ decorated	2.50	4.50	3.00

	Current Price Range		Prior Year Average
Plate, diameter 6½″			
☐ crystal	.75	2.25	1.00
☐ green	1.50	3.50	2.00
☐ decorated	1.50	3.50	2.00
Plate, diameter 8″			
☐ crystal	.75	2.25	1.00
☐ green	1.25	3.25	2.00
☐ decorated	1.25	3.25	2.00
☐ red	15.00	19.00	16.00
☐ blue	20.00	24.00	21.00
Salt and Pepper Shakers, height 4½″			
☐ crystal	10.00	14.50	11.00
☐ green	30.00	40.00	35.00
☐ decorated	20.00	25.00	21.00
Sandwich Tray, center handle			
☐ crystal	7.00	10.00	8.00
☐ green	11.00	15.00	12.50
☐ decorated	12.00	16.00	13.50
Saucer			
☐ crystal	.75	2.00	1.00
☐ green	1.00	3.00	1.50
☐ decorated	1.00	3.00	1.50
Sherbet, pedestal foot, height 4½″			
☐ crystal	3.00	5.00	3.50
☐ green	3.50	5.50	4.25
☐ decorated	3.50	5.50	4.25
Sugar Bowl, pedestal foot, height 5″			
☐ crystal	2.00	3.50	2.25
☐ green	2.75	5.00	3.25
☐ decorated	3.00	5.50	3.50
Tumbler, 5 oz., height 3½″			
☐ crystal	1.75	3.50	2.00
☐ green	2.50	4.50	3.00
☐ decorated	3.00	4.50	3.50
Tumbler, 9 oz., height 4½″			
☐ crystal	2.50	4.50	3.00
☐ green	3.50	5.50	4.00
☐ decorated	3.50	5.50	4.00
Tumbler, 12 oz., height 5″			
☐ crystal	3.00	5.00	3.50
☐ green	3.50	5.50	4.00
☐ decorated	3.50	5.50	4.00
☐ pink	5.00	7.00	6.00

	Current Price Range		Prior Year Average
Vase, height 3″			
☐ crystal...	6.00	12.00	8.00
☐ green..	6.00	12.00	8.00
☐ decorated	5.00	10.00	8.00
Vase, height 8″			
☐ crystal...	20.00	30.00	24.00
☐ green..	20.00	30.00	24.00
☐ decorated	17.50	27.50	22.50
Water Glass, height 5½″			
☐ crystal...	2.50	4.50	3.00
☐ green..	3.50	5.50	4.00
☐ decorated ..../.................................	3.50	5.50	4.00
Whiskey Glass			
☐ crystal...	2.00	3.25	2.75
☐ green..	3.00	4.00	3.50
☐ decorated	3.50	5.25	4.50

BEADED BLOCK
Imperial Glass Co.

This pattern was produced from 1927 into the 1930s. It is often mistaken for pattern or Carnival glass by dealers and so will be overpriced. It was issued in pink, green, crystal, ice blue, vaseline, iridescent amber, and opalescent colors. A typical plate or bowl features two continuous rows of blocks, one on top of the other, the top row of blocks being somewhat wider and longer, following the contour of the object. Blocks are smooth and lined on all sides by a sharply contrasting jewel-like border. The outer rim is softly scalloped, and on footed pieces, such as the vase or creamer, the round base is rayed, terminating in a scalloped edge. The center contains a sunburst design. Unlike most Depression glass, some hand work was involved in creating this line. This was necessary, for example, in the fluting of some of the bowls and in those bowls which were made by turning up the edges of the plates. Some vases have been found recently with straight rims. They are nice pieces, but it is a judgement call as to whether they are really *Beaded Block* since they lack the scalloped edges. The round lily bowl can be found in red. Watch out for pieces with the Imperial mark (IG); these were made after 1951. Prices for amber are the same as for green.

Beaded Block

	Current Price Range		Prior Year Average
Bowl, jelly, two-handled, 4½″			
☐ crystal	4.00	6.00	4.75
☐ pink	6.00	9.00	7.00
☐ green	5.00	8.00	5.75
☐ amber	5.00	8.00	5.75
☐ ice blue	11.00	15.00	12.00
Bowl, round, lily, diameter 4½″			
☐ crystal	6.00	8.50	7.00
☐ pink	8.00	10.00	8.50
☐ green	7.00	9.00	8.00
☐ opalescent	13.00	17.00	14.50
☐ red	60.00	72.00	66.00
Bowl, square shape, length 5½″			
☐ crystal	4.50	6.50	5.50
☐ pink	5.00	8.00	6.75
☐ green	5.00	8.00	6.50
☐ vaseline	7.00	10.00	8.00
Bowl, one handle, diameter 5¼″			
☐ crystal	4.50	6.50	5.50
☐ pink	6.00	9.00	7.50
☐ green	5.50	8.50	7.00
☐ ice blue	7.50	11.00	9.00
Bowl, deep, round, diameter 6″			
☐ crystal	6.00	8.50	7.00
☐ pink	7.00	10.00	8.00
☐ green	6.75	9.50	7.50
☐ opalescent	13.00	17.00	14.00

	Current Price Range		Prior Year Average

Bowl, round, diameter 6¼"
☐ crystal	4.50	6.50	5.50
☐ pink	6.00	9.00	7.50
☐ green	5.50	8.50	7.00
☐ vaseline	11.50	15.50	12.50

Bowl, round, diameter 6½"
☐ crystal	4.50	6.50	5.50
☐ pink	6.00	9.00	7.50
☐ green	5.50	8.50	7.00
☐ ice blue	11.50	15.50	12.50

Bowl, two-handled, diameter 6½"
☐ crystal	7.50	10.00	8.00
☐ pink	8.50	12.00	10.00
☐ green	8.00	11.00	9.00
☐ opalescent	13.50	17.50	15.00

Bowl, round, flared edges, diameter 7¼"
☐ crystal	6.00	8.00	7.00
☐ pink	7.00	9.50	8.00
☐ green	6.50	9.00	7.50
☐ vaseline	12.00	15.00	13.50

Bowl, squared shape, length 5½"
☐ pink	5.00	7.00	5.50
☐ opalescent	7.00	10.00	8.00

Bowl, one handle, pointed, sharply curved, diameter 5¼"
☐ pink	5.50	8.00	6.00
☐ opalescent	7.00	10.00	8.00

Bowl, round, deep, diameter 6"
☐ pink	7.00	10.00	8.00
☐ opalescent	13.00	16.00	14.00

Bowl, round shape, flared, diameter 7¼"
☐ pink	6.50	9.50	7.25
☐ opalescent	13.00	16.00	14.00

Bowl, round, plain edge, diameter 7½"
☐ crystal	6.50	9.00	7.50
☐ pink	7.50	10.00	8.50
☐ green	7.00	9.50	8.00
☐ ice blue	14.00	17.00	15.50

Bowl, round, fluted edges, diameter 7½"
☐ crystal	12.00	15.00	13.00
☐ pink	14.00	20.00	17.00
☐ green	13.50	19.00	16.50
☐ opalescent	19.00	24.00	22.00

	Current Price Range		Prior Year Average

Celery Bowl, with a single row of blocks, diameter 8¼"

☐ crystal	7.00	11.00	8.00
☐ pink	8.00	12.00	9.00
☐ green	7.50	11.50	8.50
☐ vaseline...	12.50	16.00	14.50

Creamer, wide-lipped spout

☐ crystal	8.00	12.00	10.00
☐ pink	10.00	14.00	12.00
☐ green	9.50	13.00	11.00
☐ ice blue	17.00	22.00	20.00

Jelly, diameter 4½"

☐ crystal	6.00	8.00	7.00
☐ pink	7.00	10.00	8.00
☐ green	7.00	10.00	8.00
☐ opalescent	12.00	15.00	13.00

Jelly, flared top, diameter 4½"

☐ crystal	6.50	8.50	7.50
☐ pink	7.50	10.50	8.50
☐ green	7.50	10.50	8.50
☐ vaseline...	13.00	17.00	15.00

Pitcher, pint jug, wide-lipped spout, diameter 5"

☐ crystal	60.00	70.00	65.00
☐ pink	80.00	92.00	86.00
☐ green	77.00	90.00	85.00

Plate, square, 7¾"

☐ crystal	3.00	5.00	4.00
☐ pink	4.00	7.00	5.00
☐ green	4.00	6.00	5.00
☐ ice blue	7.00	10.00	8.00

Plate, round, 8¾"

☐ crystal	6.00	8.00	7.00
☐ pink	7.00	10.00	8.00
☐ green	6.50	9.00	7.50
☐ opalescent	13.00	16.00	14.00

Sugar

☐ crystal	8.00	10.50	9.00
☐ pink	10.00	14.00	12.00
☐ green	9.50	13.50	11.50
☐ vaseline...	16.00	20.00	18.00

	Current Price Range		Prior Year Average

Vase, bouquet, height 6″
☐ crystal	7.00	10.00	8.50
☐ pink	9.00	13.00	11.50
☐ green	9.00	13.00	11.50
☐ ice blue	15.00	20.00	17.00

BEADED EDGE
Westmoreland Glass Co.

   This pattern is technically not Depression era glass, but it is included here due to collector interest. *Beaded Edge* has been manufactured on and off since the middle 1920s. The first series that was released was the fruit series. All items are hand-painted and fired. More recently, the song bird series and the floral series have been released. All pieces can also be found with a colored band circling the rim. Values depend on the item, not the date of issue or the type (i.e. song bird or floral).

Bread and Butter Plate, diameter 6″
☐ plain or colored band.........................	4.00	5.50	4.50

Breakfast plate, diameter 7¼″
☐ plain or colored band.........................	5.00	7.50	6.00

Creamer, footed
☐ plain or colored band.........................	8.50	10.50	9.25

Cup
☐ plain or colored band.........................	6.00	7.50	6.25

Dinner Plate, diameter 10″
☐ plain or colored band.........................	8.50	10.00	9.00

Preserve Dish, scooped sides, diameter 8¼″
☐ plain or colored band.........................	8.50	10.00	9.00

Relish Dish, oval, compartmented, length 9½″
☐ plain or colored band.........................	15.50	18.00	16.00

Salad Plate, diameter 8½″
☐ plain or colored band.........................	7.50	9.00	8.00

Saucer
☐ plain or colored band.........................	4.00	5.50	4.25

Serving Plate, diameter 15″
☐ plain or colored band.........................	21.00	24.00	22.00

Sugar Bowl, footed
☐ plain or colored band.........................	8.50	10.00	9.00

	Current Price Range		Prior Year Average
Tumbler, footed, 9 oz., height 6½"			
☐ plain or colored band.........................	10.50	12.50	11.00

BLOCK OPTIC
Hocking Glass Co.

This pattern, also known simply as *Block*, was manufactured from 1929 through 1933. It was advertised as being "thin blown" glassware and many collectors enjoy its lightness. It was originally issued in green, crystal, pink and yellow. Green is the most plentiful and yellow the least. In 1931 Hocking also made some pieces in topaz. The sugar and creamer have been found with a satin-finished frosting. A blue butter dish has also been reported, but only one has been found. Footed and stemmed pieces were also made with black stems and feet. These include tumblers, goblets and sherbets. It remains as one of Depression glass' best performers. It always sells well and the price increases are steady. Crystal sells for about 20–30% less than pink.

Block Optic

Berry Bowl, diameter 4¼"			
☐ green...	3.50	5.50	4.00
☐ pink...	3.00	5.00	3.50
☐ crystal...	2.75	3.50	3.00

	Current Price Range		Prior Year Average

Berry Bowl, diameter 8″

☐ green	11.00	14.00	11.50
☐ pink	8.00	11.00	9.00
☐ yellow	15.00	19.00	16.00

Bowl, cereal, 5¼″

☐ green	7.00	10.00	8.00
☐ pink	4.00	7.00	5.50

Bowl, salad, 7″

☐ green	10.00	14.00	12.00
☐ pink	7.00	10.00	8.00
☐ yellow	13.00	17.00	14.50

Butter Dish, oblong

☐ green	15.00	19.00	16.00

Candlestick, height 1¾″

☐ green	35.00	45.00	40.00
☐ pink	27.00	35.00	32.00

Candy Jar, with cover, collar base, height 2¼″

☐ green	26.00	35.00	31.00
☐ pink	24.00	32.00	28.00
☐ yellow	37.50	45.00	41.00

Creamer, three styles: round, cone-shaped and footed

☐ green	8.00	10.50	9.00
☐ pink	7.00	10.00	8.50
☐ yellow	9.00	12.00	10.00
☐ topaz	8.50	11.00	10.00

Cup

☐ green	3.50	5.50	4.00
☐ pink	3.00	5.00	3.50
☐ yellow	5.00	8.00	6.00
☐ topaz	4.00	6.00	5.00

Goblet, cocktail, height 4″

☐ green	10.00	15.00	12.00
☐ pink	7.00	10.00	8.00

Goblet, wine, height 4½″

☐ green	10.00	15.00	12.00
☐ pink	7.00	10.00	8.00

Goblet, 9 oz., height 6″

☐ green	12.00	15.00	13.00
☐ pink	7.00	10.00	8.00

	Current Price Range		Prior Year Average
Goblet, 9 oz., height 7¼″			
☐ green	17.00	22.00	19.00
☐ pink	11.00	14.00	12.00
☐ yellow	16.00	20.00	17.00
☐ topaz	17.50	22.50	20.00
Ice Bucket			
☐ green	25.00	30.00	26.00
☐ pink	20.00	25.00	21.00
Mayonnaise Compote, height 4″			
☐ green	15.00	19.00	16.00
☐ pink	32.00	40.00	36.00
Pitcher, 54 oz., height 8½″			
☐ green	22.00	27.00	24.00
☐ pink	24.00	29.00	26.00
Pitcher, 64 oz., height 7½″			
☐ green	24.00	29.00	25.50
☐ pink	24.00	29.00	25.50
Pitcher, 80 oz., height 8″			
☐ green	34.00	39.00	35.50
☐ pink	30.00	35.00	31.00
Plate, sherbet, 6″			
☐ green	1.00	2.00	1.50
☐ pink	.75	1.75	1.25
☐ yellow	1.25	2.25	1.75
☐ topaz	1.25	2.25	1.75
Plate, luncheon, 8″			
☐ green	2.50	3.50	2.75
☐ pink	2.00	3.00	2.50
☐ yellow	2.75	3.75	3.25
☐ topaz	3.75	4.75	4.25
Plate, dinner, 9″			
☐ green	10.00	13.00	11.00
☐ pink	8.00	11.50	9.00
☐ yellow	17.00	22.00	20.00
☐ topaz	13.00	18.00	15.00
Plate, grill, 9″			
☐ green	6.00	9.00	7.00
☐ pink	6.00	9.00	7.00
☐ yellow	10.00	14.00	12.00
Plate, sandwich, 10″			
☐ green	11.00	15.00	13.00
☐ pink	10.00	14.00	12.00
☐ topaz	9.00	13.00	10.00

1930 Block Optic Catalog Sheet.
Courtesy of Anchor Hocking Corporation, Lancaster, Ohio

	Current Price Range		Prior Year Average
Salt and Pepper Shakers, collar base, squat			
☐ green	27.00	33.00	29.00
☐ pink	31.00	26.00	36.00
Salt and Pepper Shakers, footed			
☐ pink	39.00	44.00	41.00
☐ yellow	50.00	60.00	53.00
Sandwich Tray, center handle			
☐ green	33.00	38.00	36.00
Saucer, diameter 6″			
☐ green	6.00	8.00	6.50
☐ pink	3.00	5.50	4.00
☐ yellow	6.50	8.50	7.00
Sherbet, conical			
☐ green	2.00	4.00	2.50
☐ topaz	6.00	9.00	7.00
Sherbet, stemmed, diameter 3″			
☐ pink	3.00	4.00	3.50
☐ green	3.50	5.50	4.50
☐ yellow	6.00	9.00	6.50
Sherbet, diameter 4½″			
☐ pink	6.00	9.00	6.50
☐ green	8.00	11.00	9.00
☐ yellow	9.00	12.00	10.00
Sugar Bowl			
☐ pink	6.50	9.50	7.25
☐ green	6.50	9.50	7.25
☐ yellow	8.00	11.50	9.00
Tumbler, footed, 5 oz., height 4″			
☐ green	8.00	12.00	10.00
☐ pink	8.00	12.00	10.00
Tumbler, footed, 9 oz.			
☐ green	10.00	13.00	11.00
☐ pink	8.00	11.00	9.50
☐ yellow	11.00	14.50	12.50
Tumbler, ice tea, 10 oz.			
☐ green	11.00	15.00	12.50
☐ pink	6.00	9.00	7.00
Tumbler, ice tea, 14 oz.			
☐ green	14.00	18.00	16.00
☐ pink	12.00	16.00	14.00
Vase, blown, height 5¾″			
☐ green	125.00	165.00	145.00

	Current Price Range		Prior Year Average

Whiskey, 2½"
☐ green	13.00	17.00	15.00
☐ pink	12.00	16.00	13.50

BOWKNOT
Unknown Manufacturer

Not only were very few pieces of *Bowknot* made, but the manufacturer is unknown. The mold etched design features knotted bows and swags with medallions. The plate, sherbet and bowls have gently scalloped rims. Evidently this pattern was made only in green.

Berry Bowl, diameter 4½"
☐ green	6.50	9.50	7.25

Cereal Bowl, 5½"
☐ green	9.00	12.00	10.00

Cup
☐ green	3.50	5.50	4.00

Salad Plate, diameter 7"
☐ green	5.00	8.00	6.00

Sherbet
☐ green	6.50	9.50	7.50

Tumbler, flat, 10 oz.
☐ green	8.50	11.50	9.00

Tumbler, footed, 10 oz.
☐ green	8.50	11.50	9.00

BUBBLE
Anchor Hocking Glass Co.

This pattern was made from 1934 through 1965 and was sold under several names. The first item issued was a pink bowl called *Bullseye* in 1934. A table setting in crystal was offered in 1937 and heat proof *Fire-King* pieces in light blue were made from 1942 to 1948. Differing dates have been reported for a dark *Forest-Green* but it was probably made in 1954. The same pattern, this time referred to as *Provincial*, was made in milk-white in 1959 and then in red in 1963 through 1965. Collectors, however, know this pattern exclusively as *Bubble*. The main colors made were crystal, dark green, light blue, ruby red and a very small amount of pink. Pieces in almost every color Anchor Hocking used have been reported but these are exceptional and are not very collectible. The pattern is made up of an overall series of raised bubble-like shapes in horizontal rows. A rayed design is contained within the circular center of the bowls and plates. The edges are scalloped, except for

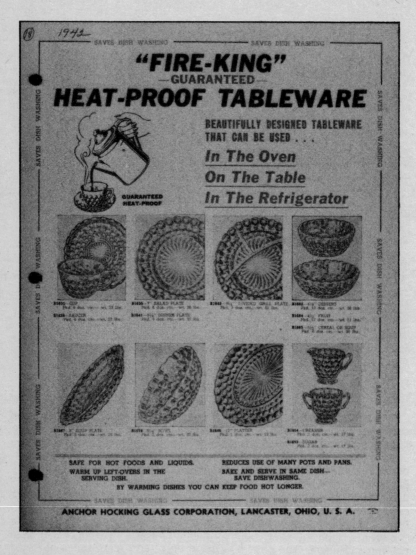

1942 Bubble Catalog Sheet.
Courtesy of Anchor Hocking Corporation, Lancaster, Ohio

the cups. The flange-edged bowls are rare as are many of the light blue pieces. Crystal sells for about half of the price of the blue.

Bubble

	Current Price Range		Prior Year Average
Bowl, berry, diameter 4″			
☐ green	3.00	4.00	3.00
☐ blue	8.00	11.00	9.00
☐ crystal	2.00	3.00	2.40
Bowl, berry, diameter 4½″			
☐ green	2.75	3.75	3.25
☐ blue	6.00	8.00	7.25
☐ red	3.00	4.25	3.50
☐ crystal	1.50	2.50	2.00
Bowl, berry, diameter 8⅜″			
☐ green	5.00	8.00	6.50
☐ blue	7.00	10.00	8.00
☐ red	4.00	7.00	5.00
☐ crystal	3.00	4.50	3.75
Bowl, cereal, 5¼″			
☐ green	2.75	3.75	3.25
☐ blue	6.00	8.00	7.25
☐ crystal	1.50	2.50	2.00
Bowl, flat soup, 7¾″			
☐ blue	6.00	8.50	7.00
☐ crystal	2.75	4.00	3.25

	Current Price Range		Prior Year Average
Bread and Butter Plate, cover, height 4″			
☐ blue	1.50	3.50	2.00
☐ green	.75	2.50	1.00
Cereal Bowl, diameter 5″			
☐ green	4.00	6.00	4.50
☐ blue	5.00	8.00	6.00
Creamer			
☐ green	5.00	7.00	5.50
☐ blue	15.00	19.00	16.00
Cup			
☐ green	5.00	7.00	5.50
☐ red	3.00	5.00	3.50
☐ blue	2.00	4.00	2.50
Fruit Bowl			
☐ green	4.00	6.00	4.50
☐ blue	5.00	7.00	5.50
☐ red	3.00	5.00	3.50
Grill Plate			
☐ blue	6.00	9.00	6.50
Juice Tumbler			
☐ red	5.00	7.00	5.50
Lemonade Tumbler, height 8″			
☐ red	12.00	15.00	12.75
Platter, oval, length 12″			
☐ blue	7.00	11.00	7.75
Saucer			
☐ green	.50	1.50	.75
☐ red	.75	2.50	1.00
☐ blue	.75	2.50	1.00
☐ pink	15.00	19.00	16.00
Soup Bowl, shallow, diameter 7″			
☐ blue	7.00	9.00	7.50
Tumbler, height 9″			
☐ red	4.00	7.00	4.75

CAMEO
Hocking Glass Co.

Cameo was manufactured from 1930 through 1934. It's also known as *Ballerina* and *Dancing Girl*, but *Cameo* is the most popular name. It was made in green, pink, yellow and crystal with a platinun ring. Pink is the hardest to find and can be quite costly. The salt shakers were reproduced but the new ones are easy to spot. The pattern is weaker, there is more glass on the bottom, and the tops are brand new. The children's dishes are also new, but since none were made originally, they're also no problem to detect.

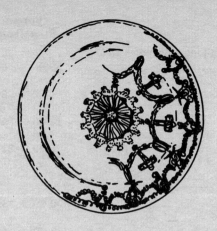

Cameo

	Current Price Range		Prior Year Average
Berry Bowl, diameter 8¾″			
☐ green	21.00	27.00	22.50
Bowl, sauce, diameter 4½″			
☐ crystal	4.00	5.25	4.60
Bowl, cream soup, diameter 4¾″			
☐ green	45.00	55.00	50.00
Bowl, cereal, diameter 5½″			
☐ green	20.00	25.00	21.50
☐ yellow	22.00	27.00	24.00
☐ crystal	4.00	6.00	5.00
Bowl, salad, diameter 7¼″			
☐ green	32.50	42.50	37.50
Bowl, flat soup, 9″			
☐ green	34.00	42.00	37.00
Bowl, oval vegetable, diameter 10″			
☐ green	13.00	16.00	14.00
☐ yellow	25.00	31.00	27.00
Bowl, console, three-legged, diameter 11″			
☐ green	35.00	45.00	38.00
☐ yellow	47.00	57.00	52.00
☐ pink	16.00	21.00	17.00
☐ crystal	14.00	19.00	15.00
Butter Dish, lidded			
☐ green	210.00	260.00	230.00
☐ yellow	700.00	1,100.00	950.00
Cake Plate, three legs, diameter 10″			
☐ green	12.00	16.00	13.00

	Current Price Range		Prior Year Average
Cake Plate, without legs, diameter 10½″			
☐ green	50.00	65.00	53.00
Candlesticks, pair, height 4″			
☐ green	60.00	80.00	70.00
Candy Jar, cover, height 4″			
☐ green	33.00	45.00	38.00
☐ yellow	45.00	55.00	47.00
☐ pink	325.00	375.00	340.00
Candy Jar, cover, height 6½″			
☐ green	85.00	95.00	97.00
Cocktail Shaker, metal lid			
☐ crystal	300.00	335.00	315.00
Cookie Jar, lidded			
☐ green	32.00	40.00	35.00
Cordial Goblet, height 3½″			
☐ green	150.00	170.00	155.00
Creamer, height 3¼″			
☐ green	15.00	19.00	15.75
☐ yellow	10.50	14.00	11.50
Creamer, height 4¼″			
☐ green	14.00	18.00	15.00
Cup			
☐ green	9.00	13.00	10.00
☐ yellow	5.50	7.50	6.00
☐ pink	47.00	53.00	49.00
Decanter, stoppered, height 10″			
☐ green	75.00	90.00	79.00
Dinner Plate, diameter 9½″			
☐ green	12.00	15.00	13.00
☐ yellow	5.00	7.00	5.50
☐ pink	25.00	35.00	27.50
Grill Plate, diameter 10½″			
☐ green	6.00	8.00	6.50
☐ yellow	5.00	7.00	5.50
☐ pink	29.00	34.00	31.00
Grill Plate, closed handles, diameter 10½″			
☐ green	44.00	54.00	45.50
☐ yellow	4.00	6.50	5.00
Ice Bowl, diameter 5½″			
☐ green	93.00	105.00	95.00
☐ pink	380.00	420.00	390.00
☐ crystal	160.00	200.00	170.00
Jam Jar, lidded, height 2″			
☐ green	82.00	95.00	85.00

	Current Price Range		Prior Year Average
Juice Pitcher, 36 oz., height 6″			
☐ green	35.00	45.00	37.00
Juice Tumbler, 5 oz., height 3¾″			
☐ green	16.00	20.00	17.50
☐ pink	55.00	65.00	67.00
Luncheon Plate, diameter 8″			
☐ green	6.00	8.00	6.50
☐ yellow	1.50	3.50	2.00
☐ pink	20.00	26.00	21.50
☐ crystal	2.50	4.50	3.00
Mayonnaise Bowl, wide, diameter 5″			
☐ green	17.00	21.00	18.00
Plate, with closed handles, diameter 11½″			
☐ green	5.50	7.50	6.00
☐ yellow	4.00	6.00	4.50
Platter, closed handles, length 12″			
☐ green	12.00	15.00	13.00
☐ yellow	12.00	15.00	13.00
Relish Dish, three compartments, footed, diameter 7½″			
☐ green	14.00	17.00	15.00
Salad Plate, diameter 7″			
☐ crystal	2.00	4.00	2.50
Salt and Pepper Shakers, footed, height 7½″			
☐ green	45.00	55.00	47.00
☐ pink	475.00	525.00	490.00
Sandwich Plate, diameter 10″			
☐ green	8.00	11.50	9.00
☐ pink	27.00	33.00	29.00
Saucer, cup ring			
☐ green	71.00	78.00	72.50
Sherbet, diameter 3⅛″			
☐ green	9.50	12.50	10.50
☐ yellow	13.00	16.00	14.00
☐ pink	21.00	27.00	22.50
Sherbet, diameter 4⅞″			
☐ green	20.00	25.00	21.50
☐ yellow	25.00	30.00	27.00
☐ pink	48.00	58.00	53.00
☐ crystal	20.00	25.00	22.00

1930 Cameo Catalog Sheet.
Courtesy of Anchor Hocking Corporation, Lancaster, Ohio

	Current Price Range		Prior Year Average
Sherbet Plate, diameter 6″			
☐ green	2.00	4.00	2.50
☐ yellow	1.00	3.00	1.50
☐ pink	41.00	48.00	42.00
☐ crystal	2.50	3.50	3.00
Sugar Bowl, diameter 3¼″			
☐ green	9.00	13.00	10.50
Sugar Bowl, diameter 4¼″			
☐ green	15.00	18.00	16.00
☐ pink	55.00	65.00	60.00
Syrup Pitcher, 20 oz., height 5¾″			
☐ green	128.00	142.00	133.00
☐ yellow	290.00	370.00	340.00
Tray, with indentations, length 7″			
☐ green	60.00	75.00	64.00
Tray, without indentations, length 7″			
☐ pink	140.00	155.00	143.00
☐ crystal	80.00	95.00	84.00
Tumbler, footed, 3 oz.			
☐ green	45.00	54.00	49.00
☐ pink	70.00	90.00	80.00
☐ crystal	30.00	45.00	35.00
Tumbler, footed, 9 oz., height 5″			
☐ green	18.00	23.00	20.00
☐ yellow	14.00	17.50	15.00
☐ pink	70.00	80.00	73.00
Tumbler, flat, 10 oz., height 4¾″			
☐ green	18.00	22.00	19.00
Tumbler, flat, 11 oz., height 5″			
☐ green	22.00	27.00	25.00
☐ yellow	52.00	60.00	55.00
☐ pink	60.00	70.00	64.00
Tumbler, footed, 11 oz., height 5¾″			
☐ green	34.00	42.00	38.00
Tumbler, flat, 15 oz., height 5¼″			
☐ green	40.00	46.00	42.50
Tumbler, footed, 15 oz., height 6⅜″			
☐ green	125.00	155.00	140.00
Vase, height 5¾″			
☐ green	95.00	120.00	110.00
Vase, height 8″			
☐ green	19.00	23.00	20.50
Water Bottle, cork stopper			
☐ green	18.00	23.00	21.00

	Current Price Range		Prior Year Average
Water Goblet, height 6″			
☐ green	32.00	38.00	33.50
☐ pink	90.00	115.00	100.00
Water Pitcher, 56 oz., height 8½″			
☐ green	40.00	47.00	42.00
Water Tumbler, 9 oz., height 4″			
☐ green	16.00	20.50	17.00
☐ pink	57.00	63.00	59.00
☐ crystal	6.00	9.00	7.00
Wine Goblet, height 4″			
☐ green	60.00	67.00	62.00
☐ pink	140.00	165.00	155.00

CHERRY BLOSSOM
Jeannette Glass Co.

Jeannette made *Cherry Blossom* from 1930 through 1938. The colors were green, pink, delphite (opaque blue), a small amount of crystal and some jadeite (opaque green). Pink is the most common. Green was made only up until 1935 and there isn't a whole lot of it around. Delphite was first made in 1936 and not much was produced, but it is highly collectible. In the early sets, the footed pieces had round edges on the feet, but later items had scalloped bases. *Cherry Blossom* is definitely one of the top patterns in all of Depression glass. As such, it is also one of the most reproduced. Some of the more common reproductions are the shakers, pitchers, a 12″ tray, the tumblers, a 7″ pitcher, a child's cup and saucer, and a covered butter dish. The shakers are the easiest to detect because there's about twice as much solid glass on the bottom than on the original. The pitcher is also easy to spot because there are only seven cherries on the underside compared to nine on the original. The new tumblers have only one ring around the rim as opposed to the three on the original. On the butter dishes, there is only one band around the bottom of the butter top. On the old dishes, there are two. There are also some cobalt blue butter dishes around and these are no problem since that color wasn't made originally. The tray is not that easy to spot, but there are differences. The new one is heavier, it's a lighter pink, the bottom is thicker, and it's of poorer quality all around. The children's set is available in pink and delphite reproductions. The colors are not quite right, though, and the pattern is weak and off center.

Berry Bowl, diameter 4¾″			
☐ pink	10.00	14.00	11.50
☐ green	11.00	16.00	13.00
☐ delphite	9.00	13.00	10.00

	Current Price Range		Prior Year Average
Berry Bowl, circular, diameter 8½″			
☐ pink	13.00	17.00	14.00
☐ green	14.00	18.00	15.00
☐ delphite	35.00	44.00	36.00
Bowl, cereal, diameter 5¾″			
☐ pink	22.00	28.00	25.00
☐ green	25.00	30.00	27.00
Bowl, flat soup, diameter 7¾″			
☐ pink	30.00	38.00	32.00
☐ green	40.00	50.00	44.00
Bowl, twin handled, diameter 9″			
☐ pink	12.00	15.00	13.00
☐ green	15.00	19.00	16.00
☐ delphite	11.00	14.00	11.75
☐ jadeite	240.00	285.00	255.00
Bowl, oval vegetable, length 9″			
☐ pink	24.00	30.00	27.00
☐ green	30.00	36.00	33.00
☐ delphite	40.00	50.00	45.00
Bowl, fruit, 3 legged, diameter 10½″			
☐ pink	42.00	50.00	46.00
☐ green	50.00	56.00	52.00
☐ jadeite	250.00	290.00	260.00
Butter Dish, lidded			
☐ pink	60.00	70.00	63.00
☐ green	70.00	80.00	73.00
Cake Plate, three legged, diameter 10¼″			
☐ pink	13.00	17.00	14.00
☐ green	14.00	18.00	15.00
Coaster			
☐ green	11.00	15.00	13.00
☐ pink	8.00	12.00	9.00
Creamer, lidded			
☐ pink	10.00	12.00	10.50
☐ green	11.50	14.50	12.00
☐ delphite	14.00	18.00	15.00
Cup			
☐ pink	11.00	15.00	12.00
☐ green	11.50	15.50	12.50
☐ delphite	12.00	16.00	13.00
Dinner Plate, diameter 9″			
☐ pink	11.00	14.00	12.00
☐ green	13.00	16.00	13.50
☐ delphite	10.50	13.50	11.50
☐ jadeite	28.00	35.00	30.00

	Current Price Range		Prior Year Average
Grill Plate, diameter 9″			
☐ pink	14.00	18.00	15.00
☐ green	16.00	19.00	17.00
Grill Plate, diameter 10″			
☐ green	37.00	44.00	39.00
Mug, 7 oz.			
☐ pink	130.00	145.00	137.00
☐ green	125.00	142.00	131.00
Pitcher, flat, 42 oz., height 8″			
☐ pink	25.00	34.00	27.00
☐ green	32.00	42.00	35.00
Pitcher, footed, 36 oz., height 8″			
☐ pink	31.00	39.00	32.50
☐ green	37.00	47.00	39.00
☐ delphite	75.00	85.00	77.00
Pitcher, scalloped base, 36 oz., height 6¾″			
☐ pink	27.00	36.00	29.00
☐ green	34.00	44.00	37.00
Pitcher, round base, 36 oz., height 6¾″			
☐ pink	27.00	36.00	29.00
☐ green	34.00	44.00	37.00
Platter, divided, diameter 13″			
☐ pink	30.00	40.00	32.00
☐ green	33.00	43.00	35.00
Platter, oval, length 9″			
☐ pink	600.00	630.00	614.00
Platter, oval, length 11″			
☐ pink	18.00	23.00	19.00
☐ green	20.00	25.00	21.00
☐ delphite	27.00	33.00	29.00
Salad Plate, diameter 7″			
☐ pink	12.00	15.00	13.00
☐ green	14.00	17.00	15.00
Salt and Pepper Shakers, scalloped base			
☐ pink	1,500.00	2,000.00	1,700.00
☐ green	700.00	1,000.00	850.00
Saucer			
☐ pink	3.00	5.00	3.50
☐ green	4.50	6.50	5.50
☐ delphite	3.50	5.25	4.50
Sherbet			
☐ pink	10.00	14.00	12.00
☐ green	12.00	16.00	14.00
☐ delphite	11.00	15.00	13.00

	Current Price Range		Prior Year Average

Sherbet Plate, diameter 6″

☐ pink	4.00	6.50	5.00
☐ green	4.50	9.00	7.50
☐ delphite	7.50	10.50	9.50

Sugar Bowl

☐ pink	15.00	20.00	17.00
☐ green	19.00	24.00	21.00
☐ delphite	22.00	27.50	24.50

Tray, handled, length 10″

☐ pink	13.00	17.00	15.00
☐ green	15.00	19.00	17.00
☐ delphite	14.00	18.50	16.00

Tumbler, flat, 4 oz., height 3½″

☐ pink	12.00	15.00	13.00
☐ green	14.00	18.00	15.00

Tumbler, footed, round base, 4 oz., height 3¾″

☐ pink	12.00	16.00	14.00
☐ green	17.00	23.00	20.00
☐ delphite	14.00	19.00	17.00

Tumbler, footed, scalloped base, 4 oz., height 3¾″

☐ pink	10.00	13.00	11.00
☐ green	14.00	17.00	15.00
☐ delphite	14.00	18.00	15.00

Tumbler, scalloped foot, 8 oz., height 4½″

☐ pink	20.00	26.00	22.00
☐ green	22.00	29.00	25.00
☐ delphite	15.00	19.00	16.00

Tumbler, flat, 9 oz., height 4½″

☐ pink	14.00	19.00	17.00
☐ green	15.00	20.00	18.00

Tumbler, round foot, 9 oz., height 4½″

☐ pink	20.00	25.00	21.00
☐ green	22.00	29.00	25.00
☐ delphite	14.00	18.00	15.00

Tumbler, flat, 12 oz., height 5″

☐ pink	35.00	43.00	38.00
☐ green	45.00	52.00	47.00

CHINEX
Macbeth-Evans Division of Corning Glass Works

This pattern was made from about 1937 through 1942. It is not at all easy to find pieces in *Chinex* (also known as *Chinex Classic*) and many people feel it's too difficult to collect. It is, however, a very attractive pattern. It is sometimes confused with *Cremax*, another decal decorated Macbeth-Evans pattern. The giveaway is the scroll design on the dishes and the color. *Chinex* is a real ivory while *Cremax* is much whiter. Both patterns strongly resemble china. *Chinex* is also available (and very popular) with a brown castle decal decoration. This is probably the hardest to find. The floral decals are more common, although still not easy to find.

	Current Price Range		Prior Year Average
Bowl, cereal, diameter 5″			
☐ ivory, plain	4.25	6.25	5.00
☐ decorated	5.00	7.50	6.00
Bowl, vegetable, diameter 7″			
☐ ivory, plain	12.00	16.00	14.00
☐ decorated	14.00	17.50	16.00
Bowl, soup, diameter 7¾″			
☐ ivory, plain	10.00	15.00	12.00
☐ decorated	13.00	17.00	15.00
Bowl, diameter 9″			
☐ ivory	10.00	14.00	11.50
☐ decorated	13.00	17.50	15.00
Bowl, diameter 11″			
☐ ivory	15.00	21.00	18.00
☐ decorated	22.00	28.00	25.00
Butter Dish			
☐ ivory, plain	45.00	55.00	47.00
☐ decorated	57.00	67.00	60.00
Butter Dish Top			
☐ ivory, plain	35.00	45.00	40.00
☐ decorated	40.00	50.00	45.00
Butter Dish Bottom			
☐ ivory, plain	8.00	14.00	10.00
☐ decorated	14.00	20.00	17.00
Creamer			
☐ ivory, plain	3.00	6.00	3.50
☐ decorated	6.00	8.00	6.50
Cup			
☐ ivory, plain	2.50	4.50	3.00
☐ decorated	3.50	5.50	4.00
Dinner Plate, diameter 9¾″			
☐ ivory, plain	2.50	4.50	3.00
☐ decorated	4.00	6.00	4.50
Sandwich Plate, diameter 11½″			
☐ ivory, plain	5.00	8.00	5.75
☐ decorated	6.50	9.50	7.25

	Current Price Range		Prior Year Average
Saucer			
☐ ivory, plain	1.00	3.00	1.50
☐ decorated	2.50	4.50	3.00
Sherbet Plate, diameter 6¼″			
☐ ivory, plain	1.00	3.00	1.50
☐ decorated	1.50	3.50	2.00
Sugar Bowl			
☐ ivory, plain	3.00	5.00	3.50
☐ decorated	5.50	8.50	6.00

CIRCLE
Hocking Glass Co.

Circle was produced during the 1930s. More and more of it turns up on the market as the years go by. During the 1970s, green was all you could find, but now, more and more pink is showing up. It is possible, also, that some crystal exists since it is listed in some early catalogs, but so far none have been reported. Some pieces have the center ray design and some do not. It's still *Circle* either way. The green is still much more common than the pink, but prices are about the same for either.

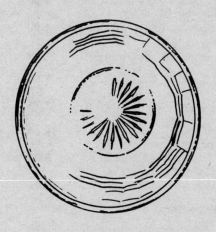

Circle

	Current Price Range		Prior Year Average
Bowl, diameter 4½″			
☐ green or pink....................................	2.50	4.00	3.35
Bowl, diameter 8½″			
☐ green or pink....................................	4.50	7.00	5.00
Creamer			
☐ green or pink....................................	4.00	6.00	5.00
Cup (2 styles)			
☐ green or pink....................................	2.00	4.00	3.00
Decanter, handled			
☐ green or pink....................................	15.00	20.00	17.50
Dinner Plate, diameter 9½″			
☐ green or pink....................................	4.50	7.50	5.25
Juice Tumbler, 4 oz.			
☐ green or pink....................................	2.50	4.50	3.00
Luncheon Plate, diameter 8¼″			
☐ green or pink....................................	3.50	5.00	4.00
Pitcher, 80 oz.			
☐ green or pink....................................	15.00	19.00	16.00
Saucer			
☐ green or pink....................................	.50	1.75	.75
Sherbet, diameter 3⅛″			
☐ green or pink....................................	2.50	4.50	3.00
Sherbet, diameter 4¾″			
☐ green or pink....................................	3.50	5.50	4.00
Sherbet Plate, diameter 6″			
☐ green or pink....................................	1.00	3.00	1.50
Sugar Bowl			
☐ green or pink....................................	4.00	6.00	4.50
Tumbler, 4 oz.			
☐ green or pink....................................	2.50	3.50	3.00
Tumbler, 8 oz.			
☐ green or pink....................................	3.75	5.00	4.50
Vase, hat shape			
☐ green or pink....................................	30.00	40.00	34.00
Water Goblet, 8 oz.			
☐ green or pink....................................	5.00	7.25	6.00
Wine Goblet, height 4½″			
☐ green or pink....................................	3.00	5.00	3.50

CLOVERLEAF
Hazel Atlas Glass Co.

Cloverleaf was made from 1930 through 1936. The colors issued were black, green, pink, yellow and crystal. It's not easy to find in any color but black is probably the scarcest and most desirable. The black saucer doesn't bear the design in the center but the sherbet plate does. Hazel Atlas listed a black candy dish but it is doubtful whether one exists. A green frosted candy dish was reported, but so far is one of a kind.

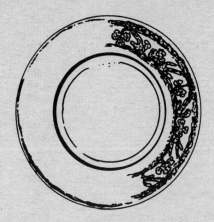

Cloverleaf

	Current Price Range		Prior Year Average
Ashtray, with match holder, diameter 4″			
☐ black	50.00	60.00	52.00
Ashtray, with match holder, diameter 5¾″			
☐ black	70.00	82.00	76.00
Bowl, deep, diameter 8″			
☐ green	37.00	47.00	39.00
Candy Dish, with cover			
☐ yellow	80.00	100.00	88.00
☐ green	35.00	43.00	38.00
Cereal Bowl, straight sides, diameter 5″			
☐ yellow	18.00	23.00	19.00
☐ green	15.00	20.00	17.00
Creamer, footed, height 3⅝″			
☐ yellow	11.00	14.00	11.50
☐ black	12.00	15.00	12.50
☐ green	6.00	8.50	6.50
Cup			
☐ black	8.00	11.00	8.50
☐ pink	4.00	6.00	4.50
☐ green	4.50	6.50	5.00
Dessert Bowl, diameter 4″			
☐ green	11.00	14.00	11.50
☐ yellow	14.00	18.00	15.00

	Current Price Range		Prior Year Average
Grill Plate, diameter 10¼"			
☐ green	13.00	17.00	14.00
☐ yellow	15.00	19.00	16.00
Luncheon Plate, diameter 8"			
☐ green	4.00	6.00	4.50
☐ pink	4.00	6.00	4.50
☐ yellow	8.00	12.00	9.00
☐ black	8.50	12.50	9.50
Salad Bowl, deep, diameter 7"			
☐ green	20.00	25.00	21.00
☐ yellow	33.00	40.00	35.00
Salt and Pepper Shakers			
☐ green	20.00	25.00	21.00
☐ yellow	75.00	85.00	78.00
☐ black	48.00	55.00	50.00
Saucer			
☐ yellow	2.00	4.00	2.50
☐ black	2.00	4.00	2.50
☐ pink	1.00	3.00	1.50
☐ green	1.50	3.50	2.00
Sherbet, footed, diameter 3"			
☐ green	3.50	5.50	4.00
☐ pink	4.00	6.00	4.50
☐ yellow	7.00	10.00	8.00
☐ black	11.00	14.00	12.00
Sugar Bowl, footed, diameter 3½"			
☐ green	6.00	8.50	6.50
☐ yellow	11.00	14.00	12.00
☐ black	11.00	14.00	12.00
Tumbler, flat, 8 oz., height 3¾"			
☐ green	25.00	31.00	27.00
☐ pink	16.00	22.00	18.00
Tumbler, flat, 9 oz., height 4"			
☐ green	22.00	32.00	26.00
☐ pink	10.00	14.00	11.00
Tumbler, footed, 10 oz., height 5¾"			
☐ green	14.00	19.00	17.00
☐ yellow	18.00	22.00	20.00

COLONIAL
Hocking Glass Co.

Colonial was made from 1934 to 1938. It strongly resembles the pressed glass pattern *Knife and Fork* that is so traditionally associated with early America table settings. The colors were crystal, green and pink. Crystal is the most common and green the least. A cup and saucer have been reported in milk-white and also a 9″ plate. Crystal with gold or platinum trim has also been reported. The small tumblers are still relatively easy to find (especially the whiskey), as are the green cups and saucers. The 4½″ berry bowl is also not too difficult. Some items are disappearing rapidly, however. The big tumblers, the cereal bowl, the soup bowl and the green dinner plates are all much harder to find than they used to be. It's not a plentiful pattern on the market, but a collection can be built with some patience.

Colonial

	Current Price Range		Prior Year Average
Berry Bowl, diameter 4½″			
☐ crystal	2.50	4.50	3.00
☐ green	7.00	10.00	8.00
☐ pink	5.00	8.00	6.00
Berry Bowl, diameter 9″			
☐ crystal	5.00	8.00	6.75
☐ pink	8.00	11.00	9.50
☐ green	10.00	13.00	11.50
Bowl, berry, diameter 3¾″			
☐ green	18.00	23.00	20.00
☐ pink	16.00	21.00	18.00
Bowl, cream soup, diameter 4¾″			
☐ crystal	15.00	19.00	16.00
☐ pink	30.00	35.00	32.00
☐ green	35.00	40.00	37.00
Bowl, cereal, diameter 5½″			
☐ crystal	11.00	16.00	13.00
☐ pink	22.00	27.00	23.00
☐ green	35.00	41.00	37.50

	Current Price Range		Prior Year Average
Bowl, flat soup, diameter 7″			
☐ crystal	14.00	20.00	16.00
☐ pink	25.00	30.00	25.00
☐ green	38.00	45.00	40.00
Bowl, oval vegetable, diameter 10″			
☐ crystal	12.00	17.00	14.00
☐ pink	23.00	28.00	24.00
☐ green	35.00	40.00	37.00
Butter Dish, with cover			
☐ pink	430.00	470.00	440.00
☐ green	38.00	46.00	40.00
Celery Holder			
☐ pink	72.00	82.00	74.00
☐ green	80.00	90.00	83.00
Cheese Dish			
☐ green	72.00	82.00	74.00
Cup			
☐ pink	4.50	7.50	5.25
☐ green	7.00	10.00	8.00
☐ milk glass	5.50	8.50	6.25
Dinner Plate, diameter 10″			
☐ pink	20.00	25.00	21.00
☐ green	36.00	45.00	37.00
Goblet, 3 oz., cocktail, height 4″			
☐ crystal	9.00	13.00	12.00
☐ green	20.00	25.00	21.00
Goblet, 4 oz., claret, height 5¼″			
☐ crystal	9.00	14.00	12.00
☐ green	21.00	26.00	23.00
Goblet, 8 oz., water, height 5¾″			
☐ crystal	10.00	15.00	12.00
☐ green	22.00	27.00	24.00
Grill Plate, diameter 10″			
☐ pink	13.00	17.00	14.00
☐ green	16.00	19.00	17.00
Iced Tea Glass, 12 oz.			
☐ pink	18.00	22.00	19.00
☐ green	27.00	33.00	29.00
Juice Glass, 5 oz., height 3″			
☐ pink	7.50	11.50	8.25
☐ green	13.00	17.00	14.00
Luncheon Plate, diameter 8½″			
☐ pink	4.00	6.50	5.00
☐ green	4.50	7.00	5.50

	Current Price Range		Prior Year Average
Mug, 12 oz., height 4½"			
☐ pink	140.00	160.00	145.00
Pitcher, 54 oz., height 7"			
☐ pink	29.00	34.50	31.50
Pitcher, ice lip, 54 oz., height 7"			
☐ pink	29.00	34.50	31.50
☐ green	31.00	38.00	32.50
Pitcher, ice lip, 68 oz., height 7¾"			
☐ pink	32.00	38.00	33.50
☐ green	43.00	51.00	45.00
Pitcher, 68 oz., height 7¾"			
☐ pink	32.00	38.00	33.50
☐ green	43.00	51.00	45.00
Platter, oval, length 12"			
☐ pink	11.00	15.00	12.00
☐ green	13.00	16.50	14.00
Salt and Pepper Shakers			
☐ crystal	40.00	50.00	45.00
☐ pink	95.00	105.00	97.00
☐ green	105.00	115.00	108.00
Saucer			
☐ pink	2.50	4.50	3.00
☐ green	2.50	4.50	3.00
☐ milk glass	2.00	4.00	2.50
Sugar Bowl, diameter 5"			
☐ pink	8.50	11.50	9.00
☐ green	9.50	12.50	10.00
Tumbler, footed, 3 oz., height 3¼"			
☐ pink	8.50	11.50	9.25
☐ green	13.00	17.00	14.00
Tumbler, 5 oz., flat, height 3"			
☐ crystal	7.00	10.00	8.00
☐ pink	9.00	13.00	10.00
☐ green	23.00	27.00	24.50
Tumbler, footed, 5 oz., height 4"			
☐ pink	11.00	14.50	12.00
☐ green	16.00	22.00	17.00
☐ crystal	7.00	10.00	8.00
Tumbler, 9 oz., flat, height 4"			
☐ crystal	7.00	10.00	8.50
☐ pink	8.00	12.00	10.00
☐ green	23.00	28.00	25.00

	Current Price Range		Prior Year Average
Tumbler, 10 oz., flat			
☐ crystal	11.00	15.00	12.50
☐ pink	17.00	23.00	19.00
☐ green	25.00	30.00	27.00
Tumbler, 10 oz., footed, height 5¼″			
☐ crystal	14.00	18.00	16.00
☐ pink	18.00	23.00	20.00
☐ green	34.00	40.00	37.00
Tumbler, 12 oz., ice tea			
☐ crystal	16.00	20.00	18.00
☐ pink	27.00	33.00	30.00
☐ green	38.00	44.00	40.00
Tumbler, 15 oz., lemonade			
☐ crystal	26.00	32.00	29.00
☐ pink	30.00	38.00	35.00
☐ green	65.00	75.00	70.00
Whiskey Glass, 1½ oz., height 2½″			
☐ crystal	3.00	5.00	4.00
☐ pink	6.00	8.00	6.50
☐ green	7.50	10.50	8.25
Wine Glass, 2½ oz., height 4½″			
☐ green	16.00	22.00	17.50

COLONIAL BLOCK

Hazel Atlas Glass Co.

Colonial Block was made during the early 1930s. It's a small pattern, but it is popular. A common mistake, and probably the reason people first noticed this pattern, was that many collectors thought they had finally found a *Block Optic* round butter dish. They hadn't; it was *Colonial Block*, but it got people to look at this pattern. The glassware itself is medium-thin and has a basic paneled block design, smooth edges, domed covers and star-motif bottoms. The pitcher and the goblet were previously thought to have been made by U.S. Glass, but this is now a point of contention. Either way, they fit into a table display very well. The creamer and the lidded sugar have been reported in milk-white, but no other pieces have surfaced. They were presumably made after the other colors, green and pink, were discontinued.

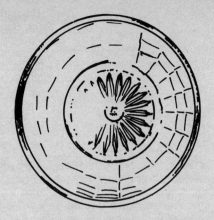

Colonial Block

	Current Price Range		Prior Year Average
Bowl, diameter 4″			
☐ pink	4.00	6.00	4.50
☐ green	4.00	6.00	4.50
Bowl, diameter 7″			
☐ pink	10.00	13.00	10.75
☐ green	10.00	13.00	10.75
Butter Dish			
☐ pink	24.00	33.00	25.00
☐ green	24.00	33.00	25.00
Butter Tub			
☐ pink	30.00	35.00	32.00
☐ green	30.00	35.00	32.00
Candy Jar, with cover			
☐ pink	22.00	28.00	23.50
☐ green	22.00	28.00	23.50
Creamer			
☐ pink	6.00	9.00	6.75
☐ green	6.00	9.00	6.75
☐ white	5.00	8.00	7.50
Goblet			
☐ pink	9.00	13.00	10.50
☐ green	9.00	13.00	10.00
Pitcher			
☐ pink	28.00	34.00	31.00
☐ green	28.00	34.00	31.00

	Current Price Range		Prior Year Average
Sugar Bowl			
☐ pink	6.00	9.00	6.75
☐ green	6.00	9.00	6.75

COLONIAL FLUTED
Federal Glass Co.

Federal made this line in the late 1920s through the early 1930s. It is often referred to simply as *Rope*. It is a luncheon set and basically the only color you will find is green. A few pieces in pink and some in crystal have been found, but only a few. The pattern is typified by a fluted panel design with roping around the edge. A dinner plate in this pattern has been searched for, but probably does not exist. There are dinner plates on the market that have the rope design but not the panels. Other dinner plates have the panels but no roping. These can be used in a setting with good results even though neither is truly *Colonial Fluted*.

Colonial Fluted

Berry Bowl, diameter 4″			
☐ green	3.00	5.00	3.50
Berry Bowl, diameter 7½″			
☐ green	7.50	10.50	8.25
Bowl, cereal, diameter 6″			
☐ green	4.75	7.00	6.00
Bowl, salad, diameter 6½″			
☐ green	11.00	15.00	13.00

	Current Price Range		Prior Year Average
Creamer			
☐ green	3.50	5.50	4.00
Cup			
☐ green	2.50	4.50	3.00
Plate, sherbet, diameter 6″			
☐ green	1.00	2.00	1.50
Plate, luncheon, diameter 8″			
☐ green	2.00	3.50	2.75
Plate, dinner, diameter 9½″			
☐ green	7.00	10.00	8.00
Saucer			
☐ green	.75	2.50	1.00
Sherbet Bowl			
☐ green	3.50	5.50	4.00
Sugar Bowl			
☐ green	2.50	4.50	3.00

COLUMBIA
Federal Glass Co.

Federal made *Columbia* for four years, from 1938 through 1942. It was first manufactured in pink, but the company soon switched over to crystal. Very little in pink is now available. The butter dishes are found with flashed-on red, green and iridescent. The tops are decal-decorated. It is not difficult to build a full collection in *Columbia*, especially the crystal. Prices are low and the supply is generally good.

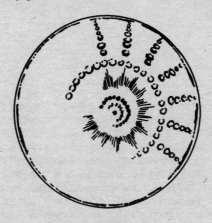

Columbia

	Current Price Range		Prior Year Average
Bowl, cereal, diameter 5″			
☐ crystal	7.00	10.00	8.00
Bowl, flat soup, diameter 8″			
☐ crystal	9.00	12.00	10.00
Bowl, salad, diameter 8½″			
☐ crystal	10.00	15.00	12.00
Bowl, ruffled, diameter 10¼″			
☐ crystal	10.00	15.00	12.00
Bread and Butter Plate, diameter 6″			
☐ crystal	.75	2.50	1.00
☐ pink	2.50	4.50	3.00
Butter Dish, lid			
☐ crystal	12.00	16.00	13.00
Cup			
☐ crystal	2.50	4.50	3.00
☐ pink	6.00	9.00	7.00
Luncheon Plate, diameter 9½″			
☐ crystal	2.50	4.50	3.00
☐ pink	11.00	14.50	12.00
Plate, diameter 11¾″			
☐ crystal	4.00	6.50	4.75
Saucer			
☐ crystal	.50	1.75	.75
☐ pink	4.00	7.00	5.00

CORONATION
Hocking Glass Co.

Also commonly referred to as *Banded Rib* or *Banded Fine Rib*. Some collectors also use the name *Saxon*. Hocking made *Coronation* from 1936 through 1942. The main colors were ruby red and pink although some crystal pieces surface occasionally, as well as a very small amount of green that has been found. The ruby red berry sets are not difficult to find. Don't bother looking for a red saucer; the red cups were sold with crystal saucers. Red was probably never made. A common mistake made by collectors is to confuse the tumblers in *Coronation* with *Lace Edge*. They are similar, but the ray design on *Coronation* extends much farther up the side of the glass. The *Lace Edge* design only covers about a third of the glass.

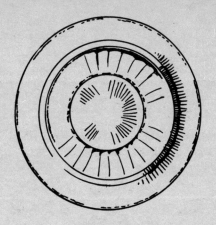

Coronation

	Current Price Range		Prior Year Average
Berry Bowl, diameter 4¼″			
☐ pink	2.50	4.50	3.50
☐ red..	3.50	6.50	4.25
Berry Bowl, diameter 8″			
☐ pink	5.50	8.50	6.25
☐ red..	10.00	13.00	11.00
Bowl, nappy, diameter 6½″			
☐ pink	3.00	4.50	3.50
☐ red..	7.00	8.50	7.50
Cup			
☐ pink	2.50	4.50	3.00
☐ red..	3.00	5.50	3.00
Luncheon Plate, diameter 8½″			
☐ pink	2.50	4.50	3.00
☐ red..	4.00	6.00	4.50
Nappy Bowl, diameter 6½″			
☐ pink	2.50	4.50	3.00
☐ red..	5.00	8.00	5.50
Saucer, diameter 6″			
☐ pink	.75	2.50	1.00
Sherbet Bowl			
☐ pink	2.50	4.50	3.00
☐ red..	3.50	5.50	4.00
Sherbet Plate, diameter 6″			
☐ pink	.75	2.50	1.00
Tumbler, footed, 10 oz., height 5″			
☐ pink	7.00	10.00	8.00

1937 Coronation Catalog Sheet.
Courtesy of Anchor Hocking Corporation, Lancaster, Ohio

CREMAX
Macbeth-Evans Corning Glassworks

This pattern was made in the late 1930s. It is very similar to *Chinex* but there are certain differences. *Cremax* is a purer white, while many pieces of *Chinex* have a scroll pattern on them that is lacking in *Cremax*. *Cremax* is probably even more difficult to find however. The most popular decal decoration found on *Cremax* is probably the castle decoration, but the floral decals are more numerous.

	Current Price Range		Prior Year Average
Bowl, cereal, diameter 5¾"			
☐ off-white	1.50	3.00	2.00
☐ decal	3.00	5.00	4.00
Bowl, soup, diameter 7"			
☐ off-white	4.50	6.50	5.50
☐ decal	6.00	8.00	7.00
Bowl, serving, diameter 9"			
☐ off white	6.00	8.00	7.00
☐ decal	8.00	10.00	8.00
Bread and Butter Plate, 6½"			
☐ off-white	.75	2.25	1.00
☐ decal	1.50	3.50	2.00
Creamer			
☐ off-white	2.00	4.00	2.50
☐ decal	4.00	7.00	5.00
Cup and Saucer			
☐ off-white	2.50	3.50	3.00
☐ decal	3.00	5.00	4.00
Plate, salad, diameter 6¼"			
☐ off-white	2.00	3.00	2.50
☐ decal	3.00	4.00	3.50
Plate, dinner, diameter 9¾"			
☐ off-white	2.75	3.75	3.25
☐ decal	4.00	5.00	4.25
Plate, cake or sandwich, diameter 11"			
☐ off-white	4.00	6.00	5.00
☐ decal	6.00	8.00	7.00
Plate, 12"			
☐ off-white	4.50	7.00	5.50
☐ decal	7.00	10.00	8.00
Sugar			
☐ off-white	2.00	4.00	2.50
☐ with decal	4.00	7.00	5.00

CUBE
Jeannette Glass Co.

Cube, also known as *Cubist* and *Modernistic Block* was made from 1929 through 1933. It is often confused with Fostoria's *American* pattern. *Cube* is heavier, and the colors are quite different (except for crystal), but sometimes it is not easy to tell the difference. If you have a piece not listed here, it could be *American*. Pink and crystal are not too hard to find now, but green is difficult. Some pieces were also made in milk-white, amber and a deep green. These are not plentiful, however. There is no dinner plate in this pattern.

Cube

	Current Price Range		Prior Year Average
Bowl, diameter 4½"			
☐ pink	3.50	5.50	4.00
Bowl, salad, diameter 6½"			
☐ pink	5.00	8.00	6.25
☐ green	9.00	13.00	10.00
Butter Dish, with lid			
☐ pink	38.00	45.00	41.00
☐ green	40.00	48.00	43.00
Butter Dish Top			
☐ pink	24.00	30.00	27.00
☐ green	26.00	32.00	29.00
Butter Dish Bottom			
☐ pink	13.00	17.00	15.00
☐ green	15.00	18.00	16.50
Candy Jar, with lid, height 6½"			
☐ pink	18.00	24.00	19.50
☐ green	21.00	27.00	22.50
Coaster, diameter 3¼"			
☐ pink	2.50	4.50	3.00
☐ green	3.50	5.50	4.00

	Current Price Range		Prior Year Average
Creamer, height 2″			
☐ pink	1.00	3.00	1.50
☐ amber	3.00	5.00	4.00
Creamer, height 3″			
☐ pink	3.50	5.50	4.00
☐ green	5.00	8.00	6.25
Cup			
☐ pink	3.50	5.50	4.00
☐ green	6.00	8.00	6.50
Dessert Bowl, diameter 4½″			
☐ pink	3.50	5.50	4.00
☐ green	4.00	6.00	4.50
Luncheon Plate, diameter 8″			
☐ pink	2.00	4.00	2.50
☐ green	3.50	5.50	4.00
Pitcher, 45 oz., height 8¾″			
☐ pink	125.00	135.00	127.00
☐ green	144.00	155.00	146.00
Powder Jar, with cover, three legged			
☐ pink	10.50	13.50	11.25
☐ green	13.00	17.00	14.00
Salt and Pepper Shakers			
☐ pink	22.00	28.00	25.00
☐ green	24.00	30.00	26.00
Saucer			
☐ pink	.75	2.25	1.00
☐ green	1.00	3.00	1.50
Sherbet Bowl, footed			
☐ pink	3.50	5.50	4.00
☐ green	5.00	7.00	5.50
Sherbet Plate, diameter 6″			
☐ pink	1.00	3.00	1.50
☐ green	1.50	3.50	2.00
Sugar Bowl, diameter 2″			
☐ pink	1.00	3.00	1.50
☐ amber	2.00	4.00	2.50
Sugar Bowl, diameter 3″			
☐ pink	3.50	5.50	4.00
☐ green	4.00	7.00	4.75
Tumbler, 10 oz., height 4″			
☐ pink	23.00	28.00	25.00
☐ green	30.00	35.00	32.00

DEBBRA
Hocking Glass Co.

This pattern was manufactured from 1931 through 1933. It was advertised as art glassware, supposedly having a fancier look than other Depression glass lines. It was issued in green, topaz (yellow) and rose (pink). Yellow is the most popular color and pink the least. Sets were originally marketed in either all-footed or all-flat packages. It is a floral design, consisting of a large thistle blossom and winged scroll and tassels. This is not an easy pattern to collect. There wasn't a lot of it made to begin with and not much of what was made has survived. Still, a usable collection can be put together with some patience.

	Current Price Range		Prior Year Average
Bowl, rose, three-legged, diameter 6½″			
☐ topaz	10.00	15.00	12.00
☐ rose	7.00	9.00	8.00
☐ green	7.00	10.00	9.00
Bowl, serving, open ribbed handles, diameter 7½″			
☐ topaz	7.00	10.00	8.00
☐ rose	5.00	8.00	6.00
☐ green	6.00	8.50	7.00
Bowl, serving, legged, diameter 8½″			
☐ topaz	6.50	9.00	7.50
☐ rose	4.00	7.00	5.50
☐ green	5.00	8.00	6.00
Cake Plate, caned base			
☐ topaz	13.00	15.50	14.00
☐ rose	11.00	14.00	12.00
☐ green	12.00	14.50	13.00
Candlestick, height 5¼″, pair			
☐ topaz	8.00	11.00	9.50
☐ rose	6.00	9.50	8.00
☐ green	6.50	9.75	8.50
Console Bowl, caned base, flared sides			
☐ topaz	14.50	17.00	15.00
☐ rose	11.00	14.00	12.00
☐ green	11.00	14.00	12.00
Rose Bowl, tri-legged, diameter 6″			
☐ topaz	19.00	23.00	20.00
☐ rose	11.00	14.00	12.00
☐ green	13.00	15.00	13.50
Serving Bowl, legged, diameter 8½″			
☐ topaz	16.00	19.00	17.00
☐ rose	7.50	9.50	8.00
☐ green	12.00	15.00	13.00

	Current Price Range		Prior Year Average

Serving Tray, rolled edge, legged, diameter 10"

☐ topaz	12.00	15.00	13.00
☐ rose	8.50	11.00	9.00
☐ green	9.50	12.00	10.00

DIAMOND QUILTED, FLAT DIAMOND
Imperial Glass Co.

For a few years, the manufacturer of this pattern was only suspected, but it has been proven to be Imperial. It was made from the late 1920s through the mid 1930s. The main colors were blue, pink, green, crystal and a small amount of black. Some amber pieces have also been found but there is very little on the market. The blue and black pieces generally have the quilting on the inside and the black plate has the pattern only on the underside. It is difficult to put together an entire set in one color in *Diamond Quilted*, so people tend to mix and match.

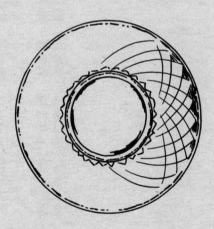

Diamond Quilted, Flat Diamond

Bowl, handle, diameter 5¾"

☐ green	4.50	6.50	5.00
☐ pink	4.50	6.50	5.00
☐ blue	7.00	10.00	8.00
☐ black	7.00	10.00	8.00

	Current Price Range		Prior Year Average

Bowl, diameter 7¼"
- ☐ green 4.50 6.50 5.00
- ☐ pink 4.50 6.50 5.00

Cake Salver, height 10"
- ☐ green 24.00 30.00 25.00

Candlesticks
- ☐ green 8.00 11.50 9.00
- ☐ pink 8.00 11.50 9.00
- ☐ blue 18.00 24.00 19.00
- ☐ black.. 18.00 24.00 19.00

Candy Jar, lidded, footed
- ☐ green 15.00 19.00 16.00
- ☐ pink 15.00 19.00 16.00

Cereal Bowl, diameter 5"
- ☐ green 3.50 5.50 4.00
- ☐ pink 3.50 5.50 4.00
- ☐ blue 6.00 9.00 7.00
- ☐ black.. 6.00 9.00 7.00

Compote, with lid, diameter 11"
- ☐ pink 34.00 44.00 36.00

Console Bowl, rolled edge
- ☐ pink 12.00 15.50 13.00
- ☐ blue 22.00 29.00 23.00
- ☐ black.. 22.00 29.00 23.50

Creamer
- ☐ green 4.50 7.50 5.25
- ☐ pink 4.50 7.50 5.25
- ☐ blue 8.00 11.50 9.00
- ☐ black.. 8.00 11.50 9.00

Cup
- ☐ green 3.00 5.00 3.50
- ☐ pink 3.00 5.00 3.50
- ☐ blue 4.50 7.50 5.25
- ☐ black.. 4.50 7.50 5.25

Goblet, 1 oz., cordial
- ☐ green 6.00 9.00 7.00
- ☐ pink 6.00 9.00 7.00

Goblet, 2 oz., wine
- ☐ green 5.00 7.00 6.00
- ☐ pink 5.00 7.00 6.00

Goblet, 3 oz., wine
- ☐ green 6.00 8.00 7.00
- ☐ pink 6.00 8.00 7.00

	Current Price Range		Prior Year Average
Goblet, 9 oz., champagne			
□ green	7.00	9.50	8.00
□ pink	7.00	9.50	8.00
Ice Bucket, with tongs			
□ green	33.00	41.00	35.00
□ pink	33.00	41.00	35.00
□ blue	52.00	58.00	53.00
□ black	52.00	58.00	53.50
Lunch Plate, diameter 8″			
□ green	3.00	5.00	3.50
□ pink	3.00	5.00	3.50
Iced Tea Glass, 12 oz.			
□ green	6.00	9.00	7.00
□ pink	6.00	9.00	7.00
Mayonnaise Set, three piece			
□ green	15.00	19.50	16.25
□ pink	15.00	19.50	16.25
Pitcher, 64 oz.			
□ green	26.00	33.00	29.00
□ pink	26.00	33.00	29.00
Punch Bowl and Stand			
□ green	250.00	300.00	275.00
□ pink	250.00	300.00	275.00
Salad Plate, diameter 7″			
□ green	3.00	5.00	3.50
□ pink	3.00	5.00	3.50
Sandwich Plate, diameter 14″			
□ pink	13.00	17.00	14.00
□ green	13.00	17.00	14.00
Saucer			
□ green	1.00	3.00	1.50
□ pink	1.00	3.00	1.50
Sherbet Plate, diameter 6″			
□ green	1.50	3.50	2.00
□ pink	1.50	3.50	2.00
Soup Bowl, diameter 4½″			
□ green	5.00	8.00	6.00
□ pink	5.00	8.00	6.00
Sugar Bowl			
□ green	4.50	7.50	5.25
□ pink	4.50	7.50	5.25
Tumbler, footed, 6 oz.			
□ green	4.50	7.50	5.25
□ pink	5.00	7.50	5.25

	Current Price Range		Prior Year Average
Tumbler, footed, 9 oz.			
☐ green	7.00	10.00	8.00
☐ pink	7.00	10.00	8.00
Tumbler, footed, 12 oz.			
☐ green	10.00	14.00	12.00
☐ pink	10.00	14.00	12.00
Water Tumbler, footed, 9 oz.			
☐ green	5.00	8.00	5.75
☐ pink	4.00	8.00	5.75
Whiskey Glass, 1½ oz., jigger			
☐ green	5.00	8.00	6.00
☐ pink	5.00	8.00	6.00

DIANA
Federal Glass Co.

Federal first released this pattern in 1933, but probably only a small number of pieces were made. In 1937 they re-started production and it lasted until 1940. The main colors were pink, crystal and amber. A common mistake made by collectors is confusing the demitasse cup and saucer for the beginnings of a children's set in this pattern. No children's set was made. The shakers are very similar to *Sharon*. The tumblers in *Diana* are getting difficult to find. Amber is especially difficult. The shakers are also disappearing. Some frosted pieces have been turning up.

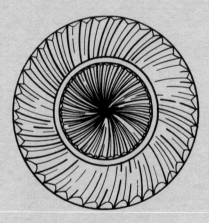

Diana

	Current Price Range		Prior Year Average
Ashtray, diameter 3½″			
☐ pink	3.00	4.00	3.50
☐ crystal	2.00	3.00	2.50
Bowl, diameter 11″			
☐ amber	6.50	9.50	7.25
Bowl, scalloped rim, diameter 12″			
☐ pink	6.00	9.00	7.00
☐ crystal	3.50	5.50	4.00
☐ amber	7.00	10.50	8.00
Bread and Butter, diameter 6″			
☐ pink	.75	2.25	1.00
☐ crystal	.50	2.00	.75
☐ amber	.75	2.25	1.00
Candy Jar, circular, with lid			
☐ pink	18.00	22.00	19.00
☐ crystal	10.50	13.50	11.25
☐ amber	20.00	25.00	21.50
Cereal Bowl, diameter 5″			
☐ pink	2.50	4.50	3.00
☐ crystal	1.50	3.50	2.00
Coaster, diameter 3½″			
☐ pink	2.50	4.50	3.00
☐ crystal	1.00	3.00	1.50
Creamer, oval			
☐ pink	2.50	4.50	3.00
☐ crystal	1.00	3.00	1.50
☐ amber	4.00	4.50	3.00
Cup			
☐ pink	2.50	4.50	3.00
☐ crystal	1.50	3.50	2.00
☐ amber	2.50	4.50	3.00
Dinner Plate, diameter 9″			
☐ pink	4.00	4.50	3.00
☐ crystal	3.00	5.00	3.50
☐ amber	5.00	8.00	5.75
Plate, diameter 5″			
☐ pink	2.50	4.50	3.00
☐ crystal	1.00	3.00	1.50
Salt and Pepper Shakers, pair			
☐ pink	35.00	42.00	38.00
☐ crystal	25.00	32.00	28.00
☐ amber	60.00	70.00	65.00

	Current Price Range		Prior Year Average
Saucer			
☐ pink	2.00	4.00	3.00
☐ crystal	1.50	2.50	2.00
☐ amber	3.00	4.50	4.00
Sherbet			
☐ pink	5.00	7.00	6.00
☐ amber	7.00	9.00	8.00
Tumbler, 9 oz., height 4⅛"			
☐ pink	10.00	15.00	12.00
☐ crystal	8.00	11.00	9.00
☐ amber	11.00	16.00	12.50

DOGWOOD
Macbeth-Evans

This is one of the most popular patterns in all of Depression glass. It was made from 1928 to 1932. The main colors were pink, green, monax (opaque white) and crystal. The pink is the most common, there is very little crystal around; monax is not very plentiful but there aren't many collectors anyway, and although the green is not abundant, it can be found. The plates are the easiest items to find in this line, especially the luncheons. Only the pitchers and tumblers have the silk-screened Dogwood design on them. Other pitchers are available in the same shape but they lack the silk-screening; they are not Dogwood. The pink cups are available in both a thin and a thick glass. The thin glass was made early in the career of this pattern and was found to be too fragile. It was replaced in production with the thicker variety. Cups in the other colors are available in the thin type only.

Dogwood

	Current Price Range		Prior Year Average
Berry Bowl, diameter 8½″			
☐ pink	29.00	34.00	30.50
☐ green	65.00	75.00	67.50
Bowl, cereal, diameter 5½″			
☐ pink	15.00	19.00	17.00
☐ green	18.00	21.00	19.50
☐ monax or cremax	10.00	16.00	13.00
Bowl, cereal, rolled edge, diameter 5½″			
☐ pink	17.00	22.00	19.00
Bread and Butter Plate, diameter 6″			
☐ pink	3.00	5.00	3.50
☐ green	4.00	6.00	4.50
Cake Plate, diameter 11″			
☐ pink	147.00	157.00	150.00
Cake Plate, diameter 13″			
☐ pink	57.00	67.00	59.50
☐ green	47.00	57.00	49.50
Creamer, diameter 2½″			
☐ pink	9.50	12.50	10.00
☐ green	31.00	39.00	33.00
Cup			
☐ pink	7.50	10.50	8.25
☐ green	13.00	17.00	14.00
Dinner Plate, diameter 9¼″			
☐ pink	15.50	19.50	16.25
Lunch Plate, diameter 8″			
☐ pink	3.00	5.00	3.50
☐ green	4.00	6.00	4.50
Pitcher, decorated, height 8″			
☐ pink	123.00	133.00	126.00
☐ green	430.00	465.00	440.00
Platter, oval, diameter 12″			
☐ pink	235.00	260.00	240.00
Salver Plate, diameter 12″			
☐ pink	16.50	20.50	17.50
Saucer			
☐ pink	3.00	5.00	3.50
☐ green	4.00	6.00	4.50
Sherbet, low footed			
☐ pink	15.50	19.50	16.50
☐ green	43.00	53.00	45.00
Sugar Bowl, diameter 2½″			
☐ pink	8.00	11.50	8.75
☐ green	32.00	39.00	33.50

	Current Price Range		Prior Year Average
Tumbler, 5 oz., decorated, height 3½"			
☐ pink	95.00	115.00	105.00
Tumbler, 20 oz., decorated, height 4"			
☐ pink	22.00	30.00	24.00
☐ green	65.00	75.00	70.00

DORIC
Jeannette Glass Co.

Jeannette made this line from 1935 through 1938. The colors were pink, green, delphite (opaque blue) and crystal. Pink and green are the easiest to find. Delphite is not abundant except for certain pieces; the sherbet for one. Green has only been found in small amounts so it's a safe bet that not much was made. Delphite was made in 1937 only. In the patterns the last year, 1938, only crystal was produced. The pattern has wide paneled sides with a band of alternating plain and snowflake decorated squares that encircle the top of a piece. The rims are smooth, however.

Doric

	Current Price Range		Prior Year Average

Berry Bowl, diameter 4⅞″
☐ pink	4.00	6.00	4.50
☐ green	4.50	7.00	5.00
☐ delphite	22.00	30.00	24.00

Berry Bowl, diameter 8¼″
☐ pink	8.00	11.00	9.00
☐ green	10.00	14.00	11.50
☐ delphite	73.00	83.00	75.00

Bowl, cream soup, diameter 5″
☐ green	125.00	15.00	135.00

Bowl, cereal, diameter 5½″
☐ pink	20.00	25.00	22.00
☐ green	23.00	28.00	26.00

Bowl, twin handled, diameter 9″
☐ pink	8.00	11.50	9.00
☐ green	8.00	11.50	9.00

Butter Dish, with lid
☐ pink	52.00	58.00	53.50
☐ green	63.00	73.00	65.00

Cake Plate, tri-legged, diameter 10″
☐ pink	10.50	13.50	11.25
☐ green	10.00	13.00	10.75

Candy Dish, with lid, diameter 8″
☐ pink	22.00	28.00	23.50
☐ green	22.00	28.00	23.50

Coaster, diameter 3″
☐ pink	8.00	11.00	8.75
☐ green	9.50	12.50	10.25

Creamer, diameter 4″
☐ pink	6.00	9.00	7.00
☐ green	7.00	10.00	8.00

Cup
☐ pink	5.00	6.50	5.50
☐ green	6.00	8.00	6.75

Dinner Plate, diameter 9″
☐ pink	6.00	9.00	7.50
☐ green	7.50	11.00	9.50

Grill Plate, diameter 9″
☐ pink	6.00	9.00	7.00
☐ green	8.50	11.50	9.00

Pitcher, collar base, 36 oz., height 6″
☐ pink	22.00	28.00	23.50
☐ green	24.00	33.00	26.00
☐ delphite	368.00	385.00	373.00

	Current Price Range		Prior Year Average
Pitcher, 48 oz., footed, height 7½″			
☐ pink	300.00	400.00	350.00
☐ green	600.00	800.00	700.00
Platter, oval, length 11″			
☐ pink	9.50	12.50	10.25
☐ green	10.50	13.50	11.25
Relish Tray			
☐ pink	4.00	6.00	4.50
☐ green	6.00	9.00	7.00
Salad Plate, diameter 7″			
☐ pink	11.00	14.00	12.00
☐ green	10.00	13.00	11.00
Salt and Pepper Shakers			
☐ pink	21.00	27.00	22.50
☐ green	24.00	31.00	25.50
Saucer			
☐ pink	1.75	3.00	2.00
☐ green	2.00	3.50	2.50
Serving Tray, length 8″			
☐ pink	6.00	9.00	7.00
☐ green	6.00	9.00	7.00
Sherbet, footed			
☐ pink	6.00	9.00	7.00
☐ green	8.00	10.00	9.00
☐ delphite	5.00	7.50	6.00
Sherbet Plate, diameter 6″			
☐ pink	1.50	3.50	2.00
☐ green	2.00	4.00	2.50
Soup Bowl, diameter 5″			
☐ green	122.00	132.00	124.00
Sugar Bowl			
☐ pink	7.00	10.00	8.00
☐ green	8.00	11.00	9.00
Tray, handled, length 10″			
☐ pink	6.00	9.00	7.00
☐ green	8.00	11.00	9.00
Tumbler, height 5″			
☐ pink	32.00	38.00	33.50
☐ green	34.00	41.00	36.00
Vegetable Bowl, oval, diameter 9″			
☐ pink	9.00	13.00	10.00
☐ green	10.50	14.50	11.50

DORIC AND PANSY
Jeannette Glass Co.

The difference between this pattern and *Doric* is that a pansy is shown in the squares that are empty in *Doric*. It was made from 1935 to 1938 in ultramarine, pink and crystal. Ultramarine is by far the most common color although none of this pattern is easy to find. The pink was only made in a children's set and in berry sets, both of which have become highly collectible. Watch out for color variations in the ultramarine. Pieces will not always match but they are still genuine. No reproductions have been found in this pattern. A few plates have been reported in green, but only time will tell if more shows up.

Doric and Pansy

	Current Price Range		Prior Year Average
Berry Bowl, diameter 4½″			
☐ ultramarine.......................................	8.00	11.00	9.00
☐ crystal	5.00	7.00	5.50
☐ pink	5.00	7.00	5.50
Berry Bowl, diameter 8″			
☐ ultramarine.......................................	54.00	64.00	55.50
☐ crystal	15.00	19.00	16.50
☐ pink	15.00	19.00	16.50
Bowl, handled, diameter 9″			
☐ ultramarine.......................................	22.00	28.00	24.00
☐ crystal	8.00	11.00	9.00
☐ pink	8.00	11.00	9.00
Butter Dish, lidded			
☐ ultramarine.......................................	600.00	700.00	650.00

	Current Price Range		Prior Year Average
Butter Dish Bottom			
☐ ultramarine...............................	200.00	300.00	250.00
Butter Dish Top			
☐ ultramarine...............................	350.00	450.00	400.00
Creamer			
☐ ultramarine...............................	150.00	185.00	158.00
☐ pink	52.00	62.00	55.00
☐ crystal....................................	52.00	62.00	55.00
Cup			
☐ ultramarine...............................	13.00	17.00	14.00
☐ pink	6.00	9.00	7.00
☐ crystal....................................	6.00	9.00	7.00
Dinner Plate, diameter 9″			
☐ ultramarine...............................	17.00	21.00	18.00
☐ pink	3.50	6.50	4.25
☐ crystal....................................	3.50	6.50	4.25
Salad Plate, diameter 7″			
☐ ultramarine...............................	23.00	33.00	25.00
Salt and Pepper			
☐ ultramarine...............................	450.00	550.00	500.00
Saucer			
☐ ultramarine...............................	3.00	5.00	3.50
☐ pink	1.25	3.25	2.00
☐ crystal....................................	1.25	3.25	2.00
Sugar Bowl			
☐ ultramarine...............................	157.00	167.00	159.00
☐ pink	52.00	62.00	55.00
☐ crystal....................................	52.00	62.00	55.00
Tray, handled, diameter 10″			
☐ ultramarine...............................	16.00	19.00	16.50
Tumbler, 9 oz., height 4½″			
☐ ultramarine...............................	31.00	39.00	32.50

DOUBLE SHIELD
L. B. Smith Glass Co.

This pattern is distinguished by its two characteristic shapes: squared with scalloped edges; round with alternating scallops and points. A shield design in relief can be found on the sides of cups, bowls and the undersides of plates. On handled items, look where the handles attach for the shield. Items are trimmed in gold and appear in black amethyst, cobalt blue, pink, amethyst and green. It was made from 1920 through 1936.

	Current Price Range		Prior Year Average

Bon Bon, two handles
☐ black..	13.00	17.00	14.00
☐ cobalt..	13.00	17.00	14.00
☐ amethyst.....................................	13.00	17.00	14.00
☐ green or pink..............................	8.00	11.00	8.75

Bowl, salad, scalloped edge, two handles, diameter 8"
☐ black..	30.00	40.00	35.00
☐ amethyst.....................................	30.00	40.00	35.00
☐ cobalt..	30.00	40.00	35.00
☐ pink	22.00	28.00	25.00
☐ green	22.00	28.00	25.00

Bowl, two handles, fluted edge, diameter 8"
☐ black..	14.50	18.50	15.50
☐ cobalt..	14.50	18.50	15.50
☐ amethyst.....................................	14.50	18.50	15.50
☐ green or pink..............................	11.00	13.50	11.75

Bowl, two handles, square, length 8"
☐ black..	14.50	18.50	15.50
☐ cobalt..	14.50	18.50	15.50
☐ amethyst.....................................	14.50	18.50	15.50
☐ green or pink..............................	11.00	13.50	11.75

Cake Plate, tab handles, diameter 10"
☐ black..	18.00	22.00	19.00
☐ amethyst.....................................	18.00	22.00	19.00
☐ cobalt..	18.00	22.00	19.00
☐ green or pink..............................	12.00	15.00	13.00

Candlesticks, double stem, pair
☐ black..	27.00	33.00	28.50
☐ amethyst.....................................	27.00	33.00	28.50
☐ cobalt..	27.00	33.00	28.50
☐ green or pink..............................	18.00	22.00	19.00

Candlesticks, pair
☐ black..	14.50	18.50	15.50
☐ cobalt..	14.50	18.50	15.50
☐ amethyst.....................................	14.50	18.50	15.50
☐ green or pink..............................	12.00	15.00	12.75

Creamer, fluted edge
☐ black..	11.00	14.00	11.50
☐ cobalt..	11.00	14.00	11.50
☐ amethyst.....................................	11.00	14.00	11.50
☐ green or pink..............................	7.00	10.00	8.00

Cup, plain
| ☐ green or pink.............................. | 3.50 | 5.50 | 4.00 |

	Current Price Range		Prior Year Average
Plate, scalloped edge, diameter 8″			
☐ black	8.00	11.00	9.00
☐ cobalt	8.00	11.00	9.00
☐ amethyst	8.00	11.00	9.00
☐ green or pink	6.00	9.00	7.00
Plate, squared, length 8″			
☐ black	8.00	11.00	9.00
☐ cobalt	8.00	11.00	9.00
☐ amethyst	8.00	11.00	9.00
☐ green or pink	6.00	9.00	7.00
Rose Bowl, tri-footed			
☐ black	14.00	18.00	15.00
☐ cobalt	14.00	18.00	15.00
☐ amethyst	14.00	18.00	15.00
☐ green or pink	11.00	14.00	12.00
Salt and Pepper Shakers			
☐ black	22.00	28.00	24.00
☐ amethyst	22.00	28.00	24.00
☐ cobalt	22.00	28.00	24.00
☐ green or pink	16.00	19.00	17.00
Saucer, scalloped edge			
☐ black	2.50	4.50	3.00
☐ amethyst	2.50	4.50	3.00
☐ cobalt	2.50	4.50	3.00
☐ green or pink	1.50	3.50	2.00
Saucer, squared shape			
☐ black	2.50	4.50	3.00
☐ amethyst	2.50	4.50	3.00
☐ cobalt	2.50	4.50	3.00
☐ green or pink	1.50	3.50	2.00
Sherbet, scalloped edge			
☐ black	9.50	12.50	10.50
☐ amethyst	9.50	12.50	10.50
☐ cobalt	9.50	12.50	10.50
☐ green or pink	4.50	7.50	5.25
Sugar, scalloped edge			
☐ black	11.00	14.00	11.50
☐ amethyst	11.00	14.00	11.50
☐ cobalt	11.00	14.00	11.50
☐ green or pink	8.00	11.00	9.00

ENGLISH HOBNAIL
Westmoreland Glass Co.

Westmoreland made this pattern for about fifty years, starting in 1928 and ending in the 1970s. No reproductions have been spotted as of yet, but the location of the original molds is unknown so it could happen. The colors you'll find most often are pink and crystal. The cobalt blue and the turquoise are very popular and command higher prices than the rest, but are in much shorter supply. Other colors that were made were red, green and amber. Along the years, Westmoreland issued many color variations. There are three shades of green, two turquoise, two pinks and two ambers. Some crystal was made in the 1930s with black bases. A common mistake is to confuse *English Hobnail* with *Miss America*. The major difference is that the rays in the center of the pieces in *English Hobnail* are of varying distance from the center. In *Miss America* the rays are of uniform length from the center. The hobs are also smoother in *English Hobnail*, which gives this pattern a smoother feel. The number and variety of pieces in this line is dazzling. There is so much to collect that it isn't advisable to go for an entire set in one color.

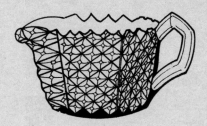

English Hobnail

	Current Price Range		Prior Year Average
Ashtray			
☐ pink, amber or green	16.50	20.50	17.50
☐ turquoise	24.50	30.50	24.50
☐ cobalt...	32.50	40.50	30.50
☐ crystal	9.00	11.00	9.50
Basket, handle, height 6″			
☐ pink	70.00	82.00	74.00
☐ amber	70.00	82.00	74.00
☐ green	70.00	82.00	74.00
☐ turquoise	85.00	110.00	100.00
☐ cobalt...	70.00	82.00	74.00
☐ crystal	40.00	50.00	44.00

	Current Price Range		Prior Year Average
Basket, handle, height 5″			
☐ pink	20.00	30.00	24.00
☐ amber	20.00	30.00	24.00
☐ green	20.00	30.00	24.00
☐ turquoise	30.00	40.00	34.00
☐ cobalt..	20.00	30.00	24.00
☐ crystal	12.00	18.00	14.50
Bowl, round, diameter 5″			
☐ pink, amber or green	8.00	11.00	8.50
☐ turquoise	12.00	16.00	13.00
☐ cobalt..	16.00	22.00	18.00
☐ crystal	4.50	6.00	5.00
Bowl, square, diameter 5″			
☐ pink, amber or green	8.00	11.00	8.50
☐ turquoise	12.00	16.00	13.00
☐ cobalt..	16.00	22.00	18.00
☐ crystal	4.50	6.00	5.00
Bowl, diameter 6″			
☐ amber or green.................................	8.00	12.00	9.00
☐ turquoise	12.00	18.00	14.00
☐ cobalt..	16.00	24.00	19.00
☐ crystal	6.00	8.00	6.50
Bowl, diameter 8″			
☐ amber or green.................................	14.00	18.00	15.00
☐ turquoise	21.00	27.00	23.00
☐ cobalt..	28.00	36.00	31.00
☐ crystal	10.00	14.00	11.00
Candlesticks, height 3½″			
☐ pink, amber or green	27.00	33.00	29.00
☐ turquoise	40.00	49.00	43.00
☐ cobalt..	27.00	33.00	29.00
☐ crystal .:...	11.50	14.00	12.00
Candlesticks, height 8″			
☐ amber or green.................................	42.00	50.00	44.00
☐ turquoise	63.00	75.00	67.00
☐ cobalt..	42.00	50.00	44.00
☐ crystal	20.00	25.00	22.00
Candy Dish, conical			
☐ pink, amber or green	42.00	50.00	44.00
☐ turquoise	63.00	75.00	67.00
☐ cobalt..	42.00	50.00	44.00
☐ crystal	16.00	20.00	17.00

	Current Price Range		Prior Year Average
Celery Dish			
☐ pink, amber or green	14.50	18.50	15.50
☐ turquoise	21.00	27.00	23.00
☐ cobalt..	14.50	18.50	15.50
☐ crystal	6.00	8.00	7.00
Cigarette Box			
☐ pink, amber or green	20.00	25.00	21.00
☐ turquoise	30.00	37.00	33.00
☐ cobalt..	40.00	50.00	43.00
☐ crystal	11.00	15.00	13.00
Cocktail Glass			
☐ pink, amber or green	13.00	17.00	14.00
☐ turquoise	19.00	25.00	21.00
☐ cobalt..	13.00	17.00	14.00
☐ crystal	8.00	11.00	9.00
Cologne Bottle			
☐ pink, amber or green	22.00	28.00	23.00
☐ turquoise	33.00	40.00	35.00
☐ cobalt..	44.00	56.00	48.00
☐ crystal	12.00	16.00	14.00
Cordial Glass			
☐ pink, amber or green	14.00	18.00	15.00
☐ turquoise	21.00	27.00	23.00
☐ cobalt..	14.00	18.00	15.00
☐ crystal	12.00	14.00	12.50
Decanter, 20 oz.			
☐ pink, amber or green	52.00	62.00	55.00
☐ turquoise	88.00	98.00	93.00
☐ cobalt..	52.00	62.00	55.00
☐ crystal	27.00	33.00	29.00
Demitasse Cup			
☐ pink	15.00	21.00	18.00
☐ amber	15.00	21.00	18.00
☐ green	15.00	21.00	18.00
Demitasse Saucer			
☐ pink	5.00	10.00	7.00
☐ amber	5.00	10.00	7.00
☐ green	5.00	10.00	7.00
Dinner Plate, diameter 10″			
☐ pink or amber...................................	15.00	19.00	16.00
☐ green or cobalt	15.00	19.00	16.00
☐ turquoise	22.00	28.00	24.00
☐ crystal	8.00	10.00	8.50

	Current Price Range		Prior Year Average
Egg Cup			
☐ pink or amber	22.00	28.00	23.00
☐ green or cobalt	22.00	28.00	23.00
☐ turquoise	33.00	42.00	35.00
☐ crystal	15.00	18.00	16.00
Goblet, 5 oz., champagne			
☐ pink	12.00	16.00	14.00
☐ amber	12.00	16.00	14.00
☐ green	12.00	16.00	14.00
☐ turquoise	17.50	23.50	21.00
☐ cobalt	12.00	16.00	14.00
☐ crystal	7.00	10.00	8.50
Goblet, 8 oz., water			
☐ pink	15.00	20.00	17.00
☐ amber	15.00	20.00	17.00
☐ green	15.00	20.00	17.00
☐ turquoise	22.00	26.00	24.00
☐ cobalt	15.00	20.00	17.00
☐ crystal	8.00	12.00	10.00
Iced Tea Glass, height 5″			
☐ pink or amber	15.00	19.00	16.50
☐ green or cobalt	15.00	19.00	16.50
☐ turquoise	22.00	28.00	24.00
☐ crystal	12.00	15.00	13.00
Lamp, electric, height 6″			
☐ pink or amber	55.00	65.00	58.00
☐ green or cobalt	55.00	65.00	58.00
☐ turquoise	80.00	90.00	82.00
☐ crystal	30.00	45.00	34.00
Lamp, oil, height 9″			
☐ cobalt	140.00	180.00	155.00
☐ crystal	85.00	95.00	87.00
Lemonade Pitcher, height 11″			
☐ pink	155.00	165.00	158.00
☐ green	170.00	182.00	173.00
Marmalade Jar, lidded			
☐ pink or amber	30.00	35.00	31.00
☐ green or cobalt	30.00	35.00	31.00
☐ turquoise	45.00	52.00	47.00
☐ crystal	20.00	25.00	22.00
Pitcher, 23 oz.			
☐ pink or amber	110.00	125.00	114.00
☐ green or cobalt	110.00	125.00	114.00
☐ turquoise	160.00	180.00	165.00
☐ crystal	60.00	70.00	62.00

	Current Price Range		Prior Year Average

Pitcher, 39 oz.
☐ pink or amber	110.00	130.00	115.00
☐ green or cobalt	110.00	130.00	115.00
☐ turquoise	165.00	190.00	172.00
☐ crystal	80.00	100.00	84.00

Pitcher, 60 oz.
☐ pink or amber	125.00	145.00	132.00
☐ green or cobalt	125.00	145.00	132.00
☐ turquoise	187.00	210.00	194.00
☐ crystal	90.00	110.00	97.00

Pitcher, 64 oz., straight sides
☐ pink	160.00	200.00	175.00
☐ amber	160.00	200.00	175.00
☐ green	160.00	200.00	175.00
☐ turquoise	180.00	225.00	195.00
☐ cobalt	180.00	225.00	195.00
☐ crystal	100.00	145.00	130.00

Pitcher, conical, height 8″
☐ green	22.00	28.00	23.00
☐ pink	18.00	22.00	19.00

Pitcher, 24 oz., height 5″
☐ green	430.00	470.00	440.00

Platter, oval, length 10″
☐ green	11.00	14.00	12.00
☐ pink	9.50	12.50	10.25
☐ delphite	90.00	100.00	92.00

Relish Bowl, oval, length 8″
☐ pink or amber	13.00	17.00	14.00
☐ green or cobalt	13.00	17.00	14.00
☐ turquoise	21.00	28.00	23.00
☐ crystal	9.00	12.00	10.00

Relish Dish, compartmentalized, length 7″
☐ pink	8.00	11.50	8.50
☐ green	8.00	11.50	8.50

Rose Bowl, tri-legged
☐ green	375.00	395.00	382.00

Salad Bowl, round rim, diameter 7″
☐ delphite	41.00	49.00	42.50
☐ pink	8.00	11.00	9.00
☐ green	10.00	12.00	10.50

	Current Price Range		Prior Year Average
Salad Plate, diameter 7½″			
☐ green	6.00	8.00	6.50
☐ pink	5.00	7.50	6.00
Salt and Pepper Shakers, collar base, height 6″			
☐ pink	28.00	32.00	29.00
Salt and Pepper Shakers, footed, height 4½″			
☐ pink	30.00	35.00	31.00
☐ green	31.00	37.00	33.00
Salt Dip, footed, diameter 2″			
☐ pink or amber	14.50	19.50	15.25
☐ green or cobalt	14.50	19.50	15.25
☐ turquoise	22.00	28.00	23.00
☐ crystal	7.00	9.00	7.50
Saucer			
☐ pink or amber	2.50	4.50	3.00
☐ green or cobalt	2.50	4.50	3.00
☐ turquoise	3.50	5.50	4.00
☐ crystal	1.25	2.50	1.75
Saucer			
☐ green	5.00	8.00	6.00
☐ pink	4.50	7.50	5.50
Sherbet			
☐ pink or amber	10.00	14.00	11.00
☐ green or cobalt	10.00	14.00	11.00
☐ turquoise	15.00	21.00	17.00
☐ crystal	6.00	8.00	6.50
Sherbet Plate, diameter 6″			
☐ green	2.50	4.50	3.00
☐ pink	2.50	4.50	3.00
Soup Bowl			
☐ pink or amber	11.00	15.00	12.00
☐ green or cobalt	11.00	15.00	12.00
☐ turquoise	16.00	22.00	18.00
☐ crystal	6.00	8.00	6.50
Soup Bowl, diameter 5″			
☐ green	240.00	260.00	245.00
Storage Dish, lidded, square, length 5″			
☐ green	41.00	48.00	42.00
☐ jadite	11.00	14.00	12.00

	Current Price Range		Prior Year Average
Sugar Bowl			
☐ green	7.00	9.00	8.00
☐ pink	6.00	9.00	7.00
Sugar Bowl, footed			
☐ pink or amber	13.00	17.00	14.00
☐ green or cobalt	13.00	17.00	14.00
☐ turquoise	22.00	29.00	24.00
☐ crystal	7.00	9.00	7.50
Tray, tab handles, square, length 5½″			
☐ green	8.50	11.50	9.00
☐ pink	8.00	11.00	8.50
Tumbler, collar base, height 4″			
☐ green	152.00	162.00	155.00
Tumbler, footed, height 3½″			
☐ green	82.00	92.00	85.00
Vase, tri-legged, flaired edge			
☐ green	375.00	395.00	381.00
Vase, octagonal, height 7″			
☐ green	375.00	395.00	381.00
Vegetable Bowl, with lid, diameter 8″			
☐ pink	20.00	25.00	22.00
☐ green	22.00	27.00	23.00
Water Tumbler, height 5″			
☐ green	12.00	15.00	13.00
☐ pink	9.50	12.50	10.25
☐ delphite	115.00	135.00	120.00
Whiskey Glass, 1½ oz.			
☐ pink	14.00	19.00	15.00
☐ amber	14.00	19.00	15.00
☐ green	14.00	19.00	15.00
☐ turquoise	21.00	29.00	23.00
☐ cobalt	14.00	19.00	15.00
☐ crystal	10.00	13.00	10.50

FIRE-KING
Hocking Glass Co.

This pattern features a series of decorative centerpiece motifs. Festoons wind about the rim from one well-spaced motif to the other, beneath a dotted ribbon bridge that closes the space between each motif. A scrolling, six-point medallion highlights the centers of plates and bowls. The rounded bases of footed items are rayed. Some items bear a platinum rim, such as the flat tumbler, cereal and salad plate. This pattern can be collected in crystal, pink, green and blue.

	Current Price Range		Prior Year Average

Candy Jar, lidded, height 4″

☐ blue	150.00	165.00	153.00
☐ pink	115.00	135.00	120.00
☐ crystal	70.00	80.00	73.00
☐ green	115.00	135.00	120.00

Cereal Bowl, diameter 5½″

☐ blue	37.00	43.00	39.00
☐ pink	27.00	32.00	28.00
☐ crystal	8.50	11.50	9.00
☐ green	27.00	32.00	28.00

Creamer, height 3¼″

☐ blue	50.00	65.00	53.00
☐ pink or green	32.00	42.00	35.00
☐ crystal	22.00	28.00	23.00

Cup

☐ blue	100.00	125.00	110.00
☐ pink or green	48.00	56.00	50.00
☐ crystal	18.00	22.00	19.00

Goblet, height 7″

☐ blue	140.00	160.00	145.00
☐ pink or green	112.00	125.00	114.00
☐ crystal	33.00	40.00	35.00

Grill Plate, diameter 10″

☐ blue	28.00	32.00	29.00
☐ pink or green	16.00	19.00	17.00
☐ crystal	10.00	14.00	11.00

Iced Tea Glass, height 6½″

☐ blue	33.00	40.00	35.00
☐ crystal	22.00	28.00	23.00
☐ pink or green	31.00	39.00	32.50

Juice Glass

☐ blue	115.00	135.00	120.00
☐ crystal	28.00	32.00	29.00
☐ pink or green	85.00	95.00	87.00

Lunch Plate, diameter 8″

☐ blue	30.00	38.00	34.00
☐ pink or green	15.00	19.00	16.00
☐ crystal	11.00	13.00	11.50

Platter, tab handled, diameter 12″

☐ blue	50.00	60.00	54.00
☐ crystal	13.00	17.00	14.00
☐ pink or green	24.00	30.00	25.00

	Current Price Range		Prior Year Average
Salad Bowl, diameter 7″			
☐ blue	57.00	63.00	58.50
☐ pink or green	37.00	43.00	39.00
☐ crystal	13.00	17.00	14.00
Sandwich Plate, diameter 10″			
☐ blue	32.00	39.00	33.50
☐ pink or green	18.00	22.00	19.00
☐ crystal	13.00	17.00	14.00
Saucer, diameter 5½″			
☐ blue	23.00	30.00	25.00
☐ crystal	8.00	12.00	9.00
☐ pink or green	13.00	17.00	14.00
Sugar Bowl, diameter 3½″			
☐ blue	62.00	85.00	70.00
☐ crystal	22.00	27.00	23.00
☐ pink or green	41.00	48.00	42.00
Tumbler, pedestal foot, height 5½″			
☐ blue	35.00	45.00	38.00
☐ crystal	18.00	22.00	20.00
☐ pink or green	37.00	43.00	38.00
Vegetable Bowl, length 10½″			
☐ blue	50.00	62.00	54.50
☐ pink or green	32.00	40.00	34.00
☐ crystal	13.00	17.00	14.00

FIRE-KING OVEN GLASS
Anchor Hocking Glass Co.

Fire-King Oven Glass is a much sought after kitchen glass made by Anchor Hocking in the 1940s. This glass complements *Fire-King* dinnerware. The center of the larger pieces, such as the roaster, skillet, pie plates and casseroles, features a center medallion with a petal-like design reaching to the edges. The sides of the pieces also have designs. Blue is the most common color, but crystal, off-white and jadeite were also used.

Bowl, diameter 6⅞″			
☐ blue	8.00	12.00	10.00
Bowl, diameter 8⅜″			
☐ blue	9.25	13.50	10.50
Bowl, diameter 10⅛″			
☐ blue	13.00	17.00	15.00
Cake Pan, 8½″			
☐ blue	11.00	15.00	12.50

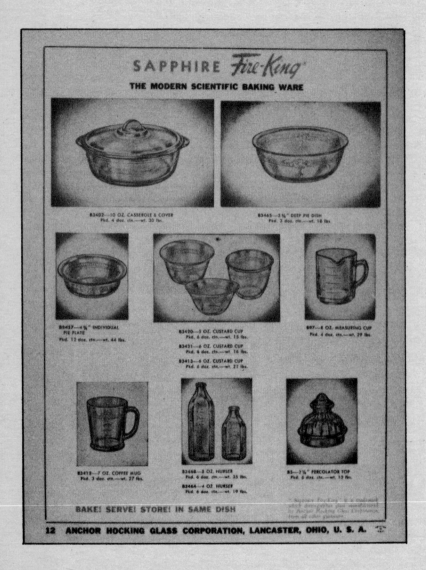

1949 Fire-King Oven Glass Catalog Sheets.

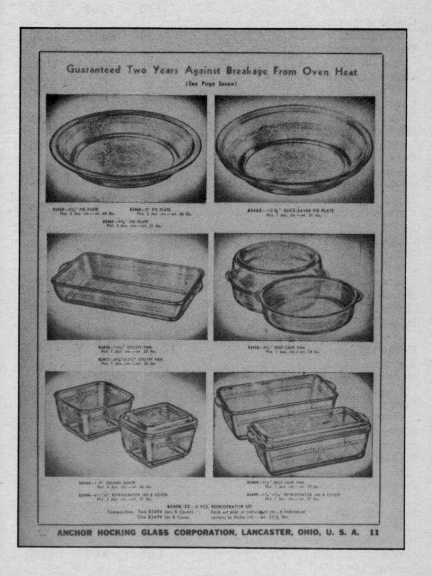

Courtesy of Anchor Hocking Corporation, Lancaster, Ohio

	Current Price Range		Prior Year Average
Cereal Bowl, 5½"			
☐ blue	9.00	12.00	10.00
Coffee Mug, 7 oz.			
☐ blue	15.00	20.00	16.50
Covered Casserole, 1 qt.			
☐ blue	11.00	14.00	12.00
Covered Casserole, 2 qt.			
☐ blue	16.00	20.00	17.00
Covered Casserole, knob handle, 1 pt.			
☐ blue	8.50	11.50	9.25
Covered Casserole, knob handle, 1 qt.			
☐ blue	9.50	12.50	10.50
Covered Casserole, knob handle, 1½ qt.			
☐ blue	13.00	16.50	14.25
Covered Casserole, knob handle, 2 qt.			
☐ blue	14.00	19.00	16.00
Custard Cup, 5 oz.			
☐ blue	2.00	4.00	2.50
Custard Cup, 6 oz., 2 styles			
☐ blue	3.00	5.50	4.00
Loaf Pan			
☐ blue	14.00	19.00	16.00
Measuring Bowl, 16 oz.			
☐ blue	13.00	17.00	14.00
Measuring Cup, no spout, 8 oz.			
☐ blue	22.00	27.00	23.00
Measuring Cup, spout, 8 oz.			
☐ blue	8.50	11.50	9.00
Measuring Cup, with three spouts, 8 oz.			
☐ blue	14.00	18.00	15.00
Nurser, 4 oz.			
☐ blue	12.00	16.00	13.50
Nurser, 8 oz.			
☐ blue	15.00	19.00	17.00
Pie Plate, 8½"			
☐ blue	5.50	8.50	6.50
Pie Plate, juice saver, 10½"			
☐ blue	32.00	38.00	33.00
Refrigerator Jar, with cover, large			
☐ blue	13.00	17.00	14.00
Refrigerator Jar, with cover, small			
☐ blue	6.00	9.00	7.00
Roaster, 10½"			
☐ blue	36.00	44.00	38.00

	Current Price Range		Prior Year Average
Uncovered Casserole, 1 pt.			
□ blue	2.50	4.50	3.00
Uncovered Casserole, 2 pt.			
□ blue	3.50	5.50	4.00

FLORAGOLD
Jeannette Glass Co.

Since this pattern was made in the 1950s, it isn't considered to be genuine Depression era glass. It is included here, however, because of a strong collector interest. The main collectible colors are crystal and iridescent. Other colors are on the market, but they are of even more recent manufacture. The pitcher is hard to get as are the iced tea glass, the cereal bowl and the dinner plate.

Ashtray/Coaster			
□ iridescent...........................	3.75	4.75	4.35
□ crystal	2.00	3.00	2.25
Bowl, square, diameter 4½″			
□ iridescent...........................	4.00	6.00	5.00
Bowl, round, diameter 5½″			
□ iridescent...........................	21.00	26.00	23.00
Bowl, square, diameter 8½″			
□ iridescent...........................	13.00	18.00	14.50
Bowl, crimped rim, diameter 8½″			
□ iridescent...........................	4.00	6.50	5.25
Bowl, deep, diameter 9½″			
□ iridescent...........................	22.00	28.00	25.00
Bowl, ruffled rim, diameter 12″			
□ iridescent...........................	4.00	6.50	5.25
Butter Dish, with top			
□ iridescent...........................	34.00	40.00	37.00
Candlesticks, two-lite, pair			
□ iridescent...........................	30.00	37.00	34.00
Candy Dish, footed, length 5¼″			
□ iridescent...........................	4.00	7.00	5.25
□ crystal	2.50	3.75	3.35
Cheese Dish, diameter 6¾″			
□ iridescent...........................	32.00	40.00	35.00
Cup			
□ iridescent...........................	2.00	4.00	3.00
Pitcher, 64 oz.			
□ iridescent...........................	30.00	37.00	34.00

	Current Price Range		Prior Year Average
Plate, dinner, diameter 8½"			
☐ iridescent...............................	12.00	17.00	14.00
Plate, sherbet, diameter 5¾"			
☐ iridescent...............................	5.00	7.50	6.00
Platter, diameter 11¼"			
☐ iridescent...............................	12.00	15.00	13.00
Salt and Pepper Shakers			
☐ iridescent...............................	34.00	40.00	37.00
Saucer			
☐ iridescent...............................	3.00	4.50	4.00
Sherbet			
☐ iridescent...............................	7.00	10.00	7.50
Tray, diameter 13½"			
☐ iridescent...............................	12.00	15.00	12.50
Tray, with indent for plate, diameter 13½"			
☐ iridescent...............................	30.00	37.00	34.00
Tumbler, 10 oz., footed			
☐ iridescent...............................	11.00	15.00	13.00
Tumbler, 11 oz., footed			
☐ iridescent...............................	11.00	15.00	13.00
Tumbler, 15 oz., footed			
☐ iridescent...............................	40.00	50.00	45.00
☐ crystal...............................	10.00	14.00	12.00
Vase or Celery			
☐ iridescent...............................	100.00	150.00	120.00
☐ crystal...............................	22.00	30.00	26.00

FLORAL
Jeannette Glass Co.

Also referred to as *Poinsetta*, Jeannette made this pattern from 1931 through 1937. The colors you will find most often are pink, green, delphite and crystal. Pieces in jadeite, amber, red, yellow and ivory have been reported but are generally not common. In some cases, they are one of a kind. Some *Floral* pieces are identical in shape to *Adam*. These include the candle holders and the covered round casserole. *Floral* features many unusual pieces. A dresser set consisting of three covered bowls resting on a 9¼" tray has been found, and more probably exist. Some of the jadeite pieces show the pattern only on the underside of the cover or on the bottom of the piece. A floral lamp has been reported but as of yet only one is known. *Floral* is a fun pattern, and popular with collectors partly because of its unpredictability. New items turn up so often that you really have to keep track. Note that the sugar lid and the candy lid are identical.

	Current Price Range		Prior Year Average

Berry Bowl, round rim, diameter 4½″
☐ delphite	22.00	27.00	23.00
☐ pink	7.00	10.00	8.00
☐ green	7.50	10.50	8.50

Bowl, cream soup, diameter 5½″
| ☐ pink | 250.00 | 350.00 | 300.00 |
| ☐ green | 250.00 | 350.00 | 300.00 |

Bowl, salad, diameter 7½″
☐ pink	10.00	14.00	12.00
☐ green	11.00	15.00	13.00
☐ delphite	40.00	50.00	45.00

Bowl, covered, diameter 8″
| ☐ pink | 22.00 | 30.00 | 24.00 |
| ☐ green | 28.00 | 36.00 | 32.00 |

Bowl, oval vegetable, length 9″
| ☐ pink | 8.00 | 12.00 | 10.00 |
| ☐ green | 10.00 | 14.00 | 12.00 |

Butter Dish, lidded
| ☐ pink | 62.00 | 72.00 | 65.00 |
| ☐ green | 68.00 | 76.00 | 70.00 |

Candlesticks, height 3⅞″
| ☐ pink | 41.00 | 49.00 | 42.50 |
| ☐ green | 58.00 | 66.00 | 60.00 |

Candy Jar, lidded
| ☐ pink | 22.00 | 31.00 | 24.00 |
| ☐ green | 28.00 | 32.00 | 29.00 |

Coaster, diameter 3″
| ☐ pink | 6.50 | 9.50 | 7.50 |
| ☐ green | 6.00 | 9.00 | 7.00 |

Comport, height 8½″
| ☐ pink | 260.00 | 290.00 | 270.00 |
| ☐ green | 290.00 | 320.00 | 290.00 |

Creamer
☐ pink	6.00	10.00	7.00
☐ green	8.00	11.00	9.00
☐ delphite	52.00	62.00	55.00

Cup
| ☐ pink | 6.00 | 9.00 | 7.00 |
| ☐ green | 7.00 | 10.50 | 8.00 |

Dinner Plate, diameter 9″
☐ pink	9.50	12.50	10.25
☐ green	11.00	14.00	12.00
☐ delphite	90.00	100.00	93.00

Dresser Set
| ☐ green | 920.00 | 980.00 | 935.00 |

	Current Price Range		Prior Year Average
Grill Plate, diameter 9″			
□ green	42.00	52.00	45.00
Ice Bucket, height 4″			
□ pink	350.00	450.00	360.00
□ green	380.00	420.00	390.00
Juice Glass, footed, height 4″			
□ green	11.50	14.50	12.25
□ pink	10.00	13.00	10.75
Lemonade Glass			
□ green	24.00	30.00	25.00
□ pink	21.00	28.00	22.50
Plate, salad, diameter 8″			
□ pink	7.00	10.00	8.00
□ green	8.00	11.00	9.00
Plate, sherbet, diameter 6″			
□ pink	3.00	5.00	4.25
□ green	3.50	5.50	4.75
Salt and Pepper Shakers, flat, height 6″, pair			
□ pink	30.00	40.00	35.00
Salt and Pepper Shakers, footed, height 4″, pair			
□ pink	30.00	38.00	32.00
□ green	37.00	44.00	40.00
Tumbler, 9 oz., flat, height 4½″			
□ green	140.00	190.00	160.00
Tumbler, 3 oz., footed, height 3½″			
□ green	110.00	140.00	120.00
Tumbler, 5 oz., footed, height 4″			
□ pink	9.00	13.00	11.00
□ green	12.00	16.00	14.00

FLORAL AND DIAMOND BAND
U.S. Glass Co.

U.S. Glass made this pattern during the 1930s. The most common colors now found are the green and the pink. Green is a bit more costly even though it seems there's more of it around. Some other colors were made in small amounts including crystal, black and an iridescent that strongly resembles Carnival glass (in fact, Carnival collectors refer to it as *Mayflower,* and many include it in their collections). A major drawback for some collectors in this line is that there is no cup and saucer. This is common for U.S. Glass. The green of this pattern will sometimes appear more blue than green. It is still green, but the coloring process they used then was not as reliable as today's techniques. Color variations were inevitable.

Floral and Diamond Band

	Current Price Range		Prior Year Average
Berry Bowl, diameter 4″			
☐ pink	3.25	5.25	4.25
☐ green	3.50	5.50	4.50
Berry Bowl, diameter 8½″			
☐ pink	7.00	9.00	8.00
☐ green	8.50	10.50	8.00
Butter Dish, with lid			
☐ pink	80.00	90.00	85.00
☐ green	85.00	95.00	90.00
Butter Dish Bottom			
☐ pink	42.00	48.00	45.00
☐ green	45.00	53.00	48.50
Butter Dish Top			
☐ pink	34.00	42.00	38.00
☐ green	37.00	46.00	41.00
Compote, height 5½″			
☐ pink	6.50	8.50	7.00
☐ green	8.00	10.00	7.50
Creamer, height 4¾″			
☐ pink	8.50	10.50	9.50
☐ green	8.50	10.50	9.50
Creamer, height 5¼″			
☐ pink	8.00	12.00	9.00
☐ green	10.00	14.00	11.00

	Current Price Range		Prior Year Average
Lunch Plate, diameter 8″			
☐ green	10.50	12.50	11.50
☐ pink	8.50	10.50	9.50
Iced Tea Glass, height 5″			
☐ pink	12.00	14.00	13.00
☐ green	13.00	15.00	14.00
Nappy, two handles, diameter 5½″			
☐ pink	5.00	7.00	6.00
☐ green	6.00	8.00	7.00
Pitcher, 40 oz.			
☐ pink	55.00	65.00	60.00
☐ green	60.00	70.00	65.00
Sherbet			
☐ green	3.50	4.50	4.00
☐ pink	3.00	4.00	3.50
Sugar Bowl, diameter 5″			
☐ pink	6.50	8.50	7.50
☐ green	7.00	9.00	8.00
Tumbler, ice tea, height 5″			
☐ pink	11.00	14.50	12.50
☐ green	12.00	15.50	13.50
Water Tumbler, height 4″			
☐ pink	8.50	10.50	9.50
☐ green	10.00	12.00	11.00

FLORENTINE NO. 1
Hazel Atlas Glass Co.

This pattern was made from 1932 to 1935. It has been known from one time to another by several different names: *Poppy No. 1*, *Florentine Hexagonal* and *Old Florentine*. It was made in crystal, green, yellow, pink and some pieces in cobalt blue. All the tumblers in *Florentine No. 1* are footed. The easiest way to tell No. 1 from No. 2 is that all the flat and footed pieces in No. 1 have serrated edges. Pieces in No. 2 have smooth edges. The pink is scarce these days, so not many people are collecting it. Cobalt is really very rare, so as to be uncollectible.

Ashtray, diameter 5½″			
☐ green	16.00	19.00	17.00
☐ yellow	20.00	25.00	21.00
☐ pink	20.00	25.00	21.00
☐ crystal	15.00	17.00	16.00

	Current Price Range		Prior Year Average
Berry Bowl, diameter 5″			
☐ green	9.00	12.00	10.00
☐ yellow	8.50	10.50	9.50
☐ pink	7.00	9.00	8.00
☐ crystal	9.00	12.00	10.00
Berry Bowl, diameter 8½″			
☐ green	16.00	24.00	19.00
☐ yellow	18.00	20.00	19.00
☐ pink	21.00	23.00	22.00
☐ crystal	13.50	15.50	14.50
Butter Dish			
☐ yellow	90.00	115.00	105.00
☐ green	95.00	110.00	100.00
☐ pink	130.00	140.00	135.00
☐ crystal	125.00	135.00	130.00
Butter Dish Bottom			
☐ green	26.00	34.00	30.00
☐ yellow	40.00	50.00	45.00
☐ pink	74.00	84.00	79.00
☐ crystal	44.00	54.00	48.00
Butter Dish Top			
☐ green	48.00	58.00	53.00
☐ yellow	70.00	80.00	74.00
☐ pink	95.00	115.00	105.00
☐ crystal	74.00	84.00	77.50
Cereal Bowl, diameter 6″			
☐ green	8.00	10.00	9.00
☐ yellow	11.00	13.00	12.00
☐ pink	11.00	13.00	12.00
☐ crystal	8.00	10.00	9.00
Coaster, diameter 4″			
☐ green	11.00	13.00	12.00
☐ yellow	14.00	16.00	15.00
☐ pink	18.00	20.00	19.00
☐ crystal	11.00	13.00	12.00
Creamer			
☐ green	6.00	8.00	6.50
☐ yellow	8.00	10.00	9.00
☐ pink	8.00	10.00	9.00
☐ crystal	6.00	8.00	7.00
Cup			
☐ green	4.50	6.50	5.50
☐ yellow	5.50	7.50	6.50
☐ pink	5.00	7.00	6.00
☐ crystal	4.50	6.50	5.50

	Current Price Range		Prior Year Average
Cup and Saucer			
☐ green	6.00	8.00	7.00
☐ pink	8.00	10.00	9.00
Dinner Plate			
☐ green	7.00	9.00	8.00
☐ yellow	10.50	12.50	11.50
☐ pink	11.00	13.00	12.00
☐ crystal	7.00	9.00	8.00
Juice Glass, height 4″			
☐ green	7.00	9.00	7.50
☐ yellow	13.50	15.50	14.50
☐ crystal	7.00	9.00	7.50
Iced Tea Glass, height 5″			
☐ green	14.50	16.50	15.50
☐ yellow	18.00	22.00	19.00
☐ crystal	14.50	16.50	15.50
Pitcher, lip, 48 oz.			
☐ green	35.00	40.00	37.50
☐ pink	90.00	100.00	95.00
☐ crystal	35.00	40.00	37.00
Plate, diameter 8″			
☐ green	4.00	6.00	4.00
☐ yellow	8.00	10.00	8.50
☐ pink	8.00	10.00	8.50
☐ crystal	4.00	6.00	4.50
Platter, oval, length 11″			
☐ green	8.00	10.00	9.00
☐ yellow	12.00	16.00	13.00
☐ pink	14.00	16.00	15.00
☐ crystal	8.00	10.00	9.00
Salt and Pepper Shakers, pedestal foot			
☐ green	27.50	31.50	29.00
☐ yellow	40.00	44.00	42.00
☐ pink	40.00	45.00	42.00
☐ crystal	27.50	31.50	29.00
Salad Plate, diameter 8″			
☐ green	4.00	6.00	4.50
☐ yellow	8.00	10.00	9.00
☐ pink	7.50	9.50	8.50
☐ crystal	4.00	6.00	4.00
Saucer			
☐ green	2.00	3.00	2.00
☐ yellow	3.00	4.00	3.50
☐ pink	3.00	4.00	3.50
☐ crystal	2.00	3.00	2.50

	Current Price Range		Prior Year Average
Sugar Bowl			
☐ green	6.00	8.00	7.00
☐ yellow	8.00	10.00	9.00
☐ pink	8.00	10.00	9.00
☐ crystal	6.00	8.00	7.00
Tumbler, 4 oz., footed, height 3¼″			
☐ green	6.00	9.00	7.50
☐ yellow	10.00	14.00	12.00
☐ pink	9.00	13.00	10.00
☐ crystal	6.00	9.00	7.00
Vegetable Bowl, with cover, length 4″			
☐ green	27.00	33.00	30.00
☐ yellow	34.00	38.00	36.00
☐ pink	34.00	38.00	36.00
☐ crystal	27.00	33.00	30.00
Water Glass, footed, height 4¾″			
☐ green	10.00	12.00	11.00
☐ yellow	14.00	15.00	13.00
☐ pink	16.00	18.00	17.00
☐ crystal	10.00	12.00	11.00

FLORENTINE NO. 2
Hazel Atlas Glass Co.

Also referred to as *Poppy No. 2,* it was in production from 1934 through 1936. The pattern on the wares is the same as *Florentine No. 1* but the shapes of the pieces are different. *Florentine No. 2* pieces are all round with smooth edges and bases. This differs from *Florentine No. 1*. The colors issued were green, crystal, yellow, cobalt blue, pink and amber. Yellow and pink demand the best prices. Amber and cobalt are very rare, but green and crystal are available. Some fired-on colors have also been reported. Some *Florentine* collectors mix No. 1 and No. 2 (in fact, the butter dish tops are interchangeable) but if you're a purist, you'll keep them separate.

Ashtray, diameter 3¼″			
☐ yellow	15.00	18.00	16.00
☐ green	7.00	10.00	8.50
☐ crystal	7.00	10.00	8.50
Ashtray, diameter 5½″			
☐ yellow	25.00	29.00	27.00
☐ green	13.00	15.00	14.00
☐ crystal	13.00	15.00	14.00

	Current Price Range		Prior Year Average
Berry Bowl, diameter 4¼″			
☐ pink	8.00	10.00	9.00
☐ yellow	12.00	14.00	13.00
☐ green	6.50	8.50	7.50
☐ crystal	6.50	8.50	7.50
Berry Bowl, diameter 8″			
☐ pink	15.00	17.00	16.00
☐ yellow	15.00	17.00	16.00
☐ green	13.00	15.00	14.00
☐ crystal	13.00	15.00	14.00
Butter Dish, with lid, length 5½″			
☐ yellow	114.00	118.00	116.00
☐ green	77.50	83.50	80.50
☐ crystal	77.50	83.50	80.50
Candlesticks, pair, height 2½″			
☐ yellow	37.50	43.50	40.50
☐ green	29.50	44.50	42.00
☐ crystal	29.50	44.50	42.00
Candy Bowl, with lid			
☐ pink	93.00	103.00	98.00
☐ yellow	120.00	130.00	125.00
☐ green	65.00	85.00	75.00
☐ crystal	65.00	85.00	75.00
Cereal Bowl, diameter 6″			
☐ pink	13.00	15.00	14.00
☐ yellow	18.00	22.00	20.00
☐ green	10.00	14.00	12.00
☐ crystal	10.00	14.00	12.00
Coaster, diameter 3¾″			
☐ yellow	18.00	21.00	19.00
☐ green	11.00	13.00	12.00
☐ crystal	11.00	13.00	12.00
Comport, height 3½″			
☐ pink	5.00	7.00	6.00
☐ yellow	16.00	18.00	17.00
☐ green	11.00	13.00	12.00
☐ crystal	11.00	13.00	12.00
☐ blue	40.00	50.00	42.00
Condiment Tray			
☐ yellow	47.00	52.00	49.00
Cup			
☐ yellow	6.00	8.00	7.00
☐ green	4.00	6.00	5.00
☐ crystal	4.00	6.00	5.00
☐ amber	30.00	35.00	32.00

	Current Price Range		Prior Year Average
Custard Cup			
☐ yellow...	57.00	63.00	60.00
☐ green	37.00	43.00	40.00
☐ crystal	37.00	43.00	40.00
Dinner Plate, diameter 10″			
☐ pink	10.00	12.00	11.00
☐ yellow...	9.00	12.00	10.50
☐ green	8.00	10.00	9.00
☐ crystal	8.00	10.00	9.00
Gravy Boat			
☐ yellow...	30.00	35.00	32.00
Gravy Boat Tray, length 11″			
☐ yellow...	30.00	33.00	31.00
Grill Plate, diameter 10″			
☐ yellow...	6.50	8.50	7.50
☐ green	4.50	6.50	5.50
☐ crystal	4.50	6.50	5.50
Juice Glass, height 3¼″			
☐ pink	6.50	8.50	7.50
☐ yellow...	12.00	14.00	13.00
☐ green	5.50	7.50	6.50
☐ crystal	5.50	7.50	6.50
Iced Tea Glass, height 5″			
☐ yellow...	20.00	25.00	22.00
☐ crystal	15.00	20.00	17.50
☐ green	15.00	20.00	17.50
Nut Bowl, fluted rim, diameter 5″			
☐ pink	8.00	12.00	9.00
☐ blue	27.00	31.00	29.00
Parfait, height 6″			
☐ yellow...	50.00	54.00	53.00
☐ green	18.00	21.00	19.00
☐ crystal	18.00	21.00	19.00
Pitcher, height 7¼″			
☐ yellow...	125.00	132.00	128.00
Pitcher, height 8″			
☐ pink	190.00	200.00	195.00
☐ yellow...	170.00	180.00	175.00
☐ green	65.00	75.00	70.00
☐ crystal	65.00	75.00	70.00
Pitcher, conical, pedestal foot, height 6½″			
☐ yellow...	80.00	88.00	84.00

	Current Price Range		Prior Year Average

Pitcher, conical, pedestal foot, height 7½″

☐ yellow..	20.00	22.00	21.00
☐ green	16.50	18.50	17.50
☐ crystal	16.50	18.50	17.50

Plate, with spoon holder, diameter 6¼″

☐ yellow..	20.00	25.00	22.00
☐ green	10.00	14.00	11.00
☐ crystal	10.00	14.00	11.00

Platter, oval, length 11″

☐ pink	9.50	11.50	10.50
☐ yellow..	11.00	14.00	12.50
☐ green	8.50	10.50	9.50
☐ crystal	8.50	10.50	9.50

Relish Dish, compartmentalized, length 11″

☐ pink	14.00	16.00	15.00
☐ yellow..	14.50	16.50	15.50
☐ green	10.50	12.50	11.50
☐ crystal	10.50	12.50	11.50

Salad Plate, diameter 8″

☐ pink	5.50	6.50	5.50
☐ yellow..	5.50	7.50	6.50
☐ green	3.50	5.50	4.50
☐ crystal	3.50	5.50	4.50

Salt and Pepper Shakers, height 3¼″

☐ yellow..	37.50	42.50	39.50
☐ green	32.50	36.50	33.75
☐ crystal	32.50	36.50	33.75

Saucer

☐ yellow..	2.75	3.75	3.25
☐ green	1.75	2.75	2.25
☐ crystal	1.75	2.75	2.25
☐ amber	13.50	15.50	14.50

Sherbet Dish, pedestal foot

☐ yellow..	7.50	9.50	8.50
☐ green	4.50	6.50	5.50
☐ crystal	4.50	6.50	5.50

Sherbet Plate, diameter 6″

☐ yellow..	3.25	4.25	3.75
☐ green	1.75	2.75	2.25
☐ crystal	1.75	2.75	2.25

	Current Price Range		Prior Year Average
Soup Bowl, diameter 4¾″			
☐ pink	7.50	9.50	8.50
☐ yellow	12.00	14.00	12.50
☐ crystal	8.00	10.00	9.50
☐ green	8.00	10.00	9.00
Sugar Bowl			
☐ yellow	7.00	9.00	8.00
☐ green	4.50	6.50	5.50
☐ crystal	4.50	6.50	5.50
Tumbler, flat base, height 3½″			
☐ crystal	5.50	7.50	6.50
☐ green	5.50	7.50	6.50
Tumbler, pedestal foot, height 3¼″			
☐ yellow	8.00	10.00	9.00
☐ green	7.00	9.00	8.00
☐ crystal	7.00	9.00	8.00
Tumbler, pedestal foot, height 4″			
☐ yellow	9.00	11.00	10.00
☐ green	7.00	9.00	8.00
☐ crystal	7.00	9.00	8.00
Tumbler, pedestal foot, height 4½″			
☐ yellow	11.00	13.00	12.00
☐ green	8.50	10.50	9.50
☐ crystal	8.50	10.50	9.50
Tumbler, height 5″			
☐ yellow	22.00	26.00	24.00
☐ green	18.00	20.00	19.00
☐ crystal	18.00	20.00	19.00
Vegetable Bowl, with lid, length 9″			
☐ yellow	40.00	44.00	42.00
☐ green	30.00	34.00	32.00
☐ crystal	30.00	34.00	32.00
Water Tumbler, height 4″			
☐ pink	7.50	9.50	8.50
☐ yellow	12.00	14.00	13.00
☐ green	7.50	9.50	8.50
☐ crystal	7.50	9.50	8.50
☐ blue	45.00	52.00	48.50

FOREST GREEN
Anchor Hocking Glass Co.

This pattern was produced from 1950 to 1957. It is therefore not true Depression glass, but high collector interest warrants its listing here. It is available mostly in green, but other colors have been reported. It is a matter of argument whether these pieces are truly *Forest Green* or not. *Forest Green*

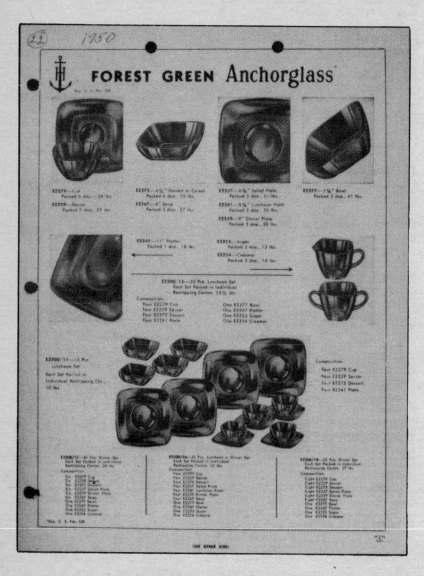

1950 Forest Green Catalog Sheet.
Courtesy of Anchor Hocking Corporation, Lancaster, Ohio

pieces are basically square. The tumblers are available with decorations of Americana scenes such as an open sleigh ride or children playing. These tumblers are worth about double what the plain ones are.

FORTUNE
Hocking Glass Co.

This line was manufactured from 1936 through 1938. It's a small pattern, can be bought inexpensively but generally doesn't cause much excitement. The colors are pink and crystal and they seem to be in equal supply on the market. You might have some trouble locating the 8″ luncheon plate, but it's the only item difficult to find.

Fortune

	Current Price Range		Prior Year Average
Berry Bowl, diameter 4″			
☐ pink or crystal....................	2.25	4.25	3.25
Bowl, two handles, diameter 4½″			
☐ pink or crystal....................	3.25	5.00	4.00
Bowl, tucked rim, diameter 5¼″			
☐ pink or crystal....................	3.75	5.25	4.50
Candy Dish, with lid, color base			
☐ pink or crystal....................	13.00	16.00	14.50
Cup			
☐ pink or crystal....................	2.25	3.50	2.75
Dessert Bowl, diameter 4½″			
☐ pink or crystal....................	3.50	4.75	4.00
Juice Tumbler, height 3½″			
☐ pink or crystal....................	3.00	4.00	3.50
Lunch Plate, diameter 8″			
☐ pink or crystal....................	4.00	5.00	4.50
Salad Bowl, diameter 7¾″			
☐ pink or crystal....................	6.00	8.00	7.00

	Current Price Range		Prior Year Average

Saucer

☐ pink or crystal..................................... 1.25 2.25 1.75

Sherbet Plate

☐ pink or crystal..................................... 1.50 3.00 2.25

Tumbler, 5 oz., juice, height 3½"

☐ pink or crystal..................................... 3.00 4.50 3.75

Tumbler, 9 oz., water, height 4"

☐ pink or crystal..................................... 3.50 4.50 4.25

FRUITS
Unknown Manufacturer

It is important to point out when talking about *Fruits* that Hazel Atlas is generally credited with the bulk of the pieces. Some tumblers have been found with pears or grapes and have been credited to Federal. No absolute proof has come to light about any manufacturer so the controversy continues. The most desirable design is the cherry motif on the tumblers. They generally bring 20%–30% more than any other decoration. The colors that have been reported are pink, green and some crystal. It's likely that what we call *Fruits* is actually a number of different lines produced by several manufacturers. The different types can be mixed with great success however.

Fruits

Berry Bowl, diameter 8"

☐ pink 26.00 32.00 29.00

☐ green 28.50 34.50 31.50

	Current Price Range		Prior Year Average
Cereal Bowl, diameter 5″			
☐ pink	9.00	12.00	10.00
☐ green	10.00	15.00	12.00
Cup			
☐ pink	3.25	4.25	3.75
☐ green	3.75	4.75	4.25
Juice Tumbler, height 3½″			
☐ pink	6.25	7.25	6.75
☐ green	6.75	7.75	7.25
Lunch Plate, diameter 8″			
☐ pink	3.25	4.25	3.75
☐ green	3.25	4.25	3.75
Pitcher, height 7″			
☐ green	37.00	41.00	39.00
Saucer			
☐ pink	1.75	2.75	2.25
☐ green	1.75	2.75	2.25
Sherbet Dish, stemmed			
☐ pink	4.75	5.75	5.25
☐ green	5.25	6.25	5.75
Tumbler, height 4″			
☐ pink	6.25	8.25	7.25
☐ green	7.25	8.25	7.75
Tumbler, height 5″			
☐ pink	20.00	23.00	21.50
☐ green	30.00	36.00	33.00

GEORGIAN
Federal Glass Co.

Also known as *Lovebirds,* Federal made this pattern from 1931 through 1935. *Georgian* got a lot of attention in 1977 when the Peach State Depression Glass Club donated a setting of it to the Smithsonian Institute in honor of President Jimmy Carter. Prices rose dramatically in this line and it became much harder to find. Some pieces, though, were never easy to find. The 6½″ berry bowl, the sugar lid and the cold cuts server are all difficult to get. The cold cuts server is a particularly interesting item. It's made of wood, 18½″ in diameter with slots for seven hot plates. It is also referred to as a lazy Susan, but Federal called it a cold cuts server. Watch out for the tumblers, they do not have the lovebirds in their designs, only the baskets are shown. Also, the dinner plates were made in two styles; one with the standard design and one with only the garland and center design.

Georgian

	Current Price Range		Prior Year Average
Berry Bowl, diameter 4″			
☐ green	4.25	5.25	4.75
Berry Bowl, diameter 7½″			
☐ green	37.00	40.00	38.50
Bowl, steep sided, diameter 6½″			
☐ green	42.00	46.00	44.00
Butter Dish, with cover			
☐ green	60.00	70.00	65.00
Cereal Bowl, diameter 5¼″			
☐ green	12.00	14.00	13.00
Creamer, pedestal foot, diameter 3″			
☐ green	7.00	9.00	8.00
Creamer, pedestal foot, diameter 4″			
☐ green	7.00	10.00	9.00
Cup			
☐ green	6.00	8.00	7.00
Dinner Plate, diameter 9¼″			
☐ green	16.00	22.00	18.00
Lunch Plate, diameter 8″			
☐ green	5.25	6.25	5.75
Plate, central medallion and band on rim, diameter 9¼″			
☐ green	14.25	15.25	14.75

	Current Price Range		Prior Year Average
Platter, tab handle, diameter 11¼"			
□ green	48.00	58.00	53.00
Saucer			
□ green	1.75	2.75	2.25
Sherbet Dish, stemmed			
□ green	7.00	10.00	8.00
Sherbet Plate, diameter 6"			
□ green	2.50	3.75	3.25
Sugar Bowl, pedestal foot, with lid, height 3"			
□ green	27.00	34.00	30.00
Sugar Bowl, pedestal foot, with lid, diameter 4"			
□ green	34.00	40.00	37.00
Sugar Lid			
□ green	21.00	23.00	22.00
Tumbler, height 4"			
□ green	36.00	42.00	37.00
Tumbler, height 5¼"			
□ green	60.00	70.00	66.00
Vegetable Bowl, length 9"			
□ green	48.00	58.00	53.00

HARP
Jeannette Glass Co.

Because it was manufactured in the mid–1950s, *Harp* isn't true Depression era glass. However, it is in demand by Depression glass collectors who are taking advantage of its relatively low values. The tray and the cake stands are really the most outstanding items in this set. Both are very useful and beautiful. There are two styles of cake stands, though, so watch for both.

Harp

	Current Price Range		Prior Year Average
Ashtray			
☐ crystal..	3.00	5.00	3.50
Cake Stand, diameter 9″			
☐ crystal..	13.00	18.00	15.00
☐ pink...	14.00	20.00	17.00
☐ blue...	15.00	21.00	18.00
Coaster, diameter 3½″			
☐ crystal..	2.00	3.00	2.50
Cup			
☐ crystal..	4.00	7.00	5.00
Plate, diameter 7″			
☐ crystal..	2.00	3.00	2.50
Saucer			
☐ crystal..	1.25	3.00	1.75
Tray, two-handled			
☐ crystal..	16.00	22.00	19.00
Vase, height 6″			
☐ crystal..	9.00	12.00	10.00

HERITAGE
Federal Glass Co.

This pattern was manufactured in the late 1930s and early 1940s. It's a small pattern but is growing in popularity. Some collectors are turned off by *Heritage* because it doesn't have tumblers, but other collectors mix and match with other patterns so it doesn't pose a great obstacle. Crystal is by far the most available. Full sets have been found in green, pink and blue but they are quite rare. The berry sets are the most available pieces in colors, but they are still far from easy to get.

Heritage

	Current Price Range		Prior Year Average
Berry Bowl, diameter 5″			
☐ crystal	3.75	4.75	4.25
☐ blue	28.00	31.00	29.50
☐ green	28.00	31.00	29.50
☐ pink	14.25	15.25	14.75
Berry Bowl, diameter 8″			
☐ crystal	11.75	12.75	12.25
☐ blue	56.00	58.00	57.00
☐ green	56.00	58.00	57.00
☐ pink	38.00	41.00	39.50
Creamer, pedestal foot			
☐ crystal	10.75	11.75	11.25
Cup			
☐ crystal	2.75	3.75	3.25
☐ blue	23.00	30.00	27.00
Dinner Plate, diameter 9″			
☐ crystal	5.75	6.75	6.25
Fruit Bowl			
☐ crystal	11.75	12.75	12.25
Lunch Plate, diameter 8″			
☐ crystal	4.25	5.25	4.75

	Current Price Range		Prior Year Average
Sandwich Plate, diameter 12″			
☐ crystal	7.75	8.75	8.25
Saucer			
☐ crystal	.75	1.50	1.00
☐ blue	10.00	16.00	13.00
Sugar Bowl			
☐ crystal	8.25	10.25	9.25

HEXAGON OPTIC
Jeannette Glass Co.

This pattern was made from 1928 through 1932. It is also referred to as *Honeycomb* or *Elongated Honeycomb*. The colors are pink and green. Some iridescent pieces were also made, but not until the 1950s. *Hex Optic* features several kitchen pieces. Especially popular are the stacking refrigerator sets. They are not easy to find, but are well worth the trouble. Attractive and useful, this pattern is made of heavy glass so don't be afraid to use it every day. The whiskey tumbler and the 9 oz. pitcher are also hard to find. Except for the pitcher, the handles in this pattern are closed.

Hexagon Optic

	Current Price Range		Prior Year Average
Berry Bowl, diameter 4¼″			
☐ pink or green....................................	1.75	2.75	2.25
Berry Bowl, diameter 7½″			
☐ pink or green....................................	4.50	7.00	5.75

	Current Price Range		Prior Year Average
Butter Dish, rectangular, lidded			
☐ pink	33.00	36.00	34.50
Creamer			
☐ pink or green.......................	3.25	4.25	3.75
Cup			
☐ pink or green.......................	2.50	3.75	3.00
Ice Bucket, chrome fittings			
☐ pink or green.......................	9.00	15.00	10.00
Lunch Plate, diameter 9″			
☐ pink or green.......................	3.25	5.25	4.25
Mixing Bowl, diameter 7¼″			
☐ pink or green.......................	10.00	14.00	12.00
Mixing Bowl, diameter 8¼″			
☐ pink or green.......................	12.00	16.00	14.00
Mixing Bowl, diameter 8¾″			
☐ pink	15.00	19.00	17.00
Mixing Bowl, diameter 10″			
☐ pink or green.......................	19.00	23.00	21.00
Pitcher, footed, 48 oz., diameter 9″			
☐ pink or green.......................	30.00	38.00	34.00
Pitcher, 32 oz., diameter 5″			
☐ pink or green.......................	29.00	25.00	22.00
Platter, diameter 11″			
☐ pink or green.......................	5.00	4.25	5.25
Refrigerator Set			
☐ pink or green.......................	28.00	31.00	29.00
Salt and Pepper			
☐ green	16.00	18.00	17.00
Saucer			
☐ pink or green.......................	1.50	2.50	2.00
Sherbet Plate, diameter 6″			
☐ pink or green.......................	2.75	3.75	3.25
Tumbler, footed, diameter 5¾″			
☐ pink or green.......................	3.25	5.25	4.25
Tumbler, height 5″			
☐ pink or green.......................	3.75	4.75	4.25
Tumbler, 7 oz., footed, height 4¾″			
☐ pink or green.......................	7.00	9.00	7.50
Tumbler, 9 oz., flat, height 3″			
☐ pink or green.......................	4.00	6.00	5.00

	Current Price Range		Prior Year Average
Whiskey Glass, jigger, height 2"			
☐ pink or green.....................................	3.00	4.50	3.75

HOBNAIL
Hocking Glass Co.

Hocking made their version of *Hobnail* from 1934 through 1936. Hocking then took many of the same molds and produced *Moonstone,* starting in 1942. Other companies also made hobnail pieces but Hocking's is the most collectible. The pink is fairly scarce but the crystal is not difficult to find. Some of the crystal pieces were made with red trim and red bases. They're worth about 50% more than the plain crystal. Many of the pieces display a rayed design either in the center or on the base.

Hobnail

Cereal Bowl, diameter 5½"			
☐ crystal	2.25	3.25	2.75
Cordial Glass, height 3½"			
☐ crystal	3.25	4.25	3.75
Creamer, pedestal foot			
☐ crystal	1.75	2.75	2.25

1934 Hobnail Catalog Sheet.
Courtesy of Anchor Hocking Corporation, Lancaster, Ohio

	Current Price Range		Prior Year Average
Cup, collar base			
☐ pink	1.75	2.75	2.25
☐ crystal	1.75	2.75	2.25
Decanter, with stopper, bulbous			
☐ crystal	10.00	13.00	12.00
Goblet, 13 oz.			
☐ crystal	4.75	6.50	5.50
☐ crystal	4.25	5.25	4.75
Iced Tea Glass, collar base, height 8″			
☐ crystal	4.25	5.25	4.75
Juice Glass, height 3½″			
☐ crystal	3.00	4.00	3.50
Lunch Plate, diameter 8″			
☐ crystal	1.25	2.25	1.75
Milk Pitcher, 18 oz.			
☐ crystal	12.00	15.00	13.50
Salad Bowl, diameter 7″			
☐ crystal	2.00	3.00	2.50
Saucer, diameter 6″			
☐ pink	1.75	2.75	2.25
☐ crystal	1.00	1.75	1.50
Sherbet Plate, diameter 6″			
☐ pink	.50	1.25	.75
☐ crystal	.75	1.50	1.25
Sugar Bowl, pedestal base			
☐ pink	1.75	2.75	2.25
☐ crystal	1.75	2.75	2.25
Water Goblet, stemmed, 10 oz.			
☐ crystal	3.75	4.75	4.25
Water Tumbler, collar base			
☐ crystal	3.75	4.75	4.25
Whiskey Glass, jigger, 1½ oz.			
☐ crystal	3.50	4.50	4.00
Wine Glass, pedestal and stem			
☐ crystal	4.50	5.75	5.00

HOLIDAY
Jeannette Glass Co.

Jeannette made this pattern, also known as *Buttons and Bows,* from 1947 to 1949. It is mainly available in pink, but other colors that were produced were shell pink, crystal and some iridized pieces made in the 1950s. There shouldn't be a problem putting together a set in *Holiday,* especially in pink. The prices are rising steadily and have been for some time so it would be best to act now. There are two styles of cups and saucers in *Holiday.* They are slightly different shades of pink, and the cup ring sizes are different so they aren't interchangeable. There are also two different kinds of sherbets, so be sure the colors match.

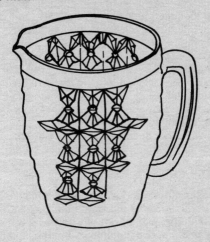

Holiday

	Current Price Range		Prior Year Average
Berry Bowl			
☐ pink	6.25	7.25	6.75
Berry Bowl, diameter 8½"			
☐ pink	14.00	19.00	16.00
Butter Dish			
☐ pink	32.00	36.00	34.00
Candlesticks, pair			
☐ pink	47.00	51.00	49.00
Console Bowl, diameter 10¾"			
☐ pink	60.00	70.00	65.00
Creamer			
☐ pink	5.25	6.25	5.75
Cup and Saucer			
☐ pink	7.25	8.25	7.75
Pitcher, 16 oz., milk, diameter 4¾"			
☐ pink	44.00	52.00	46.00
Pitcher, 52 oz., diameter 6¾"			
☐ pink	24.00	30.00	27.00
Plate, dinner, diameter 9"			
☐ pink	8.75	9.75	9.25
Plate, sherbet, diameter 6"			
☐ pink	2.00	3.50	2.75

	Current Price Range		Prior Year Average
Sandwich Tray, diameter 10½″			
☐ pink	7.00	10.00	8.00
Sherbet, footed			
☐ pink	2.25	3.25	2.75
Sugar and Creamer			
☐ pink	10.00	13.00	11.50
Tumbler, flat, height 4″			
☐ pink	20.00	25.00	22.00
Tumbler, footed, height 6″			
☐ pink	60.00	70.00	65.00

HOMESPUN
Jeannette Glass Co.

This pattern is similar to the Hazel Atlas *Fine Rib* line. The main difference is that *Homespun* has a waffle design on the bottom of the pieces and *Fine Rib* does not. The 96 oz. pitcher doesn't have the waffle design but is listed by Jeannette as being in the pattern, so it is accepted as genuine. Pink is common but only a few crystal pieces can be found. There is also a 14-piece children's set.

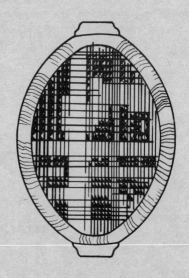

Homespun

	Current Price Range		Prior Year Average
Ashtray			
☐ pink	4.25	5.25	4.75
☐ crystal	4.25	5.25	4.75
Berry Bowl, tab handle, diameter 4½"			
☐ pink	3.75	4.75	4.25
☐ crystal	3.75	4.75	4.25
Berry Bowl, diameter 8¼"			
☐ pink	8.50	10.50	9.25
Butter Dish, with cover			
☐ pink	37.00	41.00	39.00
☐ crystal	37.00	41.00	39.00
Cereal Bowl, diameter 5"			
☐ pink	6.75	7.75	7.25
☐ crystal	6.75	7.75	7.25
Coaster/Ashtray			
☐ pink	4.25	5.25	4.75
Creamer, footed			
☐ pink	5.75	6.75	6.25
☐ crystal	5.75	6.75	6.25
Cup			
☐ pink	3.25	4.25	3.75
☐ crystal	3.25	4.25	3.75
Plate, sherbet, diameter 6"			
☐ pink	1.75	2.50	2.00
Plate, dinner, diameter 9¼"			
☐ pink	7.00	10.00	8.50
Sugar Bowl, with lid			
☐ pink	12.00	15.00	13.00
Tumbler, 5 oz., footed, height 4"			
☐ pink	5.00	8.00	6.75
Tumbler, 8 oz., flat, water, height 4¼"			
☐ pink	7.00	9.25	8.25
Tumbler, 9 oz., footed, height 6¼"			
☐ pink	12.00	17.00	14.50
Tumbler, 13 oz., flat, ice tea, height 5¼"			
☐ pink	13.00	18.00	15.00
Tumbler, 15 oz., footed, height 6½"			
☐ pink	14.00	18.00	15.50

INDIANA CUSTARD
Indiana Glass Co.

This pattern is found in ivory or custard only, although in the 1950s a version appeared in white. It is called *Flower and Leaf Band* after the decorative motif that encircles the squarely scalloped rim of plates and bowls, or the mid-section of other items. To actually qualify as custard glass, a piece contains a certain amount of uranium which will cause it to fluoresce under backlight, and it must also produce a ring when struck, rather than a dull thud. It was manufactured in the early 1930s.

	Current Price Range		Prior Year Average
Berry Bowl, diameter 4⅞"			
☐ ivory	5.00	7.00	6.00
Berry Bowl, diameter 8¾"			
☐ ivory	19.00	23.00	21.00
Bread and Butter Plate, diameter 5¾"			
☐ ivory	4.00	6.00	5.00
Butter Dish, with lid			
☐ ivory	50.00	60.00	54.00
Cereal Bowl, diameter 5¾"			
☐ ivory	12.00	16.00	14.00
Creamer			
☐ ivory	12.00	15.00	13.00
Cup			
☐ ivory	30.00	35.00	32.00
Dinner Plate, diameter 9¾"			
☐ ivory	14.00	16.00	15.00
Luncheon Plate, diameter 8⅞"			
☐ ivory	8.00	11.00	9.25
Platter, oval, length 11½"			
☐ ivory	24.00	28.00	25.50
Salad Plate, diameter 7½"			
☐ ivory	9.00	13.00	10.00
Saucer			
☐ ivory	5.25	7.25	6.50
Sherbet			
☐ ivory	69.00	77.00	71.00
Soup Bowl, flat, diameter 7½"			
☐ ivory	15.00	21.00	17.50
Vegetable Bowl, diameter 9½"			
☐ ivory	18.00	21.00	19.50

IRIS
Jeannette Glass Co.

Also known as *Iris and Herringbone,* Jeannette first produced this pattern in crystal and pink from 1928 through 1932. Some green is rumored to have been made as well, but as yet, no pieces have been reported. Crystal is by far the easiest to find. Jeannette produced some iridescent colors in the 1950s and then again in the 1960s and 70s. These pieces can be spotted instantly since no iridized pieces were originally made, but Jeannette also made crystal sets in 1960–70 and these are impossible to detect so don't even try. The one exception to that is the candy dish. The original had a rayed foot and the new one has a plain foot. The 8″ beaded bowl and the 7½″ soup are both very rare, as is the luncheon plate. Some pieces have also been found with a satin finish.

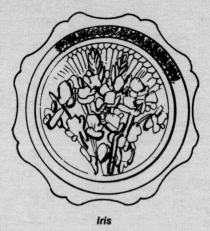

Iris

	Current Price Range		Prior Year Average
Berry Bowl, beaded edge, diameter 4½″			
☐ crystal	40.00	46.00	42.00
☐ iridescent	5.00	7.00	6.00
Berry Bowl, diameter 8″			
☐ crystal	55.00	65.00	60.00
☐ iridescent	7.00	9.00	8.00
Bowl, ruffled rim, diameter 5½″			
☐ crystal	5.00	7.00	6.00
☐ iridescent	6.00	8.00	7.00
Butter Dish, with cover			
☐ crystal	27.00	31.00	29.00
☐ iridescent	30.00	33.00	31.50
Candlesticks, pair			
☐ crystal	16.00	20.00	17.50
☐ iridescent	20.00	24.00	22.00
Candy Jar, with cover			
☐ crystal	60.00	70.00	65.00
Cereal Bowl, diameter 5″			
☐ crystal	25.00	33.00	29.00
Coaster			
☐ crystal	30.00	36.00	32.50
Creamer, footed			
☐ crystal	6.25	7.25	6.75
☐ iridescent	6.75	8.75	7.75

	Current Price Range		Prior Year Average
Cup			
☐ crystal...	8.00	10.00	9.00
☐ iridescent.......................................	6.75	8.75	7.75
Demitasse Cup, with saucer			
☐ crystal...	13.50	15.50	14.50
☐ iridescent.......................................	50.00	62.00	55.00
Dinner Plate, diameter 9″			
☐ crystal...	27.00	31.00	29.00
☐ iridescent.......................................	16.25	20.00	18.00
Fruit Bowl, diameter 11½″			
☐ crystal...	30.00	36.00	33.00
Fruit Bowl, ruffled rim, diameter 11″			
☐ crystal...	7.00	9.00	8.00
☐ iridescent.......................................	5.25	6.25	5.75
Goblet, cocktail, height 4¼″			
☐ crystal...	12.00	16.00	14.00
Goblet, 4 oz., height 5¾″			
☐ crystal...	13.00	17.00	14.00
Goblet, 8 oz., height 5¾″			
☐ crystal...	14.00	17.50	15.25
Luncheon Plate, diameter 8″			
☐ crystal...	33.00	40.00	35.00
Pitcher, footed, height 9½″			
☐ crystal...	17.00	23.00	20.00
☐ iridescent.......................................	23.00	29.00	25.00
Salad Bowl, diameter 9″			
☐ crystal...	6.00	9.00	7.00
☐ iridescent.......................................	6.50	8.50	7.50
Sandwich Plate, diameter 11¾″			
☐ crystal...	10.00	13.00	11.50
☐ iridescent.......................................	9.50	11.50	10.50
Sherbet Bowl, footed, diameter 2½″			
☐ crystal...	12.00	14.00	13.00
☐ iridescent.......................................	7.00	10.00	8.50
Sherbet Bowl, footed, diameter 4″			
☐ crystal...	9.00	12.00	10.50
Sherbet Plate, diameter 5½″			
☐ crystal...	9.00	5.25	6.25
☐ iridescent.......................................	6.00	8.00	7.00
Soup Bowl, diameter 7½″			
☐ crystal...	70.00	76.00	72.00
☐ iridescent.......................................	25.00	32.00	27.00
Sugar Bowl, with lid			
☐ crystal...	12.00	14.00	13.00
☐ iridescent.......................................	10.00	15.00	11.50

	Current Price Range		Prior Year Average

Tumbler, flat, height 4″
☐ crystal 40.00   50.00   45.00
Tumbler, footed, height 6″
☐ crystal 10.00   12.00   11.00
☐ iridescent 10.00   12.00   11.00
Tumbler, footed, height 7″
☐ crystal 13.25   14.25   13.75
☐ iridescent 12.00   14.00   13.00
Vase, height 9″
☐ crystal 14.25   15.25   14.75
☐ iridescent 13.25   14.25   13.75
☐ pink 47.00   53.00   50.00
Wine Glass, height 4″
☐ crystal 11.25   13.25   12.25
☐ iridescent 12.25   14.25   13.25
Wine Goblet, height 4½″
☐ crystal 11.00   13.00   12.00

JUBILEE
Lancaster Glass Co.

This pattern was manufactured in the early 1930s. Basically the only color you will find it in is yellow, although some pink has been reported and more may exist. There are many patterns that resemble *Jubilee,* some even by Lancaster, but there is only one real one. The design features a flower with twelve petals and an open center. The center of the item is plain. The edges feature a six-point scallop.

Cake Tray, open handle, diameter 11″
☐ yellow 22.00   28.00   24.00
Cheese and Cracker Set
☐ yellow 35.00   45.00   40.00
Creamer
☐ yellow 14.00   18.00   16.00
Cup
☐ yellow 9.00   12.00   11.00
Fruit Bowl, open handle, diameter 9″
☐ yellow 30.00   37.00   34.00
Goblet, 6 oz., height 5″
☐ yellow 25.00   32.00   27.50
Goblet, stem and pedestal, height 6″
☐ yellow 20.00   25.00   21.50

	Current Price Range		Prior Year Average
Goblet, stem and pedestal, height 6¼"			
☐ yellow..	40.00	47.00	43.00
Lunch Plate, diameter 8½"			
☐ yellow..	7.00	10.00	8.00
Mayonnaise Compote, with ladle			
☐ yellow..	65.00	80.00	65.00
Salad Plate, diameter 7¼"			
☐ yellow..	5.00	8.00	6.00
Sandwich Plate, diameter 13"			
☐ yellow..	20.00	26.00	23.00
Sandwich Tray, center open handle			
☐ yellow..	23.00	29.00	25.00
Saucer			
☐ yellow..	2.25	3.50	2.75
Sugar Bowl			
☐ yellow..	14.50	17.50	15.50

LACE EDGE
Hocking Glass Co.

Hocking made this pattern, also known as *Open Lace,* from 1935 through 1938. Some crystal pieces were made, but pink is by far the more common color. Other glass companies made lace-edge patterns and some of them can be confused with Hocking's quite easily. Many collectors feel, however, that Hocking's is lower quality glass and can be detected by its cheaper "feel." Also, the other companies made a wide range of colors, so if you have any other color than pink and crystal, it's not Hocking. As you can see by the price, the 9" compote is very, very rare. The vase will often bring over $100 these days, as will the three-legged bowl. The sugar and creamer are also not easily found. Some *Lace Edge* pieces can be found with a satin finish. These sell for about half of the price of the pink.

Lace Edge

	Current Price Range		Prior Year Average
Bowl, plain, diameter 9½″			
☐ pink	10.00	13.00	11.50
Bowl, ribbed, diameter 9½″			
☐ pink	10.00	13.00	11.50
Bowl, three-legged, diameter 10½″			
☐ pink	120.00	130.00	125.00
Butter Dish, with cover			
☐ pink	43.00	46.00	44.50
Candlesticks, pair			
☐ pink	110.00	120.00	115.00
Cereal Bowl, diameter 6⅜″			
☐ pink	11.00	13.00	12.00
Comport, diameter 7″			
☐ pink	13.00	16.00	14.50
Comport, with cover, footed			
☐ pink	20.00	30.00	25.00
Comport, diameter 9″			
☐ pink	400.00	500.00	450.00
Cookie Jar, with cover			
☐ pink	32.00	42.00	37.00
Creamer			
☐ pink	13.00	15.00	14.00
Cup			
☐ pink	14.50	16.50	15.50
Dinner Plate, diameter 10½″			
☐ pink	16.00	18.00	17.00

1936 Lace Edge Catalog Sheet.
Courtesy of Anchor Hocking Corporation, Lancaster, Ohio

	Current Price Range		Prior Year Average
Fish Bowl, one gallon and 8 oz.			
☐ crystal	15.00	20.00	17.00
Flower Vase, with crystal frog			
☐ pink	15.00	17.00	16.00
Grill Plate, diameter 10½″			
☐ pink	10.00	14.00	12.00
Luncheon Plate, diameter 8¾″			
☐ pink	10.00	14.00	12.00
Plate, with four compartments, rim in closed Lace, diameter 13″			
☐ pink	15.00	18.00	16.50
Platter, five compartments, length 13¾″			
☐ pink	15.00	20.00	17.00
Platter, length 13¾″			
☐ pink	16.00	18.00	17.00
Relish Dish, three compartments, deep, diameter 7½″			
☐ pink	30.00	40.00	35.00
Relish Tray, three compartments, diameter 10½″			
☐ pink	16.00	18.00	17.00
Salad Bowl, diameter 7¾″			
☐ pink	11.00	15.00	13.00
Salad Plate, diameter 7¼″			
☐ pink	9.00	14.00	12.00
Saucer			
☐ pink	5.00	8.00	6.50
Sherbet Bowl, footed			
☐ pink	40.00	50.00	45.00
Sugar Bowl			
☐ pink	11.00	15.00	13.00
Tumbler, flat, height 3½″			
☐ pink	6.00	8.00	7.00
Tumbler, flat, height 4½″			
☐ pink	7.00	10.00	8.00
Tumbler, footed, height 5″			
☐ pink	37.00	47.00	42.00
Vase, height 7″			
☐ pink	210.00	270.00	245.00

LACED EDGE
Imperial Glass Co.

Imperial made this pattern in the early and middle 1930s. It was primarily made in blue, although some green pieces can be found. The edge of these pieces is a white opalescent. Imperial called this design *Sea Foam* and it was very successful. Imperial added it to several of its lines. This pattern isn't easy to collect, but some pieces are more difficult to locate than others. The vase is particularly hard to spot.

Laced Edge

	Current Price Range		Prior Year Average
Bowl, diameter 5″			
☐ blue	14.00	17.00	15.50
Bowl, oval, length 11″			
☐ blue	35.00	45.00	40.00
Bread and Butter Plate, 6½″			
☐ blue	6.50	9.50	7.50
Candleholder, double branch			
☐ blue	27.00	33.00	28.00
Creamer			
☐ blue	13.00	17.00	14.00
Cup			
☐ blue	13.00	17.00	14.00
Dinner Plate, 10″			
☐ blue	18.00	22.00	19.00
Fruit Bowl, 4½″			
☐ blue	7.50	10.50	8.25
Platter, diameter 13″			
☐ blue	44.00	52.00	48.00
Salad Plate, 8″			
☐ blue	10.50	13.50	11.50
Saucer			
☐ blue	3.00	5.00	3.50
Soup Bowl, 7″			
☐ blue	13.00	17.00	14.00

	Current Price Range		Prior Year Average

Sugar
☐ blue 13.00   17.00   14.00
Tumbler, 9 oz.
☐ blue 18.00   22.00   19.00
Tumbler, water, footed
☐ blue 18.00   22.00   19.00
Vase, 5½"
☐ blue 20.00   25.00   21.00
Vegetable Bowl, 9"
☐ blue 27.00   33.00   28.00

LAKE COMO
Hocking Glass Co.

This scenic pattern is white with blue decoration and can be identified by its depiction of a lakeside garden. Guarded steps lead to a platform featuring three Greek columns in perspective; the top pedestal of the stairway is mounted with a large, decorative urn. A sailboat is seen in the distance against a backdrop of rolling hills and clouds. Plate rims are encircled with five consecutive blue bands of white flowers, five to each grouping. It is a small pattern but very attractive and so, therefore, very popular. It is difficult to find, so you must be prepared to search. Prices are low on these pieces and should be going up.

Cereal Bowl, diameter 5¼"
☐ white 4.00   6.00   4.50
Creamer, pedestal base
☐ white 7.00   9.00   8.00
Cup
☐ white 6.00   8.00   7.00
Dinner Plate, diameter 9½"
☐ white 8.00   10.00   9.00
Platter, diameter 11"
☐ white 13.00   16.00   14.50
Salad Plate, diameter 7½"
☐ white 4.00   6.00   4.50
Salt and Pepper Shakers
☐ white 21.00   23.00   22.00
Saucer
☐ white 2.00   4.00   2.50
Sugar Bowl, pedestal foot
☐ white 7.00   9.00   8.00

1937 Lake Como Catalog Sheet.
Courtesy of Anchor Hocking Corporation, Lancaster, Ohio

	Current Price Range		Prior Year Average

Vegetable Bowl, diameter 9¼"
☐ white.. 11.00 13.00 12.00

LAUREL
McKee Glass Co.

A continuous laurel trim, consisting of a band of berries with stippled leaves, encircles the rim of these items which were cast in French ivory, jade green, white opal, and very rarely, poudre (powder) blue. The children's sets feature fired-on rims of either orange, red, blue, or green. In another motif, a Scottie dog is fired on under the glass. The colored band rim can be found on some of the adult items. There isn't much left on the market in *Laurel,* however. The tumblers, shakers and three-legged bowl are particularly scarce. The children's set is easier to find than a lot of the standard items.

Berry Bowl, diameter 5"
☐ ivory...................... 3.25 5.25 4.25
☐ white or jade 2.75 3.75 3.25
☐ blue 5.00 7.00 6.00
Berry Bowl, diameter 9"
☐ ivory...................... 11.00 13.00 12.00
☐ white or jade 8.00 10.00 9.00
☐ blue 15.00 18.00 16.50
Bowl, three-legged, diameter 6"
☐ ivory...................... 7.00 9.00 7.50
☐ white or jade 5.00 7.00 6.00
Bowl, three-legged, diameter 10½"
☐ ivory...................... 23.00 26.00 24.50
☐ white or jade 17.00 21.00 19.00
☐ blue 30.00 33.00 31.50
Bowl, diameter 11"
☐ ivory...................... 24.00 28.00 26.00
☐ white or jade 15.00 17.00 16.00
☐ blue 24.00 28.00 26.00
Candlesticks, pair, height 4"
☐ ivory...................... 19.00 23.00 21.00
☐ white or jade 15.00 17.00 16.00
☐ blue 19.00 23.00 21.00
Cereal Bowl, diameter 6"
☐ ivory...................... 4.50 6.00 4.75
☐ white or jade 3.00 5.00 4.00
☐ blue 7.25 8.25 7.75

	Current Price Range		Prior Year Average
Cheese Dish, with cover			
☐ ivory...	40.00	50.00	45.00
☐ white or jade	30.00	40.00	35.00
Creamer, small			
☐ ivory...	6.00	8.00	7.00
☐ white or jade	5.00	7.00	6.00
Creamer, large			
☐ ivory...	7.00	9.00	8.00
☐ white or jade	6.00	8.00	7.00
☐ blue	11.00	13.00	12.00
Cup			
☐ ivory...	4.00	6.00	4.50
☐ white or jade	3.00	5.00	3.50
☐ blue	10.00	12.00	10.50
Dinner Plate, diameter 9⅛″			
☐ ivory...	3.50	5.50	4.50
☐ white or jade	3.00	6.50	4.50
☐ blue	8.00	10.00	9.00
Grill Plate, diameter 9⅛″			
☐ ivory...	3.00	5.00	4.00
☐ white or jade	3.00	4.00	3.25
☐ blue	6.00	8.00	7.00
Platter, oval, length 10¾″			
☐ ivory...	15.00	17.00	16.00
☐ white or jade	12.00	15.00	13.00
☐ blue	18.00	21.00	19.50
Salad Plate, diameter 7½″			
☐ ivory...	4.50	5.50	4.75
☐ white or jade	2.50	3.50	2.75
☐ blue	6.00	8.00	7.00
Salt and Pepper Shakers			
☐ ivory...	39.00	47.00	42.00
☐ white or jade	44.00	52.00	47.00
Saucer			
☐ ivory...	2.00	3.00	2.50
☐ white or jade	2.00	3.00	2.50
☐ blue	4.00	6.00	4.50
Sherbet Dish			
☐ ivory...	8.00	10.00	9.00
☐ white or jade	5.00	7.00	6.00
Sherbet Plate, diameter 6″			
☐ ivory...	3.00	4.00	3.25
☐ white or jade	2.00	3.00	2.25
☐ blue	3.00	5.00	4.00

	Current Price Range		Prior Year Average
Sugar Bowl, small			
□ ivory....................................	6.00	8.00	7.00
□ white or jade	5.00	7.00	6.00
□ blue	11.00	13.00	12.00
Sugar Bowl, large			
□ ivory....................................	7.00	9.00	7.50
□ white or jade	6.00	8.00	7.00
□ blue	12.00	14.00	13.00
Tumbler, flat, height 4½″			
□ ivory....................................	21.00	23.00	22.00
Tumbler, flat, height 5″			
□ ivory....................................	26.00	28.00	27.00
Vegetable Bowl, oval, length 9¾″			
□ ivory....................................	14.00	16.00	15.00
□ white or jade	10.00	13.00	11.50
□ blue	20.00	25.00	22.00

LORAIN
Indiana Glass Co.

Indiana made *Lorain* in 1932. It is also referred to as *Basket.* It's available in crystal, yellow and green. Yellow is the most common color and crystal the least, and yet yellow consistently commands much higher prices. The bowls are reported to be scarce in this pattern, especially the 8″ berry. An interesting characteristic of this pattern is square-shaped plates with scalloped corners. Basically, though, this pattern is scarce.

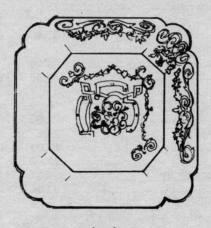

Lorain

	Current Price Range		Prior Year Average

Berry Bowl, diameter 8″
| ☐ green | 59.00 | 69.00 | 60.00 |
| ☐ yellow | 90.00 | 115.00 | 105.00 |

Cereal Bowl, diameter 6″
| ☐ green | 20.00 | 30.00 | 21.00 |
| ☐ yellow | 37.00 | 41.00 | 39.00 |

Creamer, footed
| ☐ green | 9.00 | 12.00 | 10.00 |
| ☐ yellow | 16.00 | 18.00 | 16.50 |

Cup
| ☐ green | 7.00 | 10.00 | 8.00 |
| ☐ yellow | 9.00 | 12.00 | 10.00 |

Dinner Plate, diameter 10¼″
| ☐ green | 30.00 | 35.00 | 31.00 |
| ☐ yellow | 35.00 | 45.00 | 42.00 |

Luncheon Plate, diameter 8⅜″
| ☐ green | 11.00 | 13.00 | 12.00 |
| ☐ yellow | 18.00 | 21.00 | 19.00 |

Platter, length 11½″
| ☐ green | 16.00 | 22.00 | 19.00 |
| ☐ yellow | 26.00 | 32.00 | 29.50 |

Relish Bowl, four compartments, diameter 8″
| ☐ green | 12.00 | 16.00 | 13.00 |
| ☐ yellow | 15.00 | 25.00 | 22.00 |

Salad Bowl, diameter 7¼″
| ☐ green | 27.00 | 31.00 | 28.00 |
| ☐ yellow | 37.00 | 41.00 | 39.00 |

Salad Plate, diameter 7¾″
| ☐ green | 6.00 | 8.00 | 6.50 |
| ☐ yellow | 9.00 | 12.00 | 10.00 |

Saucer
| ☐ green | 3.00 | 5.00 | 3.25 |
| ☐ yellow | 4.00 | 5.00 | 4.25 |

Sherbet Dish, footed
| ☐ green | 12.00 | 15.00 | 13.00 |
| ☐ yellow | 20.00 | 27.00 | 23.50 |

Sherbet Plate, diameter 5½″
| ☐ green | 3.00 | 5.00 | 3.50 |
| ☐ yellow | 5.00 | 7.00 | 5.75 |

Snack Tray, indented for a cup, diameter 11½″
| ☐ crystal with fired-on colors | 8.00 | 12.00 | 10.00 |

	Current Price Range		Prior Year Average
Sugar Bowl, footed			
☐ green	10.00	12.00	10.50
☐ yellow................................	13.00	15.00	18.00
Vegetable Bowl, oval, length 9¾"			
☐ green	24.00	29.00	26.00
☐ yellow................................	35.00	42.00	39.00

LOUISA
Jeannette Glass Co.

Jeannette made this pattern in the 1950s so it is not Depression era glassware. We include it because of strong collector interest. It was also referred to as *Floragold.* The most popular pieces are the iridescents, but some red-yellow, pink and crystal were also made. The iridescent was made to look like the Carnival glass pattern *Louisa* after which this pattern was named. The shakers are extremely hard to find.

Louisa

Ashtray, diameter 4"			
☐ iridescent..........................	4.00	6.00	4.50
Bowl, square, diameter 4½"			
☐ iridescent..........................	3.00	5.00	3.00
Butter Dish, with cover, oblong			
☐ iridescent..........................	14.00	18.00	15.50
Butter Dish, with cover, round			
☐ iridescent..........................	30.00	38.00	33.00

	Current Price Range		Prior Year Average
Candlesticks, pair			
☐ iridescent.............................	27.00	32.00	28.00
Candy Dish, footed, diameter 5¼″			
☐ iridescent.............................	3.50	5.75	4.50
Candy Dish, with cover, diameter 6¾″			
☐ iridescent.............................	26.00	34.00	29.00
Cereal Bowl, round, diameter 5½″			
☐ iridescent.............................	15.00	18.00	16.00
Creamer			
☐ iridescent.............................	5.00	7.00	5.50
Cup			
☐ iridescent.............................	4.00	6.00	4.75
Dinner Plate, diameter 8½″			
☐ iridescent.............................	15.00	17.00	16.00
Fruit Bowl, ruffled rim, diameter 5½″			
☐ iridescent.............................	3.50	6.00	4.50
Fruit Bowl, ruffled rim, diameter 8½″			
☐ iridescent.............................	3.50	6.00	4.50
Fruit Bowl, ruffled rim, diameter 12″			
☐ iridescent.............................	5.00	8.00	6.00
Pitcher, 64 oz.			
☐ iridescent.............................	20.00	26.00	21.00
Platter, diameter 11¼″			
☐ iridescent.............................	12.00	16.00	13.00
Salad Bowl, deep, diameter 9½″			
☐ iridescent.............................	25.00	31.00	27.00
Salt and Pepper Shakers			
☐ iridescent.............................	32.00	39.00	34.50
Saucer, diameter 5¼″			
☐ iridescent.............................	5.00	8.00	6.00
Sherbet Dish, footed			
☐ iridescent.............................	7.00	10.00	8.00
Sherbet Plate, diameter 5¾″			
☐ iridescent.............................	4.00	6.00	4.50
Sugar Bowl, with cover			
☐ iridescent.............................	10.00	15.00	12.25
Tray, length 13½″			
☐ iridescent.............................	11.00	15.00	13.00
Tumbler, footed, 10 oz.			
☐ iridescent.............................	10.00	15.00	12.00
Tumbler, footed, 11 oz.			
☐ iridescent.............................	11.00	15.00	13.00
Tumbler, footed, 15 oz.			
☐ iridescent.............................	35.00	45.00	40.00

	Current Price Range		Prior Year Average

Vase
☐ iridescent.. **60.00** **80.00** **70.00**

LYDIA RAY
Hazel Atlas Glass Co.

This pattern was made from 1930 to 1935. The most available color is green. Amethyst and blue weren't made in complete sets. The dinner plates in this pattern are very hard to come by, as are the pitchers. The bowls are available without much problem. If you're willing to substitute for the dinner plate, it isn't too difficult to build up a usable set in *Lydia Ray*.

Ashtray/Coaster
☐ green.. 24.00 28.00 26.00
Berry Bowl, diameter 4½"
☐ green.. 3.75 5.00 4.25
Berry Bowl, diameter 8"
☐ green.. 10.00 15.00 12.00
Butter Dish, with top
☐ green.. 40.00 50.00 45.00
Creamer
☐ green.. 6.00 9.00 7.00
Cup
☐ green.. 4.00 5.00 4.00
Decanter, with stopper
☐ green.. 35.00 41.00 37.00
Dinner Plate, diameter 10"
☐ green.. 11.00 14.00 12.50
Goblet, cocktail, 3¼ oz.
☐ green.. 10.00 15.00 12.00
Goblet, wine, 2½"
☐ green.. 10.00 15.00 12.00
Grill Plate, diameter 10"
☐ green.. 7.00 10.00 8.00
Pitcher, 60 oz., height 7¾"
☐ green.. 20.00 26.00 23.00
☐ other colors....................................... 23.00 30.00 25.00
Pitcher, 80 oz., height 8"
☐ green.. 28.00 34.00 30.00
☐ other colors....................................... 31.00 36.00 33.00
Platter, oval, 11"
☐ green.. 10.00 14.00 12.00

	Current Price Range		Prior Year Average
Salad Plate, diameter 8½"			
☐ green	4.00	6.00	4.75
Salt and Pepper Shakers, pair			
☐ green	25.00	30.00	27.00
Saucer			
☐ green	1.75	2.50	2.10
Sherbet Plate, diameter 6"			
☐ green	1.75	2.50	2.10
Sherbet, diameter 3"			
☐ green	5.00	6.25	5.75
Sugar			
☐ green	12.00	16.00	13.00
Tumbler, 5 oz., footed, height 4"			
☐ green	7.00	10.00	8.25
Tumbler, 5 oz., height 3½"			
☐ green	7.00	10.00	8.25
☐ other colors	6.00	9.00	7.00
Tumbler, 9 oz., footed, height 4⅛"			
☐ green	7.00	10.00	8.25
☐ other colors	6.00	9.00	7.00
Tumbler, 10 oz., height 5"			
☐ green	9.00	13.00	11.00
☐ other colors	8.00	12.00	10.00
Tumbler, 12 oz., height 5¼"			
☐ green	11.00	15.50	13.00
☐ other colors	10.00	14.00	12.00
Whiskey, 1½ oz., height 2½"			
☐ green	5.00	7.00	6.25

MADRID
Federal Glass Co.

Sometimes called *Meandering Vine,* this pattern consists of a dainty and scrolling leafy trim which is generally, but not always, set about a prominent diamond design. It was cast from the same molds used to make *Parrot.* The round knob on the butter cover is a Federal trademark. It can be found in green, pink, amber, crystal and "madonna" blue. Federal started making this line in 1932 and stopped in 1939. Just before they went out of business in the 1970s, they made some new *Madrid* pieces for the bicentennial called *Recollection* in amber. There was no real problem in identifying these pieces because they were clearly marked with a small '76 on the back. In 1982, Indiana Glass acquired the molds and started manufacturing new *Madrid* in large numbers. They took the '76 off so it's now more difficult to spot the new copies. Indiana's crystal color is a little darker than the original and is difficult to detect without close comparison. The new pink pieces are a very bland pink, so they're not a big problem. Also, several items that Indiana is now making were not made originally. For instance, the sugar and creamer were not made in pink originally, so if you've got a pink creamer, it's definitely new.

	Current Price Range		Prior Year Average
Ashtray, fluted rim, square, length 6″			
☐ green	75.00	80.00	75.00
☐ amber	135.00	175.00	155.00
☐ crystal	135.00	175.00	155.00
Berry Bowl, diameter 9⅜″			
☐ pink	13.00	16.50	14.50
☐ amber	12.00	15.00	13.00
☐ crystal	11.00	14.00	12.50
Butter Dish, with lid			
☐ green	60.00	70.00	65.00
☐ amber	58.00	62.00	59.00
☐ crystal	58.00	62.00	59.00
Candlesticks, height 2¼″, pair			
☐ pink	12.00	15.00	13.00
☐ amber	13.00	19.00	16.50
☐ crystal	13.00	18.00	16.00
Cake Plate, diameter 12″			
☐ green	15.00	17.00	16.00
☐ pink	7.00	9.00	8.00
☐ amber	7.00	9.00	8.00
☐ crystal	140.00	150.00	145.00
Console Bowl, diameter 11″			
☐ pink	7.00	9.00	8.00
☐ amber	9.00	13.00	11.00
☐ crystal	9.00	13.00	11.00
Cookie Jar, with lid			
☐ pink	23.00	28.00	24.00
☐ amber	30.00	34.00	31.00
☐ crystal	30.00	34.00	31.00
Creamer, pedestal foot			
☐ green	7.00	9.00	7.50
☐ blue	10.00	12.00	11.00
☐ crystal	5.00	7.00	6.00
☐ amber	5.00	7.00	6.00
Cup			
☐ green	5.00	7.00	5.50
☐ pink	5.00	7.00	5.50
☐ blue	9.00	12.00	9.50
☐ amber or crystal	4.00	6.00	4.50

	Current Price Range		Prior Year Average
Dinner Plate, diameter 11″			
☐ green	24.00	28.00	25.00
☐ blue	30.00	40.00	35.00
☐ amber or crystal	22.00	26.00	23.00
Gelatin Mold, height 2½″			
☐ amber or crystal	7.00	9.00	8.00
Gravy Boat, with platter			
☐ amber or crystal	625.00	800.00	840.00
Grill Plate, diameter 11″			
☐ green	12.00	15.00	12.50
☐ amber or crystal	7.00	9.00	7.50
Hot Plate			
☐ green	25.00	30.00	26.00
☐ amber or crystal	23.00	26.00	24.00
Hot Plate, with spoon holder			
☐ green	25.00	30.00	26.00
☐ amber or crystal	25.00	30.00	26.00
Jam Dish, diameter 6½″			
☐ green	11.00	15.00	12.00
☐ blue	20.00	25.00	21.00
☐ crystal	14.00	17.00	15.00
Jello Mold, height 2¼″			
☐ amber or crystal	8.00	11.00	9.00
Juice Pitcher, height 5″			
☐ amber or crystal	27.00	32.00	29.00
Lunch Plate, diameter 9″			
☐ green	7.00	9.00	7.50
☐ pink	5.00	7.00	5.50
☐ blue	11.00	13.00	11.50
☐ amber or crystal	4.50	6.50	5.00
Pitcher, ice lip, height 9″			
☐ green	170.00	190.00	175.00
☐ amber or crystal	45.00	55.00	47.50
Pitcher, rounded body, height 9″			
☐ green	170.00	190.00	175.00
☐ amber or crystal	45.00	55.00	47.00
Pitcher, squared body, height 8½″			
☐ green	110.00	120.00	113.00
☐ pink	30.00	33.00	31.00
☐ blue	135.00	145.00	137.00
☐ amber or crystal	35.00	40.00	36.00

	Current Price Range		Prior Year Average

Pitcher, 60 oz., square, height 6″

☐ green	90.00	120.00	110.00
☐ pink	24.00	30.00	28.00
☐ blue	120.00	155.00	130.00
☐ amber	32.00	38.00	34.00
☐ crystal	32.00	38.00	34.00

Platter, oval, length 12″

☐ pink	8.00	10.00	9.00
☐ green	11.00	14.00	12.00
☐ blue	16.00	19.00	17.00
☐ amber or crystal	9.00	11.00	9.50

Relish Plate, two compartments, length 11″

☐ green	8.00	11.00	9.00
☐ pink	7.00	9.00	8.00
☐ amber or crystal	7.00	9.00	8.00

Salad Bowl, diameter 8″

☐ green	14.00	16.00	14.50
☐ blue	21.00	24.00	21.50
☐ amber or crystal	10.00	13.00	11.00

Salad Bowl, steep sided, diameter 9″

☐ amber or crystal	17.00	20.00	18.00

Salad Plate, diameter 7″

☐ green	7.00	9.00	7.50
☐ pink	7.00	9.00	7.50
☐ blue	11.00	13.00	11.50
☐ amber or crystal	7.00	9.00	7.50

Salt and Pepper Shakers, flat, height 3¼″

☐ green	50.00	60.00	55.00
☐ amber or crystal	30.00	35.00	32.00

Salt and Pepper Shakers, footed, height 3¼″

☐ green	70.00	80.00	75.00
☐ blue	105.00	115.00	108.00
☐ amber or crystal	50.00	60.00	55.00

Sauce Bowl, diameter 5″

☐ green	5.00	6.00	5.50
☐ pink	4.50	6.50	5.00
☐ blue	6.00	8.00	7.00
☐ amber	4.00	6.00	5.00

	Current Price Range		Prior Year Average
Saucer			
☐ green	3.00	4.00	3.50
☐ pink	2.00	3.00	2.50
☐ blue	4.00	5.00	4.50
☐ amber or crystal	2.00	3.00	2.50
Sherbet Dish, stemmed			
☐ green	6.00	8.00	6.50
☐ blue	9.00	10.00	9.50
☐ amber or crystal	6.00	8.00	6.00
Sherbet Plate, diameter 6"			
☐ green	2.50	3.50	2.75
☐ pink	2.50	3.50	2.75
☐ blue	5.50	7.50	6.00
☐ amber or crystal	2.00	3.00	2.25
Soup Bowl, diameter 4½"			
☐ amber or crystal	10.00	15.00	12.00
Soup Bowl, diameter 7"			
☐ green	9.00	11.00	9.50
☐ blue	10.00	13.00	11.00
☐ amber or crystal	9.00	11.00	9.25
Sugar Bowl			
☐ green	7.00	9.00	7.50
☐ blue	9.00	11.00	9.50
☐ amber or crystal	6.00	8.00	6.50
Sugar Lid			
☐ green	22.00	26.00	23.00
☐ blue	65.00	75.00	70.00
☐ amber or crystal	22.00	26.00	23.00
Tumbler, height 4"			
☐ green	26.00	29.00	27.00
☐ blue	15.00	20.00	16.00
☐ amber or crystal	10.00	12.00	11.00
Tumbler, height 4½"			
☐ green	16.00	20.00	17.00
☐ pink	10.00	12.00	11.00
☐ blue	16.00	20.00	17.00
☐ amber or crystal	10.00	12.00	11.00
Tumbler, height 5½"			
☐ green	20.00	25.00	22.00
☐ blue	18.00	22.00	19.00
☐ amber or crystal	15.00	17.00	16.00
Tumbler, pedestal foot, height 4"			
☐ green	31.00	33.00	31.50
☐ amber or crystal	16.00	18.00	17.00

	Current Price Range		Prior Year Average
Tumbler, pedestal foot, height 5½″			
☐ green	28.00	32.00	29.00
☐ amber or crystal.................................	18.00	22.00	19.00
Vegetable Bowl, egg shape, length 10″			
☐ green	12.00	14.00	13.00
☐ blue	18.00	22.00	19.00
☐ pink	10.00	13.00	11.00
☐ amber or crystal.................................	10.00	14.00	12.00

MANHATTAN
Anchor Hocking Glass Co.

Manhattan was made from 1939 through 1941. Basically, the only color you're going to find is crystal, although some pink is around. Some green was also made, but very few pieces have surfaced. Collectors used to refer to *Manhattan* as *Ribbed,* but *Manhattan* has stuck as the correct name all over the country. This pattern is a lot more popular than it used to be and prices reflect that surge. Probably the most popular item in the line is the five-section relish tray with ruby inserts. Westmoreland made some pieces in a similar design that blend quite well with *Manhattan.*

Manhattan

	Current Price Range		Prior Year Average
Ashtray, diameter 4″			
☐ crystal	6.00	8.50	7.00
Ashtray, square, 4″			
☐ crystal	6.00	8.00	7.00

"MANHATTAN"

A new line of water-crystal tableware; beautifully styled pieces with deep circular mitres; ultra-modern — as new as tomorrow. The unusual brilliance and striking design cannot fail to instantly appeal.

3779 CUP—Open Handle
Pkd. 4 doz. ctn.—Wt. 19 lbs.

3729—SAUCER
Pkd. 4 doz. ctn.—Wt. 21 lbs.

3730—SHERBET
Pkd. 4 doz. ctn.—Wt. 18 lbs.

3729—6" SHERBET PLATE
Pkd. 4 doz. ctn.—Wt. 21 lbs.

3718—4" ASH TRAY
Pkd. 12 doz. ctn.—Wt. 40 lbs.

3742—8" VASE
Pkd. 1 doz. ctn.—Wt. 31 lbs.

3718—3½" COASTER (they nest)
Pkd. 12 doz. ctn.—Wt. 24 lbs.

3741—10¼" DINNER PLATE
Pkd. 2 doz. ctn.—Wt. 40 lbs.

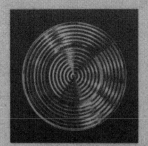

3730—8" SALAD PLATE
Pkd. 4 doz. ctn.—Wt. 39 lbs.

1938 Manhattan Catalog Sheet.
Courtesy of Anchor Hocking Corporation, Lancaster, Ohio

	Current Price Range		Prior Year Average
Berry Bowl, handled, diameter 5″			
☐ crystal	4.00	6.00	5.00
☐ pink	5.00	7.00	6.00
Bowl, tab handled, diameter 8″			
☐ crystal	10.00	12.00	10.50
☐ pink	12.00	14.00	12.25
Candlesticks, pair, height 4″			
☐ crystal	8.00	12.00	9.00
Candy Dish, flat, with cover			
☐ crystal	15.00	21.00	17.00
Candy Dish, tri-legged			
☐ pink	4.00	7.00	5.50
Coaster, diameter 3½″			
☐ crystal	2.00	3.00	2.50
☐ pink	2.50	3.50	2.75
Comport, height 5¾″			
☐ crystal	7.00	9.00	8.00
☐ pink	9.00	11.00	9.50
Creamer, egg shape			
☐ crystal	3.00	5.00	3.50
☐ pink	5.00	7.00	5.50
Cup			
☐ crystal	7.00	10.00	8.00
Fruit Bowl, diameter 9½″			
☐ crystal	11.00	16.00	12.75
☐ pink	12.50	17.00	13.50
Goblet, footed cocktail, height 4″			
☐ crystal	5.00	8.00	6.50
Pitcher, juice, 40 oz.			
☐ crystal	12.00	16.00	13.00
☐ pink	20.00	30.00	21.00
Pitcher, tilt, 80 oz.			
☐ crystal	18.00	20.00	19.00
☐ pink	30.00	40.00	31.00
Relish Tray, four compartments, length 14″			
☐ crystal	6.00	8.00	6.50
☐ pink	8.00	10.00	7.00
Relish Tray, five compartments, length 14″			
☐ crystal	8.00	10.00	8.50
☐ pink	13.00	15.00	14.00

	Current Price Range		Prior Year Average
Relish Tray Inserts, round or triangular			
☐ crystal	2.25	3.50	2.75
☐ pink	2.25	4.00	3.00
☐ ruby	2.00	3.00	2.50
Salad Bowl, diameter 9″			
☐ crystal	8.00	10.00	9.00
☐ pink	8.00	11.00	9.00
Salt and Pepper Shakers, height 2″, pair			
☐ crystal	10.00	15.00	12.50
☐ pink	25.00	31.00	28.00
Sauce Bowl, diameter 4½″			
☐ crystal	4.00	5.00	4.50
☐ pink	5.00	6.00	5.50
Sherbet Plate, diameter 6″			
☐ crystal	2.00	3.00	2.50
Sugar Bowl, oval			
☐ crystal	3.00	5.00	3.25
☐ pink	5.00	7.00	5.50
Tumbler, pedestal foot, height 6½″			
☐ crystal	6.00	8.00	6.50
☐ pink	7.00	10.00	7.50
Vase, height 8″			
☐ crystal	7.00	10.00	8.00
Wine Glass, stemmed, height 3½″			
☐ crystal	6.00	8.00	6.50

MAYFAIR
Federal Glass Co.

When Federal came out with their *Mayfair* line in 1934, they didn't take into account that Hocking already had a *Mayfair* so they had to change the name. They ended up completely redesigning the pattern and calling it *Rosemary*. As a result, since so little Federal *Mayfair* was made, not too much is on the market today. The colors you will find are crystal, green and amber. Green is generally harder to come by than the other colors. There are certain pieces that were made in between the old *Mayfair* and the newer *Rosemary*. These are often referred to as transition pieces having characteristics of both patterns but more closely resembling *Mayfair*.

Mayfair (Federal)

	Current Price Range		Prior Year Average
Cereal Bowl, diameter 6″			
☐ green	13.00	16.00	14.00
☐ amber	11.00	14.00	12.00
☐ crystal	5.00	9.00	6.75
Creamer, pedestal foot			
☐ green	7.00	11.00	8.00
☐ amber	7.00	11.00	8.00
☐ crystal	6.00	9.00	7.00
Cup			
☐ green	6.00	8.50	7.00
☐ amber	4.00	6.00	4.50
☐ crystal	3.00	4.00	3.25
Dinner Plate, diameter 9½″			
☐ green	7.00	10.00	8.50
☐ amber	7.00	9.00	8.00
☐ crystal	5.00	8.00	6.50
Grill Plate, diameter 9½″			
☐ green	8.00	11.00	9.00
☐ amber	8.00	10.00	8.50
☐ crystal	6.00	8.00	7.00
Platter, oval, length 12″			
☐ green	13.00	15.00	13.00
☐ amber	11.00	14.00	12.00
☐ crystal	7.00	10.00	8.50
Salad Plate, diameter 6¾″			
☐ green	3.50	5.50	4.00
☐ amber	3.00	4.00	3.25
☐ crystal	1.75	2.75	2.00

	Current Price Range		Prior Year Average
Sauce Bowl, diameter 5″			
☐ green	5.00	7.00	6.00
☐ amber	4.00	6.00	5.25
☐ crystal	3.50	4.50	4.00
Saucer			
☐ green	1.50	2.50	1.75
☐ amber	1.75	2.75	2.00
☐ crystal	1.00	2.25	1.00
Soup Bowl, diameter 5″			
☐ green	11.50	13.50	12.00
☐ amber	11.50	13.50	12.00
☐ crystal	8.00	10.00	8.50
Sugar Bowl, pedestal foot			
☐ green	7.00	9.00	8.00
☐ amber	8.00	10.00	8.50
☐ crystal	6.00	8.00	6.50
Tumbler, 9 oz., height 4½″			
☐ green	12.50	15.00	13.00
☐ amber	9.00	11.00	9.50
☐ crystal	5.00	8.00	6.00
Vegetable Bowl, oval, length 10″			
☐ green	12.00	15.00	13.00
☐ amber	11.50	13.50	12.00
☐ crystal	8.00	10.00	8.50

MAYFAIR
Hocking Glass Co.

Also referred to as *Open Rose*. This is probably the most popular Depression glass pattern ever made. Not only is it the most popular now, but it was the most popular in the 1930s. It was produced in large quantities from 1931 through 1937. The colors were blue, green, yellow, pink and crystal. The yellow and green are the very rare and probably the most valuable pieces in all Depression glass. The blue is the most popular even though it's also not cheap (although it can't compare with green's values). Pink and crystal are the most reasonably priced but have fewer collectors than the blue. Some pieces can be found with a satin finish. These sell for about 20–30% less than the pink. Crystal sells for about the same as pink. Reproductions have been made of the whiskey tumblers and the cookie jars. They are easy to detect because the colors and patterns are weak. If you are familiar with the "feel" of Hocking *Mayfair,* you will notice the pattern feels almost smooth to the touch on the reproductions. The original pattern feels much more raised. The new whiskeys are much heavier than the old and have thicker bottoms.

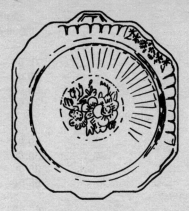

Mayfair (Hocking)

	Current Price Range		Prior Year Average
Bowl, shallow, diameter 11″			
☐ green	18.00	22.00	19.00
☐ yellow	75.00	85.00	80.00
☐ blue	40.00	48.00	44.00
☐ pink	31.00	37.00	34.00
Butter Dish, with cover, diameter 6⅞″			
☐ green	875.00	925.00	885.00
☐ yellow	875.00	925.00	885.00
☐ blue	190.00	210.00	195.00
☐ pink	40.00	50.00	42.00
Cake Plate, handles, diameter 12″			
☐ green	22.00	26.00	24.00
☐ blue	37.00	42.00	38.50
☐ pink	23.00	26.00	24.00
Cake Plate, pedestal foot, diameter 10″			
☐ green	47.00	52.00	49.00
☐ blue	38.00	42.00	39.00
☐ pink	15.00	20.00	16.50
Candy Dish, with lid			
☐ green	400.00	450.00	410.00
☐ yellow	285.00	320.00	290.00
☐ blue	120.00	140.00	125.00
☐ pink	32.00	38.00	34.00
Celery Bowl, two compartments, length 9″			
☐ green	95.00	105.00	97.50
☐ yellow	95.00	105.00	97.50

	Current Price Range		Prior Year Average

Celery Dish, 10"

☐ green	75.00	85.00	80.00
☐ yellow	80.00	90.00	85.00
☐ blue	26.00	34.00	30.00
☐ pink	22.00	29.00	25.00

Celery Dish, two compartments, length 10"

☐ green	80.00	90.00	85.00
☐ yellow	80.00	90.00	85.00
☐ blue	25.00	30.00	26.00
☐ pink	65.00	70.00	67.00

Cereal Bowl, diameter 5¼"

☐ green	47.00	53.00	49.00
☐ yellow	47.00	53.00	49.00
☐ blue	28.00	32.00	29.00
☐ pink	13.00	15.00	14.00

Cocktail Glass, height 4"

☐ green	225.00	275.00	230.00
☐ pink	48.00	54.00	50.00

Console Bowl, tri-legged, diameter 8⅞"

☐ pink	2,000.00	2,500.00	2,200.00

Cookie Jar, with cover

☐ green	400.00	460.00	430.00
☐ yellow	450.00	525.00	485.00
☐ blue	140.00	180.00	160.00
☐ pink	25.00	32.00	29.00

Cordial Glass, height 3½"

☐ green	340.00	350.00	345.00
☐ pink	340.00	350.00	345.00

Creamer, pedestal foot

☐ green	145.00	155.00	147.50
☐ yellow	145.00	155.00	147.50
☐ pink	13.00	15.00	14.00
☐ blue	45.00	50.00	46.00

Cup

☐ green	90.00	120.00	100.00
☐ yellow	90.00	120.00	100.00
☐ blue	33.00	38.00	34.00
☐ pink	11.00	13.00	12.00

Decanter, with glass stopper, 32 oz.

☐ pink	100.00	140.00	115.00
☐ green	260.00	330.00	300.00

Decanter Stopper

☐ pink	35.00	45.00	40.00
☐ green	90.00	110.00	100.00

	Current Price Range		Prior Year Average
Dinner Plate, diameter 9″			
☐ green	95.00	100.00	97.00
☐ yellow	95.00	100.00	97.00
☐ blue	40.00	43.00	41.00
☐ pink	38.00	42.00	39.00
Fruit Bowl, fluted edge, deep sides, diameter 12¼″			
☐ green	20.00	25.00	22.00
☐ yellow	85.00	95.00	87.50
☐ blue	48.00	53.00	49.00
☐ pink	35.00	40.00	36.50
Goblet, cylindrical, height 7¼″			
☐ blue	95.00	100.00	96.50
☐ pink	125.00	130.00	126.50
Goblet, stemmed, height 4″			
☐ pink	70.00	75.00	71.00
Grill Plate, diameter 9″			
☐ green	50.00	55.00	52.00
☐ yellow	50.00	55.00	52.00
☐ blue	20.00	25.00	22.00
☐ pink	20.00	25.00	22.00
Grill Plate, tab handles, diameter 11″			
☐ yellow	75.00	85.00	79.00
Iced Tea Glass, footed, height 6″			
☐ green	175.00	180.00	176.50
☐ blue	78.00	83.00	79.50
☐ pink	26.00	30.00	27.50
Iced Tea Glass, height 5½″			
☐ blue	83.00	90.00	86.00
☐ pink	27.00	32.00	28.50
Juice Glass, height 3¾″			
☐ blue	60.00	70.00	62.00
☐ pink	20.00	25.00	22.00
Juice Tumbler, pedestal foot, height 3″			
☐ pink	53.00	60.00	56.00
Lunch Plate, diameter 8″			
☐ green or yellow	55.00	60.00	56.50
☐ blue	23.00	26.00	24.00
☐ pink	14.50	16.50	15.00
Pitcher, bulbous body, 80 oz., height 8¼″			
☐ green or yellow	355.00	360.00	356.50
☐ blue	125.00	130.00	127.00
☐ pink	62.00	67.00	64.00

ROSE "MAYFAIR" TABLEWARE

R2070—CUP
Pkd. 4 doz. ctn.—wt. 19 lbs.
R2020—SAUCER
Pkd. 4 doz. ctn.—wt. 22 lbs.

R2041—9½" DINNER PLATE
Pkd. 2 doz. ctn.—wt. 31 lbs.
R2040—8½" LUNCHEON PLATE
Pkd. 4 doz. ctn.—wt. 53 lbs.

R2001—9 OZ. TABLE TUMBLER
Pkd. 12 doz. ctn.—wt. 45 lbs.
R2003—5 OZ. FRUIT JUICE
Pkd. 12 doz. ctn.—wt. 30 lbs.
R2008—13½ OZ. ICED TEAS
Pkd. 6 doz. ctn.—wt. 34 lbs.

R2088—15 OZ. FOOTED ICED TEA
Pkd. 4 doz. ctn.—wt. 38 lbs.
R2081—10 OZ. FOOTED TUMBLER
Pkd. 4 doz. ctn.—wt. 33 lbs.

R2080—80 OZ. PITCHER
Pkd. 1 doz. ctn.—wt. 36 lbs.
R2084—60 OZ. PITCHER
Pkd. 1 doz. ctn.—wt. 23 lbs.

R2050—37 OZ. PITCHER
Pkd. 2 doz. ctn.—wt. 40 lbs.

R2065—5½ OZ. SHERBET
Pkd. 4 doz. ctn.—wt. 24 lbs.
R2030—6½" SHERBET PLATE
Pkd. 4 doz. ctn.—wt. 27 lbs.

R2052—SUGAR
Pkd. 2 doz. ctn.—wt. 14 lbs.
R2053—CREAMER
Pkd. 2 doz. ctn.—wt. 14 lbs.
R2025—SALT AND PEPPER
Chrome Top
Pkd. 6 doz. ctn.—wt. 14 lbs.
(Half salt and half pepper)

R2078—10" NAPPY
Pkd. 2 doz. ctn.—wt. 51 lbs.

R2077—7" NAPPY
(As illustrated)
Pkd. 4 doz. ctn.—wt. 50 lbs.
R2075—5½" NAPPY
(Without handles)
Pkd. 6 doz. ctn.—wt. 40 lbs.

R2046—13½"x9" MEAT DISH
Pkd. 2 doz. ctn.—wt. 48 lbs.

R2013—11"x7½" VEGETABLE DISH
Pkd. 2 doz. ctn.—wt. 36 lbs.

THE HOCKING GLASS COMPANY, LANCASTER, OHIO

1935 Mayfair Catalog Sheets.

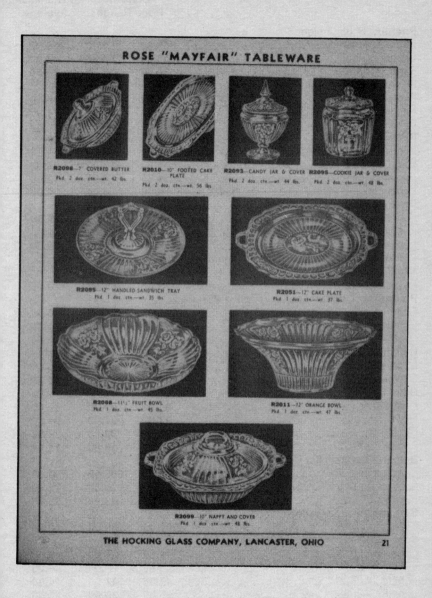

ROSE "MAYFAIR" TABLEWARE

R2098—7" COVERED BUTTER
Pkd. 2 doz. ctn.—wt. 42 lbs.

R2010—10" FOOTED CAKE PLATE
Pkd. 2 doz. ctn.—wt. 56 lbs.

R2093—CANDY JAR & COVER
Pkd. 2 doz. ctn.—wt. 44 lbs.

R2095—COOKIE JAR & COVER
Pkd. 2 doz. ctn.—wt. 48 lbs.

R2095—12" HANDLED SANDWICH TRAY
Pkd. 1 doz. ctn.—wt. 35 lbs.

R2051—12" CAKE PLATE
Pkd. 1 doz. ctn.—wt. 37 lbs.

R2088—11½" FRUIT BOWL
Pkd. 1 doz. ctn.—wt. 45 lbs.

R2011—12" ORANGE BOWL
Pkd. 1 doz. ctn.—wt. 47 lbs.

R2099—10" NAPPY AND COVER
Pkd. 1 doz. ctn.—wt. 48 lbs.

THE HOCKING GLASS COMPANY, LANCASTER, OHIO

21

	Current Price Range		Prior Year Average
Pitcher, 37 oz., height 6″			
☐ green or yellow.............................	355.00	360.00	356.50
☐ blue..	85.00	90.00	87.00
☐ pink..	28.00	33.00	29.50
Pitcher, 60 oz., height 8″			
☐ green or yellow.............................	315.00	320.00	316.50
☐ pink..	33.00	37.00	34.00
☐ blue..	950.00	1000.00	965.00
Plate, diameter 6″			
☐ green..	50.00	60.00	55.00
☐ yellow...	50.00	60.00	55.00
☐ blue..	11.50	14.50	12.00
☐ pink..	6.00	9.00	7.00
Plate, spoon holder, diameter 6½″			
☐ green..	60.00	65.00	61.50
☐ blue..	22.00	26.00	24.00
☐ pink..	38.00	42.00	39.50
Platter, oval, closed handles, diameter 12½″			
☐ yellow...	155.00	185.00	170.00
Platter, oval, open handles, length 12″			
☐ green or yellow.............................	115.00	120.00	116.50
☐ blue..	33.00	37.00	34.50
☐ pink..	14.00	18.00	14.50
Relish, length 8½″			
☐ green or yellow.............................	90.00	110.00	100.00
☐ pink..	145.00	165.00	155.00
Relish, four compartments, length 8½″			
☐ green or yellow.............................	96.00	100.00	97.00
☐ yellow...	93.00	97.00	94.50
☐ blue..	28.00	33.00	29.50
☐ pink..	16.00	19.00	17.00
Salt and Pepper, flat			
☐ green or yellow.............................	575.00	625.00	590.00
☐ blue..	170.00	180.00	172.50
☐ pink..	37.00	43.00	38.50
Salt and Pepper, pedestal foot			
☐ pink..	1,800.00	2100.00	1,900.00
Sandwich Server, central loop handle			
☐ green..	19.00	21.00	19.50
☐ yellow...	80.00	90.00	85.00
☐ blue..	43.00	47.00	44.00
☐ pink..	25.00	30.00	26.50
Saucer			
☐ pink..	16.00	20.00	17.00

	Current Price Range		Prior Year Average

Sherbet Dish, flat, diameter 2½"
☐ blue	50.00	55.00	52.00
☐ pink	85.00	90.00	87.50

Sherbet Dish, footed, height 3"
☐ pink	11.50	13.50	12.00

Sherbet Dish, pedestal foot, diameter 4½"
☐ green or yellow	120.00	130.00	125.00
☐ blue	45.00	50.00	46.50
☐ pink	53.00	58.00	54.00

Sherbet Plate, diameter 6½"
☐ pink	8.00	11.00	9.00

Sherbet Plate, off-center indent, diameter 6½"
☐ green	40.00	50.00	44.00
☐ blue	15.00	20.00	18.00
☐ pink	14.00	19.00	17.00

Sherry Glass, height 5½"
☐ green	360.00	390.00	375.00
☐ pink	360.00	390.00	375.00

Soup Bowl, diameter 5"
☐ pink	30.00	36.00	33.00

Sugar Bowl, pedestal foot
☐ green or yellow	145.00	155.00	147.50
☐ blue	42.00	46.00	43.00
☐ pink	14.00	16.00	14.50

Tumbler, pedestal foot, height 5"
☐ blue	65.00	70.00	66.50
☐ pink	20.00	25.00	22.00

Vase (Sweet Pea)
☐ green	145.00	155.00	147.50
☐ blue	60.00	68.00	62.00
☐ pink	120.00	128.00	122.00

Vegetable Bowl, oval, length 9"
☐ green or yellow	70.00	80.00	72.00
☐ blue	30.00	40.00	32.00
☐ pink	15.00	17.00	15.50

Vegetable Bowl, diameter 10"
☐ yellow	85.00	90.00	86.50
☐ pink	12.00	15.00	12.50
☐ blue	37.00	43.00	38.50

Vegetable Bowl, with cover, diameter 10"
☐ yellow	220.00	230.00	222.50
☐ blue	70.00	80.00	72.50
☐ pink	58.00	63.00	58.50

	Current Price Range		Prior Year Average
Water Glass, height 4″			
☐ blue	60.00	65.00	61.50
☐ pink	18.00	22.00	19.00
Water Glass, height 5″			
☐ green	150.00	160.00	155.00
☐ blue	82.00	88.00	83.50
☐ pink	85.00	90.00	86.50
Water Glass, stemmed, height 6″			
☐ green	250.00	260.00	255.00
☐ pink	38.00	43.00	39.00
Whiskey Glass, jigger, height 2″			
☐ pink	50.00	60.00	55.00
Wine Glass, stemmed, height 4″			
☐ green	250.00	260.00	255.00
☐ pink	50.00	55.00	51.00

MISS AMERICA
Hocking Glass Co.

Hocking made this pattern from 1933 through 1936. It is sometimes referred to as *Diamond*. It is definitely one of the top patterns in Depression glass. A common mistake of beginning collectors, by the way, is to confuse *Miss America* with *English Hobnail*. Pink and crystal can be found without difficulty except for a few pieces such as the butter dish and the candy dish. Green is scarce, but red is very rare. Some pieces can be found with a satin finish. These sell for about 20–30% less than crystal. Some ice blue pieces have surfaced, but they are also very rare. Reproductions of the shakers, the butter dish and the pitcher have been found. To tell the new butter dish top from the old, feel where the knob is. If there is a hollow space there, it's an original. If there is glass forming a small bump, it is a reproduction. The new butter dish bottom exhibits a ray design without definite ends to the rays. When held up to the light, the original shows a well-proportioned star. The old shakers have about half as much glass on the bottom as the original. The new pitchers have a plain edge above the handle. The original pitchers have a small bump there.

Miss America

	Current Price Range		Prior Year Average
Berry Bowl, diameter 4½″			
☐ green	6.00	8.00	6.75
Berry Bowl, diameter 6¼″			
☐ green	8.00	10.00	8.50
☐ pink	9.00	12.00	10.00
☐ crystal	4.00	6.00	5.00
Butter Dish, with lid			
☐ pink	400.00	445.00	420.00
☐ crystal	170.00	190.00	180.00
Cake Plate, pedestal foot, height 8″			
☐ pink	25.00	30.00	26.50
☐ crystal	13.00	18.00	15.00
Candy Jar, with lid, height 11″			
☐ pink	95.00	100.00	96.50
☐ crystal	45.00	50.00	46.50
Celery Dish, oblong, 10½″			
☐ pink	11.00	16.00	14.00
☐ crystal	6.00	8.00	7.00
Coaster, diameter 5¾″			
☐ pink	17.00	22.00	19.00
☐ crystal	9.00	13.00	12.00
Comport, height 5″			
☐ pink	12.00	16.00	14.00
☐ crystal	7.00	11.00	9.50
Creamer, pedestal foot			
☐ pink	11.00	13.00	12.00
☐ crystal	5.50	7.50	6.00

	Current Price Range		Prior Year Average
Cup			
☐ green	7.00	9.00	7.50
☐ pink	14.00	16.00	14.50
☐ crystal	6.50	8.50	7.00
Dinner Plate, diameter 10½″			
☐ pink	16.50	22.50	19.00
☐ crystal	7.00	11.00	9.00
Fruit Bowl, curves in at top			
☐ pink	40.00	50.00	45.00
☐ crystal	22.00	32.00	27.00
Fruit Bowl, steep sided, diameter 8¾″			
☐ pink	35.00	40.00	37.00
☐ crystal	20.00	25.00	21.50
Grill Plate, diameter 10¼″			
☐ pink	13.00	17.00	15.00
☐ crystal	5.00	8.00	6.50
Iced Tea Glass, 14 oz., height 6¾″			
☐ pink	45.00	50.00	46.50
☐ crystal	19.00	22.00	20.00
Juice Glass, 5 oz., height 4¾″			
☐ red	145.00	155.00	147.50
☐ pink	45.00	55.00	50.00
☐ crystal	12.00	18.00	14.50
Juice Tumbler, 5 oz., juice, height 4 oz.			
☐ pink	30.00	40.00	32.00
☐ crystal	10.00	15.00	12.00
Pitcher, 65 oz., height 8″			
☐ pink	80.00	90.00	85.00
☐ crystal	48.00	53.00	49.50
Pitcher, ice lip, 65 oz., height 8½″			
☐ pink	90.00	95.00	92.00
☐ crystal	55.00	60.00	56.50
Plate, diameter 6½″			
☐ green	5.00	7.00	5.50
Platter, oblong, length 12″			
☐ pink	12.00	16.00	14.00
☐ crystal	8.00	11.00	9.50
Relish Dish, four compartments, length 8½″			
☐ pink	12.00	14.00	13.00
☐ crystal	6.00	9.00	7.00
Relish Dish, round, two compartments, diameter 11″			
☐ pink	120.00	130.00	122.50
☐ crystal	10.00	13.00	11.00

	Current Price Range		Prior Year Average
Rose Bowl, diameter 8"			
☐ pink	40.00	50.00	42.50
☐ red	275.00	325.00	290.00
☐ crystal	28.00	33.00	29.00
Salad Plate, diameter 8½"			
☐ red	50.00	60.00	51.00
☐ green	7.00	9.00	7.50
☐ pink	13.00	15.00	13.50
☐ crystal	4.00	6.00	4.50
Salt and Pepper Shakers, pair			
☐ green	250.00	300.00	270.00
☐ pink	37.00	44.00	42.00
☐ crystal	20.00	25.00	21.50
Saucer			
☐ pink	3.50	5.50	4.00
☐ crystal	2.00	3.00	2.25
Sherbet Dish			
☐ pink	11.50	13.50	12.00
☐ crystal	5.50	7.50	6.00
Sherbet Plate, diameter 5¾"			
☐ green	4.00	6.00	4.50
☐ pink	4.00	6.00	4.50
☐ crystal	2.50	3.50	2.75
Sugar Bowl			
☐ pink	11.00	14.00	12.00
☐ crystal	5.00	7.00	5.50
☐ red	120.00	130.00	122.50
Vegetable Bowl, oval, length 10"			
☐ pink	15.50	19.50	17.00
☐ crystal	9.00	13.00	10.00
Water Glass, 10 oz., height 5¾"			
☐ red	135.00	155.00	140.00
☐ pink	35.00	40.00	36.50
☐ crystal	16.50	22.50	19.00
Water Tumbler, 5 oz., juice, height 4"			
☐ green	12.50	14.50	13.00
☐ pink	22.00	26.00	23.00
☐ crystal	10.00	13.00	11.00

PINK AND CRYSTAL TABLEWARE

"MISS AMERICA" LINE

Pink* or Crystal

This is a very handsome, universally popular pattern with many appealing features. The diamond-like blocks or "Hobnails" reflect the light rays to a surprising degree, lending to the "Miss America" line a remarkable sparkle and brilliance. The individual pieces are ornate and rich looking. The line is made in a wide variety of items, including every useful tableware piece, permitting the housewife to set her table very completely and beautifully.

▼

MISS AMERICA			DOZ. TO CTN.	WGT. PER CTN.
2550		Cup	4	19 lb
2551		Saucer	4	24 "
2552	5¾"	Coaster	4	25 "
2535	5½"	Fruit or Cereal	4	36 "
2522	5¾"	Sherbet Plate	4	24 "
2560		Salt and Pepper—Chrome Top	4	9 "
2502	5 oz.	Fruit Juice	4	20 "
2506	10 oz.	Table Tumbler	4	29 "
2513	5½ oz.	Footed Sherbet	3	24 "
2516	10 oz.	Footed Tumbler	3	17 "
2561		Creamer	2	13 "
2562		Sugar	2	15 "
2508	14 oz.	Iced Tea	3	32 "
2524	8½"	Luncheon Plate	2	29 "
2526	10¼"	Dinner Plate	2	31 "
2529	10¼"	Grill Plate	2	40 "
2544	10½"	Celery Tray	2	34 "
2566	12¼"	Meat Dish	2	57 "
2547	10¼"	Vegetable Dish	2	46 "
2545	8¾"	Relish	2	42 "
2546		Footed Comport	2	25 "
2591	65 oz.	Pitcher, Ice Lipped	1	48 "

*If Pink color is desired, place prefix "R" before each stock number.

10   THE HOCKING GLASS COMPANY, LANCASTER, OHIO

1935 Miss America Catalog Sheets.

Courtesy of Anchor Hocking Corporation, Lancaster, Ohio

	Current Price Range		Prior Year Average

Wine Glass, 3 oz., height 3¼″

☐ red	145.00	155.00	147.50
☐ pink	40.00	50.00	46.50
☐ crystal	10.00	15.00	13.50

MODERNTONE
Hazel Atlas Co.

This simple but elegant pattern is also known as *Wedding Band,* which may allude to the characteristic horizontal bands which encircle each piece. Centers are plain. It appears in cobalt blue, amethyst, and some crystal, pink, and platonite fired-on colors.

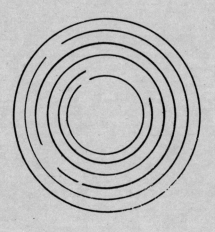

Moderntone

Ashtray, with match holder, height 7½″

☐ cobalt	83.00	93.00	85.00

Berry Bowl, diameter 4¾″

☐ cobalt	11.00	15.50	12.50
☐ amethyst	5.00	8.50	5.75

Berry Bowl, diameter 8½″

☐ amethyst	15.00	20.00	16.25
☐ cobalt	20.00	25.00	21.50

Butter Dish, metal cover

☐ cobalt	53.00	60.00	55.00

	Current Price Range		Prior Year Average
Cereal Bowl, diameter 6″			
☐ amethyst...	22.00	27.00	23.50
☐ cobalt...	29.00	35.00	30.50
Cheese Dish, diameter 7″			
☐ cobalt...	64.00	71.00	65.50
Creamer			
☐ amethyst...	5.00	7.00	5.50
☐ cobalt...	6.00	9.00	7.00
Cup			
☐ amethyst...	5.00	7.00	5.50
☐ cobalt...	6.00	9.00	7.00
Custard Cup			
☐ amethyst...	7.50	10.50	8.25
☐ cobalt...	8.00	11.00	8.75
Dinner Plate, diameter 9″			
☐ amethyst...	5.50	7.50	6.00
☐ green	7.50	10.50	8.25
Lunch Plate, diameter 7½″			
☐ cobalt...	4.00	6.00	4.50
☐ amethyst...	4.00	6.00	4.50
Platter, oblong, length 11″			
☐ amethyst...	10.00	13.00	10.75
☐ cobalt...	15.00	20.00	16.50
Platter, oblong, length 12″			
☐ amethyst...	16.00	20.00	17.00
☐ cobalt...	22.00	28.00	22.50
Salad Plate, diameter 6½″			
☐ amethyst...	3.50	5.50	4.50
☐ cobalt...	5.00	8.00	5.50
Salt and Pepper Shakers, pair			
☐ amethyst...	22.00	28.00	23.50
☐ cobalt...	22.00	28.00	23.50
Sandwich Plate, diameter 10″			
☐ amethyst...	8.50	11.50	9.25
☐ cobalt...	13.00	17.00	14.00
Saucer			
☐ amethyst...	1.00	3.00	1.50
☐ cobalt...	1.00	3.00	1.50
Sherbet Plate, diameter 5½″			
☐ amethyst...	5.00	8.00	6.00
☐ cobalt...	6.00	9.00	7.00
Soup Bowl, diameter 4″			
☐ cobalt...	9.50	13.00	10.00
☐ amethyst...	8.00	11.00	9.00

	Current Price Range		Prior Year Average
Soup Bowl, scalloped rim, diameter 5″			
☐ cobalt..	13.00	17.00	14.00
☐ amethyst..	10.00	13.00	10.50
Soup Bowl			
☐ amethyst..	5.50	7.50	6.00
☐ cobalt..	6.00	9.00	7.00
Sugar Bowl, diameter 7″			
☐ amethyst..	23.00	27.00	24.00
☐ cobalt..	29.00	35.00	30.50
Tumbler, height 8″			
☐ cobalt..	13.00	17.00	14.00
Whiskey Glass, jigger, height 1½″			
☐ cobalt..	10.00	13.00	11.00

MOONDROPS
New Martinsville Glass Co.

This pattern was made from 1932 through 1940. The colors that were produced were blue, red, pink, green, amber, amethyst and crystal. Blue and
red are, of course, the collectors' favorites. This is a big pattern and can be
collected without great difficulty. Watch out for the butter dish cover in glass;
it is rare.

	Current Price Range		Prior Year Average
Ashtray, 4″			
☐ blue and red....................................	14.00	19.00	17.00
☐ all other colors................................	10.00	14.00	12.00
Ashtray, 6″			
☐ blue and red....................................	30.00	40.00	34.00
☐ all other colors................................	13.00	18.00	16.00
Berry Bowl, deep, diameter 4″			
☐ blue and red....................................	22.00	28.00	25.00
☐ all other colors................................	8.00	11.00	9.00
Berry Bowl, diameter 5″			
☐ blue and red....................................	17.00	22.00	20.00
☐ all other colors................................	8.00	12.00	10.00
Bowl, three-footed, diameter 7″			
☐ blue and red....................................	30.00	37.00	34.00
☐ all other colors................................	11.00	16.00	13.00
Bowl, three-footed, console, diameter 10″			
☐ blue and red....................................	28.00	34.00	30.00
☐ all other colors................................	12.00	16.00	14.00

	Current Price Range		Prior Year Average
Bowl, three-footed, ruffled rim			
☐ blue and red.....................................	44.00	50.00	46.00
☐ all other colors.................................	18.00	23.00	21.00
Bowl, diameter 11¾″			
☐ blue and red.....................................	45.00	52.00	46.00
☐ all other colors.................................	25.00	30.00	27.50
Butter Dish			
☐ blue and red.....................................	300.00	400.00	350.00
☐ all other colors.................................	200.00	250.00	230.00
Candlesticks, height 2″, curved edge, pair			
☐ blue and red.....................................	20.00	25.00	23.00
☐ all other colors.................................	16.00	20.00	18.00
Candlesticks, height 5″, "wings," pair			
☐ blue or red......................................	46.00	54.00	50.00
☐ all other colors.................................	25.00	34.00	29.00
Candlesticks, height 5¼″, triple-lite, "wings," pair			
☐ blue or red......................................	75.00	85.00	80.00
☐ all other colors.................................	37.00	44.00	40.00
Candlesticks, height 8½″, metal stem, pair			
☐ blue or red......................................	40.00	50.00	45.00
☐ all other colors.................................	28.00	35.00	32.00
Comport, diameter 4″			
☐ blue or red......................................	15.00	20.00	27.00
☐ all other colors.................................	8.00	14.00	10.00
Decanter, height 7¾″			
☐ blue or red......................................	40.00	47.00	44.00
☐ all other colors.................................	26.00	34.00	30.00
Decanter, height 11″			
☐ blue or red......................................	45.00	55.00	50.00
☐ all other colors.................................	27.00	34.00	30.00
Goblet, 3 oz., wine, metal stem, height 5¼″			
☐ blue and red.....................................	6.00	10.00	8.00
☐ all other colors.................................	3.00	7.50	5.00
Goblet, 9 oz., water, metal stem, height 5⅞″			
☐ blue and red.....................................	12.00	16.00	14.00
☐ all other colors.................................	9.00	14.00	11.50
Goblet, 4 oz., wine, height 4″			
☐ blue and red.....................................	13.00	18.00	15.00
☐ all other colors.................................	8.00	13.00	11.00
Goblet, sundae, height 4½″			
☐ blue and red.....................................	20.00	26.00	23.00
☐ all other colors.................................	10.00	14.00	12.00

	Current Price Range		Prior Year Average

Goblet, 9 oz., water, height 6¼″
☐ blue and red.. 26.00 33.00 29.00
☐ all other colors................................... 12.00 18.00 15.00
Mayonnaise, three-footed, diameter 3″
☐ blue or red... 45.00 55.00 50.00
☐ all other colors................................... 17.00 22.00 20.00
Pitcher, 24 oz., height 7″
☐ blue and red.. 100.00 140.00 120.00
☐ all other colors................................... 80.00 120.00 100.00
Pitcher, 50 oz., ice lip, height 8″
☐ blue and red.. 140.00 170.00 155.00
☐ all other colors................................... 100.00 140.00 120.00
Pitcher, 53 oz., no ice lip, height 8″
☐ blue and red.. 130.00 160.00 145.00
☐ all other colors................................... 100.00 140.00 120.00
Plate, off-center indent, diameter 6″
☐ blue and red.. 12.00 16.00 14.50
☐ all other colors................................... 6.00 9.00 7.00
Plate, sherbet, diameter 6¼″
☐ blue and red.. 8.00 12.00 10.00
☐ all other colors................................... 5.00 8.00 6.00
Plate, salad, diameter 7⅛″
☐ blue and red.. 14.00 18.00 16.00
☐ all other colors................................... 5.00 8.00 6.00
Plate, luncheon, diameter 8½″
☐ blue and red.. 12.00 17.00 15.00
☐ all other colors................................... 5.00 8.00 6.00
Plate, dinner, diameter 9½″
☐ blue and red.. 15.00 19.00 17.00
☐ all other colors................................... 9.00 13.00 12.00
Relish, three-footed, three compartments
☐ blue and red.. 23.00 27.00 25.00
☐ all other colors................................... 12.00 16.00 14.00
Saucer
☐ blue and red.. 3.00 5.00 4.00
☐ all other colors................................... 2.50 4.50 3.00
Tray, two-handled, oblong, length 15″
☐ blue and red.. 60.00 80.00 70.00
☐ all other colors................................... 25.00 33.00 29.00
Tumbler, 1 oz., height 1¾″
☐ blue and red.. 22.00 26.00 24.00
☐ all other colors................................... 10.00 14.00 12.00
Tumbler, 2 oz., height 2½″
☐ blue and red.. 9.00 14.00 12.00
☐ all other colors................................... 5.00 8.00 6.00

	Current Price Range		Prior Year Average
Tumbler, 3 oz., juice, footed, height 3¼″			
☐ blue and red......................................	14.00	18.00	16.50
☐ all other colors...................................	8.00	12.00	14.00
Tumbler, 5 oz., height 3⅝″			
☐ blue and red......................................	10.00	14.00	12.00
☐ all other colors...................................	5.00	8.00	6.00
Tumbler, 7 oz., height 4⅜″			
☐ blue and red......................................	10.00	14.00	12.00
☐ all other colors...................................	5.00	8.00	6.00
Tumbler, 9 oz., height 4¾″			
☐ blue and red......................................	10.00	16.00	13.50
☐ all other colors...................................	6.00	9.00	7.00
Tumbler, 10 oz., height 4⅞″			
☐ blue and red......................................	13.00	17.00	15.00
☐ all other colors...................................	8.00	13.00	10.00
Tumbler, 12 oz., height 5⅛″			
☐ blue and red......................................	18.00	13.00	20.00
☐ all other colors...................................	13.00	18.00	15.00

MOONSTONE
Anchor Hocking Glass Co.

This striking crystal glassware features opalescent trim on rims and hob-nails. It was issued from the *Hobnail* molds, and can be distinguished from other *Hobnail* patterns by the many-rayed star in relief in the center and/or on the feet of most items. It was produced from 1941 through 1946. Mainly white opalescent was made, although a very small amount of green opalescent appears to have been made as well. The bowls are becoming the one type of item in *Moonstone* that is becoming hard to find. Rising popularity is resulting in higher prices and lower supply. A very similar pattern was made by Fenton. Many collectors are mixing the two patterns with great success.

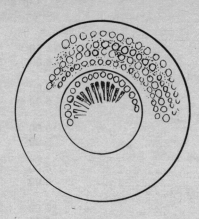

Moonstone

	Current Price Range		Prior Year Average
Berry Bowl, diameter 5½″			
☐ opalescent crystal	5.50	8.50	6.50
Bon Bon, heart shape			
☐ opalescent crystal	5.50	8.50	6.25
Bowl, flat, diameter 7¾″			
☐ opalescent crystal	6.50	9.50	7.25
Bowl, fluted edge, diameter 9½″			
☐ opalescent crystal	11.00	14.00	12.00
Bowl, fluted rim, with handle, diameter 6½″			
☐ opalescent crystal	5.50	8.50	6.25
Bud Vase, height 5″			
☐ opalescent crystal	7.00	10.00	8.00
Candlesticks, pair			
☐ opalescent crystal	13.00	17.00	14.00
Candy Jar, with lid, diameter 5″			
☐ opalescent crystal	16.00	18.50	16.75
Cigarette Bowl, with lid			
☐ opalescent crystal	12.00	16.00	13.75
Creamer			
☐ opalescent crystal	5.00	8.00	6.50
Cup			
☐ opalescent crystal	5.00	7.50	5.25
Dessert Bowl, fluted rim, diameter 5″			
☐ opalescent crystal	4.50	7.50	5.25

	Current Price Range		Prior Year Average
Goblet, height 5½"			
☐ opalescent crystal	13.00	16.00	14.00
Lunch Plate, diameter 8"			
☐ opalescent crystal	6.50	9.50	7.75
Puff Box, with lid, round, diameter 4¾"			
☐ opalescent crystal	13.00	17.00	14.00
Relish Bowl, two compartments, diameter 7"			
☐ opalescent crystal	6.00	9.00	7.00
Relish Dish, clover shapes, three compartments			
☐ opalescent crystal	7.00	10.00	8.00
Sandwich Plate, diameter 10"			
☐ opalescent crystal	13.00	17.00	14.00
Saucer			
☐ opalescent crystal	1.75	2.50	2.25
Sherbet Dish, pedestal foot			
☐ opalescent crystal	4.50	7.50	5.25
Vase, bud, height 5½"			
☐ opalescent crystal	7.00	10.00	8.25

NEW CENTURY
Hazel Atlas Glass Co.

Items in this pattern are characterized by a banded ribbon design that encircles the rim or body of a piece, finished with a concentric ring border. On footed pieces, the round bases are also ringed. Centers are rayed. Collectors can find this pattern abundantly in green, but also in crystal, pink, cobalt and amethyst. Green is the most popular color in this pattern.

New Century

	Current Price Range		Prior Year Average
Ashtray, diameter 5⅜″			
☐ crystal or green.................................	20.00	25.00	22.00
Berry Bowl, diameter 4½″			
☐ crystal or green.................................	3.00	6.00	5.00
Butter Dish, with cover			
☐ crystal or green.................................	44.00	54.00	55.50
Casserole Bowl, with cover, diameter 9″			
☐ crystal or green.................................	40.00	50.00	43.00
Cocktail Glass, 3¼ oz.			
☐ crystal or green.................................	11.00	14.00	12.00
Creamer			
☐ crystal or green.................................	4.50	6.50	5.00
Cup			
☐ crystal or green.................................	2.50	4.50	3.00
☐ pink or cobalt	11.00	15.00	13.00
Decanter, with stopper			
☐ crystal or green.................................	33.00	41.00	35.00
Dinner Plate, diameter 10″			
☐ crystal or green.................................	8.00	11.50	9.00
Grill Plate, diameter 10″			
☐ crystal or green.................................	6.00	9.00	7.00
Pitcher, with ice lip, 60 oz., height 7¾″			
☐ crystal or green.................................	23.00	27.00	24.00
☐ pink or cobalt	23.00	27.00	24.00
Pitcher, without ice lip, 60 oz., height 7¾″			
☐ crystal or green.................................	25.00	30.00	26.00
☐ pink or cobalt	25.00	30.00	26.00
Pitcher, with ice lip, 80 oz., height 8″			
☐ crystal or green.................................	25.00	30.00	26.00
Pitcher, without ice lip 80 oz., height 8″			
☐ crystal or green.................................	25.00	30.00	26.00
Plate, diameter 7⅛″			
☐ crystal or green.................................	4.50	6.50	5.00
Platter, oval, length 11″			
☐ crystal or green.................................	8.50	11.50	9.00
Salad Plate, diameter 8½″			
☐ crystal or green.................................	4.50	6.50	5.00
Salt and Pepper Shakers, pair			
☐ crystal or green.................................	23.00	27.00	24.75
Saucer			
☐ crystal or green.................................	1.70	2.60	2.10
☐ pink or cobalt	4.00	6.50	5.25
Sherbet Dish, diameter 3″			
☐ crystal or green.................................	4.50	6.50	5.00

	Current Price Range		Prior Year Average
Sherbet Plate, diameter 6″			
☐ crystal or green.................................	1.00	3.00	1.50
Soup Bowl, diameter 4¾″			
☐ crystal or green.................................	7.00	10.00	8.00
Tumbler, 5 oz., height 3½″			
☐ crystal or green.................................	7.00	9.25	8.00
☐ pink or cobalt	8.00	10.50	9.00
Tumbler, 5 oz., footed, height 4″			
☐ crystal or green.................................	8.50	11.00	9.50
☐ pink or cobalt	9.00	12.00	10.00
Tumbler, 9 oz., height 4⅛″			
☐ crystal or green.................................	7.50	10.00	9.00
☐ pink or cobalt	7.00	9.50	8.50
Tumbler, 10 oz., height 5″			
☐ crystal or green.................................	9.00	12.00	10.50
☐ pink or cobalt	10.00	13.00	11.50
Whiskey, 1½″, height 2½″			
☐ crystal or green.................................	7.00	10.00	8.50
Wine Glass, 2½ oz.			
☐ crystal or green.................................	10.00	13.00	10.50

NEWPORT
Hazel Atlas Glass Co.

In this pattern, hairpin lines are pressed into the glass, creating an inter-connected series of undulating, triangular motifs that follow the contour of a piece. Plate edges and bowls are slightly scalloped and centers are generally plain. It can be collected in cobalt blue, amethyst, pink and white. *Newport* was manufactured from 1936 through 1940.

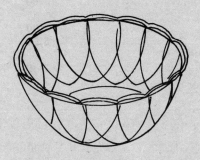

Newport

	Current Price Range		Prior Year Average
Berry Bowl, diameter 4¼"			
☐ cobalt...	8.50	11.00	9.50
☐ amethyst...	6.75	9.00	8.00
Berry Bowl, diameter 8¼"			
☐ cobalt...	22.00	30.00	27.00
☐ amethyst...	22.00	25.00	23.00
Cereal Bowl, diameter 5¼"			
☐ cobalt...	18.00	23.00	20.00
☐ amethyst...	13.00	16.00	14.00
Creamer			
☐ cobalt...	8.00	11.00	9.00
☐ amethyst...	6.50	9.50	7.00
Cup			
☐ cobalt...	6.00	9.00	8.00
☐ amethyst...	5.00	7.00	6.00
Luncheon Plate, diameter 8½"			
☐ cobalt...	6.50	8.50	7.50
☐ amethyst...	6.25	8.00	7.00
Platter, oval, length 11¾"			
☐ cobalt...	23.00	29.00	26.00
☐ amethyst...	17.00	22.00	19.00
Salt and Pepper Shakers			
☐ cobalt...	30.00	35.00	31.00
☐ amethyst...	28.00	32.00	30.00
Sandwich Plate, diameter 11½"			
☐ cobalt...	17.00	22.00	18.00
☐ amethyst...	12.00	16.00	13.00
Saucer			
☐ cobalt...	1.75	2.75	2.35
☐ amethyst...	1.60	2.60	2.10
Sherbet Dish			
☐ cobalt...	7.00	10.00	8.00
☐ amethyst...	6.00	9.00	7.00
Sherbet Plate, diameter 6"			
☐ cobalt...	2.50	4.50	3.00
☐ amethyst...	2.00	4.00	3.00
Soup Bowl, diameter 4¾"			
☐ cobalt...	10.00	14.00	12.00
☐ amethyst...	8.00	11.00	9.00
Sugar Bowl			
☐ cobalt...	8.00	11.00	9.00
☐ amethyst...	6.50	9.50	7.00
Tumbler, 9 oz., height 4½"			
☐ cobalt...	20.00	25.00	22.00
☐ amethyst...	17.00	21.00	19.00

NORMANDIE
Federal Glass Co.

Federal made this pattern from 1933 through 1939. It features a lattice design alternated with a floral design. The edges of the plates and bowls are slightly scalloped. The glass is thin and was made in pink, amber, iridescent, crystal and a small amount of green. Iridescent or *Sunburst* as Federal called it, is the only color in which you can put together a good collection without a great amount of difficulty. *Sunburst* was marketed as a premium and sold to the Great Northern Products Co. It closely resembles Carnival glass and a lot of people think that's what it is. The pink items in *Normandie* will cause a lot of searching and spending, as they're quite rare and expensive. The pink sugar lid is just about impossible. The amber, the pitcher is the stumbling block, with lots of people looking for it without much success. Some collectors refer to this pattern as *Bouquet and Lattice*.

	Current Price Range		Prior Year Average
Berry Bowl, diameter 5″			
☐ amber	3.00	5.00	4.00
☐ pink	3.50	6.50	4.75
☐ iridescent	3.25	5.50	4.00
Berry Bowl, diameter 8½″			
☐ amber	9.00	11.50	9.00
☐ pink	11.00	15.00	12.00
☐ iridescent	8.00	11.00	9.00
Cereal Bowl, diameter 6½″			
☐ amber	6.00	9.00	7.00
☐ pink	8.00	10.00	9.00
☐ iridescent	6.00	8.00	7.00
Creamer, footed			
☐ amber	5.25	7.25	6.00
☐ pink	7.50	10.00	8.25
☐ iridescent	6.25	8.75	7.00
Cup			
☐ amber	4.50	7.00	5.00
☐ pink	5.00	8.00	6.00
☐ iridescent	4.00	7.00	4.50
Dinner Plate, diameter 11″			
☐ amber	13.00	17.00	14.50
☐ pink	40.00	50.00	45.00
☐ iridescent	11.00	15.00	12.00
Grill Plate, diameter 11″			
☐ amber	8.50	11.50	10.00
☐ pink	9.00	12.00	8.00
☐ iridescent	9.00	12.00	10.50

	Current Price Range		Prior Year Average
Iced Tea Glass, 12 oz., height 5″			
☐ amber	15.00	18.00	16.00
☐ pink	40.00	50.00	45.00
Luncheon Plate, diameter 9¼″			
☐ amber	6.00	8.00	7.00
☐ pink	9.00	12.00	10.00
☐ iridescent	8.00	10.00	9.00
Pitcher, 80 oz., height 8″			
☐ amber	45.00	50.00	46.00
☐ pink	63.00	73.00	67.00
Platter, length 11¾″			
☐ amber	8.50	12.50	10.50
☐ pink	12.00	16.00	13.00
☐ iridescent	8.50	12.50	10.50
Salad Plate, diameter 8″			
☐ amber	5.00	7.00	5.50
☐ pink	6.00	9.00	7.00
☐ iridescent	20.00	25.00	21.00
Salt and Pepper Shakers			
☐ amber	32.00	39.00	33.50
☐ pink	45.00	55.00	50.00
Saucer			
☐ amber	1.00	3.00	1.50
☐ pink	1.50	3.50	2.00
☐ iridescent	1.00	3.00	1.50
Sherbet Dish			
☐ amber	4.50	6.50	5.00
☐ pink	6.00	9.00	7.00
☐ iridescent	5.50	8.50	9.00
Sherbet Plate, diameter 6″			
☐ amber	1.00	3.00	1.50
☐ pink	1.00	3.00	1.50
☐ iridescent	1.00	3.00	1.50
Sugar Bowl, with lid			
☐ amber	55.00	65.00	57.00
☐ pink	90.00	100.00	93.00
Tumbler, 5 oz., height 4″			
☐ amber	10.00	14.00	11.00
☐ pink	23.00	27.00	24.00
Vegetable Bowl, oval, diameter 10″			
☐ amber	10.00	14.00	12.00
☐ pink	20.00	24.00	22.00
☐ iridescent	12.00	16.00	13.50

	Current Price Range		Prior Year Average
Water Glass, 9 oz., height 4¼″			
☐ amber	9.00	13.00	10.00
☐ pink	18.00	22.00	19.00

NO. 610, PYRAMID
Indiana Glass Co.

This pattern, known to most collectors as *Pyramid*, was made from 1928 to 1932. The colors are pink, green, yellow, a small amount of crystal, some milk-white pieces that were made in the 1950s and some black produced in the 1970s for Tiara. Green and pink are not difficult to find, but yellow is quite scarce. The footed ice tea glasses are rare in all colors. The ice tub is only made in yellow and is no doubt the hardest piece in *Pyramid* to find (not to mention afford). Other than those pieces, however, *Pyramid* is in good supply. Watch out for nicks and scratches on these pieces; this pattern chips easily.

No. 610, Pyramid

	Current Price Range		Prior Year Average
Berry Bowl, diameter 4¾″			
☐ pink	12.00	16.00	14.00
☐ green	13.00	17.00	15.00
☐ yellow...	22.00	27.00	25.00
Berry Bowl, diameter 8½″			
☐ pink	20.00	25.00	22.00
☐ green	24.00	30.00	27.00
☐ yellow...	36.00	44.00	40.00

	Current Price Range		Prior Year Average
Bowl, oval, length 9½"			
☐ pink	23.00	29.00	25.00
☐ green	23.00	29.00	25.00
☐ yellow	40.00	50.00	44.00
Creamer			
☐ pink	17.00	22.00	20.00
☐ green	17.00	22.00	20.00
☐ yellow	20.00	26.00	24.00
Ice Bucket			
☐ yellow	400.00	480.00	420.00
Pitcher			
☐ pink	170.00	220.00	142.00
☐ green	160.00	170.00	165.00
☐ yellow	340.00	360.00	345.00
Relish Bowl, diameter 9½"			
☐ pink	22.00	28.00	24.00
☐ green	24.00	30.00	28.00
☐ yellow	40.00	50.00	45.00
Relish Tray, handles, four compartments			
☐ pink	27.00	34.00	30.00
☐ green	32.00	37.00	35.00
☐ yellow	36.00	43.00	40.00
Sugar Bowl			
☐ pink	14.00	19.00	16.00
☐ green	19.00	23.00	21.00
☐ yellow	20.00	26.00	24.50
Tray, holds sugar bowl and creamer, center handle			
☐ pink	15.00	20.00	16.00
☐ green	22.00	27.00	24.00
☐ yellow	38.00	45.00	43.00
Tumbler, footed, 8 oz.			
☐ pink	19.00	23.00	21.00
☐ green	28.00	33.00	31.00
☐ yellow	37.00	43.00	40.00
Tumbler, footed, 11 oz.			
☐ pink	32.50	38.00	35.00
☐ green	41.00	48.00	44.00
☐ yellow	45.00	50.00	47.00

NO. 612
Indiana Glass Co.

Collectors have called this pattern *Horseshoe* but most people still refer to it as *No. 612.* It was manufactured from 1930 to 1933. Green is the most commonly found color today, with yellow second in number. Small amounts of pink and crystal were produced, but they are rare today. The footed items in this line have square bases except for the pitcher. The butter dish in *No. 612* is particularly hard to find. You might see some plates without the center design. They are genuine; Indiana made two styles, one with the center motif and one without. The values are equal for both styles.

No. 612

	Current Price Range		Prior Year Average
Berry Bowl, diameter 4½″			
☐ green	14.50	18.50	15.50
☐ yellow	12.00	15.00	13.00
Berry Bowl, diameter 9½″			
☐ green	20.00	25.00	21.50
☐ yellow	22.00	27.00	23.50
Butter Dish, with cover			
☐ green	475.00	525.00	490.00
Cereal Bowl, diameter 6½″			
☐ green	13.00	17.00	14.00
☐ yellow	13.00	17.00	14.00
Creamer, footed			
☐ green	10.00	13.00	11.00
☐ yellow	11.00	14.00	12.00
Cup			
☐ green	5.50	8.50	6.25
☐ yellow	6.00	9.00	7.00
Dinner Plate, diameter 10⅜″			
☐ green	12.50	16.50	13.50
☐ yellow	13.00	17.00	14.00
Grill Plate, diameter 10⅜″			
☐ green	15.50	20.50	16.50
☐ yellow	18.00	22.00	19.00
Luncheon Plate, diameter 9⅜″			
☐ green	6.00	9.00	7.00
☐ yellow	6.00	9.00	7.00

	Current Price Range		Prior Year Average
Pitcher, 64 oz., height 8½″			
☐ green	170.00	195.00	178.00
☐ yellow	180.00	220.00	190.00
Platter, oval, length 10¾″			
☐ green	13.00	16.00	14.00
☐ yellow	13.00	17.00	14.00
Relish Dish, footed, three compartments			
☐ green	13.00	17.00	14.00
☐ yellow	22.00	28.00	23.50
Salad Bowl, diameter 7½″			
☐ green	11.00	14.00	12.00
☐ yellow	13.00	17.00	14.00
Salad Plate, diameter 8⅜″			
☐ green	4.50	7.50	5.25
☐ yellow	5.50	8.50	6.25
Sandwich Plate, diameter 11″			
☐ green	7.50	10.50	8.00
☐ yellow	9.00	13.00	10.00
Saucer			
☐ green	2.00	4.00	2.50
☐ yellow	2.50	4.50	3.00
Sherbet Dish			
☐ green	8.50	11.50	9.00
☐ yellow	9.00	13.00	10.00
Sherbet Plate, diameter 6″			
☐ green	2.00	4.00	2.50
☐ yellow	3.50	5.50	4.00
Sugar Bowl, without lid			
☐ green	8.50	11.50	9.00
☐ yellow	9.00	12.00	10.00
Tumbler, 9 oz., height 4½″			
☐ green	63.00	70.00	65.00
Tumbler, 12 oz., height 4¾″			
☐ green	73.00	80.00	75.00
Tumbler, footed, 9 oz.			
☐ green	10.50	13.50	11.00
☐ yellow	13.00	16.00	14.00
Tumbler, footed, 12 oz.			
☐ green	65.00	75.00	68.00
☐ yellow	68.00	75.00	70.00
Vegetable Bowl, diameter 8½″			
☐ green	14.00	18.00	15.00
☐ yellow	20.00	25.00	21.00

	Current Price Range		Prior Year Average
Vegetable Bowl, oval, length 10½″			
☐ green	11.00	14.00	11.50
☐ yellow	14.00	18.00	15.00

NO. 616, VERNON
Indiana Glass Co.

Also referred to as *Vernon*, this pattern was made from 1931 through 1933. It consists of a series of four floral sprays with foliage arranged quarterly around the perimeter. The central medallion is a combination of latticework and blossoms, the very middle framed with squared-off twigs. It was not made in large numbers, so it is pretty scarce today. Green is more popular than yellow. Crystal, although very lovely, dosen't attract as many collectors as the colored glass.

	Current Price Range		Prior Year Average
Creamer, footed			
☐ yellow	18.00	22.00	20.00
☐ crystal	11.00	15.00	13.00
☐ green	18.00	23.00	22.00
Cup			
☐ yellow	11.00	15.00	13.00
☐ crystal	6.00	9.00	7.25
☐ green	14.00	19.00	16.00
Luncheon Plate, diameter 8″			
☐ yellow	7.75	9.75	8.75
☐ crystal	6.00	9.00	7.00
☐ green	7.50	10.00	8.00
Sandwich Plate, diameter 11″			
☐ yellow	16.50	20.50	17.50
☐ crystal	8.00	12.00	10.00
☐ green	18.00	23.00	20.00
Saucer			
☐ yellow	4.50	6.50	5.50
☐ crystal	2.25	2.75	2.50
☐ green	19.00	23.00	21.00
Sugar Bowl, footed			
☐ yellow	19.50	23.50	21.50
☐ crystal	10.00	15.00	12.00
☐ green	18.00	25.00	21.00
Tumbler, footed, diameter 5″			
☐ yellow	22.00	26.00	23.00
☐ crystal	10.00	13.00	11.00
☐ green	23.00	28.00	24.50

NO. 618, PINEAPPLE AND FLORAL
Indiana Glass Co.

Indiana's official name for this pattern was *No. 618*, but collectors call it *Pineapple and Floral, Wildflower* or *Many Flowers*, among others. It was made from 1932 through 1937. The first issues were in crystal only, but by the end of the production run, amber was also being made. Pieces can also be found in a fired-on ruby red and a milk-white and olive green that were made as late as the 1970s. A piece in green was reported in the 1970s but it was probably an exception. Some pink items are now being made by Indiana so you know they're not original. The vase is very often used in funeral homes. As of this writing, the fired-on red has only been found in a few pieces. Any additional pieces that are found will sell for about the same as amber.

No. 618, Pineapple and Floral

	Current Price Range		Prior Year Average
Ashtray, diameter 4½″			
□ crystal	11.00	15.00	12.00
Berry Bowl, diameter 4¾″			
□ crystal	18.00	22.00	19.00
□ red	12.00	16.00	13.00
□ amber	12.00	16.00	13.00
Cereal Bowl, diameter 6″			
□ crystal	16.50	20.50	17.50
□ red	13.00	17.00	14.00
□ amber	13.00	17.00	14.00
Comport, diamond-shaped			
□ crystal	.75	2.25	1.00
□ red	5.00	8.00	6.00
□ amber	5.00	8.00	6.00

	Current Price Range		Prior Year Average
Creamer, diamond-shaped			
☐ crystal	5.00	8.00	6.00
☐ red....................................	7.00	10.00	8.00
☐ amber	7.00	10.00	8.00
Cup			
☐ crystal	6.00	9.00	7.00
☐ red....................................	5.50	8.50	6.50
☐ amber	6.00	8.00	6.50
Dinner Plate, diameter 9⅜″			
☐ crystal	8.50	11.50	9.00
☐ amber	11.00	14.00	12.00
Platter, tab handles, diameter 11″			
☐ crystal	8.50	11.50	9.00
☐ red....................................	10.00	13.00	11.00
☐ amber	10.00	13.00	11.00
Relish Platter, compartments, diameter 11½″			
☐ crystal	12.00	16.00	13.00
☐ amber	8.00	11.00	9.00
Salad Bowl			
☐ crystal	2.00	4.00	2.50
☐ red....................................	6.00	9.00	8.00
☐ amber	7.00	10.00	8.00
Salad Plate, diameter 8⅜″			
☐ crystal	4.00	6.00	4.50
☐ amber	4.50	7.50	5.00
Sandwich Plate, diameter 11½″			
☐ crystal	11.00	14.00	12.00
☐ amber	12.00	15.00	13.00
Saucer			
☐ crystal	2.00	4.00	2.50
☐ red....................................	2.00	4.00	2.50
☐ amber	2.00	4.00	2.50
Sherbet Dish, footed			
☐ crystal	13.00	17.00	14.00
☐ amber	13.00	17.00	14.00
Sherbet Plate, diameter 6″			
☐ crystal	2.00	4.00	2.50
☐ amber	3.00	5.00	3.50
Soup Bowl			
☐ crystal	13.00	17.00	15.00
☐ amber	15.50	19.50	16.50

	Current Price Range		Prior Year Average

Sugar Bowl, diamond-shaped
☐ crystal	5.00	8.00	6.00
☐ red	7.00	10.00	8.00
☐ amber	7.00	10.00	8.00

Tumbler, 10½ oz., height 4¼"
☐ crystal	20.00	25.00	21.50
☐ red	22.00	28.00	23.00
☐ amber	22.00	28.00	23.00

Tumbler, 12 oz., height 5"
☐ crystal	23.00	30.00	25.00

Vase
☐ crystal	22.00	28.00	25.00

Vegetable Bowl, oval, length 10"
☐ crystal	18.00	23.00	20.00
☐ amber	14.00	19.00	16.00

NO. 620, DAISY
Indiana Glass Co.

Although this pattern was issued under *No. 620,* collectors prefer to call it *Daisy,* as it features an arch effect in the center banded by large daisies in low relief. A central rayed design highlights the plates and bowls, encircled by a wide, sawtooth band. It appeared in crystal during the 1930s; amber, during the war years; and recently was produced in white opaque and dark green.

Berry Bowl, diameter 4½"
☐ crystal	4.00	5.25	4.50
☐ amber	6.00	9.00	7.00

Berry Bowl, deep, diameter 7⅜"
☐ crystal	5.00	7.50	6.00
☐ amber	8.00	11.50	10.50

Berry Bowl, deep, diameter 9⅜"
☐ crystal	5.00	8.00	5.75
☐ amber	18.00	22.00	19.00

Cake Plate, diameter 11½"
☐ crystal	3.00	6.00	4.50
☐ amber	7.00	10.00	8.00

Cereal Bowl, diameter 6"
☐ crystal	7.00	10.00	8.00
☐ amber	17.00	22.00	19.00

	Current Price Range		Prior Year Average

Creamer, footed
☐ crystal	2.75	4.25	3.50
☐ amber	5.00	8.00	6.00

Cup
☐ crystal	1.50	3.50	2.00
☐ amber	3.50	5.50	4.00

Dinner Plate, diameter 9⅜"
☐ crystal	3.00	5.00	4.00
☐ amber	4.00	7.00	5.25

Grill Plate, diameter 10⅜"
☐ crystal	3.00	5.00	3.50
☐ amber	7.50	10.50	8.25

Luncheon Plate, diameter 8⅜"
☐ crystal	1.00	3.00	1.50
☐ amber	3.50	5.50	4.00

Platter, diameter 10¾"
☐ crystal	5.00	8.00	6.00
☐ amber	8.50	11.50	9.25

Relish Dish, three compartments, diameter 8⅜"
☐ crystal	4.00	6.50	5.50
☐ amber	11.00	16.00	13.00

Salad Plate, diameter 7⅜"
☐ crystal	1.75	3.00	1.50
☐ amber	4.50	6.50	5.00

Saucer
☐ crystal	.75	1.50	1.00
☐ amber	1.25	2.00	1.55

Sherbet Dish, footed
☐ crystal	1.50	3.50	2.00
☐ amber	5.50	8.50	6.25

Sherbet Plate, diameter 6"
☐ crystal	.50	1.75	.75
☐ amber	1.75	3.00	1.50

Soup Bowl, diameter 4½"
☐ crystal	2.00	4.00	2.50
☐ amber	4.50	7.50	5.25

Sugar Bowl, footed
☐ crystal	2.00	4.00	2.50
☐ amber	5.00	8.00	5.50

Tumbler, footed, 9 oz.
☐ crystal	7.00	9.50	8.00
☐ amber	11.00	14.00	13.00

	Current Price Range		Prior Year Average
Tumbler, footed, 12 oz.			
☐ crystal	8.50	11.50	9.25
☐ amber	25.00	30.00	26.00
Vegetable Bowl, oval, diameter 10"			
☐ crystal	5.00	7.00	5.50
☐ amber	11.00	14.00	11.50

OLD CAFE
Hocking Glass Co

Old Cafe was made from 1936 through 1938 in crystal and pink. Two years later, in 1940, some pieces in ruby red were made. The dinner plates are very hard to find in this pattern. Chances are, if you can get them, you'll have no real problem putting a full set together. Tumblers are beginning to attract a lot of attention, so they probably won't be around in good supply for very long. There are certain pieces that many collectors feel are not really *Old Cafe,* but are simply similar pieces made by Hocking. They can be mixed and matched with the set very successfully, however. One of these pieces is the cookie jar. The bottom is fine, looks perfectly genuine, but the top has a cross-hatching that standard *Old Cafe* doesn't have. No listings have been found in old Hocking catalogs, so the controversy continues.

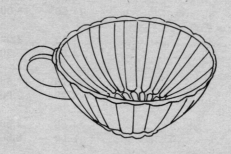

Old Cafe

	Current Price Range		Prior Year Average
Berry Bowl, diameter 3¾"			
☐ pink or crystal..................................	1.00	3.00	1.50
☐ red..	3.00	5.00	3.50
Bowl, loop handle, diameter 5"			
☐ pink or crystal..................................	2.00	4.00	2.50
Bowl, tab handled, diameter 9"			
☐ pink or crystal..................................	6.00	9.00	7.00
☐ red..	9.00	13.00	10.00

	Current Price Range		Prior Year Average
Bowl, two loop handles, diameter 5″			
☐ pink or crystal.....................	2.00	4.00	2.50
Candy Dish, shallow, diameter 8″			
☐ pink or crystal.....................	4.00	6.00	4.50
☐ red..................	8.50	11.50	9.00
Cereal Bowl, diameter 5″			
☐ pink or crystal.....................	3.00	5.00	3.50
☐ red..................	7.00	10.00	8.00
Cup			
☐ pink or crystal.....................	2.50	4.50	3.10
☐ red..................	4.50	6.50	5.00
Dinner Plate, diameter 10″			
☐ pink or crystal.....................	11.00	14.00	12.00
Juice Tumbler, height 3″			
☐ pink or crystal.....................	3.00	5.00	3.50
Lamp			
☐ pink or crystal.....................	8.00	12.00	9.00
☐ red..................	15.00	20.00	16.00
Olive Dish, oval, length 6″			
☐ pink or crystal.....................	3.00	5.00	3.50
Pitcher, height 6″			
☐ pink or crystal.....................	43.00	51.00	45.00
Pitcher, height 8″			
☐ pink or crystal.....................	63.00	73.00	65.00
Saucer			
☐ pink or crystal.....................	1.00	3.00	1.50
Sherbet Dish, footed			
☐ pink or crystal.....................	3.00	5.00	3.50
Sherbet Plate, diameter 6″			
☐ pink or crystal.....................	.75	2.00	1.00
Vase, height 7¼″			
☐ pink or crystal.....................	7.00	10.00	8.00
☐ red..................	12.00	15.00	13.00
Water Tumbler, height 4″			
☐ pink or crystal.....................	4.00	6.00	4.50

OVIDE
Hazel Atlas Glass Co.

Ovide was made from 1929 through 1935. It is opaque and is made in three very different designs. The first is referred to as the Art Deco design. It is the one pictured in the line drawing. The ray design extends all the way around the perimeter of the plate. The second style is a plainer one. A pair of orange bands circle the edge of the object. A small circular area with three flying birds is shown on each item, the rest of the item is plain. The third style is a plain item with a green band around the edge. Some pieces were also made in a black. It is heat-resistant and is used widely in restaurants. The Art Deco pattern has always been in demand but not much of it was made, so it's in short supply today. The plainer styles don't attract as many collectors.

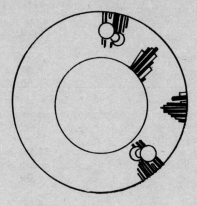

Ovide

	Current Price Range		Prior Year Average
Berry Bowl, diameter 4¾"			
☐ decorated	5.00	8.00	6.00
Berry Bowl, diameter 8"			
☐ decorated	14.00	18.00	15.50
☐ black...	12.00	15.00	13.00
Candy Dish, cover			
☐ decorated	22.00	28.00	25.00
☐ black...	20.00	25.00	21.00
☐ green	13.00	15.50	14.00
Cereal Bowl, diameter 6"			
☐ decorated	6.00	9.00	7.00
Creamer			
☐ decorated	7.00	10.00	8.00
☐ black...	6.00	9.00	7.00
☐ green	1.50	3.50	2.00
Dinner Plate, diameter 9"			
☐ decorated	7.00	10.00	8.00
☐ black...	6.00	9.00	7.00
Fruit Bowl, pedestal foot			
☐ decorated	6.00	10.00	7.75
☐ black...	5.00	8.00	6.00
☐ green	.75	2.00	1.00

	Current Price Range		Prior Year Average
Luncheon Plate, diameter 8″			
☐ decorated	5.00	7.50	5.50
☐ black	4.00	6.00	4.50
☐ green	.75	2.50	1.00
Platter, length 11″			
☐ decorated	9.25	12.00	10.75
☐ black	8.00	11.00	9.00
Salt and Pepper Shakers, pair			
☐ decorated	20.00	25.00	22.00
☐ black	18.00	22.00	19.00
☐ green	6.00	9.00	7.00
Saucer			
☐ decorated	3.00	5.00	4.00
☐ black	2.00	4.00	2.50
☐ green	.75	2.25	1.00
Sherbet Dish			
☐ decorated	6.00	9.00	7.25
☐ black	5.00	8.00	5.50
☐ green	.75	2.50	1.00
Sherbet Plate, diameter 6″			
☐ decorated	2.00	4.00	3.00
☐ black	1.50	3.50	2.00
☐ green	.50	1.75	.75
Sugar Bowl			
☐ decorated	7.00	10.00	8.00
☐ black	6.00	9.00	7.00
☐ green	1.50	3.50	2.00
Tumbler			
☐ decorated	25.00	32.00	27.00

OYSTER AND PEARL
Anchor Hocking Glass Co.

This pattern was manufactured from 1938 to 1940 in crystal and pink. In 1940, Anchor Hocking made some pieces in ruby red, and then later in the 1940s, some pieces in the opaque white and white with green or pink were made. It is a pattern that has never achieved much popularity due to its lack of a dinner setting. It is basically made up of occasional pieces. The ruby red is the most collectible color, with the pink and crystal next in popularity. Not too many pieces were made in the white with green or pink, so they're not too popular.

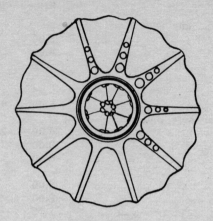

Oyster and Pearl

	Current Price Range		Prior Year Average
Bowl, heart shape, tab handle, diameter 5″			
☐ pink	4.00	6.00	4.50
☐ opaque pink	4.00	6.00	4.50
☐ opaque green	4.00	6.00	4.50
☐ crystal	4.00	6.00	4.50
Bowl, handled, diameter 5½″			
☐ pink	3.00	4.25	3.60
☐ ruby	6.50	8.00	7.25
☐ crystal	2.50	3.50	3.00
Bowl, tab handle, steep sides, diameter 6″			
☐ pink	6.50	10.00	7.00
☐ crystal	6.50	10.00	7.00
Candleholders, pair, height 3″			
☐ pink	13.00	17.00	14.00
☐ ruby	26.00	33.00	27.50
☐ opaque pink	11.00	14.00	12.00
☐ opaque green	11.00	14.00	12.00
☐ crystal	13.00	17.00	14.00
Relish Dish, oval, length 10″			
☐ pink	4.50	6.50	5.00
☐ crystal	4.50	6.50	5.00
Sandwich Plate, diameter 13″			
☐ pink	8.50	11.50	9.00
☐ ruby	22.00	28.00	23.00
☐ crystal	8.50	11.50	9.00

PARROT
Federal Glass Co.

Sylvan was the official name given to this pattern by Federal Glass Co., but collectors refer to it as *Parrot.* It was made from 1931 through 1932. The colors are green, amber, a small amount of crystal and there is one known piece in blue. A few years ago, green was abundant, so not too many collectors bought the amber. Now that green is not as easy to find as it used to be, more people are turning to the amber, causing its supplies to run low. Watch out for the luncheon plates with a pattern similar to *Parrot* also in green! These are rumored to have been made by Indiana and are definitely not part of the *Parrot* line. They are thinner glass, and the color is a lighter shade of green.

Parrot

	Current Price Range		Prior Year Average
Berry Bowl, diameter 5″			
☐ green	11.00	14.00	12.00
☐ amber	8.50	11.50	9.00
Berry Bowl, diameter 8″			
☐ green	45.00	50.00	46.00
☐ amber	46.00	54.00	48.00
Butter Dish, with cover			
☐ green	215.00	240.00	220.00
☐ amber	530.00	570.00	543.00
Creamer, footed			
☐ green	18.00	22.00	19.00
☐ amber	20.00	25.00	21.00
Cup			
☐ green	20.00	25.00	21.00
☐ amber	20.00	25.00	21.00

	Current Price Range		Prior Year Average
Dinner Plate, diameter 9″			
☐ green	27.00	33.00	30.00
☐ amber	22.00	28.00	23.00
Grill Plate, round, diameter 10½″			
☐ green	20.00	25.00	23.00
Grill Plate, square, diameter 10½″			
☐ amber	15.00	20.00	17.00
Luncheon Plate, diameter 9″			
☐ green	24.00	28.00	26.00
☐ amber	20.00	25.00	23.00
Pitcher, 80 oz., height 8½″			
☐ green	730.00	770.00	740.00
Plate, square, length 10¼″			
☐ green	30.00	35.00	31.00
☐ amber	30.00	35.00	31.00
Platter, oblong, length 11¼″			
☐ green	24.00	31.00	26.00
☐ amber	37.00	43.00	39.00
Salad Plate, diameter 7½″			
☐ green	12.00	16.00	13.00
Salt and Pepper Shakers, pair			
☐ green	195.00	235.00	215.00
Saucer			
☐ green	6.00	9.00	7.00
☐ amber	6.00	9.00	7.00
Sherbet Dish, footed			
☐ green	14.50	18.50	15.50
☐ amber	14.50	18.50	15.50
Sherbet Dish, height 4¼″			
☐ green	120.00	135.00	123.00
Sherbet Plate, diameter 5¾″			
☐ green	8.50	11.50	9.00
☐ amber	8.50	11.50	9.00
Soup Bowl, diameter 7″			
☐ green	22.00	28.00	23.00
☐ amber	22.00	28.00	23.00
Sugar Bowl, with cover			
☐ green	18.00	22.00	19.00
☐ amber	17.50	21.50	18.50
Tumbler, 10 oz., height 4¼″			
☐ green	80.00	95.00	88.00
☐ amber	85.00	100.00	93.00
Tumbler, 12 oz., diameter 5¾″			
☐ green	93.00	103.00	95.00
☐ amber	93.00	103.00	95.00

	Current Price Range		Prior Year Average
Tumbler, footed, 14 oz., height 5¾"			
☐ green	83.00	95.00	85.00
☐ amber	85.00	97.00	87.00
Vegetable Bowl, diameter 10"			
☐ green	34.00	39.00	33.00
☐ amber	37.00	44.00	38.00

PATRICIAN
Federal Glass Co.

Collectors used to refer to this pattern as *Spoke* but *Patrician* has turned out to be the official name. It was made from 1933 through 1937. Golden glow (amber) and springtime green were the first colors produced. Some pink and crystal were made in 1934 or 1935 and by 1936 only the amber was being made. Some blue was also made, but it appears to be a small amount. The amber is still plentiful today, so it must have been made in large numbers. The dinner plates in amber are still available, but an educated guess is that they won't stay that way. Dinner plates in every pattern are becoming scarce so it makes sense for *Patrician* to follow suit.

Patrician

	Current Price Range		Prior Year Average
Berry Bowl, diameter 5″			
☐ green	6.00	9.00	7.00
☐ pink	8.00	11.00	9.00
☐ amber	6.00	9.00	7.00
☐ crystal	6.00	9.00	7.00
Berry Bowl, diameter 8½″			
☐ green	16.00	19.00	17.00
☐ pink	16.00	19.00	17.00
☐ amber	22.00	28.00	24.00
☐ crystal	22.00	28.00	24.00
Butter Dish, with cover			
☐ green	85.00	95.00	87.00
☐ pink	180.00	220.00	190.00
☐ amber	62.00	72.00	65.00
☐ crystal	62.00	72.00	65.00
Cereal Bowl, diameter 6″			
☐ green	15.50	19.50	16.50
☐ pink	15.50	19.50	16.50
☐ amber	13.00	17.00	14.00
☐ crystal	13.00	17.00	14.00
Cookie Jar, with cover			
☐ green	250.00	300.00	265.00
☐ amber	48.00	55.00	50.00
☐ crystal	48.00	55.00	50.00
Creamer, footed			
☐ green	8.00	11.00	9.00
☐ pink	7.00	10.00	8.00
☐ amber	5.00	8.00	6.00
☐ crystal	5.00	8.00	6.00
Cup			
☐ green	6.50	9.50	7.50
☐ pink	6.00	9.00	7.00
Dinner Plate, diameter 10½″			
☐ green	18.00	22.00	19.00
☐ pink	14.00	18.00	15.00
☐ amber	4.00	6.00	4.50
☐ crystal	4.00	6.00	4.50
Grill Plate, diameter 10½″			
☐ green	8.00	11.00	9.00
☐ pink	8.00	11.00	9.00
☐ amber	6.00	9.00	7.00
☐ crystal	6.00	9.00	7.00
Jam Dish, diameter 6¼″			
☐ amber	15.00	19.00	16.50

	Current Price Range		Prior Year Average

Luncheon Plate, diameter 9"
☐ green	5.00	8.00	6.00
☐ pink	5.00	8.00	6.00
☐ amber	5.50	8.50	6.50
☐ crystal	5.50	8.50	6.50

Pitcher, 75 oz., height 8"
☐ green	75.00	85.00	78.00
☐ pink	93.00	105.00	95.00
☐ amber	73.00	82.00	75.00
☐ crystal	73.00	82.00	75.00

Pitcher, 75 oz., height 8¼"
☐ green	83.00	95.00	85.00
☐ pink	93.00	105.00	95.00
☐ amber	72.00	84.00	75.00
☐ crystal	72.00	84.00	75.00

Platter, oval, length 11½"
☐ green	10.50	14.50	11.50
☐ pink	8.50	11.50	9.50
☐ amber	8.50	11.50	9.50
☐ crystal	8.50	11.50	9.50

Salad Plate, diameter 7½"
☐ green	8.00	11.00	9.00
☐ pink	11.00	14.00	12.00
☐ amber	8.00	11.00	9.00
☐ crystal	8.00	11.00	9.00

Salt and Pepper Shakers, pair
☐ green	38.00	46.00	40.00
☐ pink	70.00	80.00	73.00
☐ amber	36.00	44.00	38.00
☐ crystal	36.00	44.00	38.00

Saucer
☐ green	4.00	6.00	4.50
☐ pink	4.00	6.00	4.50
☐ amber	4.00	6.00	4.50
☐ crystal	4.00	6.00	4.50

Sherbet Dish
☐ green	8.50	11.00	9.00
☐ pink	8.50	11.00	9.00
☐ amber	7.50	10.50	8.00
☐ crystal	7.50	10.50	8.00

Sherbet Plate, diameter 6"
☐ green	3.50	5.50	4.00
☐ pink	3.50	5.50	4.00
☐ amber	5.00	8.00	6.00
☐ crystal	5.00	8.00	6.00

	Current Price Range		Prior Year Average
Soup Bowl, diameter 4¾″			
☐ green	13.00	17.00	14.00
☐ pink	13.00	17.00	14.00
☐ amber	8.50	11.50	9.00
☐ crystal	8.50	11.50	9.00
Sugar Bowl, with cover			
☐ green	38.00	46.00	41.00
☐ pink	38.00	46.00	41.00
☐ amber	28.00	35.00	30.00
☐ crystal	28.00	35.00	30.00
Tumbler, 5 oz., height 4″			
☐ green	18.00	22.00	20.00
☐ pink	18.00	22.00	20.00
☐ amber	18.00	22.00	20.00
☐ crystal	18.00	22.00	20.00
Tumbler, footed, 8 oz., height 5¼″			
☐ green	33.00	42.00	35.00
☐ amber	26.00	33.00	28.00
☐ crystal	26.00	33.00	28.00
Tumbler, 14 oz., height 5½″			
☐ green	25.00	33.00	27.00
☐ pink	27.00	33.00	28.00
☐ amber	25.00	30.00	26.00
☐ crystal	25.00	30.00	26.00
Vegetable Bowl, oval			
☐ green	13.00	17.00	14.00
☐ pink	13.00	17.00	14.00
☐ amber	15.50	19.50	16.50
☐ crystal	15.50	19.50	16.50

PETALWARE
Macbeth-Evans Glass Co.

Macbeth-Evans made this pattern from 1930 to about 1938. It was made in monax (white), cremax (beige), small amounts of cobalt blue, green and yellow. A few pieces of fired-on red have been reported. Petalware is available in several styles: 1) bands of blue, green and pink, 2) bands of red, blue, green and yellow, 3) a gold trim, and 4) a brightly colored fruit or floral design (which is the most popular). Only the monax and cremax have the fired-on floral and fruit decorations. Lampshades are also common in this pattern.

	Current Price Range		Prior Year Average
Berry Bowl, diameter 8¾"			
☐ crystal	6.00	9.00	7.00
☐ pink	7.00	10.00	8.00
☐ beige or white, plain	11.00	14.00	12.00
☐ beige or white with decoration	13.00	17.00	14.00
Cereal Bowl, diameter 5¾"			
☐ crystal	2.50	4.50	3.00
☐ pink	3.25	5.00	3.50
☐ beige or white, plain	3.50	5.50	4.00
☐ beige or white with decoration	5.00	8.00	6.00
Creamer, footed			
☐ crystal	1.50	3.50	2.00
☐ pink	2.00	4.00	3.00
☐ beige or white, plain	3.50	5.50	4.00
☐ beige or white with decoration	6.00	9.00	7.00
Cup			
☐ crystal	1.50	3.50	2.00
☐ pink	2.00	4.00	3.00
☐ beige or white, plain	3.50	5.50	4.00
☐ beige or white with decoration	4.50	7.50	5.00
Dinner Plate, diameter 9"			
☐ crystal	3.00	4.50	3.50
☐ pink	3.00	4.50	3.50
☐ beige or white, plain	2.50	4.50	3.00
☐ beige or white with decoration	6.00	9.00	7.00
Mustard, with metal lid			
☐ crystal	6.00	9.00	7.00
☐ pink	7.00	10.00	8.00
☐ cobalt blue	9.00	12.00	10.00
Pitcher, 80 oz.			
☐ crystal	18.00	23.00	20.00
Platter, oval, length 13"			
☐ crystal	4.00	7.00	5.00
☐ pink	4.50	7.50	5.75
☐ beige or white, plain	6.00	9.00	7.00
☐ beige or white with decoration	11.00	14.00	12.00
Salad Plate, diameter 8"			
☐ crystal	1.25	2.25	1.50
☐ pink	1.60	2.60	2.00
☐ beige or white, plain	2.00	4.00	2.50
☐ beige or white with decoration	4.50	7.50	5.00

	Current Price Range		Prior Year Average

Salver, diameter 11″
☐ crystal	2.75	4.75	3.00
☐ pink	3.00	5.00	3.50
☐ beige or white, plain	4.00	6.00	4.50
☐ beige or white with decoration	8.50	11.50	9.00

Salver, diameter 12″
| ☐ beige or white, plain | 5.00 | 8.00 | 6.00 |
| ☐ beige or white with decoration | 11.00 | 14.00 | 12.00 |

Saucer
☐ crystal	.75	2.25	1.00
☐ pink	1.00	2.50	1.35
☐ beige or white, plain	.75	2.25	1.00
☐ beige or white with decoration	1.50	3.50	2.00

Sherbet Dish, footed, diameter 4½″
☐ crystal	2.00	4.00	2.50
☐ pink	2.50	4.50	3.00
☐ beige or white, plain	3.50	5.50	4.00
☐ beige or white with decoration	6.00	9.00	7.00

Sherbet Plate
☐ crystal	1.00	2.25	1.50
☐ pink	1.50	2.75	2.00
☐ beige or white, plain	1.00	3.00	1.50
☐ beige or white with decoration	3.00	5.00	3.50

Soup Bowl, diameter 4½″
☐ crystal	3.50	5.50	4.00
☐ pink	4.00	6.00	5.00
☐ beige or white, plain	4.00	7.00	5.00
☐ beige or white with decoration	6.00	9.00	7.00

Soup Bowl, diameter 7″
| ☐ beige or white, plain | 5.00 | 8.00 | 6.00 |
| ☐ beige or white with decoration | 8.50 | 11.50 | 9.00 |

Sugar Bowl
☐ crystal	1.50	3.50	2.00
☐ pink	2.00	4.00	3.00
☐ beige or white, plain	3.50	5.50	4.00
☐ beige or white with decoration	6.00	9.00	7.00

Tidbit, several styles
| ☐ crystal | 13.00 | 21.00 | 15.00 |

Tumblers, all styles
| ☐ crystal | 4.00 | 10.00 | 7.00 |

PRETZEL
Indiana Glass Co.

Indiana's name for this pattern was just *No. 622.* Some collectors also referred to it as *Ribbon Candy* but *Pretzel* is the name that has stuck. It was made basically only in crystal although a couple of exceptional pieces have turned up in green and in blue. Indiana made this pattern starting in the 1930s and continuing with some pieces into the 1970s. The pieces made in the '70s are the items you will find most readily. They include the 10¼" tray and the 8½" pickle. Some pieces in this pattern are very hard to find, the most difficult being the pitcher. You can, however, put together a nice collection of *Pretzel* without too much time and money being spent.

Pretzel

	Current Price Range		Prior Year Average
Berry Bowl, 9¾"			
☐ crystal	6.00	9.00	7.00
Celery Tray, 10¼"			
☐ crystal	3.00	4.50	3.75
Creamer			
☐ crystal	3.50	5.50	4.00
Cup			
☐ crystal	2.50	4.50	3.00
Dinner Plate, 9⅜"			
☐ crystal	2.50	4.50	3.00
Pickle, diameter 8½"			
☐ crystal	2.50	4.50	3.50
Pitcher, 39 oz.			
☐ crystal	45.00	55.00	50.00
Plate, 6"			
☐ crystal	2.50	4.25	3.25
Salad Plate, 8⅜"			
☐ crystal	2.00	4.00	3.00
Sandwich Plate, 11½"			
☐ crystal	3.50	6.50	4.25
Saucer			
☐ crystal	.50	2.00	.75

	Current Price Range		Prior Year Average

Sherbet
☐ crystal................................. 2.00 4.00 2.50
Soup Bowl, diameter 7½"
☐ crystal................................. 2.50 4.50 3.00
Sugar
☐ crystal................................. 2.50 4.50 3.00
Tumbler, 5 oz., height 3½"
☐ crystal................................. 4.50 6.50 5.25
Tumbler, 9 oz., height 4¼"
☐ crystal................................. 8.00 11.00 9.00
Tumbler, 12 oz., height 5¼"
☐ crystal................................. 9.00 12.00 10.50

PRIMO
U.S. Glass Co.

Manufactured in the early 1930s, *Primo* or *Paneled Aster* was made in yellow and green. The pattern features a floral and scroll design separated by pointed lines that suggest panels.

Bowl, 4½"
☐ yellow or green...................... 6.75 8.75 7.50
Bowl, 7¾"
☐ yellow or green...................... 11.00 15.00 13.00
Cake Plate, three-footed, diameter 10"
☐ yellow or green...................... 12.00 15.00 13.00
Coaster/Ashtray
☐ yellow or green...................... 6.00 8.50 7.25
Creamer
☐ yellow or green...................... 6.00 9.00 7.00
Cup
☐ yellow or green...................... 6.00 9.00 7.00
Dinner Plate, 10"
☐ yellow or green...................... 8.50 12.50 10.50
Grill Plate
☐ yellow or green...................... 7.00 10.00 8.00
Saucer
☐ yellow or green...................... 1.00 3.00 1.50
Sherbet
☐ yellow or green...................... 5.00 8.00 6.00
Sugar
☐ yellow or green...................... 6.00 9.00 7.00

	Current Price Range		Prior Year Average

Tumbler, 9 oz., height 5″
☐ yellow or green 10.00   13.00   11.00

PRINCESS
Hocking Glass Co.

The central medallion is a rosette formed by emanating rows of lilies and foliage circling a five-point star. This is achieved by delicate mold work tastefully executed. The modified square shape of the bowls and plates has a most interesting series of scroll bands, alternating triangles and trapezoids, fitting together as well as a jig-saw puzzle. This is a truly lovely pattern, an asset to your collection. Hocking made this pattern from 1931 through 1934. The first color to be issued was green, followed by yellow and then by pink. A few pieces have been found in blue but they were probably experimental. Certain pieces can also be found with a platinum rim which will usually add about 10–20% to their value. Pieces with the platinum rim can be found in all colors. Some pieces were also made with a satin finish. It seems that collectors either love satin finishing or they hate it. Depending on who is selling and buying, satin-finished pieces will either cost a little more or a little less. It depends on the buyer more than the seller. Always keep in mind that it's the collectors who set prices, not the dealers. Two distinct shades of the yellow are available. One is an amber-yellow and the other is a very light yellow. Both are attractive, but collectors do not generally like to mix the two. Hocking didn't mean to issue two colors, but one batch came out different than the other. The stemware in this line has either a checkered or a rayed pattern on the base. Either way, both are genuine. The most difficult pieces in this pattern to find are the ashtray and the 4½″ berry bowl.

Ashtray, diameter 4½″
☐ pink 53.00   63.00   55.00
☐ green 46.00   54.00   48.00
☐ topaz or amber 63.00   73.00   65.00
Berry Bowl, diameter 4½″
☐ pink 8.50   11.50   9.00
☐ green 14.50   18.50   16.00
☐ topaz or amber 23.00   31.00   25.00
Bowl, hat-shaped, diameter 9½″
☐ pink 13.00   16.00   14.00
☐ green 22.00   28.00   23.00
☐ topaz or amber 70.00   80.00   73.00

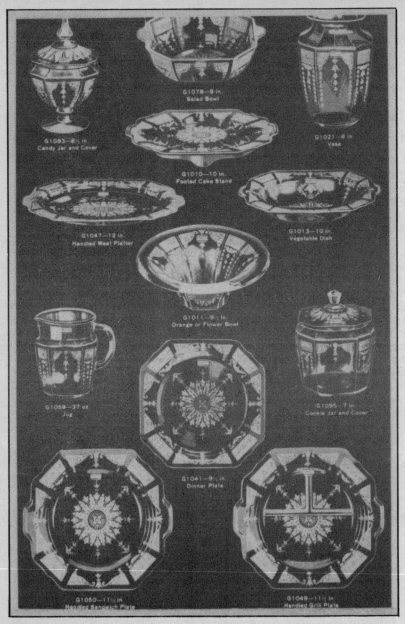

1930 Princess Catalog Sheet.
Courtesy of Anchor Hocking Corporation, Lancaster, Ohio

	Current Price Range		Prior Year Average
Butter Dish, with cover			
☐ pink	61.00	69.00	62.00
☐ green	63.00	72.00	65.00
☐ topaz or amber	400.00	450.00	410.00
Cake Stand, diameter 10″			
☐ pink	10.00	14.00	11.50
☐ green	13.00	16.00	14.00
Candy Dish, with cover			
☐ pink	32.00	40.00	34.00
☐ green	31.00	39.00	33.00
Cereal Bowl, diameter 5″			
☐ pink	12.00	15.00	12.50
☐ green	16.50	20.50	17.25
☐ topaz or amber	20.00	25.00	21.00
Cookie Jar, with cover			
☐ pink	36.00	44.00	38.00
☐ green	31.00	39.00	33.00
☐ blue	380.00	420.00	390.00
Creamer, oval			
☐ pink	8.00	11.00	9.00
☐ green	7.00	10.00	8.00
☐ topaz or amber	8.00	11.00	9.00
Cup			
☐ pink	5.00	8.00	6.00
☐ green	7.50	10.50	8.00
☐ topaz or amber	6.00	9.00	7.00
☐ blue	55.00	65.00	68.00
Dinner Plate, diameter 9½″			
☐ pink	9.50	12.50	10.50
☐ green	15.50	19.50	16.50
☐ topaz or amber	9.50	12.50	10.50
Grill Plate, diameter 9½″			
☐ pink	5.50	8.00	6.00
☐ green	8.00	11.00	9.00
☐ topaz or amber	5.50	8.00	6.00
☐ blue	55.00	65.00	68.00
Grill Plate, tab handles, diameter 11½″			
☐ pink	4.00	6.00	4.50
☐ green	6.00	9.00	7.00
☐ topaz or amber	4.50	7.50	5.50
Iced Tea Glass, 13 oz., height 5¼″			
☐ pink	14.50	18.50	15.50
☐ green	20.00	26.00	22.00
☐ topaz or amber	21.00	28.00	22.00

	Current Price Range		Prior Year Average
Juice Glass, 5 oz., height 3″			
☐ pink	13.00	16.00	14.00
☐ green	18.00	22.00	19.00
☐ topaz or amber	20.00	25.00	21.00
Pitcher, 24 oz., footed, 7″			
☐ pink	375.00	450.00	410.00
☐ green	375.00	450.00	410.00
Pitcher, 37 oz., height 6″			
☐ pink	21.00	27.00	22.00
☐ green	31.00	39.00	32.00
☐ topaz or amber	480.00	520.00	490.00
Pitcher, 60 oz., height 8″			
☐ pink	32.00	38.00	33.00
☐ green	33.00	39.00	35.00
☐ topaz or amber	55.00	65.00	57.00
Platter, tab handles, length 12″			
☐ pink	9.50	12.50	11.50
☐ green	11.00	14.00	11.50
☐ topaz or amber	26.00	34.00	28.00
Relish, plain, length 7½″			
☐ green	62.00	70.00	65.00
☐ topaz	100.00	115.00	105.00
☐ amber	100.00	115.00	105.00
Relish Tray, with compartments, length 7¹/₂″			
☐ pink	11.00	14.00	12.00
☐ green	15.00	20.00	17.00
☐ topaz or amber	43.00	53.00	45.00
Salad Bowl, octagonal, diameter 9″			
☐ pink	15.00	20.00	17.00
☐ green	21.00	26.00	23.00
☐ topaz	60.00	70.00	64.00
☐ amber	60.00	70.00	64.00
Salad Bowl, diameter 9″			
☐ pink	14.50	18.50	15.50
☐ green	20.00	25.00	21.00
☐ topaz or amber	62.00	72.00	65.00
Salad Plate, diameter 8″			
☐ pink	5.00	8.00	6.00
☐ green	7.00	10.00	8.00
☐ topaz or amber	6.00	9.00	7.00
Salt and Pepper Shakers			
☐ pink	27.00	33.00	29.00
☐ green	34.00	41.00	35.00
☐ topaz or amber	46.00	54.00	48.00

	Current Price Range		Prior Year Average
Sandwich Plate, handles, diameter 11½"			
☐ pink	6.00	9.00	7.00
☐ green	8.00	11.00	9.00
☐ topaz or amber	7.00	10.00	8.00
Sherbet Dish, footed			
☐ pink	9.50	12.50	10.50
☐ green	12.00	15.00	13.00
☐ topaz or amber	24.00	31.00	26.00
Sherbet Plate, diameter 5½"			
☐ pink	2.50	4.50	3.00
☐ green	4.00	6.00	4.50
☐ topaz or amber	3.50	5.50	4.00
Sugar Bowl, with cover			
☐ pink	14.00	18.00	15.00
☐ green	15.00	19.00	16.00
☐ topaz or amber	15.00	19.00	16.00
Tumbler, footed, 9 oz., height 4¾"			
☐ pink	38.00	44.00	40.00
☐ green	46.00	54.00	48.00
Tumbler, footed, 10 oz., height 5¼"			
☐ pink	14.00	18.00	15.00
☐ green	18.00	24.00	19.00
☐ topaz or amber	15.00	20.00	16.50
Tumbler, footed, 12½ oz., height 6½"			
☐ pink	27.00	33.00	29.00
☐ green	44.00	52.00	46.00
Vase, height 8"			
☐ pink	15.00	20.00	16.50
☐ green	20.00	24.00	21.00
Vegetable Bowl, oval, length 10"			
☐ pink	13.00	17.00	14.00
☐ green	15.00	20.00	16.50
☐ topaz or amber	33.00	41.00	35.00
Water Glass, 9 oz., height 4"			
☐ pink	11.00	14.00	12.00
☐ green	15.00	20.00	16.50
☐ topaz or amber	18.00	22.00	19.00

QUEEN MARY
Hocking Glass Co.

Sometimes referred to as *Vertical Big Rib,* this pattern was manufactured in pink and crystal from 1936 through 1939 and then some pieces of ruby red were made in the late 1940s. Only a few pieces were made in the red, but full settings were made in the pink and crystal. Pink is much easier to find than the crystal, although certain pink pieces are good at hiding. For example, the pink butter dish and 9½" plate are both very difficult to spot. As of yet, no pink shakers have ever been reported. Dinner plates are tough in both colors as are footed tumblers.

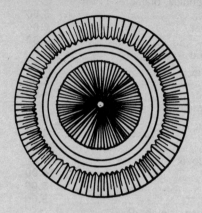

Queen Mary

	Current Price Range		Prior Year Average
Ashtray, round, diameter 3½"			
☐ crystal	2.00	3.25	2.50
Ashtray, oval, 2" × 3¾"			
☐ pink	2.50	3.50	3.00
☐ crystal	1.75	2.50	2.00
Berry Bowl, diameter 5"			
☐ pink	2.50	4.50	3.00
☐ crystal	1.50	3.50	2.00
Berry Bowl, diameter 9"			
☐ pink	6.00	9.00	7.00
☐ crystal	5.00	7.00	5.50
Bowl, diameter 7"			
☐ pink	4.00	6.00	4.50
☐ crystal	3.00	5.00	3.50
Bowl, round, no handles, diameter 4"			
☐ pink	2.00	4.00	2.50
☐ crystal	1.00	3.00	1.50
Bowl, two vertical handles, diameter 5"			
☐ pink	3.00	5.00	3.50
☐ crystal	2.00	4.00	2.50
Bowl, vertical handle, diameter 4"			
☐ pink	2.00	4.00	2.50
☐ crystal	1.00	3.00	1.50

	Current Price Range		Prior Year Average
Butter Dish, with cover			
☐ pink	70.00	80.00	72.00
☐ crystal	18.00	22.00	19.00
Candlesticks, double stem, pair, height 4″			
☐ crystal	8.50	11.50	9.25
☐ red..	23.00	30.00	25.00
Candy Dish, with cover			
☐ pink	18.00	22.00	19.00
☐ crystal	10.50	14.00	11.50
Celery Dish, length 10″			
☐ pink	3.50	5.50	4.00
☐ crystal	2.50	4.50	3.00
Cereal Bowl, diameter 6″			
☐ pink	2.50	4.50	3.00
☐ crystal	1.50	3.50	2.00
Cigarette Jar, oval, with lid, 2″ × 3″			
☐ pink	4.00	7.00	5.00
☐ crystal	2.50	4.50	3.00
Coaster, diameter 3½″			
☐ pink	2.00	2.75	2.35
☐ crystal	1.50	2.50	2.00
Coaster/Ashtray, square, 4¼″			
☐ pink	2.50	3.50	3.00
☐ crystal	2.00	3.00	2.50
Comport, height 5″			
☐ pink	4.00	6.00	4.50
☐ crystal	3.50	5.50	4.00
Creamer, oval			
☐ pink	4.00	5.50	4.00
☐ crystal	3.00	4.75	3.50
Cup			
☐ pink	4.00	6.00	4.50
☐ crystal	3.50	5.50	4.00
Dinner Plate, diameter 10″			
☐ pink	15.00	20.00	16.50
☐ crystal	5.00	8.00	6.00
Juice Glass, 5 oz., height 3″			
☐ pink	3.00	5.00	3.50
☐ crystal	1.50	3.50	2.00
Pickle Dish, oval, 5″ × 10″			
☐ pink	5.00	7.25	6.00
☐ crystal	3.50	5.50	4.25
Plate, diameter 6″			
☐ pink	1.50	3.50	2.00
☐ crystal	1.50	3.50	2.00

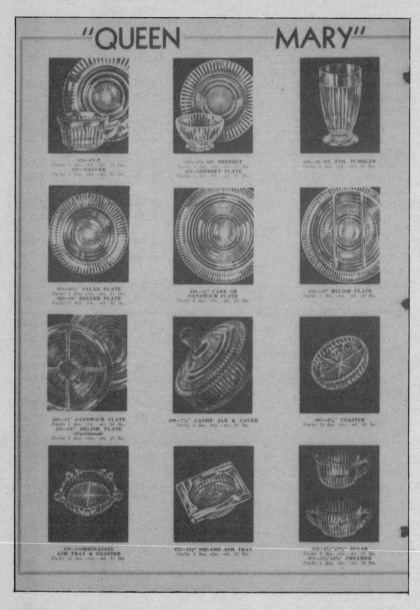

1937 Queen Mary Catalog Sheets.

PRISMATIC LINE

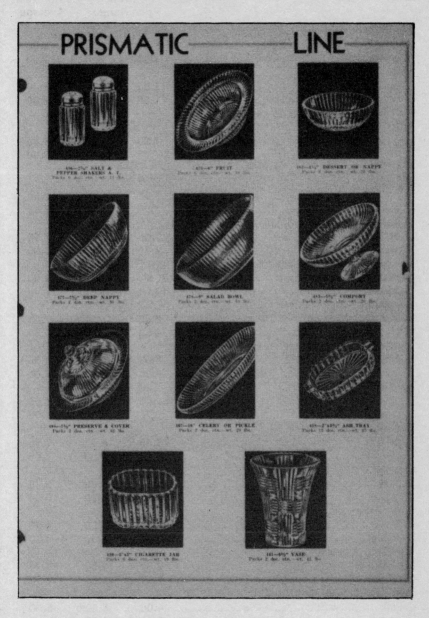

498—3⅝" SALT &
PEPPER SHAKERS A. T.
Packs 6 doz. ctn. wt. 11 lbs.

419—6" FRUIT
Packs 4 doz. ctn. wt. 34 lbs.

397—4⅜" DESSERT OR NAPPY
Packs 4 doz. ctn. wt. 28 lbs.

477—7½" DEEP NAPPY
Packs 2 doz. ctn. wt. 30 lbs.

478—9" SALAD BOWL
Packs 1 doz. ctn. wt. 34 lbs.

493—5¾" COMPORT
Packs 2 doz. ctn. wt. 25 lbs.

499—5⅜" PRESERVE & COVER
Packs 2 doz. ctn. wt. 32 lbs.

387—10" CELERY OR PICKLE
Packs 2 doz. ctn. wt. 29 lbs.

419—2"x5½" ASH TRAY
Packs 12 doz. ctn. wt. 37 lbs.

139—4"x2" CIGARETTE JAR
Packs 6 doz. ctn. wt. 19 lbs.

141—4½" VASE
Packs 2 doz. ctn. wt. 42 lbs.

Courtesy of Anchor Hocking Corporation, Lancaster, Ohio

	Current Price Range		Prior Year Average
Plate, diameter 7″			
☐ pink	1.50	3.50	2.00
☐ crystal	1.50	3.50	2.00
Plate, diameter 9½″			
☐ pink	12.00	15.00	13.00
☐ crystal	11.00	14.00	12.00
Relish Dish, three compartments, diameter 14″			
☐ pink	7.00	10.00	8.00
☐ crystal	7.00	10.00	8.00
Relish Platter, three compartments, length 12″			
☐ pink	7.00	10.00	8.00
☐ crystal	7.00	10.00	8.00
Salad Plate, diameter 8″			
☐ pink	3.00	5.00	3.50
☐ crystal	2.50	4.50	3.00
Salt and Pepper Shakers, pair			
☐ pink	70.00	78.00	74.00
☐ crystal	14.00	20.00	17.00
Sandwich Plate, diameter 12″			
☐ pink	6.00	8.00	7.00
☐ crystal	4.50	7.00	6.00
Sandwich Plate, diameter 14″			
☐ pink	7.00	10.00	8.00
☐ crystal	6.00	8.50	7.00
Saucer			
☐ pink	.75	2.25	1.00
☐ crystal	.75	2.25	1.00
Serving Plate, diameter 13″			
☐ pink	6.50	9.50	7.50
☐ crystal	6.00	9.00	7.00
Sherbet Dish, footed			
☐ pink	3.00	5.00	3.50
☐ crystal	2.50	4.50	3.00
Sugar Bowl, oval, length 3″			
☐ pink	3.50	5.50	4.00
☐ crystal	3.00	5.00	3.50
Tumbler, pedestal foot, height 5″			
☐ pink	12.00	15.00	13.00
☐ crystal	8.50	12.50	9.50
Tumbler, 9 oz., water, height 4″			
☐ pink	4.00	6.50	5.00
☐ crystal	3.00	5.00	3.50

RAINDROPS
Federal Glass Co.

This pattern is an overall treatment of the glass in round imprints occurring on the interior of the piece. This gives the pieces a mottled appearance and shows off the color to its advantage. The little circles are neatly arranged in symmetrical rows, the shapes are straightforward.

	Current Price Range		Prior Year Average
Cereal Bowl, diameter 6″			
☐ green	2.00	4.00	2.50
Creamer			
☐ green	3.50	5.50	4.00
Cup			
☐ green	2.00	4.00	2.50
Fruit Bowl, diameter 4¼″			
☐ green	1.00	3.00	1.50
Lunch Plate, diameter 8″			
☐ green	1.50	3.50	2.00
Salt and Pepper Shakers			
☐ green	34.00	41.00	35.00
Saucer			
☐ green	.75	2.25	1.00
Sherbet Dish			
☐ green	2.50	4.50	3.00
Sherbet Plate, diameter 6″			
☐ green	.75	2.25	1.00
Sugar Bowl			
☐ green	2.50	4.50	3.00
Sugar Bowl, cover			
☐ green	18.00	22.00	19.00
Tumbler, height 3″			
☐ green	2.00	4.00	2.50
Whiskey Glass, jigger			
☐ green	2.50	4.50	3.00

RIBBON
Hazel Atlas Glass Co.

This pattern was made from 1930 through 1931. It was made basically only in luncheon sets but included a few extras. It was produced mostly in green, but some black was made as well. Some crystal pieces have begun to turn up but not enough to hope for a complete set. Some pink has been reported, but so far only the shakers. The candy dish is very much in demand these days, as are the tumblers. The molds used to make *Ribbon* are the same Hazel Atlas used to make *Cloverleaf* and *Ovide*.

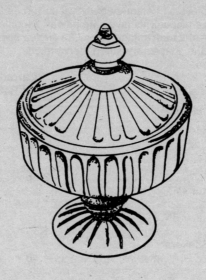

Ribbon

	Current Price Range		Prior Year Average
Berry Bowl, diameter 4″			
☐ green	2.00	4.00	3.00
Berry Bowl, diameter 8″			
☐ green	8.00	12.00	7.00
☐ black	11.50	14.50	12.25
Candy Dish, with cover			
☐ green	21.00	27.00	24.00
Creamer, pedestal foot			
☐ green	2.50	4.50	3.00
☐ black	7.50	10.50	8.50
Cup			
☐ green	1.50	3.50	2.00
Lunch Plate, diameter 8″			
☐ green	1.00	3.00	1.50
☐ black	6.50	9.50	7.50
Salt and Pepper Shakers			
☐ green	13.00	17.00	14.00
☐ black	24.00	31.00	26.00

	Current Price Range		Prior Year Average
Saucer			
□ green	.75	2.25	1.00
Sherbet Dish, pedestal foot			
□ green	2.00	4.00	2.50
Sherbet Plate, diameter 6″			
□ green	.50	2.00	.75
Sugar Bowl, pedestal foot			
□ green	5.00	9.00	7.00
□ black	7.50	10.50	8.50
Tumbler, height 6″, 10 oz.			
□ green	5.00	8.00	6.00
Tumbler, height 7″, 13 oz.			
□ green	10.00	15.00	13.00

ROCK CRYSTAL
McKee Glass Co.

Rock Crystal was made in crystal starting around 1910 and in colors around the early 1920s. The main colors produced were crystal, green, red, yellow, blue, amber and pink. Within those main colors there are a *lot* of shade variations. For instance, there are at least four shades of the red, ranging from a light amberina to a dark ruby. Some milk glass, some frosted pieces and some cobalt pieces have all been found but in very small numbers. The pattern is overall and has the look of an ice mold, with floral and scroll designs. On footed pieces, the pedestal is octagonal, the collar bases are on a heavy band. The butter dish, the pitchers, the 14″ punch bowl and the salt and pepper shakers are all difficult to find. Red is by far the most popular color. Crystal is the least desired and the other colors all fare about the same. For space saving, only the red is listed here. Prices for the blue, green, yellow, amber and pink are all about the same.

Rock Crystal

	Current Price Range		Prior Year Average
Bon Bon, diameter 7″			
☐ red..	34.00	41.00	35.00
☐ all other colors..................................	18.00	22.00	19.00
☐ crystal	11.00	14.00	12.00
Bowl, diameter 4″			
☐ red..	18.00	22.00	19.00
☐ all other colors..................................	8.50	11.50	9.00
☐ crystal	6.00	9.00	7.00
Bowl, diameter 4½″			
☐ red..	20.00	25.00	21.00
☐ all other colors..................................	8.50	11.50	9.00
☐ crystal	6.50	9.50	7.50
Bowl, diameter 5″			
☐ red..	22.00	28.00	23.00
☐ all other colors..................................	11.00	14.00	12.00
☐ crystal	8.00	11.00	9.00
Bread and Butter Plate, diameter 6″			
☐ red..	9.50	12.50	10.50
☐ all other colors..................................	5.00	8.00	6.00
☐ crystal	3.50	5.50	4.00
Cake Stand, diameter 11″			
☐ red..	53.00	63.00	55.00
☐ all other colors..................................	30.00	35.00	31.00
☐ crystal	18.00	22.00	19.00

	Current Price Range		Prior Year Average
Candelabra, double stem			
☐ red..	100.00	125.00	115.00
☐ all other colors................................	46.00	54.00	48.00
☐ crystal...	30.00	35.00	31.00
Candelabra, triple stem			
☐ red..	120.00	150.00	135.00
☐ all other colors................................	51.00	59.00	52.00
☐ crystal...	32.00	38.00	34.00
Candlestick, height 6″			
☐ red..	62.00	73.00	64.00
☐ all other colors................................	42.00	48.00	43.00
☐ crystal...	24.00	30.00	25.00
Candlestick, height 8½″			
☐ red..	130.00	150.00	135.00
☐ all other colors................................	70.00	80.00	72.00
☐ crystal...	53.00	62.00	55.00
Candy Dish, with cover			
☐ red..	95.00	105.00	97.00
☐ all other colors................................	41.00	49.00	43.00
☐ crystal...	22.00	27.00	23.00
Champagne Glass, stemmed			
☐ red..	25.00	30.00	26.00
☐ all other colors................................	15.00	20.00	16.00
☐ crystal...	11.00	14.00	12.00
Cocktail Glass, stemmed			
☐ red..	32.00	38.00	33.00
☐ all other colors................................	15.00	20.00	16.00
☐ crystal...	10.50	13.15	11.50
Comport, diameter 7″			
☐ red..	49.00	56.00	51.00
☐ all other colors................................	35.00	40.00	36.00
☐ crystal...	25.00	30.00	26.00
Cordial Glass, stemmed			
☐ red..	36.00	44.00	38.00
☐ all other colors................................	22.00	28.00	23.00
☐ crystal...	13.00	17.00	14.00
Creamer, pedestal foot			
☐ red..	39.00	46.00	41.00
☐ all other colors................................	23.00	27.00	24.00
☐ crystal...	13.00	17.00	14.00
Cruet, with stopper, 6 oz.			
☐ red..	200.00	235.00	210.00
☐ all other colors................................	70.00	80.00	76.00
☐ crystal...	40.00	50.00	45.00

	Current Price Range		Prior Year Average
Cup			
☐ red...	30.00	35.00	31.00
☐ all other colors................................	13.00	17.00	14.00
☐ crystal	10.50	13.50	11.50
Dinner Plate, diameter 10″, center design			
☐ red...	58.00	66.00	60.00
☐ all other colors................................	41.00	49.00	42.00
☐ crystal	34.00	41.00	36.00
Egg Cup, 3½ oz., footed			
☐ red...	35.00	45.00	40.00
☐ all other colors................................	22.00	28.00	24.00
☐ crystal	11.00	16.00	14.00
Finger Bowl, with tray, diameter 5″			
☐ red...	32.00	39.00	33.00
☐ all other colors................................	18.00	22.00	19.00
☐ crystal	13.00	17.00	14.00
Goblet, pedestal, height 7″			
☐ red...	41.00	49.00	42.00
☐ all other colors................................	20.00	25.00	21.00
☐ crystal	12.00	15.00	13.00
Goblet, stemmed, 8 oz.			
☐ red...	41.00	49.00	42.00
☐ all other colors................................	20.00	25.00	21.00
☐ crystal	12.00	15.00	13.00
Iced Tea Glass, pedestal, height 8½″			
☐ red...	50.00	60.00	53.00
☐ all other colors................................	20.00	24.00	21.00
☐ crystal	13.00	17.00	14.00
Jelly Jar, height 5″, footed			
☐ red...	32.00	38.00	33.00
☐ alll other colors	18.00	22.00	19.00
☐ crystal	12.00	15.00	13.00
Juice Glass, height 3½″			
☐ red...	30.00	35.00	31.00
☐ all other colors................................	16.00	20.00	17.00
☐ crystal	10.50	13.50	11.00
Lamp			
☐ red...	230.00	270.00	240.00
☐ all other colors................................	115.00	140.00	120.00
☐ crystal	52.00	62.00	55.00
Oil and Vinegar Cruet, with glass stopper			
☐ crystal	36.00	44.00	38.00

	Current Price Range		Prior Year Average

Old Fashion Glass, 5 oz.

☐ red..	31.00	39.00	33.00
☐ all other colors.................................	16.00	20.00	17.00
☐ crystal..	10.50	13.50	11.25

Pickle Dish, diameter 7″

☐ red..	34.00	41.00	35.00
☐ all other colors.................................	20.00	24.00	21.00
☐ crystal..	13.00	17.00	14.00

Pitcher, with lid, height 9″

☐ red..	275.00	325.00	385.00
☐ all other colors.................................	160.00	190.00	165.00
☐ crystal..	110.00	140.00	115.00

Plate, diameter 7″

☐ red..	12.00	15.00	13.00
☐ all other colors.................................	7.50	10.50	8.50
☐ crystal..	5.00	8.00	6.00

Plate, diameter 8½″

☐ red..	18.00	22.00	19.00
☐ all other colors.................................	8.00	11.00	9.00
☐ crystal..	6.00	9.00	7.00

Plate, diameter 9″

☐ red..	32.00	38.00	33.00
☐ all other colors.................................	15.00	20.00	16.00
☐ crystal..	11.00	14.00	12.00

Plate, diameter 10½″

☐ red..	34.00	42.00	36.00
☐ all other colors.................................	16.00	21.00	17.00
☐ crystal..	12.00	15.00	13.00

Plate, diameter 11½″

☐ red..	36.00	44.00	38.00
☐ all other colors.................................	18.00	22.00	19.00
☐ crystal..	13.00	16.00	14.00

Relish Bowl, six compartments, diameter 14″

☐ all other colors.................................	34.00	42.00	35.00
☐ crystal..	20.00	25.00	21.00

Salad Bowl, diameter 7″

☐ red..	27.00	33.00	28.00
☐ all other colors.................................	20.00	25.00	21.00
☐ crystal..	13.00	17.00	14.00

Salad Bowl, diameter 8″

☐ red..	32.00	39.00	33.00
☐ all other colors.................................	20.00	25.00	21.00
☐ crystal..	13.00	17.00	14.00

	Current Price Range		Prior Year Average
Salad Bowl, diameter 9″			
☐ red	36.00	44.00	38.00
☐ all other colors	21.00	26.00	22.00
☐ crystal	15.00	20.00	16.00
Salad Bowl, diameter 10½″			
☐ red	41.00	49.00	42.00
☐ all other colors	22.00	28.00	23.00
☐ crystal	16.50	20.50	17.50
Salt and Pepper Shakers			
☐ green	70.00	80.00	72.00
☐ amber	70.00	80.00	72.00
☐ pink	70.00	80.00	72.00
☐ crystal	36.00	44.00	38.00
Salt Dip			
☐ crystal	18.00	22.00	19.00
Sandwich Tray, central handle			
☐ red	70.00	80.00	72.00
☐ all other colors	27.00	33.00	28.00
☐ crystal	18.00	22.00	19.00
Saucer			
☐ red	8.50	11.50	9.00
☐ all other colors	5.00	8.00	6.00
☐ crystal	3.50	5.50	4.00
Sherbet Dish, pedestal stem, 3½ oz.			
☐ red	27.00	33.00	28.00
☐ all other colors	15.00	20.00	16.00
☐ crystal	8.00	11.00	9.00
Spooner			
☐ crystal	23.00	30.00	24.00
Sugar Bowl, large			
☐ red	31.00	39.00	32.00
☐ all other colors	18.00	22.00	19.00
☐ crystal	11.50	14.50	12.25
Sugar Bowl, with lid			
☐ red	45.00	55.00	47.00
☐ all other colors	31.00	39.00	32.00
☐ crystal	22.00	27.00	23.00
Sundae Dish, 6 oz.			
☐ red	24.00	31.00	25.50
☐ all other colors	13.00	17.00	14.00
☐ crystal	8.00	11.00	9.00
Tumbler, straight side, 9 oz.			
☐ red	32.00	39.00	33.00
☐ all other colors	20.00	24.00	21.00
☐ crystal	13.00	17.00	14.00

	Current Price Range		Prior Year Average
Tumbler, straight side, 12 oz.			
☐ red..	41.00	49.00	42.00
☐ all other colors...............................	22.00	28.00	23.00
☐ crystal...	18.00	22.00	19.00
Vase, cornucopia			
☐ crystal...	32.00	40.00	35.00
☐ pink	45.00	55.00	50.00
☐ green...	43.00	53.00	48.00
Vase, pedestal foot, height 11″			
☐ red..	105.00	130.00	110.00
☐ all other colors...............................	36.00	44.00	38.00
☐ crystal...	28.00	35.00	29.50
Whiskey Glass, 2½ oz.			
☐ red..	31.00	39.00	32.00
☐ all other colors...............................	13.00	17.00	14.00
☐ crystal...	8.00	11.00	9.00
Wine Glass, stemmed			
☐ red..	33.00	37.00	34.00
☐ all other colors...............................	23.00	26.00	24.00
☐ crystal...	13.00	16.00	14.00

ROSE CAMEO
Belmont Tumbler

Some controversy still remains as to the manufacturer of this pattern. However, Belmont Tumbler is the best bet. This line probably gets its name from its resemblance to the standard *Cameo* pattern. It is a very small line and was not made in great quantity, apparently, because it is not easy to find now. The tumblers are probably the most plentiful items and the 6″ straight-sided bowl the hardest to find. Green is the only color reported so far.

Rose Cameo

	Current Price Range		Prior Year Average
Berry Bowl, diameter 5″			
☐ green	2.75	4.00	2.85
Bowl, straight sides, diameter 6″			
☐ green	9.00	13.00	11.00
Cereal Bowl, diameter 5″			
☐ green	5.00	7.00	5.25
Salad Plate, diameter 7″			
☐ green	3.50	5.50	4.00
Sherbet Dish			
☐ green	3.50	5.50	4.00
Tumbler, diameter 5″			
☐ green	9.00	10.00	9.25

ROSEMARY
Federal Glass Co.

This pattern, at one time referred to commonly as *Dutch Rose* was made from 1935 through 1936. The first color issued was golden glow (amber) followed by rose glow (pink) and springtime glow (green). Some iridescent pieces have also been found. Amber was made in the greatest quantities and continues today to be the most available. Green and pink, however, are generally thought of as being more desirable. One thing to watch out for in this pattern—the sugars have no handles or lid so they can easily be confused with the sherbets. The cereal bowl and the tumblers have become rare in this line. If you notice some small inconsistencies in the pattern on some of your pieces, don't worry about it. It seems that a lot of *Rosemary* has that. The molds that were used to make this pattern were Federal's original *Mayfair* pattern and were reworked to make *Rosemary*.

Rosemary

	Current Price Range		Prior Year Average
Berry Bowl, diameter 5″			
☐ pink	3.00	5.00	3.50
☐ green	4.00	5.00	4.25
☐ amber	3.00	5.00	3.50
Cereal Bowl, diameter 6″			
☐ pink	9.00	11.00	9.50
☐ green	12.00	13.00	12.25
☐ amber	9.00	11.00	9.50
Creamer, pedestal foot			
☐ pink	7.00	10.00	8.00
☐ green	8.50	10.50	9.00
☐ amber	5.50	7.50	6.00
Cup			
☐ pink	5.00	7.00	5.75
☐ green	6.00	8.00	6.50
☐ amber	4.00	6.00	5.00
Dinner Plate			
☐ pink	8.00	11.00	9.25
☐ green	9.00	11.00	9.50
☐ amber	5.00	6.00	5.25

	Current Price Range		Prior Year Average
Grill Plate			
☐ pink	7.00	10.00	8.00
☐ green	9.00	11.00	9.50
☐ amber	5.00	7.00	5.50
Platter, oval, length 12″			
☐ pink	11.00	12.50	11.00
☐ green	13.50	16.50	15.00
☐ amber	8.50	10.50	9.50
Salad Plate, diameter 7″			
☐ pink	2.75	3.75	3.00
☐ green	5.00	7.00	5.50
☐ amber	3.00	5.00	3.50
Saucer			
☐ pink	2.50	3.50	3.00
☐ green	3.00	5.00	4.00
☐ amber	2.00	3.00	2.50
Soup Bowl, diameter 5″			
☐ pink	12.00	14.00	11.00
☐ green	12.50	14.50	13.00
☐ amber	7.00	8.00	7.25
Sugar, pedestal foot			
☐ pink	7.00	9.00	7.50
☐ green	8.50	10.50	9.00
☐ amber	5.50	7.50	6.00
Tumbler, height 4″			
☐ pink	17.00	19.00	17.50
☐ green	12.50	14.50	13.00
☐ amber	9.00	11.00	9.50
Vegetable Bowl, diameter 10″			
☐ pink	11.00	14.00	12.00
☐ green	3.00	4.00	3.25
☐ amber	1.50	2.50	1.75

ROULETTE
Hocking Glass Co.

Hocking made this pattern from about 1935 through 1939. It was made in mostly green and crystal, but some pink does exist. Many collectors have reported *Roulette* pieces in many different colors, but so far none have been genuine. For example, a lot of blue tumblers that closely resembled *Roulette* were found in the early and middle 1970s. It is widely known that Hocking didn't make that shade of blue but Hazel Atlas did, so the tumblers have been attributed to Hazel Atlas. The pitcher is the most difficult item in this pattern to find.

	Current Price Range		Prior Year Average

Cup
| ☐ green | 3.00 | 5.00 | 3.50 |
| ☐ pink or crystal | 3.00 | 5.00 | 3.50 |

Fruit Bowl, diameter 9″
| ☐ green | 8.00 | 10.50 | 9.00 |
| ☐ pink or crystal | 7.50 | 9.50 | 8.00 |

Iced Tea Glass, height 5″
| ☐ green | 9.25 | 12.00 | 10.25 |
| ☐ pink or crystal | 9.00 | 11.00 | 9.50 |

Juice Glass, height 3½″
| ☐ green | 4.50 | 6.00 | 5.00 |
| ☐ pink or crystal | 4.00 | 5.00 | 4.25 |

Lunch Plate, diameter 8″
| ☐ green | 4.00 | 5.50 | 4.75 |
| ☐ pink or crystal | 3.00 | 5.00 | 3.50 |

Old Fashion Glass, height 3½″
| ☐ green | 5.00 | 7.00 | 5.50 |
| ☐ pink or crystal | 5.00 | 7.00 | 5.50 |

Pitcher, height 8″
| ☐ green | 19.00 | 24.00 | 20.00 |
| ☐ pink or crystal | 20.00 | 25.00 | 21.00 |

Sandwich Plate, diameter 12″
| ☐ green | 7.50 | 6.50 | 8.50 |
| ☐ pink or crystal | 7.50 | 6.50 | 8.50 |

Saucer
| ☐ green | 2.50 | 3.50 | 3.00 |
| ☐ pink or crystal | 2.00 | 3.00 | 2.50 |

Sherbet
| ☐ green | 3.50 | 4.50 | 3.75 |
| ☐ pink or crystal | 3.50 | 4.50 | 3.75 |

Sherbet Plate, diameter 6″
| ☐ green | 4.00 | 5.25 | 4.50 |
| ☐ pink or crystal | 3.50 | 4.50 | 3.75 |

Tumbler, footed, 5 ½″
| ☐ green | 9.50 | 11.75 | 10.50 |
| ☐ pink or crystal | 9.50 | 10.50 | 10.50 |

Water Glass, height 4½″
| ☐ green | 12.25 | 14.25 | 13.25 |
| ☐ pink or crystal | 11.50 | 13.50 | 12.00 |

Whiskey Glass, jigger, height 2″
| ☐ green | 6.50 | 5.50 | 7.50 |
| ☐ pink or crystal | 6.50 | 5.50 | 7.50 |

ROUND ROBIN
Unknown Manufacturer

This pattern was probably made in the early or middle 1930s. The manufacturer is still being investigated. It is a very small pattern to begin with, and not many pieces are around on the market today. The colors made were green, crystal and some iridescent. The green is the most common. The most unusual aspect of this pattern is that the cup is footed.

Round Robin

	Current Price Range		Prior Year Average
Berry Bowl, diameter 4″			
☐ green	3.00	4.00	3.25
☐ iridescent	3.00	4.00	3.25
Creamer, pedestal foot			
☐ green	4.00	5.00	4.25
☐ iridescent	5.00	6.00	5.25
Cup			
☐ green	2.50	3.50	2.75
☐ iridescent	3.50	4.50	3.75
Lunch Plate, diameter 8″			
☐ green	2.00	3.00	2.25
☐ iridescent	5.00	2.50	3.50
Saucer			
☐ green	1.00	2.00	1.25
☐ iridescent	1.00	2.00	3.25

	Current Price Range		Prior Year Average

Sherbet, pedestal foot

☐ green	3.00	4.00	3.25
☐ iridescent	3.00	5.00	3.50

Sugar Bowl, pedestal foot

☐ green	4.00	5.00	4.25
☐ iridescent	4.00	6.00	4.50

ROYAL LACE
Hazel Atlas Glass Co.

This pattern was made from 1934 to 1941. It is a very popular line, probably because of the great number of blue pieces manufactured. The other colors produced were green, crystal, pink and some amethyst (referred to as burgundy by Hazel Atlas). There were several style changes in many of the items in *Royal Lace* so don't be surprised when you encounter different shapes. The pattern shows a large sunflower, geometrically designed and covering most of the available space. There are several motifs that make up the flower including a delicate scrollwork in the center and contrasting ridges in triangular shapes. The most difficult pieces to find in *Royal Lace* are the pitchers.

Berry Bowl, diameter 5″

☐ blue	23.00	30.00	28.00
☐ green	20.00	26.00	23.00
☐ pink	14.00	20.00	16.00
☐ crystal	10.00	14.00	11.50

Berry Bowl, diameter 10″

☐ blue	40.00	47.00	43.50
☐ green	25.00	30.00	27.00
☐ pink	15.00	20.00	17.00
☐ crystal	10.00	15.00	12.00

Butter Dish, with lid

☐ blue	350.00	450.00	400.00
☐ green	200.00	260.00	230.00
☐ pink	80.00	110.00	100.00
☐ crystal	60.00	85.00	75.00

Candlesticks, rolled edge, pair

☐ blue	100.00	125.00	110.00
☐ green	47.00	53.00	48.50
☐ pink	33.00	37.00	34.50
☐ crystal	35.00	40.00	36.00

	Current Price Range		Prior Year Average
Candlesticks, scalloped rim, pair			
☐ blue	80.00	90.00	85.00
☐ green	47.00	53.00	48.50
☐ pink	32.00	38.00	33.50
☐ crystal	20.00	25.00	22.00
Candlesticks, smooth rim, pair			
☐ blue	70.00	80.00	72.50
☐ green	40.00	45.00	42.00
☐ pink	22.00	26.00	24.00
☐ crystal	15.00	20.00	17.00
Cookie Jar, with lid			
☐ blue	210.00	220.00	212.00
☐ green	50.00	55.00	51.00
☐ pink	35.00	40.00	37.00
☐ crystal	23.00	28.00	24.50
Creamer, tri-legged			
☐ blue	23.00	28.00	24.00
☐ green	15.00	19.00	16.00
☐ pink	10.00	12.00	10.50
☐ crystal	7.00	9.00	7.50
Cup			
☐ blue	20.00	25.00	21.50
☐ green	12.00	15.00	13.00
☐ pink	8.00	12.00	9.00
☐ crystal	4.00	6.00	4.50
Dinner Plate, diameter 10″			
☐ blue	20.00	28.00	33.00
☐ green	16.00	19.00	17.00
☐ pink	10.00	13.00	11.00
☐ crystal	6.00	8.00	6.50
Grill Plate, diameter 10″			
☐ blue	20.00	25.00	21.50
☐ green	14.00	16.00	14.50
☐ pink	7.50	9.50	8.00
☐ crystal	4.00	6.00	4.50
Lunch Plate, diameter 8″			
☐ blue	20.00	24.00	21.00
☐ green	8.00	10.00	9.00
☐ pink	5.00	7.00	6.00
☐ crystal	3.00	5.00	3.50
Pitcher, bulbous, 86 oz.			
☐ blue	125.00	130.00	127.00
☐ green	90.00	100.00	91.00
☐ pink	50.00	60.00	51.00
☐ crystal	39.00	44.00	40.00

	Current Price Range		Prior Year Average

Pitcher, bulbous, 96 oz., height 8½"
☐ blue	115.00	160.00	156.50
☐ green	118.00	122.00	119.00
☐ pink	60.00	65.00	61.00
☐ crystal	43.00	48.00	44.00

Pitcher, cylindrical, 48 oz.
☐ blue	80.00	85.00	82.00
☐ green	62.00	65.00	70.00
☐ pink	38.00	43.00	39.00
☐ crystal	28.00	33.00	29.00

Pitcher, 54 oz., height 8"
☐ blue	85.00	95.00	90.00
☐ green	75.00	85.00	80.00
☐ pink	50.00	60.00	55.00
☐ crystal	32.00	42.00	36.00

Pitcher, bulbous, height 8", 68 oz.
☐ blue	115.00	120.00	116.00
☐ green	72.00	78.00	74.00
☐ pink	37.00	43.00	37.00
☐ crystal	38.00	42.00	39.50

Platter, oblong, length 13"
☐ blue	33.00	38.00	34.00
☐ green	23.00	28.00	24.00
☐ pink	14.00	16.00	14.50
☐ crystal	10.00	15.00	11.00

Rose Bowl, tri-legged, rolled edge, diameter 10"
☐ blue	155.00	160.00	157.00
☐ green	58.00	63.00	59.50
☐ pink	23.00	28.00	24.00
☐ crystal	70.00	80.00	70.00

Rose Bowl, tri-legged, scalloped rim, diameter 10"
☐ blue	140.00	145.00	139.50
☐ green	35.00	40.00	36.50
☐ pink	18.00	22.00	18.50
☐ crystal	16.00	18.00	17.00

Rose Bowl, tri-legged, smooth rim, diameter 10"
☐ blue	40.00	45.00	42.00
☐ green	28.00	32.00	29.50
☐ pink	17.00	20.00	18.00
☐ crystal	11.00	14.00	12.00

	Current Price Range		Prior Year Average
Salt and Pepper Shakers			
☐ blue	195.00	205.00	196.50
☐ green	110.00	115.00	111.50
☐ pink	35.00	40.00	36.50
☐ crystal	30.00	35.00	31.50
Saucer			
☐ blue	6.00	9.00	7.25
☐ green	4.00	6.00	4.50
☐ pink	3.00	5.00	3.50
☐ crystal	2.00	3.00	2.50
Sherbet, tri-legged			
☐ blue	23.00	28.00	24.00
☐ green	16.00	19.00	17.00
☐ pink	8.00	10.00	8.50
☐ crystal	6.00	8.00	6.50
Sherbet, with chrome fittings			
☐ blue	20.00	25.00	22.00
☐ crystal	3.00	5.00	3.25
☐ amethyst	22.00	28.00	23.50
Sherbet Plate, diameter 6″			
☐ blue	7.00	9.00	7.50
☐ green	5.00	7.00	5.50
☐ pink	3.00	5.00	3.50
☐ crystal	2.00	3.00	2.50
Soup Bowl, diameter 5″			
☐ blue	24.00	30.00	27.00
☐ green	20.00	25.00	21.00
☐ pink	10.50	12.50	11.00
☐ crystal	6.50	8.50	7.00
Sugar Bowl			
☐ blue	24.00	30.00	27.00
☐ green	14.00	16.00	15.00
☐ pink	6.00	8.00	6.50
☐ crystal	6.00	8.00	6.50
Sugar Cover			
☐ blue	75.00	80.00	76.50
☐ pink	20.00	25.00	21.00
☐ green	25.00	30.00	26.50
☐ crystal	10.00	15.00	11.00
Tumbler, height 3½″			
☐ blue	25.00	30.00	27.00
☐ pink	11.00	14.00	12.00
☐ green	18.00	23.00	19.50
☐ crystal	6.00	8.00	7.00

	Current Price Range		Prior Year Average
Tumbler, height 4⅛″			
☐ blue	23.00	28.00	24.50
☐ green	16.00	18.00	17.00
☐ pink	9.00	11.00	10.00
☐ crystal	7.00	9.00	8.00
Tumbler, height 4⅞″			
☐ blue	43.00	48.00	44.00
☐ green	25.00	30.00	27.00
☐ pink	16.00	18.00	17.00
☐ crystal	12.00	13.00	12.50
Tumbler, height 5⅜″			
☐ blue	40.00	50.00	44.00
☐ green	23.00	28.00	24.00
☐ pink	18.00	22.00	19.50
☐ crystal	11.50	13.50	12.00
Vegetable Bowl, oblong, length 11″			
☐ blue	40.00	50.00	45.00
☐ green	18.00	22.00	19.00
☐ pink	14.00	16.00	15.00
☐ crystal	12.00	14.00	12.50

ROYAL RUBY
Anchor Hocking Glass Co.

Royal Ruby refers to the deep red glassware made by Anchor Hocking and by no other company. It was made from 1938 through to the 1970s. There was also a line of dinnerware made by Anchor Hocking and marketed under that name. If you have a piece of glass in the *Royal Ruby* color but in a different pattern, look it up under the name of the pattern. The first items to come out in this line were the round-shaped dinner sets and accessories. The pattern did well and it wasn't until 1949 that Anchor introduced the square-shaped dinner line. The square sets are more scarce now but are still highly collectible. The *Royal Ruby* vegetable bowl and salad bowl are probably the most difficult to find items in the pattern. In 1977, Anchor came out with some re-issues of *Royal Ruby*. Included were the tumblers, an ashtray, and a punch cup. Supposedly the reissues were marked but a lot of them weren't. They are, however, lighter in color and quite a bit lighter in weight.

Ashtray, length 4¾″			
☐ ruby	2.00	3.00	2.25
Berry Bowl, diameter 4″			
☐ ruby	3.00	5.00	3.50

	Current Price Range		Prior Year Average

Berry Bowl, diameter 8″
☐ ruby 11.00 13.50 12.00
Cocktail Glass, 3 oz.
☐ ruby 5.00 7.00 5.50
Creamer, flat
☐ ruby 5.00 7.00 5.50
Creamer, footed
☐ ruby 6.00 8.00 6.50
Cup
☐ ruby 3.00 4.00 3.25
Dinner Plate, diameter 9″
☐ ruby 6.00 8.00 6.50
Goblet, knobbed stem
☐ ruby 6.00 8.00 6.50
Iced Tea Glass, 14 oz.
☐ ruby 7.00 9.00 7.50
Juice Glass, 5 oz.
☐ ruby 4.00 6.00 4.50
Lamp
☐ ruby 18.00 22.00 19.00
Lunch Plate, diameter 8″
☐ ruby 3.00 5.00 3.50
Pitcher, tilted, height 7″
☐ ruby 18.00 22.00 19.00
Pitcher, upright, height 7″
☐ ruby 18.00 22.00 19.00
Pitcher, tilted, 96 oz.
☐ ruby 23.00 28.00 24.00
Pitcher, upright, 96 oz.
☐ ruby 28.00 33.00 29.00
Punch Bowl, with base
☐ ruby 33.00 38.00 34.00
Punch Cup
☐ ruby 1.50 2.50 1.75
Salad Plate, diameter 7″
☐ ruby 2.00 4.00 3.00
Saucer, round
☐ ruby 1.00 2.00 1.25
Saucer, square
☐ ruby 1.00 2.00 1.25
Sherbet Dish, pedestal foot
☐ ruby 5.00 7.00 6.00
Sherbet Plate, diameter 6″
☐ ruby 1.00 3.00 1.50

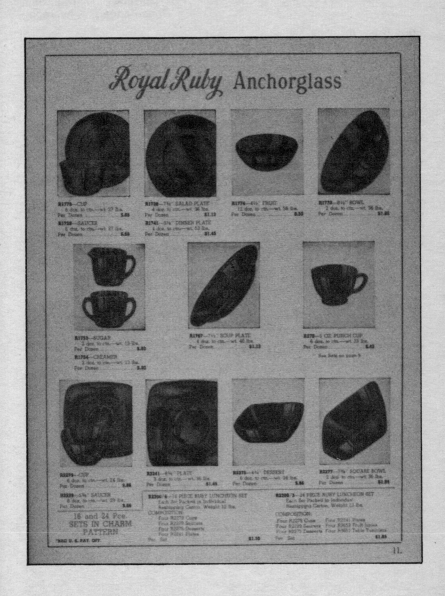

1950 Royal Ruby Catalog Sheet.
Courtesy of Anchor Hocking Corporation, Lancaster, Ohio

	Current Price Range		Prior Year Average
Soup Bowl, diameter 7½"			
☐ ruby................................	8.00	10.00	8.50
Sugar Bowl, flat			
☐ ruby................................	5.00	7.00	5.50
Sugar Bowl, footed			
☐ ruby................................	6.00	8.00	7.00
Water Glass, 9 oz.			
☐ ruby................................	4.00	6.00	4.50
Water Glass, 10 oz.			
☐ ruby................................	4.00	6.00	4.50
Wine Glass, pedestal foot, 2½ oz.			
☐ ruby................................	7.00	9.00	7.50
Vase, bulbous, height 4"			
☐ ruby................................	3.00	5.00	3.50
Vase, bulbous, height 9"			
☐ ruby................................	7.00	9.00	7.50
Vegetable, oblong, length 8"			
☐ ruby................................	12.00	13.00	12.25

S PATTERN, STIPPLED ROSE BAND
Macbeth-Evans Glass Co.

Also referred to as *Stippled Rose Band,* this pattern was made from 1930 through 1932. The colors were crystal, crystal with either blue, gold or platinum trim, amber, yellow (two shades), fired-on red and small amounts of pink and green. The pieces you will run across most often will be either in crystal or crystal with trim. They are very elegant and have attracted many collectors. The amber and yellow are in good supply so there shouldn't be too much trouble collecting them. The other colors are all rare. The pitchers are the hardest items to come by. One pitcher has been reported with the pattern silk-screened onto it, which is unusual. Many collectors aren't interested in *S Pattern* as an entire pattern, just in the pitchers and tumblers.

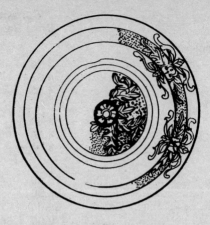

S Pattern, Stippled Rose Band

	Current Price Range		Prior Year Average
Berry Bowl, diameter 8½″			
☐ crystal	5.00	7.00	6.25
☐ crystal with trim	12.50	14.00	12.50
☐ yellow or amber	11.50	13.50	12.00
Cake Plate, diameter 11″			
☐ crystal	28.00	33.00	29.00
☐ crystal with trim	31.00	36.00	33.00
☐ yellow or amber	30.00	34.00	31.50
Cake Plate, diameter 13″			
☐ crystal	45.00	50.00	46.00
☐ crystal with trim	53.00	63.00	58.00
☐ yellow or amber	50.00	60.00	52.00
Cereal Bowl, diameter 5½″			
☐ crystal	2.00	3.00	2.50
☐ crystal with trim	3.50	5.50	4.50
☐ yellow or amber	3.00	5.00	3.50
Creamer			
☐ crystal	3.00	5.00	3.50
☐ crystal with trim	5.00	7.00	6.00
☐ yellow or amber	4.50	6.50	5.00
Cup			
☐ crystal	2.00	3.00	2.25
☐ crystal with trim	3.40	5.25	3.50
☐ yellow or amber	3.00	5.00	3.25

	Current Price Range		Prior Year Average

Dinner Plate, diameter 9¼″

☐ crystal	3.00	5.00	3.25
☐ crystal with trim	4.50	6.50	4.60
☐ yellow or amber	4.00	6.00	4.25

Grill Plate

☐ crystal	2.00	3.00	2.35
☐ crystal with trim	4.50	6.25	5.00
☐ yellow or amber	4.00	6.00	4.25

Pitcher, 80 oz.

☐ crystal	35.00	40.00	36.50
☐ crystal with trim	66.00	75.00	71.00
☐ yellow or amber	65.00	70.00	66.00
☐ green	470.00	500.00	492.50

Sandwich Plate, diameter 8″

☐ crystal	2.00	3.00	2.00
☐ crystal with trim	2.25	3.25	2.50
☐ yellow or amber	2.00	3.00	2.25

Saucer

☐ crystal	1.00	3.00	1.25
☐ crystal with trim	1.75	3.25	1.50
☐ yellow or amber	1.00	3.00	1.25

Sherbet Dish, footed

☐ crystal	3.00	5.00	3.25
☐ crystal with trim	4.35	6.35	4.65
☐ yellow or amber	4.00	6.00	4.25

Sherbet Plate, diameter 6″

☐ crystal	1.00	3.00	1.25
☐ crystal with trim	1.75	3.00	2.35
☐ yellow or amber	1.50	2.50	1.75

Sugar Bowl

☐ crystal	3.00	5.00	3.25
☐ crystal with trim	5.25	7.35	6.00
☐ yellow or amber	5.00	7.00	5.25

Tumbler, 9 oz., height 4″

☐ crystal	3.00	5.00	3.25
☐ crystal with trim	5.25	7.50	6.10
☐ yellow or amber	5.00	7.00	5.25
☐ green	55.00	60.00	56.50

Tumbler, 10 oz., height 4¼″

☐ crystal	3.00	5.00	3.50
☐ crystal with trim	5.50	7.25	6.00
☐ yellow or amber	5.00	7.00	5.50

	Current Price Range		Prior Year Average
Tumbler, 12 oz., height 5″			
☐ crystal	4.00	6.00	4.25
☐ crystal with trim	6.35	7.25	6.65
☐ yellow or amber	6.00	7.00	6.25

SANDWICH
Anchor Hocking Glass Co.

Anchor Hocking's *Sandwich* has a long and involved history. It was first manufactured in berry sets in pink and royal ruby in 1939–40. In the 1950s, a dark forest green and crystal were both made. A small amount of white glass was also made in the 1950s. Amber was made during the 1960s. In 1977, Anchor made a new cookie jar. The new one is 10¼″ high and the old is 9½″ high, so there's no problem in identifying it. Some other pieces were reissued by Anchor in the 1950s. These included the 4⅞″ nappy, the 5 oz. and 9 oz. tumblers and the 4¼″ plate. These are considered collectible. The green cookie jar lid has never materialized. It was probably never made and the bottom piece was marketed as a vase.

Sandwich (Hocking)

	Current Price Range		Prior Year Average

Berry Bowl, diameter 4½″

☐ crystal	2.50	3.50	2.75
☐ pink	2.00	3.00	2.25
☐ red	8.00	10.00	8.50
☐ amber	2.00	3.00	2.25
☐ green	1.00	3.00	1.25

Bowl, diameter 6½″

☐ crystal	4.00	6.00	4.25
☐ amber	5.00	7.00	5.25
☐ green	18.00	23.00	19.00

Bowl, scalloped rim, diameter 6½″

☐ crystal	4.00	6.00	4.50
☐ amber	5.00	7.00	5.25
☐ green	18.00	23.00	19.00

Bowl, diameter 8″

☐ crystal	5.00	7.00	6.00
☐ pink	6.00	8.00	7.00
☐ red	28.00	33.00	29.00
☐ green	33.00	38.00	34.00

Bowl, scalloped rim, diameter 8″

☐ crystal	5.00	7.00	6.00
☐ pink	6.00	8.00	7.00
☐ red	28.00	33.00	29.00
☐ green	33.00	38.00	34.00

Butter Dish

☐ crystal	30.00	35.00	31.50

Cereal Bowl, diameter 6″

☐ crystal	11.00	14.00	12.00
☐ amber	5.00	7.00	5.00

Cookie Jar, with cover

☐ crystal	28.00	33.00	29.00
☐ gold	25.00	30.00	26.00

Creamer

☐ crystal	3.50	4.50	3.75
☐ green	13.50	15.50	14.00

Cup

☐ crystal	1.00	3.00	1.25
☐ amber	3.00	5.00	3.50
☐ green	12.00	13.00	12.25

Custard Cup

☐ crystal	3.00	4.00	3.25
☐ green	1.00	2.00	1.50

Dessert Plate, diameter 7″

☐ crystal	5.00	7.00	5.50
☐ amber	2.00	3.00	2.50

1957 Sandwich Catalog Sheet.
Courtesy of Anchor Hocking Corporation, Lancaster, Ohio

	Current Price Range		Prior Year Average
Dinner Plate, diameter 9″			
☐ crystal	8.00	10.00	8.50
☐ amber	3.50	4.50	3.75
☐ green	33.00	38.00	34.00
Juice Glass, 5 oz.			
☐ crystal	4.00	6.00	4.25
☐ green	1.50	2.50	1.75
Pitcher, height 6″			
☐ crystal	43.00	48.00	44.00
☐ green	90.00	95.00	91.50
Pitcher, ice lip, 64 oz.			
☐ crystal	40.00	45.00	41.50
☐ green	160.00	170.00	162.50
Salad Bowl, diameter 7″			
☐ crystal	5.00	7.00	6.00
☐ green	28.00	33.00	29.00
Sandwich Plate, diameter 12″			
☐ crystal	6.50	8.50	6.75
☐ amber	6.50	8.50	6.75
Saucer			
☐ crystal	1.00	3.00	1.25
☐ amber	2.50	3.50	2.75
☐ green	3.50	5.50	4.00
Serving Bowl, oval, length 8¼″			
☐ crystal	4.00	6.00	4.75
Sherbet Dish, footed			
☐ crystal	5.00	7.00	5.50
Sugar Bowl			
☐ crystal, with lid	11.50	13.50	12.00
☐ green, no lid	13.50	15.50	14.00
Tumbler, footed, 9 oz.			
☐ crystal	13.00	14.00	13.25
Water Glass, 9 oz.			
☐ crystal	6.00	7.00	6.25
☐ green	2.00	3.00	2.25

SANDWICH
Indiana Glass Co.

Indiana's *Sandwich* was made starting in the 1920s and is still being made today. The original colors were crystal, light green, pink and amber. In the early 1930s red was introduced and later on, in the 1950s, teal blue. Crystal is still being made today and has become almost uncollectible as a result. Some of the new pieces, including the 68 oz. pitcher and the wine goblet, are bigger than the old pieces, but most are impossible to tell apart. Indiana is also putting out a gold color now, but since that wasn't one of the original colors, it's no problem to spot as a reissue. The crystal, however, is so close to the original that collectors won't touch any crystal *Sandwich* anymore. Collectors with large sets of original crystal *Sandwich* are afraid (and rightfully so) of losing their investments. Indiana is also coming out with new amber and blue pieces. It seems that the only safe colors right now are the green and pink. It seems irresponsible for Indiana to ruin the secondary market on its glass. They are advertising the new glass as being collectible but it's exactly the opposite; it's ruining what once was collectible.

Sandwich (Indiana)

	Current Price Range		Prior Year Average
Berry Bowl, 4¼″			
☐ crystal	1.50	3.50	2.00
☐ pink or green	2.00	4.00	2.50
Bowl, 6″			
☐ pink or green	2.50	4.50	3.00
Bowl, six-sided, 6″			
☐ crystal	2.00	4.00	2.50
☐ teal	6.00	9.00	7.00
Bread and Butter Plate, 7″			
☐ crystal	3.00	5.00	3.50
☐ pink or green	2.50	4.50	3.00
Butter Dish, with cover			
☐ pink or green	145.00	165.00	150.00
☐ teal	180.00	210.00	190.00
Candlesticks, 3½″			
☐ crystal	9.00	11.50	10.00
☐ pink or green	13.00	17.00	14.00

	Current Price Range		Prior Year Average
Cocktail Tumbler, footed, 3 oz.			
☐ pink or green......................................	13.00	17.00	14.00
Creamer			
☐ pink or green......................................	5.00	8.00	6.00
Cup			
☐ pink or green.....................................	3.50	5.50	4.00
☐ teal...	5.00	9.00	6.50
☐ red..	18.00	22.00	19.00
Decanter, with stopper			
☐ pink or green......................................	70.00	85.00	73.00
Goblet, 9 oz.			
☐ pink or green......................................	13.00	17.00	14.00
Iced Tea Tumbler, footed, 12 oz.			
☐ pink or green......................................	20.00	25.00	21.00
Luncheon Plate, 8⅜″			
☐ crystal..	2.00	4.00	2.50
☐ pink or green......................................	3.50	5.50	4.00
Pitcher, 68 oz.			
☐ pink or green......................................	75.00	85.00	77.00
Sandwich Plate, 13″			
☐ pink or green......................................	11.00	14.00	12.00
Sandwich Serving Plate, handle in center			
☐ crystal..	20.00	25.00	21.00
☐ pink or green......................................	25.00	30.00	26.00
Saucer			
☐ pink or green......................................	1.50	3.50	2.00
☐ teal...	2.50	4.50	3.00
☐ red..	4.50	7.50	5.00
Sherbet			
☐ crystal..	2.50	4.50	3.00
☐ pink or green......................................	4.00	6.00	4.50
☐ teal...	4.50	7.50	5.00
Sherbet Plate, 6″			
☐ pink or green......................................	1.50	3.50	2.00
☐ teal...	3.50	5.50	4.00
Water Tumbler, 8 oz.			
☐ pink or green......................................	11.00	14.00	12.00
Wine Goblet, 4 oz.			
☐ pink or green......................................	15.00	20.00	16.00

SHARON
Federal Glass Co.

Sharon was one of the most popular patterns during the Depression and has stayed one of the most popular even now. Many people started off their collections with a piece of *Sharon,* although then, they would probably have called it *Cabbage Rose*. It was made from 1935 through 1939. Full settings were made in pink, amber and green. Some pieces were also made in crystal, but not very many. The pink and amber exist in good quantities today and it shouldn't be too much trouble to get a nice collection together. A complete set is a possibility in pink and amber, but complete sets are often more difficult to come by in Depression glass than it first appeared. A complete set in green would be very difficult to get, but it is around. This is a very durable glass. It will show signs of wear but will remain in good condition even with lots of use. The footed tumblers in this pattern weren't introduced until 1937. The rare items in *Sharon* include the cheese dish, the butter dish, the 6½" tumbler in green and all salt and pepper shakers. There have been reproductions in *Sharon* but generally they are not too worrisome, being fairly apparent as being not genuine. The butter dish and cheese dish were reproduced in the late 1970s. The colors were blue, green, dark green, pink and amber. The new green and pink are lighter than the originals; the amber is too dark; the dark green and the blue are no problem since these colors were not in the original issues. In the early 1980s, salt and pepper shakers in pink and green and the cream and sugar in pink were reproduced. Again, look for inaccurate color duplication and poor patterns.

Sharon

	Current Price Range		Prior Year Average
Berry Bowl, diameter 5"			
☐ pink	6.00	8.00	7.00
☐ amber	5.00	7.00	5.50
☐ green	7.00	10.00	8.25

	Current Price Range		Prior Year Average
Berry Bowl, diameter 8½"			
☐ pink	15.00	17.00	15.50
☐ amber	3.50	5.50	4.00
☐ green	19.50	23.50	21.50
Bread and Butter Plate, diameter 6"			
☐ pink	3.00	5.00	4.00
☐ amber	2.00	4.00	3.00
☐ green	3.00	5.00	4.00
Butter Dish, with cover			
☐ pink	35.00	42.00	38.00
☐ amber	38.00	43.00	39.50
☐ green	65.00	70.00	67.00
Cake Plate, footed, diameter 11½"			
☐ pink	23.00	28.00	24.00
☐ amber	15.00	17.00	16.00
☐ green	43.00	50.00	46.00
Candy Jar, with cover			
☐ pink	38.00	43.00	39.50
☐ amber	33.00	38.00	34.00
☐ green	115.00	120.00	116.50
Cereal Bowl, diameter 6"			
☐ pink	14.00	15.00	14.25
☐ amber	9.00	11.00	9.75
☐ green	15.00	19.00	17.00
Cheese Dish, with cover			
☐ pink	575.00	625.00	585.00
☐ amber	120.00	160.00	140.00
Creamer, footed			
☐ pink	9.00	11.00	13.00
☐ amber	9.00	10.00	9.25
☐ green	13.00	14.00	13.25
Cup			
☐ pink	10.00	13.00	11.00
☐ amber	7.00	9.00	8.00
☐ green	11.00	14.00	13.00
Dinner Plate, diameter 9½"			
☐ pink	11.00	13.00	11.50
☐ amber	8.50	10.50	9.00
☐ green	11.00	13.00	11.50
Fruit Bowl, diameter 10"			
☐ pink	23.00	28.00	24.00
☐ amber	14.00	16.00	15.00
☐ green	20.00	25.00	22.00

	Current Price Range		Prior Year Average
Jam Dish, diameter 7½″			
☐ pink	78.00	83.00	79.00
☐ amber	22.00	28.00	23.00
☐ green	30.00	35.00	32.00
Pitcher, no ice lip, 80 oz.			
☐ pink	95.00	105.00	97.50
☐ amber	93.00	98.00	93.50
☐ green	305.00	335.00	317.50
Pitcher, with ice lip, 80 oz.			
☐ pink	100.00	110.00	103.50
☐ amber	90.00	95.00	92.00
☐ green	290.00	310.00	295.00
Platter, oval, length 12½″			
☐ pink	12.00	16.00	13.00
☐ amber	10.00	12.00	11.00
☐ green	15.00	17.00	15.50
Salad Plate, diameter 7½″			
☐ pink	12.00	17.00	14.00
☐ amber	8.00	11.00	9.00
☐ green	9.00	13.00	11.00
Salt and Pepper Shakers			
☐ pink	35.00	40.00	37.00
☐ amber	30.00	35.00	32.00
☐ green	53.00	58.00	55.00
Saucer			
☐ pink	4.50	6.50	5.35
☐ amber	3.50	4.50	4.00
☐ green	4.50	6.50	5.25
Sherbet Dish, footed			
☐ pink	9.00	11.00	9.50
☐ amber	7.50	9.50	8.00
☐ green	18.00	22.00	19.00
Soup Bowl, diameter 5″			
☐ pink	28.00	33.00	29.00
☐ amber	15.50	17.50	16.00
☐ green	30.00	35.00	31.00
Soup Bowl, diameter 7½″			
☐ pink	25.00	30.00	26.50
☐ amber	20.00	25.00	22.00
Sugar Bowl, with lid			
☐ pink	30.00	35.00	31.00
☐ amber	20.00	25.00	21.00
☐ green	23.00	28.00	24.00

	Current Price Range		Prior Year Average
Tumbler, 9 oz., height 4⅛"			
☐ pink	18.00	22.00	19.00
☐ amber	17.00	20.00	18.00
☐ green	38.00	43.00	39.00
Tumbler, 12 oz., height 5¼", thin			
☐ pink	30.00	34.00	32.00
☐ amber	20.00	25.00	22.00
☐ green	63.00	68.00	64.00
Tumbler, footed, 15 oz., height 6½"			
☐ pink	32.00	38.00	33.00
☐ amber	45.00	50.00	46.00
☐ green	170.00	210.00	190.00
Vegetable Bowl, oval, length 9½"			
☐ pink	15.00	20.00	17.00
☐ amber	9.00	11.00	9.50
☐ green	17.00	22.00	19.00

SHIPS
Hazel Atlas Glass Co.

This pattern was manufactured in the late 1930s. It was issued in cobalt blue with white or white and red decoration. The pattern consists of maritime scenes including fish, water skiers, windmills, and the most common, sailboats.

	Current Price Range		Prior Year Average
Cocktail Mixer with Stirrer			
☐ blue with white	16.00	21.00	18.00
☐ blue with white and red	20.00	24.00	22.00
Cocktail Shaker			
☐ blue with white	21.00	26.00	22.00
☐ blue with white and red	24.00	28.00	25.00
Cup			
☐ blue with white	7.00	10.00	7.50
☐ blue with white and red	9.00	12.50	10.50
Ice Bowl			
☐ blue with white	20.00	27.00	24.00
☐ blue with white and red	25.00	31.00	28.00
Pitcher with Lip, 86 oz.			
☐ blue with white	32.00	40.00	34.00
☐ blue with white and red	35.00	43.00	37.00
Pitcher, no lip, 82 oz.			
☐ blue with white	30.00	37.00	33.00
☐ blue with white and red	33.00	40.00	36.00

	Current Price Range		Prior Year Average
Plate, 6"			
☐ blue with white	8.00	13.00	11.00
☐ blue with white and red......................	10.00	14.00	12.00
Plate, 9"			
☐ blue with white	14.00	20.00	16.00
☐ blue with white and red......................	16.00	22.00	17.50
Saucer			
☐ blue with white	7.00	11.00	9.00
☐ blue with white and red......................	9.00	13.00	11.00
Tumbler, juice, 5 oz.			
☐ blue with white	5.00	9.00	7.00
☐ blue with white and red......................	6.00	10.00	7.50
Tumbler, 6 oz.			
☐ blue with white	5.00	9.00	7.00
☐ blue with white and red......................	6.00	10.00	7.50
Tumbler, old fashion, 8 oz.			
☐ blue with white	8.00	13.00	10.00
☐ blue with white and red......................	10.00	15.00	12.00
Tumbler, water, 9 oz.			
☐ blue with white	5.00	9.00	7.00
☐ blue with white and red......................	6.00	10.00	8.00
Tumbler, iced tea, 10 oz.			
☐ blue with white	7.00	12.00	9.00
☐ blue with white and red......................	9.00	14.00	11.00
Tumbler, iced tea, 12 oz.			
☐ blue with white	10.00	15.00	12.00
☐ blue with white and red......................	12.00	17.00	14.00

SIERRA
Jeannette Glass Co.

This pattern was made from 1930 to 1932. It is called *Pinwheel* by some collectors. Full settings were made in pink and green. If there is a problem with this pattern, it's that the individual edges chipped easily. It was probably for this reason that Jeannette stopped production. Because of its short production period, not much *Sierra* was made. Therefore, present day supplies are not high. The pitcher and the tumblers are especially hard to find in *Sierra.* The 6" sherbet plate was probably not made, even though it has been listed in several guides for years. The cups in this pattern have smooth edges, not serrated. This makes for much safer drinking. It seems as though *Sierra* and *Adam* were sister designs. The *Sierra* butter dish has the *Sierra* pattern on the inside and the *Adam* motif on the outside. A *Sierra* pitcher has been reported with the *Adam* motif clearly marked on the outside.

Sierra

	Current Price Range		Prior Year Average
Berry Bowl, diameter 8½″			
☐ pink	9.00	11.00	9.50
☐ green	12.00	15.00	13.00
Butter Dish, with cover			
☐ pink	40.00	48.00	44.00
☐ green	49.00	55.00	52.00
Cereal Bowl, diameter 5½″			
☐ pink	5.00	7.00	5.00
☐ green	6.00	8.00	6.00
Creamer			
☐ pink	8.00	10.00	9.00
☐ green	11.50	13.50	12.00
Cup			
☐ pink	5.00	7.00	5.50
☐ green	7.50	9.50	8.00
Dinner Plate, diameter 9″			
☐ pink	10.00	13.00	11.00
☐ green	9.00	13.00	12.00
Pitcher, 32 oz., height 6½″			
☐ pink	35.00	40.00	36.50
☐ green	60.00	70.00	63.00
Platter, oval, length 11″			
☐ pink	20.00	26.00	22.00
☐ green	14.00	18.00	15.50
Salt and Pepper Shakers, pair			
☐ pink	23.00	32.00	29.00
☐ green	35.00	41.00	37.00

	Current Price Range		Prior Year Average
Saucer			
☐ pink	2.50	4.50	3.00
☐ green	3.00	5.00	3.50
Serving Tray, with handles			
☐ pink	8.00	11.00	9.00
☐ green	9.50	12.50	10.50
Sugar Bowl, with cover			
☐ pink	20.00	25.00	21.50
☐ green	18.00	22.00	19.50
Tumbler, footed, 9 oz., height 4½″			
☐ pink	18.00	22.00	19.50
☐ green	25.00	30.00	26.50
Vegetable Bowl, oval, length 9¼″			
☐ pink	24.00	30.00	28.00
☐ green	38.00	43.00	39.50

SPIRAL
Hocking Glass Co.

Made from 1928 to 1930, *Spiral* is sometimes referred to as *Spiral Optic.* Many companies made a spiral pattern and it is sometimes difficult to tell them apart. One way to tell the difference is that Hocking's spirals go clockwise while Imperial's spiral pattern, for example, goes counter-clockwise. Another tell-tale sign is that Hocking's plates don't have a collar. However, dealers and collectors alike will mix in Hocking's pattern with others. This can be done with great success, so consider it as an alternative to a straight Hocking collection. Dinner and luncheon sets were produced in green and perhaps a small amount of pink. The sandwich server is a very unusual piece and is not easy to find. The pitcher and tumblers in this pattern are made of a lighter glass than the other pieces. Also, watch out for the two styles of cream and sugar. The first style they issued was with straight sides, the second was footed.

Berry Bowl, diameter 4¾″			
☐ green	3.00	5.00	3.60
Berry Bowl, diameter 8″			
☐ green	6.00	9.00	7.00
Creamer			
☐ green	3.00	5.00	3.50
Creamer, footed			
☐ green	3.00	5.00	3.50
Cup			
☐ green	2.50	4.50	3.00

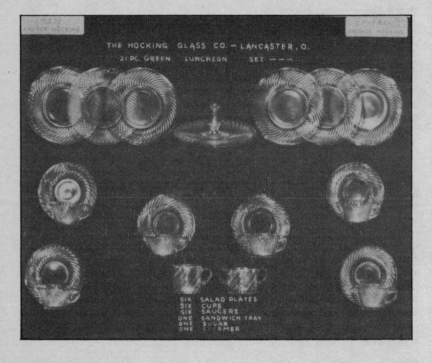

1929 Spiral Catalog Sheet.
Courtesy of Anchor Hocking Corporation, Lancaster, Ohio

	Current Price Range		Prior Year Average
Ice Bucket			
☐ green	12.50	14.50	13.00
Jam Jar, with cover			
☐ green	16.50	18.50	17.00
Juice Glass, 5 oz., height 3″			
☐ green	2.00	3.00	2.00
Luncheon Plate, diameter 8″			
☐ green	1.50	2.50	2.00
Mixing Bowl, diameter 7″			
☐ green	5.00	9.00	6.00
Pitcher, 58 oz., height 7½″			
☐ green	16.50	18.50	17.00
Salt and Pepper Shakers			
☐ green	15.00	17.00	15.50
Sandwich Server, center handle			
☐ green	12.00	16.00	14.00
Saucer			
☐ green	1.00	2.00	1.50
Sherbet Plate, diameter 6″			
☐ green	2.00	3.00	2.50
Sugar Bowl			
☐ green	3.00	5.00	3.50
Sugar Bowl, footed			
☐ green	3.00	5.00	3.50
Water Glass, 9 oz., height 5″			
☐ green	3.00	5.00	3.50

STARLIGHT
Hazel Atlas Glass Co.

This pattern was made from 1938 to early 1940. It wasn't made in great numbers, so supplies are now limited. Settings were made mostly in crystal, although some pink exists. Other pieces have been reported in white, green and cobalt. It appears that only the bowls exist in cobalt. The 13″ plate in this pattern can be listed in three ways depending on where you look, either as a cake plate, a salad liner or as a sandwich tray. The shakers are becoming quite rare.

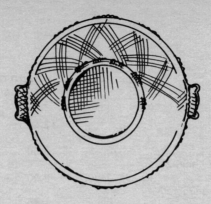

Starlight

	Current Price Range		Prior Year Average
Bowl, tab handles, diameter 8½"			
☐ crystal	2.50	3.50	2.75
☐ pink	7.50	9.50	8.00
☐ blue	7.50	9.50	8.00
Bowl, diameter 12"			
☐ crystal	14.00	17.00	16.00
Bread and Butter Plate, diameter 6"			
☐ crystal	1.50	2.50	1.75
☐ pink	2.50	3.50	2.75
Cereal Bowl, diameter 5½"			
☐ crystal	2.00	3.00	2.25
☐ pink	2.50	4.50	3.00
Creamer, oval			
☐ crystal	2.50	3.50	2.75
Cup			
☐ crystal	2.00	3.00	2.25
☐ pink	3.00	4.00	3.25
Dinner Plate, diameter 9"			
☐ crystal	3.00	4.00	3.25
☐ pink	5.50	6.50	5.75
Luncheon Plate, diameter 8½"			
☐ crystal	2.00	3.00	2.25
☐ pink	3.00	4.00	3.25
Relish Dish			
☐ crystal	2.00	3.00	2.25
☐ pink	4.00	5.00	4.25

	Current Price Range		Prior Year Average

Salad Bowl, diameter 11½″
☐ crystal	10.50	12.50	11.00
☐ pink	16.50	18.50	17.00
☐ blue	16.50	18.50	17.00

Salt and Pepper Shakers
☐ crystal	14.00	16.00	14.50

Sandwich Plate, diameter 13″
☐ crystal	3.50	4.50	3.75
☐ pink	6.50	8.50	7.00

Saucer
☐ crystal	.75	1.50	.85
☐ pink	1.50	2.50	1.75

Sherbet
☐ crystal	3.00	4.00	3.25

Sugar Bowl, oval
☐ crystal	2.50	3.50	2.75

STRAWBERRY
U.S. Glass Co.

This pattern was manufactured in the early 1930s. It has a sister pattern called *Cherryberry.* It's the same pattern with cherries substituted for strawberries. Settings were made in crystal, pink, green and some pieces were also made in an iridescent color resembling Carnival glass. Some pieces have also been reported with a satin finish. They are generally worth a little less than the crystal. The 6⅜″ bowl is rare, as are the tumblers. The butter dish is unusual because on the top it has the *Strawberry* design but the bottom is rayed like *Aunt Polly* or *Floral and Diamond.* The large sugar, when it is seen without its lid, can be mistaken for a spooner, since it has no handles.

Berry Bowl, diameter 4″
☐ crystal	4.00	5.00	4.25
☐ pink or green	6.00	7.00	6.25

Bowl, diameter 6¼″
☐ crystal	18.00	22.00	19.50
☐ pink or green	33.00	40.00	34.00

Bowl, diameter 6⅜″
☐ crystal	20.00	28.00	25.00
☐ pink	25.00	33.00	29.00

	Current Price Range		Prior Year Average
Bowl, diameter 7½"			
☐ crystal...	8.00	10.00	9.00
☐ pink...	12.00	15.00	13.00
☐ green...	12.00	15.00	13.00
☐ iridescent...	10.00	13.00	11.00
Butter Dish, with cover			
☐ crystal...	95.00	100.00	96.00
☐ pink...	120.00	130.00	123.50
Comport, diameter 5¾"			
☐ crystal...	7.50	9.50	8.00
☐ pink or green.....................................	11.50	13.50	12.00
Creamer, small			
☐ crystal...	7.50	9.50	8.00
☐ pink or green.....................................	10.00	12.00	10.75
Creamer, large, height 4⅜"			
☐ crystal...	10.00	11.00	10.25
☐ pink or green.....................................	14.00	16.00	14.75
Olive Dish, with one handle			
☐ crystal...	6.00	7.00	6.25
☐ pink or green.....................................	8.00	10.00	8.75
Pickle Dish, oval, length 8¼"			
☐ crystal...	6.00	8.00	6.50
☐ pink or green.....................................	8.00	10.00	8.75
Pitcher, height 7¾"			
☐ crystal...	145.00	155.00	142.00
☐ pink or green.....................................	130.00	135.00	132.00
☐ iridescent...	145.00	155.00	142.00
Salad Bowl, diameter 6½"			
☐ crystal...	6.50	8.50	7.00
☐ pink or green.....................................	9.00	11.00	9.50
Salad Plate, diameter 7½"			
☐ crystal...	5.50	7.50	6.00
☐ pink or green.....................................	7.50	9.50	8.00
Sherbet Plate, diameter 6"			
☐ crystal...	3.00	4.00	3.25
☐ pink or green.....................................	4.00	6.00	4.50
Sugar Bowl, without lid, small			
☐ crystal...	9.00	11.00	9.50
☐ pink or green.....................................	11.50	13.50	12.00
Sugar Bowl, with cover, large			
☐ crystal...	20.00	23.00	21.00
☐ pink or green.....................................	30.00	35.00	32.00
Tumbler, 9 oz., height 3⅝"			
☐ crystal...	12.50	14.50	13.00
☐ pink or green.....................................	18.00	22.00	19.00

SUNFLOWER
Jeannette Glass Co.

This pattern was made in the late 1920s and in the early 1930s. Luncheon sets were made in pink and green. Green is probably a little more popular with collectors but values are about equal for both. Some opaque colors have been reported but only a few pieces exist. By far the most common item in this line is the 10″ cake plate. You will have no trouble finding it at shops or shows. The hardest piece to find is the 7″ trivet or hot plate. The price for the trivet is already very high and will probably stay there unless someone finds a store of them.

Sunflower

	Current Price Range		Prior Year Average
Ashtray, diameter 5″			
☐ pink	6.00	8.00	6.50
☐ green	7.00	10.00	8.00
Cake Plate, three-legged, diameter 10″			
☐ pink	6.00	8.00	7.00
☐ green	8.00	10.00	8.50
Creamer			
☐ pink	7.00	9.00	8.00
☐ green	7.00	9.00	8.00
☐ opaque	60.00	67.00	64.00
Cup			
☐ pink	6.00	8.00	7.00
☐ green	7.00	10.00	8.00
Dinner Plate, diameter 9″			
☐ pink	7.00	9.00	8.00
☐ green	9.00	11.00	9.50

	Current Price Range		Prior Year Average
Saucer			
☐ pink	2.50	3.50	2.75
☐ green	3.00	4.00	3.50
Sugar Bowl			
☐ pink	8.00	9.00	8.25
☐ green	8.00	9.00	8.25
Trivet, three-legged, length 7″			
☐ pink	120.00	145.00	130.00
☐ green	120.00	145.00	130.00
Tumbler, footed, 8 oz., height 4¾″			
☐ pink	12.50	14.50	13.00
☐ green	13.50	15.50	14.00

SWIRL
Jeannette Glass Co.

Also known as *Petal Swirl,* this pattern was made from 1937 to 1938. Settings were made in ultramarine (blue-green) and pink. Some pieces were also made in delphite (opaque blue) and amber. Ultramarine is the most available color. It is possible to get a set in pink but it would take a lot of looking. Delphite is certainly not common, but enough pieces are around to put together a small set. One thing to watch out for in the ultramarine is different shades; there are at least two. Collectors generally don't like to mix them. The hardest to find pieces in *Swirl* are the butter dish and the covered candy dish. The iced tea tumblers and the shakers are also not easy to come across. The plates in this pattern come in two styles: either with round or fluted edges.

Swirl

Ashtray, diameter 5⅜″

☐ pink	5.00	7.00	5.50

	Current Price Range		Prior Year Average

Bowl, footed, tab handles, diameter 10″
| ☐ pink | 15.00 | 21.00 | 18.00 |
| ☐ aquamarine | 20.00 | 27.00 | 24.00 |

Bowl, footed, diameter 10½″
| ☐ pink | 12.00 | 15.00 | 13.00 |
| ☐ aquamarine | 18.00 | 21.00 | 19.00 |

Butter Dish
| ☐ pink | 115.00 | 135.00 | 125.00 |
| ☐ aquamarine | 190.00 | 210.00 | 195.00 |

Candleholders, single branch, pair
| ☐ blue | 75.00 | 80.00 | 76.00 |

Candleholders, double branch, pair
| ☐ pink | 20.00 | 24.00 | 21.50 |
| ☐ aquamarine | 22.00 | 26.00 | 23.50 |

Candy Dish, with cover
| ☐ pink | 50.00 | 60.00 | 52.00 |
| ☐ aquamarine | 70.00 | 75.00 | 72.00 |

Candy Dish, without lid, three-legged
| ☐ pink | 5.00 | 7.00 | 5.50 |
| ☐ aquamarine | 8.00 | 9.00 | 8.25 |

Cereal Bowl, diameter 5¼″
☐ pink	4.00	6.00	4.50
☐ aquamarine	6.50	8.50	7.00
☐ delphite	7.50	9.50	8.00

Coaster, diameter 3¼″
| ☐ pink | 5.00 | 6.00 | 5.25 |
| ☐ aquamarine | 6.00 | 9.00 | 7.50 |

Creamer, footed
☐ pink	6.00	7.00	6.25
☐ aquamarine	9.00	10.00	9.25
☐ delphite	7.00	8.00	7.25

Cup
☐ pink	3.00	5.00	3.50
☐ aquamarine	6.00	8.00	6.00
☐ delphite	4.00	6.00	4.50

Dinner Plate, diameter 9¼″
☐ pink	5.50	7.50	6.00
☐ aquamarine	10.00	12.00	10.50
☐ delphite	5.00	8.00	5.50

Pitcher, footed, 48 oz.
| ☐ aquamarine | 800.00 | 900.00 | 850.00 |

Plate, diameter 7¼″
| ☐ pink | 4.00 | 6.00 | 5.00 |
| ☐ aquamarine | 7.00 | 9.00 | 8.00 |

	Current Price Range		Prior Year Average
Plate, diameter 10½"			
☐ delphite	9.00	11.00	9.50
Platter, oval, length 12"			
☐ delphite	18.00	22.00	19.00
Salad Bowl, diameter 9"			
☐ pink	8.50	10.50	9.00
☐ aquamarine......................	14.00	16.00	14.50
☐ delphite	15.00	17.00	15.50
Salad Plate, diameter 8"			
☐ pink	4.00	6.00	5.00
☐ aquamarine......................	8.00	10.00	9.00
☐ delphite	3.50	5.50	4.00
Salt and Pepper Shakers			
☐ aquamarine......................	25.00	31.00	27.00
Sandwich Plate, diameter 12½"			
☐ pink	7.00	8.00	7.25
☐ aquamarine......................	12.50	14.50	13.00
Saucer			
☐ pink	1.50	2.50	1.70
☐ aquamarine......................	2.00	3.00	2.25
☐ delphite	1.75	2.50	2.00
Sherbet Dish, footed			
☐ pink	4.50	6.50	5.00
☐ aquamarine......................	8.00	10.00	9.00
Sherbet Plate, height 6½"			
☐ pink	2.00	3.00	2.25
☐ aquamarine......................	3.00	4.00	3.50
☐ delphite	3.50	4.50	4.00
Soup Bowl, tab handles			
☐ pink	11.50	13.50	12.00
☐ aquamarine......................	13.00	13.50	15.50
Sugar Bowl, footed			
☐ pink	5.50	7.50	6.00
☐ aquamarine......................	9.00	10.00	9.25
☐ delphite	7.00	8.00	7.25
Tumbler, 9 oz., height 4"			
☐ pink	6.50	8.50	7.00
☐ aquamarine......................	10.50	12.50	11.00
Tumbler, 9 oz., height 4⅝"			
☐ pink	9.00	11.00	10.00
Tumbler, footed, 9 oz.			
☐ pink	11.50	13.50	12.00
☐ aquamarine......................	18.00	22.00	19.00

	Current Price Range		Prior Year Average
Tumbler, 12 oz., height 4¾″			
☐ pink	14.00	16.00	15.00
☐ aquamarine......................................	33.00	38.00	34.00
Vase, footed, height 6½″			
☐ pink	10.50	12.50	11.00
☐ aquamarine......................................	14.00	16.00	15.00
Vase, footed, height 8½″			
☐ aquamarine......................................	16.50	18.50	17.00

TEA ROOM
Indiana Glass Co.

Tea Room was made from 1927 through 1931. Settings were made in pink, green and crystal. A small amount of amber has been found. Pink and green are more commonly found than crystal. This is a large pattern, with many different items. It was obviously made for use in an ice cream parlor or tea room (hence the name). It seems strange, therefore, that not very much of *Tea Room* has survived for us to collect. Plates, cups and saucers are all rare. So are all the vases and the pitcher in crystal and amber. The creamer and sugar bowl are the easiest items to find.

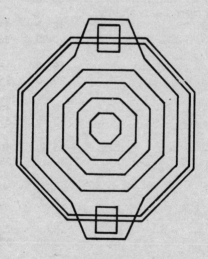

Tea Room

	Current Price Range		Prior Year Average

Banana Split Bowl, flat, diameter 7½″
☐ pink 30.00 37.00 34.00
☐ green 42.00 48.00 45.00
☐ crystal 10.00 16.00 14.00
Banana Split Bowl, footed, diameter 7½″
☐ pink 30.00 37.00 34.00
☐ green 42.00 48.00 45.00
☐ crystal 10.00 16.00 14.00
Candlesticks
☐ pink 23.00 28.00 24.00
☐ green 28.00 33.00 29.00
Celery Bowl, length 8½″
☐ pink 16.00 18.00 16.50
☐ green 20.00 25.00 21.50
Creamer, rectangular
☐ pink 9.00 11.00 9.50
☐ green 11.50 13.50 12.00
Creamer, round, diameter 4″
☐ pink 9.00 11.00 9.50
☐ green 11.50 13.50 12.00
☐ amber 38.00 43.00 39.00
Creamer and Sugar Bowl Set, with tray
☐ pink 48.00 53.00 49.00
☐ green 50.00 55.00 51.50
Cup
☐ pink 16.50 18.50 17.00
☐ green 20.00 25.00 22.00
Goblet, height 8″
☐ pink 40.00 45.00 42.00
☐ green 50.00 55.00 51.50
Ice Bucket
☐ pink 35.00 40.00 36.50
☐ green 30.00 35.00 32.00
Lamp, electric fittings
☐ pink 28.00 33.00 29.00
☐ green 30.00 35.00 32.00
Lunch Plate, diameter 8″
☐ pink 18.00 23.00 19.00
☐ green 18.00 23.00 19.00
Mustard Bowl, with lid
☐ pink 65.00 70.00 67.00
☐ green 75.00 80.00 77.00
Parfait Glass
☐ pink 30.00 35.00 32.00
☐ green 35.00 40.00 36.00

	Current Price Range		Prior Year Average
Pitcher, two quart capacity			
☐ pink	90.00	100.00	92.50
☐ green	75.00	80.00	76.00
☐ amber	175.00	240.00	200.00
Plate, loop handled, diameter 11″			
☐ pink	28.00	33.00	28.50
☐ green	30.00	35.00	32.00
Relish Dish, two compartment			
☐ pink	12.00	13.00	12.25
☐ green	15.00	17.00	15.50
Salad Bowl, steep-sided, diameter 9″			
☐ pink	35.00	40.00	36.50
☐ green	45.00	50.00	47.50
Salt and Pepper Shakers, pair			
☐ pink	35.00	40.00	36.50
☐ green	35.00	40.00	36.50
Saucer			
☐ pink	10.00	12.00	10.50
☐ green	10.00	12.00	10.50
Sherbet Dish, footed			
☐ pink	12.50	14.50	13.00
☐ green	15.00	17.00	15.50
Sherbet Plate, diameter 6″			
☐ pink	11.00	13.00	11.50
☐ green	11.00	13.00	11.50
Sugar, with lid			
☐ pink	30.00	35.00	32.00
☐ green	35.00	40.00	36.50
Sugar Bowl, diameter 4″			
☐ pink	9.00	11.00	9.50
☐ green	11.50	13.50	12.00
☐ amber	38.00	43.00	39.00
Sugar Bowl, rectangular			
☐ pink	9.00	11.00	9.50
☐ green	11.50	13.50	12.00
Sundae Dish, pedestal foot, scalloped edge			
☐ pink	20.00	25.00	22.00
☐ green	25.00	30.00	27.00
Tray, for sugar and creamer			
☐ pink	33.00	40.00	37.00
☐ green	37.00	44.00	40.00
Tumbler, collar base			
☐ pink	35.00	40.00	37.00
☐ green	45.00	50.00	47.00

	Current Price Range		Prior Year Average
Tumbler, pedestal foot, 6 oz.			
☐ pink	14.00	16.00	14.50
☐ green	16.50	18.50	17.00
Tumbler, pedestal foot, 8 oz.			
☐ pink	12.00	17.00	14.00
☐ green	15.00	21.00	16.50
☐ amber	27.00	37.00	32.00
☐ crystal	5.00	10.00	8.00
Tumbler, pedestal foot, 9 oz.			
☐ pink	15.50	17.50	16.00
☐ green	18.00	22.00	19.00
☐ amber	43.00	48.00	44.00
Tumbler, pedestal foot, 11 oz.			
☐ pink	20.00	25.00	22.00
☐ green	25.00	30.00	26.50
Tumbler, pedestal foot, 12 oz.			
☐ pink	25.00	30.00	26.50
☐ green	28.00	33.00	29.50
Vase, height 9″			
☐ pink	35.00	40.00	36.50
☐ green	45.00	50.00	46.50
Vase, height 11″			
☐ pink	50.00	55.00	52.00
☐ green	60.00	65.00	62.00
Vegetable Bowl, oblong, length 10″			
☐ pink	33.00	38.00	34.00
☐ green	38.00	43.00	39.50

THISTLE
Macbeth-Evans Glass Co.

Macbeth-Evans made this pattern from approximately 1929 through the early 1930s. Settings were made in pink and green. A small amount of crystal and yellow has been reported. You will notice that *Thistle* pieces are the same shapes as *Dogwood;* the same molds were used. Pink is considered more collectible than the green since more of it is around, but even the pink is not easy to come across. The pitcher and the cake plate are hard to get, as is the 9½″ bowl. The pattern is an overall foliage design with bunches of fat thistles. It is very light and feathery. The wide outer band that decorates the smooth edge is a wreath of thistles with stippled bodies and ridged puffs connected with pairs of oak leaves. The bowls have only the wreath with no center medallion.

	Current Price Range		Prior Year Average
Cake Plate, diameter 12″			
☐ pink	68.00	73.00	69.00
☐ green	83.00	88.00	84.00
Cereal Bowl, diameter 5½″			
☐ green	14.00	16.00	14.50
☐ pink	11.00	13.00	11.50
Cup			
☐ pink	13.00	15.00	13.50
☐ green	16.50	18.50	17.00
Fruit Bowl, diameter 10″			
☐ green	95.00	105.00	96.50
☐ pink	155.00	160.00	156.50
Grill Plate, diameter 11″			
☐ pink	11.50	13.50	12.00
☐ green	11.50	13.50	12.00
Lunch Plate, diameter 7½″			
☐ pink	7.00	9.00	7.50
☐ green	11.50	13.50	12.00
Saucer			
☐ pink	6.50	8.50	7.00
☐ green	6.50	8.50	7.00

THREADING
Indiana Glass Co.

From a distance, these pieces have the appearance of a satin finish, showing off the lovely colors from the Indiana Glass Company. At close inspection, it can be seen that the matte surface is achieved by row after row of tiny ridges, rather like the grooves on a record album. The pieces are devoid of decoration other than moldwork.

Threading

	Current Price Range		Prior Year Average
Bowl, diameter 4″			
☐ all colors..	9.00	11.00	9.50
Bowl, diameter 9½″			
☐ all colors..	20.00	24.00	21.00
Candlesticks, height 4″			
☐ all colors..	20.00	24.00	21.00
Candy Jar, with cover			
☐ all colors..	33.00	37.00	34.00
Compote, diameter 7″			
☐ all colors..	11.00	14.00	11.50
Compote Tray			
☐ all colors..	16.50	18.50	17.00
Creamer			
☐ all colors..	11.00	12.00	11.25
Fan Vase, height 5½″			
☐ all colors..	30.00	34.00	31.50
Fruit Bowl, pedestal foot, height 6″			
☐ all colors..	20.00	25.00	22.00
Fruit Bowl, diameter 9″			
☐ all colors..	18.50	20.50	19.00
Goblet, height 6″			
☐ all colors..	16.50	18.50	17.00
Pitcher, with lid			
☐ all colors..	78.00	83.00	79.50
Sandwich Tray			
☐ all colors..	25.00	30.00	26.50

	Current Price Range		Prior Year Average

Sherbet Dish
| □ all colors.. | 13.50 | 15.50 | 14.00 |

Sugar Bowl
| □ all colors.. | 10.00 | 12.00 | 10.50 |

Tumbler, pedestal foot, height 4½″
| □ all colors.. | 11.50 | 13.50 | 12.00 |

Tumbler, pedestal foot, height 5½″
| □ all colors.. | 18.50 | 20.50 | 19.00 |

Vase, height 12″
| □ all colors.. | 28.00 | 33.00 | 29.50 |

THUMBPRINT
Federal Glass Co.

Also known as *Pear Optic*, this pattern was made from 1928 to 1929. It is an overall design of oval indentations lined up in horizontal rows. Green is the only color produced but some green with gold trim has been reported. It is a small line and not very available to collectors today. The first items issued were the cup and saucer as a premium. It can be a confusing pattern, since several companies marketed very similar designs. If you want a usable service, you will probably have to mix and match with the various *Pear Optic* patterns. The creamer and sugar bowl are rare.

Berry Bowl, diameter 4¾″
| □ green .... | 1.50 | 3.00 | 2.25 |

Berry Bowl, diameter 8″
| □ green .... | 5.00 | 7.00 | 5.50 |

Cereal Bowl, diameter 5″
| □ green .... | 2.00 | 3.00 | 2.25 |

Creamer, pedestal foot
| □ green .... | 6.00 | 9.00 | 7.25 |

Cup
| □ green .... | 2.00 | 3.00 | 2.25 |

Dinner Plate, diameter 9¼″
| □ green .... | 4.00 | 6.00 | 5.00 |

Luncheon Plate, diameter 8″
| □ green .... | 2.00 | 3.50 | 2.75 |

Sherbet Plate, diameter 6″
| □ green .... | 1.00 | 2.25 | 1.65 |

Sugar Bowl, pedestal foot
| □ green .... | 3.00 | 5.00 | 3.75 |

Tumbler, height 4″
| □ green .... | 3.00 | 4.00 | 3.25 |

	Current Price Range		Prior Year Average
Tumbler, height 5″			
☐ green...	3.50	4.50	3.75
Tumbler, height 5½″			
☐ green...	3.00	5.00	3.75
Whiskey Glass, height 2½″			
☐ green...	2.50	3.50	2.75

TWISTED OPTIC
Imperial Glass Co.

Also known as *Swirl No. 1*, this pattern was made in the late 1920s. Settings were made in green, amber, pink, yellow and a couple of pieces in blue have surfaced. It is very easy to confuse this pattern with Hocking's *Spiral*. The swirls in *Twisted Optic* usually go counter-clockwise but some pieces are exceptions so it's not at all easy to tell the difference. Some collectors say that the best angle to look at the swirls is from the underside. Give that a try. The footed, covered candy jar and the pitcher are probably the most difficult pieces to find in *Twisted Optic*.

	Current Price Range		Prior Year Average
Candlesticks, height 3″			
☐ all colors...	9.00	11.00	9.50
Candy Jar, with cover			
☐ all colors...	14.00	16.00	14.50
Cereal Bowl, diameter 5″			
☐ all colors...	1.50	2.50	1.75
Creamer			
☐ all colors...	3.50	5.50	4.00
Jam Jar, lidded, with spoon holder			
☐ all colors...	16.00	18.00	17.00
Lunch Plate			
☐ all colors...	1.50	2.50	1.75
Pitcher, 2 quart capacity			
☐ all colors...	16.50	18.50	17.00
Salad Bowl, diameter 7″			
☐ all colors...	4.50	6.50	5.00
Salad Plate, diameter 7″			
☐ all colors...	1.50	2.50	1.75
Sandwich Tray, central handle			
☐ all colors...	11.50	13.50	12.00
Sandwich Tray, two handles on rim			
☐ all colors...	4.50	6.50	5.00
Saucer			
☐ all colors...	1.50	.75	1.25

	Current Price Range		Prior Year Average
Sherbet Plate, diameter 6″			
☐ all colors...............................	1.00	2.00	1.25
Soup Bowl, diameter 5″			
☐ all colors...............................	4.50	6.50	5.00
Sugar Bowl			
☐ all colors...............................	3.50	5.50	4.00
Tumbler, height 4½″			
☐ all colors...............................	4.00	5.00	4.25
Tumbler, height 5½″			
☐ all colors...............................	6.00	7.00	6.25

VICTORY
Diamond Glassware Co.

This pattern was made from 1929 through 1932. Settings were made in green, cobalt blue and amber. Some pieces were made in black. Some pieces have also been reported with gold trim. This pattern was small and not many pieces remain today. The edges on these pieces have a petal fluting. The gravy boat and platter are the most desirable pieces in the pattern. The candlesticks are also hard to find.

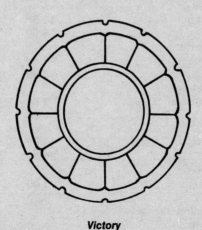

Victory

Bread and Butter, diameter 6″			
☐ pink, green or amber	2.00	3.00	2.25
☐ blue or black	2.50	3.50	2.75

	Current Price Range		Prior Year Average

Candlesticks, pair, height 3″
| ☐ pink, green or amber .... | 14.00 | 16.00 | 14.50 |
| ☐ blue or black .... | 24.00 | 26.00 | 24.50 |

Cereal Bowl, diameter 6″
| ☐ pink, green or amber .... | 4.50 | 6.50 | 5.00 |
| ☐ blue or black .... | 6.50 | 9.50 | 7.00 |

Compote, height 6″
| ☐ pink, green or amber .... | 7.50 | 9.00 | 8.00 |
| ☐ blue or black .... | 9.00 | 11.00 | 9.50 |

Console Bowl, diameter 12″
| ☐ pink, green or amber .... | 14.00 | 16.00 | 14.50 |
| ☐ blue or black .... | 25.00 | 30.00 | 26.50 |

Creamer
| ☐ pink, green or amber .... | 6.50 | 8.50 | 7.00 |
| ☐ blue or black .... | 9.00 | 11.00 | 9.50 |

Cup
☐ pink, green or amber	4.00	6.00	4.50
☐ blue	9.00	13.00	10.50
☐ black..	10.00	14.00	11.00

Dinner Plate, diameter 9″
| ☐ pink, green or amber .... | 9.00 | 11.00 | 9.50 |
| ☐ blue or black .... | 10.50 | 12.50 | 11.00 |

Goblet, 7 oz., height 5″
| ☐ pink, green or amber .... | 11.50 | 13.50 | 12.00 |
| ☐ blue or black .... | 16.50 | 18.50 | 17.00 |

Gravy Boat and Platter
| ☐ pink, green or amber .... | 90.00 | 100.00 | 92.50 |
| ☐ blue or black .... | 95.00 | 100.00 | 96.50 |

Lunch Plate, diameter 8″
| ☐ pink, green or amber .... | 3.50 | 4.50 | 3.75 |
| ☐ blue or black .... | 4.00 | 6.00 | 4.50 |

Platter, diameter 12″
| ☐ pink, green or amber .... | 16.00 | 22.00 | 18.00 |
| ☐ blue or black .... | 30.00 | 38.00 | 34.00 |

Salad Plate, diameter 7″
| ☐ pink, green or amber .... | 3.00 | 4.00 | 3.25 |
| ☐ blue or black .... | 5.00 | 6.00 | 5.25 |

Sandwich Tray, central handle
| ☐ pink, green or amber .... | 14.00 | 16.00 | 14.50 |
| ☐ blue or black .... | 33.00 | 38.00 | 34.00 |

Saucer
☐ pink, green or amber	1.50	2.50	1.75
☐ blue or black	3.00	5.00	3.50
☐ black..	4.00	6.50	5.00

	Current Price Range		Prior Year Average

Soup Bowl, flat, diameter 8"

☐ pink, green or amber	8.00	9.00	8.25
☐ blue or black	9.00	10.00	9.25

VITROCK
Hocking Glass Co.

This pattern is a simple floral wreath rounding the outer rim. It is molded in high relief giving the piece a good texture. The rest of the glass is smooth, heavy and devoid of design. It was made from about 1935 to 1937. The most commonly found color today is the milk-white. Some fired-on colors do exist, mostly green and red.

	Current Price Range		Prior Year Average
Berry Bowl, diameter 4"			
☐ white...	2.00	4.25	3.00
Cereal Bowl, diameter 7½"			
☐ white...	2.00	3.00	2.25
Creamer, oval			
☐ white...	3.00	4.25	3.65
Cup			
☐ white...	1.50	2.50	1.75
Dinner Plate, diameter 10"			
☐ white...	3.00	5.00	4.00
Fruit Bowl, diameter 6"			
☐ white...	2.50	3.50	2.75
Lunch Plate, diameter 8¾"			
☐ white...	2.00	4.25	3.10
Platter, oval, length 11½"			
☐ white...	11.00	13.00	11.50
Salad Plate, diameter 7"			
☐ white...	1.00	2.00	1.25
Saucer			
☐ white...	1.00	1.75	1.35
Soup Bowl, diameter 5½"			
☐ white...	7.00	10.00	8.75
Soup Plate, diameter 9"			
☐ white...	2.00	4.00	2.50
Sugar Bowl, oval			
☐ white...	2.50	3.50	2.75

VITROCK
The New Tableware and Kitchenware...

VITROCK is one of the finest, fastest selling Tableware and Kitchenware lines we have ever offered. It is literally "taking the country by storm."

VITROCK is a snowy-white, lustrous material that is very tough and durable. It is translucent, like Fine China. It is of the same material throughout, consequently cannot "check" or "craze" as Semi-Vitreous Dinnerware frequently does.

VITROCK W1600 Tableware pattern, shown on this page, is a modern adaptation of one of the most beautiful Embossed Tableware Patterns ever produced. Women admire and want this handsome pattern for their table just as soon as they see it.

VITROCK Kitchenware reflects cleanliness and will add an undeniable charm to the Kitchen equipment of any home. The modern vogue in gleaming white or effectively colored Stoves and Ranges, Refrigerators, Porcelain or Polished Metal Sinks and Drain Boards, naturally causes housewives to demand the most beautiful Mixing Bowls, Seasoning Shakers, Refrigerator Jars, Fruit Juice Extractors, and other articles of Kitchenware that they can buy. VITROCK admirably fills this need.

VITROCK TABLEWARE

ITEM	DESCRIPTION	DOZ. CTN.	WT. CTN.
W1679	Cup	6	34 lb
W1629	Saucer	6	37 lb
W1658	Sugar	2	17 lb
W1659	Creamer	2	15 lb
W1638	7½" Bread & Butter or Cream Soup Plate	4	33 lb
W1639	8¾" Luncheon or Salad Plate	2	25 lb
W1649	10" Dinner Plate	2	38 lb
W1668	Cream Soup	4	29 lb
W1669	9" Soup Plate	2	53 lb
W1674	4" Dessert	6	34 lb
W1675	6" Fruit Dish	6	50 lb
W1691	7½" Cereal Bowl	4	55 lb
W1677	9½" Vegetable Bowl	2	48 lb
W1647	11½" Meat Platter	2	42 lb

VITROCK KITCHENWARE

ITEM	DESCRIPTION	DOZ. CTN.	WT. CTN.
W505	6½" Mixing Bowl	3	39 lb
W506	7½" Mixing Bowl	3	54 lb
W507	8½" Mixing Bowl	2	48 lb
W508	9½" Mixing Bowl	2	62 lb
W509	10½" Mixing Bowl	1	40 lb
W510	11½" Mixing Bowl	1	49 lb
W13	Orange Reamer	2	39 lb
W39	Egg Cup	4	27 lb
W47	Leftover Dish & Cover	2	31 lb
W49	Ash Tray	2	21 lb
W515	Drippings Jar & Cover	2	40 lb
W523	Shaker—Salt, Pepper, Spice, Sugar, Flour	2	14 lb

Manufactured by
THE HOCKING GLASS COMPANY, LANCASTER, OHIO

Printed in U.S.A.

1936 Vitrock Catalog Sheet.
Courtesy of Anchor Hocking Corporation, Lancaster, Ohio

	Current Price Range		Prior Year Average
Vegetable Bowl, diameter 9½″			
□ white...	4.00	6.00	4.50

WATERFORD
Hocking Glass Co.

This pattern, also known as *Waffle*, was made from 1936 to 1944. Pink was the first color issued in 1936 and only a few items of the line were manufactured. By 1939, the pink had been phased out and crystal had taken over. Some yellow was also made during that period. Later on in the 1950s, some milk-white pieces were made, the 5¼″ goblet was reissued and a 13½″ relish in dark green was produced. The relish was issued with inserts but these are often missing. It is not at all uncommon to find *Manhattan* inserts instead. The pink, since it wasn't in production for very long, is now pretty rare. The crystal is readily available, however, and makes a lovely setting.

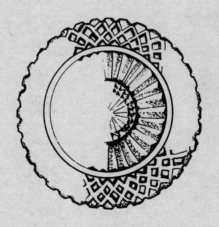

Waterford

Ashtray, diameter 4″			
□ crystal	2.00	3.00	2.25
Berry Bowl, diameter 4¾″			
□ crystal	3.00	4.00	3.25
□ pink	4.50	6.50	5.00

	Current Price Range		Prior Year Average

Berry Bowl, diameter 8½″

☐ crystal	5.00	6.00	5.25
☐ pink	11.00	13.00	11.50

Cake Plate, tab handled, diameter 10″

☐ crystal	4.00	6.00	4.50
☐ pink	9.00	10.00	9.25

Cereal Bowl, diameter 5½″

☐ crystal	5.50	7.50	6.00
☐ pink	11.00	13.00	11.50

Coaster, diameter 4″

☐ crystal	1.00	2.00	1.25
☐ pink	3.50	4.50	3.75

Creamer, oblong shape

☐ crystal	2.00	3.00	2.25
☐ pink	7.00	8.00	7.25

Creamer, "Miss America"

☐ crystal	6.00	7.00	6.25

Cup

☐ crystal	3.00	4.00	3.25
☐ pink	8.50	10.50	9.00

Dinner Plate, diameter 9½″

☐ crystal	4.50	5.50	4.75
☐ pink	9.00	11.00	9.50

Goblet, height 5¼″

☐ crystal	9.00	10.00	9.25

Goblet, "Miss America"

☐ crystal	20.00	24.00	22.00
☐ pink	37.00	43.00	38.50

Juice Pitcher, 42 oz.

☐ crystal	14.00	16.00	14.50

Pitcher, with ice lip, 80 oz.

☐ crystal	20.00	24.00	21.50
☐ pink	95.00	100.00	96.50

Salad Plate, diameter 7″

☐ crystal	1.50	2.50	1.75
☐ pink	3.00	4.00	3.25

Salt and Pepper Shakers, large, pair

☐ crystal	7.00	10.00	8.00

Salt and Pepper Shakers, small, pair

☐ crystal	3.75	4.50	4.00

Saucer

☐ crystal	.50	1.50	.75
☐ pink	3.00	4.00	3.25

	Current Price Range		Prior Year Average
Sherbet Dish, pedestal foot			
☐ crystal	2.00	3.00	2.25
☐ pink	6.00	7.00	6.25
Sherbet Plate, diameter 6″			
☐ crystal	1.00	2.00	1.25
☐ pink	3.00	4.00	3.25
Sugar Bowl, covered			
☐ crystal	4.00	6.00	4.50
☐ pink	15.00	18.00	16.00
Sugar Bowl, "Miss America"			
☐ crystal	6.00	8.00	6.50
Tumbler, pedestal foot, 10 oz., height 5″			
☐ crystal	5.00	7.00	5.50
☐ pink	9.00	13.00	10.00

WINDSOR
Jeannette Glass Co.

Windsor, also known as *Windsor Diamond*, was manufactured from 1936 through 1946. The first colors to be issued were the pink and green. After a year, the green was discontinued and crystal added. By 1940, only the crystal remained in production. Crystal was the only color made until the line was ended in 1946. In the 1950s, a few milk-white pieces were made. A few pieces of ice blue, red and delphite (opaque blue) have been reported but they exist in very small numbers. During the production period of this pattern, Jeannette would drop items and add others quite frequently. The footed tumblers, for instance, were not added until the early 1940s. You will find two kinds of sugar covers. One has a rounded finial and the other a pointed one. They are valued about the same. The 5½″ comport is a very unusual piece. When turned upside down, it is the base for the punch bowl. The set was sold with twelve cups. You will also find the berry bowl in two styles, one with pointed edges and the other with rounded edges. They are also valued at about the same price. Pink is hard to find because it didn't have a very long run at the factory. The pink candlesticks are especially hard to locate.

Windsor

	Current Price Range		Prior Year Average
Ashtray, 5¾″			
☐ pink	28.00	33.00	29.00
☐ crystal	10.50	12.50	11.00
☐ green	35.00	40.00	37.00
Berry Bowl, diameter 4¾″			
☐ pink	4.00	6.00	4.50
☐ crystal	2.00	3.00	2.25
☐ green	5.00	7.00	5.50
Berry Bowl, diameter 8½″			
☐ pink	9.00	11.00	9.50
☐ crystal	4.00	5.00	4.25
☐ green	10.00	12.00	10.50
Bowl, boat-shaped, 7¼″ × 11¾″			
☐ pink	17.00	19.00	17.50
☐ crystal	10.00	12.00	10.50
☐ green	17.50	22.50	18.00
Bowl, tri-legged, diameter 7⅛″			
☐ pink	13.00	15.00	13.50
☐ crystal	3.50	4.50	3.75
Cake Plate, diameter 13″			
☐ pink	10.50	12.50	11.00
☐ crystal	4.00	6.00	4.75
☐ green	11.50	13.50	12.00
Candlesticks, pair, 3″			
☐ pink	60.00	67.00	64.00
☐ crystal	10.50	13.50	12.00

	Current Price Range		Prior Year Average
Candy Jar, with cover			
☐ pink	18.00	22.00	19.00
☐ crystal	7.50	9.50	8.00
Bowl, diameter 12½″			
☐ pink	48.00	53.00	49.00
☐ crystal	9.00	11.00	9.50
Bowl, diameter 5″			
☐ pink	11.50	12.50	11.75
☐ crystal	4.00	5.00	4.25
☐ green	12.50	13.50	13.00
Bowl, sugar, lidded			
☐ pink	3.50	4.50	3.75
Cereal Bowl, two sizes, diameter 5⅜″ or 5⅛″			
☐ pink	11.00	15.00	13.00
☐ crystal	4.00	5.50	4.50
☐ green	10.00	14.00	12.00
Coaster			
☐ pink	4.50	5.50	4.75
☐ crystal	2.00	3.00	2.25
Creamer			
☐ pink or crystal.................................	2.50	3.50	2.75
☐ green	7.00	8.00	7.25
Pitcher, 16 oz., height 4⅝″			
☐ pink	75.00	80.00	76.00
☐ crystal	16.50	18.50	17.00
Pitcher, 52 oz., height 6⅝″			
☐ pink	17.50	19.50	18.00
☐ crystal	10.00	12.00	10.50
☐ green	42.00	47.00	44.50
Plate, diameter 13½″			
☐ pink	14.00	15.00	14.25
☐ crystal	7.00	8.00	7.25
☐ green	14.00	16.00	14.75
Plate, dinner, diameter 9″			
☐ pink	9.00	10.00	9.25
☐ crystal	3.00	4.00	3.25
☐ green	9.00	10.00	9.25
Plate, oval, diameter 11⅜″			
☐ pink	9.00	10.00	9.25
☐ crystal	4.00	5.00	4.25
☐ green	9.00	11.00	9.50

	Current Price Range		Prior Year Average
Plate, salad, diameter 7″			
☐ pink	9.00	10.00	9.25
☐ crystal	2.50	3.50	2.75
☐ green	9.00	11.00	9.75
Plate, sandwich, with handle, diameter 10¼″			
☐ pink	8.00	10.00	8.50
☐ crystal	3.50	4.50	3.75
☐ green	9.00	11.00	9.50
Plate, serving, diameter 15½″			
☐ crystal	4.50	5.50	4.75
Plate, sherbet, diameter 6″			
☐ pink	2.00	3.00	2.25
☐ crystal	1.00	2.00	1.25
☐ green	3.00	4.00	3.25
Relish Platter, divided, length 11½″			
☐ crystal	5.00	6.00	5.25
Salt and Pepper, pair			
☐ pink	25.00	30.00	27.00
☐ crystal	11.50	13.50	12.00
☐ green	33.00	38.00	34.00
Tray, oval, 4¼″ × 9″			
☐ pink	6.00	7.00	6.25
☐ crystal	2.50	3.50	2.75
☐ green	7.00	8.00	7.25
Tray, square, 4″			
☐ pink	4.00	5.00	4.25
☐ crystal	2.00	3.00	2.25
☐ green	6.00	7.00	6.25
Tumbler, 5 oz., height 3¼″			
☐ pink	9.00	10.00	9.25
☐ crystal	3.50	4.50	3.75
☐ green	9.00	11.00	9.50
Tumbler, 9 oz., height 4″			
☐ pink	8.00	9.00	8.25
☐ crystal	4.00	5.00	5.25
☐ green	9.50	10.50	9.75
Tumbler, 12 oz., height 5″			
☐ pink	14.00	16.00	14.50
☐ crystal	5.00	6.00	5.25
☐ green	18.00	22.00	19.50

ELEGANT PATTERNS

AMERICAN
Fostoria Glass Co.

Fostoria's *American* has been made from 1915 to the present. Crystal was the first color made, followed by blue, green, amber, white and some yellow around 1930. Some pieces in red are still being made today. The crystal is no problem to find but the blue, green, yellow and amber are all difficult to locate in any quantity.

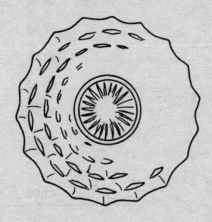

American

	Current Price Range		Prior Year Average
Appetizer, individual, 3¼"			
☐ crystal	15.00	40.00	20.00
Ashtray, square, 5"			
☐ crystal	17.00	25.00	19.00
Baby Set, tumbler and bowl			
☐ crystal	40.00	50.00	42.00
Banana Split Bowl, 9"			
☐ crystal	28.00	42.00	32.00
Bell			
☐ crystal	17.00	27.00	19.00
Bon Bon Dish, 3 toes, 6"			
☐ crystal	8.00	13.00	9.50
Bowl, rolled edge, 11½"			
☐ crystal	30.00	45.00	33.00
Bread and Butter Plate, 6"			
☐ crystal	5.00	7.50	6.00

	Current Price Range		Prior Year Average
Bud Vase, footed, flared, 6″			
☐ crystal	13.00	17.00	14.00
Bud Vase, footed, flared, 8½″			
☐ crystal	20.00	26.00	21.00
Butter Dish, with lid, round			
☐ crystal	95.00	108.00	98.00
Butter Dish, oblong, ¼ lb.			
☐ crystal	30.00	40.00	32.00
Cake Plate, footed, 12″			
☐ crystal	37.00	46.00	39.00
Candlesticks, pair, 3″			
☐ crystal	22.00	35.00	25.00
Candlesticks, pair, 6″			
☐ crystal	50.00	70.00	57.00
Centerpiece Bowl, 3 corners, 11″			
☐ crystal	30.00	45.00	34.00
Coaster, 3¾″			
☐ crystal	4.00	8.00	5.00
Cocktail Goblet, footed, 3 oz., 2⅞″			
☐ crystal	11.00	14.00	12.00
Cologne Bottle, 8 oz., 7½″			
☐ crystal	43.00	60.00	46.00
Comport, flat, 8½″			
☐ crystal	40.00	50.00	42.00
Comport, flat, 9½″			
☐ crystal	40.00	50.00	42.00
Condiment Tray, 4 sections			
☐ crystal	30.00	40.00	32.00
Cream Soup			
☐ crystal	20.00	30.00	22.50
Creamer, 9½ oz., 4¼″			
☐ crystal	9.00	14.00	11.00
Creamer, tea			
☐ crystal	6.00	9.00	7.00
Cup, footed, 7 oz.			
☐ crystal	6.00	10.00	7.00
Decanter, with stopper, 24 oz., 9¼″			
☐ crystal	68.00	85.00	72.00
Dinner Plate, 9½″			
☐ crystal	18.00	24.00	20.00
Finger Bowl, 4½″			
☐ crystal	17.00	24.00	18.00
Finger Bowl Plate, 6½″			
☐ crystal	8.00	12.00	9.00

	Current Price Range		Prior Year Average
Fruit Bowl, footed, 12″			
☐ crystal	85.00	110.00	90.00
Fruit Bowl, footed, 16″			
☐ crystal	60.00	90.00	68.00
Fruit Nappy, flared, 4¾″			
☐ crystal	8.00	12.00	9.00
Goblet, footed, 10 oz., 6⅞″			
☐ crystal	14.00	19.00	15.00
Goblet, low, 9 oz., 5½″			
☐ crystal	9.00	13.00	10.00
Handkerchief Box, with cover, 5½″ × 4½″ × 2″			
☐ crystal	110.00	140.00	115.00
Hurricane Lamp, 12″			
☐ crystal	70.00	80.00	72.00
Ice Bucket			
☐ crystal	40.00	50.00	42.00
Iced Tea Tumbler, footed, flared, 12 oz., 5¾″			
☐ crystal	13.00	17.00	14.00
Jam Pot, with cover, 4½″			
☐ crystal	40.00	50.00	42.00
Jelly Comport, regular, 4¼″			
☐ crystal	12.00	18.00	13.00
Juice Tumbler, footed, 5 oz., 4¾″			
☐ crystal	10.00	14.00	11.00
Lemon Dish, with cover, 5½″			
☐ crystal	26.00	34.00	28.00
Mayonnaise Dish, with liner			
☐ crystal	24.00	32.00	25.00
Mayonnaise Ladle			
☐ crystal	10.50	14.50	11.50
Muffin Tray, handled			
☐ crystal	21.00	29.00	22.50
Mustard Dish, with cover and spoon, 3¾″			
☐ crystal	28.00	35.00	30.00
Napkin Ring			
☐ crystal	5.00	8.00	6.00
Nappy, flared, 7″			
☐ crystal	30.00	40.00	32.00
Nappy, flared, 9″			
☐ crystal	30.00	45.00	33.00
Nappy, shallow, 7″			
☐ crystal	27.00	35.00	28.00
Nappy, 3 corners, handle, 5″			
☐ crystal	8.00	12.00	9.00

	Current Price Range		Prior Year Average
Oil Cruet, 7 oz., 6¾"			
☐ crystal	35.00	45.00	37.00
Old Fashion Tumbler, flat, 6 oz., 3⅜"			
☐ crystal	9.00	13.00	10.00
Oyster Cocktail, 4½ oz., 3½"			
☐ crystal	11.00	14.00	12.00
Pickle Jar, with cover, 6"			
☐ crystal	135.00	165.00	142.00
Pitcher, with lip, 3 pints, 6½"			
☐ crystal	45.00	55.00	47.00
Pitcher, with lip, ½ gallon, 8¼"			
☐ crystal	70.00	80.00	72.00
Platter, oval, 12"			
☐ crystal	60.00	70.00	62.00
Preserve Bowl, with cover and handle, 5½"			
☐ crystal	30.00	45.00	33.00
Puff Box, with cover, 3" × 3" × 2⅞"			
☐ crystal	68.00	85.00	72.00
Punch Bowl, with base, 3¾ gallons, 18"			
☐ crystal	230.00	260.00	240.00
Punch Cup, flared, 6 oz.			
☐ crystal	6.00	9.00	7.00
Relish Tray, for olives, oval, 6"			
☐ crystal	8.00	12.00	9.00
Relish Tray, for pickles, oval, 8"			
☐ crystal	11.00	15.00	12.00
Relish Tray, oval, 3 sections, 11"			
☐ crystal	28.00	35.00	30.00
Rose Bowl, 3½"			
☐ crystal	13.00	22.00	15.00
Rose Bowl, 5"			
☐ crystal	18.00	25.00	19.00
Salad Plate, 8½"			
☐ crystal	13.00	17.00	14.00
Salt and Pepper, round bottom, 3½"			
☐ crystal	13.00	17.00	14.00
Salt Dish, individual			
☐ crystal	3.00	7.00	4.00
Sandwich Platter, 11½"			
☐ crystal	20.00	30.00	22.00
Saucer			
☐ crystal	2.50	4.50	3.00
Serving Bowl, with handle, 9"			
☐ crystal	20.00	30.00	22.00

	Current Price Range		Prior Year Average
Sherbet, low, flared, 5 oz., 3¼"			
☐ crystal	7.50	11.50	8.50
Sherbet, with handle, 4½ oz., 3½"			
☐ crystal	13.00	17.00	14.00
Sugar, tea			
☐ crystal	5.50	8.50	6.00
Sugar, with cover and handle, 5¼"			
☐ crystal	19.00	25.00	21.00
Sugar Shaker, 4¾"			
☐ crystal	110.00	140.00	120.00
Sundae, 6 oz., 3⅛"			
☐ crystal	8.00	11.50	9.00
Sweet Pea Vase, 4½"			
☐ crystal	88.00	105.00	92.00
Toothpick, 2¼"			
☐ crystal	16.00	23.00	17.00
Urn, square, 7½"			
☐ crystal	30.00	40.00	32.00
Utility Tray, handled, round, 9"			
☐ crystal	21.00	29.00	22.00
Vase, 8"			
☐ crystal	32.00	45.00	34.00
Vase, 10"			
☐ crystal	42.00	55.00	44.00
Vegetable Bowl, oval, 2 sections, 10"			
☐ crystal	27.00	37.00	30.00
Water Bottle, 44 oz., 9¼"			
☐ crystal	130.00	160.00	138.00
Water Tumbler, footed, 9 oz., 4⅜"			
☐ crystal	9.00	15.00	10.00
Wedding Bowl, pedestal, 6½"			
☐ crystal	28.00	37.00	30.00
Whiskey Tumbler, flat, 2 oz., 2½"			
☐ crystal	7.00	11.00	8.00
Wine Goblet, footed, 2½ oz., 4¾"			
☐ crystal	12.00	17.00	13.00

BAROQUE
Fostoria Glass Co.

This elegant pattern features ornamental scrolls and designs on simple, delicately scalloped pieces. It was made from about 1935 through 1966. The colors were crystal, blue, yellow and green. The footed punch bowl in blue is going to be particularly hard to find and will cost quite a bit to take home. The pitcher is also quite rare in *Baroque*.

Baroque

	Current Price Range		Prior Year Average
Ashtray, oval			
☐ blue	13.00	17.00	14.00
☐ yellow...	11.00	14.00	12.00
☐ crystal	7.00	10.00	8.00
Bowl, flared, 12″			
☐ blue	26.00	34.00	28.00
☐ yellow...	21.00	29.00	22.00
☐ crystal	15.00	20.00	16.00
Bowl, handles, 10½″			
☐ blue	31.00	39.00	32.00
☐ yellow...	26.00	34.00	28.00
☐ crystal	17.00	23.00	18.00
Bowl, oval, 6½″			
☐ blue	13.00	20.00	14.00
☐ yellow...	11.00	16.00	12.00
☐ crystal	8.00	12.00	9.00
Bread and Butter Plate, 6″			
☐ blue	5.00	7.00	5.50
☐ yellow...	3.50	5.50	4.00
☐ crystal	2.00	4.00	2.50
Cake Plate, handles, 10″			
☐ blue	20.00	25.00	21.00
☐ yellow...	15.00	20.00	16.00
☐ crystal	11.00	14.00	12.00
Candelabra, 3 lights, 9¼″			
☐ blue	68.00	82.00	71.00
☐ yellow...	54.00	66.00	56.00
☐ crystal	40.00	50.00	42.00

	Current Price Range		Prior Year Average
Candlestick, 4″			
☐ blue	22.00	29.00	23.00
☐ yellow	18.00	22.00	19.00
☐ crystal	13.00	17.00	14.00
Candlesticks, 5½″			
☐ blue	26.00	34.00	28.00
☐ yellow	22.00	28.00	23.00
☐ crystal	18.00	22.00	19.00
Celery Dish, oval, 11″			
☐ blue	22.00	29.00	23.00
☐ yellow	14.00	19.00	15.00
☐ crystal	11.00	14.00	12.00
Cereal Bowl, 6″			
☐ blue	26.00	34.00	28.00
☐ yellow	20.00	25.00	21.00
☐ crystal	14.00	20.00	15.00
Cocktail Tumbler, footed, 3¾ oz., 3″			
☐ blue	15.00	20.00	16.00
☐ yellow	12.00	16.00	13.00
☐ crystal	8.00	12.00	9.00
Compote, 6½″			
☐ blue	18.00	22.00	19.00
☐ yellow	14.00	18.00	15.00
☐ crystal	8.00	11.00	10.00
Cream Soup			
☐ blue	26.00	34.00	28.00
☐ yellow	20.00	25.00	21.00
☐ crystal	14.00	19.00	15.00
Creamer, footed, 3¾″			
☐ blue	14.00	18.00	15.00
☐ yellow	11.00	14.00	12.00
☐ crystal	6.00	10.00	7.00
Cruet, with stopper, 3½ oz., 5½″			
☐ blue	230.00	270.00	240.00
☐ yellow	230.00	270.00	240.00
☐ crystal	23.00	29.00	24.00
Dinner Plate, 9″			
☐ blue	26.00	34.00	28.00
☐ yellow	20.00	25.00	21.00
☐ crystal	13.00	17.00	14.00
Floating Garden Bowl, 10″			
☐ blue	35.00	45.00	37.00
☐ yellow	31.00	39.00	32.00
☐ crystal	21.00	29.00	22.00

	Current Price Range		Prior Year Average
Ice Bucket, metal handle			
☐ blue	78.00	97.00	82.00
☐ yellow	55.00	65.00	57.00
☐ crystal	31.00	39.00	32.00
Iced Tea Tumbler, 14 oz., 5¾″			
☐ blue	31.00	39.00	32.00
☐ yellow	25.00	30.00	26.00
☐ crystal	15.00	20.00	16.00
Juice Tumbler, 5 oz., 3¾″			
☐ blue	20.00	25.00	21.00
☐ yellow	18.00	22.00	19.00
☐ crystal	11.00	14.00	12.00
Luncheon Plate, 8″			
☐ blue	9.00	13.00	10.00
☐ yellow	7.00	11.00	8.00
☐ crystal	5.00	9.00	6.00
Mayonnaise, 5½″			
☐ blue	24.00	31.00	26.00
☐ yellow	20.00	24.00	21.00
☐ crystal	17.00	21.00	18.00
Nappy, 5″			
☐ blue	14.00	20.00	15.00
☐ yellow	11.00	15.00	12.00
☐ crystal	8.00	12.00	9.00
Old Fashion Tumbler, 6¾ oz., 3½″			
☐ blue	21.00	29.00	22.00
☐ yellow	18.00	22.00	19.00
☐ crystal	11.00	14.00	12.00
Pickle Dish, 8¼″			
☐ blue	14.00	19.00	15.50
☐ yellow	11.00	16.00	12.00
☐ crystal	7.50	11.50	8.50
Pitcher, 44 oz.			
☐ blue	625.00	675.00	635.00
☐ yellow	525.00	575.00	535.00
☐ crystal	135.00	165.00	145.00
Punch Cup, 6 oz.			
☐ blue	18.00	22.00	19.00
☐ crystal	6.00	9.00	7.00
Relish Tray, 3 sections, handled			
☐ blue	24.00	31.00	26.00
☐ yellow	20.00	25.00	21.00
☐ crystal	11.00	14.00	12.00

	Current Price Range		Prior Year Average

Rose Bowl, 3¾″
☐ blue	26.00	34.00	28.00
☐ yellow	19.00	26.00	21.00
☐ crystal	13.00	17.00	14.00

Rose Bowl, 8¾″
☐ yellow	26.00	34.00	28.00

Salad Plate, 7″
☐ blue	7.00	11.00	8.00
☐ yellow	6.00	10.00	7.00
☐ crystal	4.00	7.00	5.00

Salt and Pepper Shakers
☐ blue	100.00	130.00	110.00
☐ yellow	87.00	103.00	90.00
☐ crystal	30.00	40.00	32.00

Saucer
☐ blue	4.50	6.50	5.00
☐ yellow	3.00	5.00	3.50
☐ crystal	1.00	3.00	1.50

Serving Plate, center handle, 11″
☐ crystal	14.00	19.00	15.00

Sherbet, 5 oz.
☐ blue	16.00	21.00	17.00
☐ yellow	12.00	16.00	13.00
☐ crystal	7.00	10.00	8.00

Sugar, footed, 3½″
☐ blue	12.00	15.00	13.00
☐ yellow	9.00	13.00	10.00
☐ crystal	6.00	9.00	6.50

Tray, oval, 11¼″
☐ blue	20.00	25.00	21.00
☐ yellow	15.00	20.00	16.00
☐ crystal	11.00	14.00	12.00

Vase, 8¼″
☐ blue	26.00	34.00	28.00
☐ yellow	21.00	28.00	22.00
☐ crystal	16.00	20.00	17.00

Water Goblet, 9 oz.
☐ blue	26.00	34.00	28.00
☐ yellow	18.00	22.00	19.00
☐ crystal	13.00	17.00	14.00

Water Tumbler, 9 oz.
☐ blue	25.00	30.00	26.00
☐ yellow	20.00	25.00	21.00
☐ crystal	12.00	16.00	13.00

CANDLEWICK
Imperial Glass Co.

This pattern was introduced in 1936. The vast majority of its production has been in crystal but several interesting new colors have come to light recently. Pieces have been found in blue, pink, yellow, cobalt blue and black. *Candlewick* was made until Imperial went out of business in 1984. At that time, Lancaster Colony acquired the old Imperial molds and sold them, some of them to different glass companies. The fate of *Candlewick* is still undecided. Prices have been steadily on the increase but doubt over the eventual whereabouts of the molds will no doubt have a sobering effect on many collectors.

Candlewick

	Current Price Range		Prior Year Average
Ashtray			
☐ crystal	4.00	6.50	5.00
Ashtray, heart-shaped, 5½″			
☐ crystal	3.50	6.00	4.50
Ashtray, oblong, 4½″			
☐ crystal	3.50	6.00	4.50
Ashtray, round, 2¾″			
☐ crystal	2.50	4.50	3.25
Ashtray, square, 4½″			
☐ crystal	4.00	6.00	4.50
Baked Apple Bowl, rolled edge, 6″			
☐ crystal	11.00	14.00	12.00
Banana Bowl, 10″			
☐ crystal	16.00	20.00	17.50
Bell, 4″			
☐ crystal	14.00	18.00	15.00
Bon Bon Bowl, handled, 5″			
☐ crystal	14.00	18.00	15.00
Bouillon Bowl			
☐ crystal	11.50	14.50	12.50

	Current Price Range		Prior Year Average

Bowl, basket shape, handle, 11″
☐ crystal 37.00   45.00   40.00

Bowl, bell-shaped, 10″
☐ crystal 14.00   17.00   15.00

Bowl, square, fancy edge, footed, 9″
☐ crystal 14.00   18.00   15.50

Bread and Butter Plate, 6″
☐ crystal 5.00   8.00   6.50

Butter Dish, with cover, round, 5½″
☐ crystal 16.00   20.00   17.00

Butter Knife
☐ crystal 18.00   23.00   19.00

Candleholder, 5½″
☐ crystal 14.00   17.00   15.00

Candleholder, flat
☐ crystal 9.50   12.00   10.50

Candleholder, flower-shaped, 4″
☐ crystal 7.00   10.00   8.00

Candleholder, mushroom shape
☐ crystal 7.00   10.00   8.00

Candy Box, with round lid, 6½″
☐ crystal 16.00   19.00   17.00

Candy Jar, footed with cover
☐ crystal 18.00   23.00   19.00

Celery Bowl, oval, 11″
☐ crystal 20.00   26.00   22.00

Claret Goblet, 5 oz.
☐ crystal 16.00   19.00   17.00

Coaster, 4″
☐ crystal 4.00   6.50   5.00

Cocktail Goblet, 4 oz.
☐ crystal 16.00   19.00   17.00

Compote, 4½″
☐ crystal 8.50   11.50   9.50

Compote, beaded stem, 8″
☐ crystal 16.00   20.00   17.00

Condiment Tray, 5½″ × 9¼″
☐ crystal 14.00   17.00   15.00

Cream Soup, 5″
☐ crystal 11.00   14.00   12.00

Creamer, footed
☐ crystal 5.00   7.50   6.00

Cruet, with stopper, etched "oil"
☐ crystal 18.00   23.00   19.00

	Current Price Range		Prior Year Average
Cruet, with stopper, etched "vinegar"			
☐ crystal	18.00	23.00	19.00
Decanter, with stopper			
☐ crystal	21.00	26.00	22.00
Dinner Plate, 10"			
☐ crystal	11.00	14.00	12.00
Egg Cup			
☐ crystal	11.00	14.00	12.00
Finger Bowl			
☐ crystal	9.00	12.00	10.00
Floating Garden Bowl, 12"			
☐ crystal	16.00	20.00	17.00
Fruit Bowl, beaded stem, 10"			
☐ crystal	16.00	20.00	17.00
Fruit Bowl, handles, 4¾"			
☐ crystal	10.50	13.00	11.50
Fruit Bowl, 6½"			
☐ crystal	11.00	14.00	12.00
Goblet, 11 oz.			
☐ crystal	11.00	15.00	12.00
Hurricane Lamp, flared and crimped edge globe, 3 pieces			
☐ crystal	48.00	62.00	53.00
Iced Tea Tumbler, beaded foot, 14 oz.			
☐ crystal	13.00	16.00	14.00
Jam Bowl, 3 sections, 10½"			
☐ crystal	20.00	25.00	22.00
Jelly Bowl, with lid, 5½"			
☐ crystal	14.00	18.00	15.00
Juice Tumbler, beaded foot, 5 oz.			
☐ crystal	14.00	18.00	15.00
Luncheon Plate, 9"			
☐ crystal	7.00	10.00	8.00
Mayonnaise Dish, with liner, 7"			
☐ crystal	16.00	20.00	17.00
Mayonnaise Ladle, 6¼"			
☐ crystal	2.50	4.50	3.00
Mint Bowl, 6"			
☐ crystal	8.50	11.50	9.50
Mustard Jar, with spoon			
☐ crystal	25.00	30.00	26.00
Nappy, footed, 8½"			
☐ crystal	12.50	15.00	13.50
Old Fashion Tumbler, 7 oz.			
☐ crystal	11.00	14.00	12.00

	Current Price Range		Prior Year Average

Parfait, 6 oz.

☐ crystal 14.00   18.00   15.00

Pickle Bowl, 7½"

☐ crystal 11.00   13.50   12.00

Pickle Bowl, 8½"

☐ crystal 11.00   14.00   12.00

Pitcher, beaded handle, lip, 40 oz.

☐ crystal 31.00   36.00   32.00

Pitcher, short, round, 14 oz.

☐ crystal 18.00   23.00   19.00

Pitcher, 20 oz.

☐ crystal 23.00   29.00   25.00

Pitcher, 64 oz.

☐ crystal 31.00   36.00   32.00

Plate, oval, 12"

☐ crystal 16.00   19.00   17.00

Punch Cup

☐ crystal 3.50   5.50   4.00

Punch Set, 8 cup, ladle, lid

☐ crystal 110.00   150.00   120.00

Relish Bowl, 7"

☐ crystal 14.00   17.00   15.00

Relish Bowl, footed, 3 sections, 10"

☐ crystal 18.00   23.00   19.50

Relish Bowl, oval, 12"

☐ crystal 18.00   23.00   20.00

Relish Tray, 13"

☐ crystal 25.00   35.00   27.00

Rose Bowl, footed, crimped edge, 7¼"

☐ crystal 15.00   19.00   16.00

Salad Bowl, 10½"

☐ crystal 18.00   23.00   20.00

Salad, Fork and Spoon

☐ crystal 11.00   14.00   12.00

Salad Plate, 8"

☐ crystal 6.00   9.00   7.00

Salad Plate, oval, 9"

☐ crystal 12.00   15.00   13.00

Salt and Pepper, beaded stem, chrome top

☐ crystal 5.00   8.00   6.00

Sugar, beaded handle, 6 oz.

☐ crystal 4.50   7.00   5.50

Tea Cup

☐ crystal 6.50   8.50   7.00

	Current Price Range		Prior Year Average
Tid-bit Server, 2 tier			
☐ crystal	35.00	45.00	38.00
Tray, 5″			
☐ crystal	11.00	15.00	12.00
Vase, tab-shaped, 6½″			
☐ crystal	16.00	20.00	17.00
Vase, pitcher shape, handle			
☐ crystal	18.00	24.00	20.00
Water Goblet, 9 oz.			
☐ crystal	16.00	20.00	17.00
Wine Goblet, beaded foot, 5 oz.			
☐ crystal	15.00	19.00	16.00
Wine Goblet, 4 oz.			
☐ crystal	15.00	19.00	16.00

CAPRICE
Cambridge Glass Co.

The big news for *Caprice* collectors is, of course, the sale of about eight or ten of Imperial's original molds by the Summit Art Glass Co. of Ohio. They are now making eight *Caprice* pieces. Since these are made in the original molds, they will probably be impossible to tell from the original issues. They are making the new pieces in blue and crystal. This can only mean bad things for the *Caprice* collector. Let's watch and hope that only a small amount of these pieces is made. Prices had been on a sharp upturn before the sale. It would appear, at least for the time being, that pink and light green are still a safe buy. You shouldn't count on a full dinner service in either color, but a luncheon set isn't out of the question.

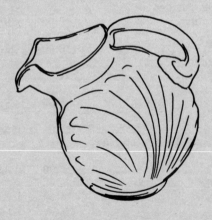

Caprice

	Current Price Range		Prior Year Average

Ashtray, triangle shape, 4½″
| ☐ blue | 13.00 | 18.00 | 14.00 |
| ☐ crystal | 9.00 | 12.00 | 10.00 |

Bon Bon Dish, square with handle, 6″
| ☐ blue | 26.00 | 34.00 | 28.00 |
| ☐ crystal | 16.00 | 20.00 | 17.00 |

Bread and Butter Plate, 6½″
| ☐ blue | 17.00 | 21.00 | 18.00 |
| ☐ crystal | 11.00 | 14.00 | 12.00 |

Cake Plate, footed, 13″
| ☐ blue | 230.00 | 275.00 | 240.00 |
| ☐ crystal | 95.00 | 110.00 | 98.00 |

Candy Box, footed, with lid, 6″
| ☐ blue | 82.00 | 92.00 | 84.00 |
| ☐ crystal | 47.00 | 55.00 | 50.00 |

Claret Goblet, 4½ oz.
| ☐ blue | 40.00 | 50.00 | 42.00 |
| ☐ crystal | 23.00 | 30.00 | 25.00 |

Coaster, 3½″
| ☐ blue | 23.00 | 28.00 | 25.00 |
| ☐ crystal | 13.00 | 18.00 | 15.00 |

Cocktail Goblet, 3½ oz.
| ☐ blue | 37.00 | 45.00 | 39.00 |
| ☐ crystal | 22.00 | 29.00 | 24.00 |

Creamer, medium
| ☐ blue | 13.00 | 18.00 | 14.50 |
| ☐ crystal | 6.00 | 9.00 | 7.00 |

Decanter, with stopper, 36 oz.
| ☐ blue | 130.00 | 170.00 | 140.00 |
| ☐ crystal | 72.00 | 90.00 | 77.00 |

Dinner Plate, 9½″
| ☐ blue | 87.00 | 110.00 | 90.00 |
| ☐ crystal | 35.00 | 45.00 | 37.00 |

Luncheon Plate, 8½″
| ☐ blue | 23.00 | 30.00 | 24.00 |
| ☐ crystal | 13.00 | 19.00 | 14.00 |

Pitcher, ball-shaped, 32 oz.
| ☐ blue | 170.00 | 185.00 | 175.00 |
| ☐ crystal | 87.00 | 100.00 | 90.00 |

Rose Bowl, footed, 8″
| ☐ blue | 93.00 | 105.00 | 95.00 |
| ☐ crystal | 56.00 | 68.00 | 60.00 |

Salad Bowl, footed, 8″
| ☐ blue | 40.00 | 50.00 | 42.00 |
| ☐ crystal | 22.00 | 32.00 | 25.00 |

	Current Price Range		Prior Year Average
Salad Plate, 7½"			
☐ blue	18.00	24.00	20.00
☐ crystal	13.00	17.00	14.00
Sherbet, tall, 7 oz.			
☐ blue	23.00	30.00	25.00
☐ crystal	18.00	24.00	20.00
Sugar, medium size			
☐ blue	13.00	18.00	15.00
☐ crystal	6.50	9.00	7.50
Tumbler, footed, 3 oz.			
☐ blue	21.00	26.00	22.00
☐ crystal	15.00	20.00	16.00
Tumbler, footed, 5 oz.			
☐ blue	21.00	26.00	22.00
☐ crystal	15.00	20.00	16.00
Tumbler, footed, 10 oz.			
☐ blue	30.00	37.00	32.00
☐ crystal	18.00	24.00	20.00
Tumbler, footed, 12 oz.			
☐ blue	33.00	40.00	35.00
☐ crystal	21.00	27.00	22.00
Vase, 5½"			
☐ blue	57.00	65.00	59.00
☐ crystal	43.00	49.00	45.00
Vase, 8½"			
☐ blue	87.00	95.00	89.00
☐ crystal	53.00	60.00	54.00
Wine Goblet, 3 oz.			
☐ blue	43.00	52.00	45.00
☐ crystal	25.00	32.00	27.00

CHEROKEE ROSE
Tiffin Glass Co.

This elegant glassware pattern was manufactured by the Tiffin Glass Company. The alternating design, around the rim of the plates and covering the other pieces, features a rose design and a cameo design. There is no decoration on the center of the plates. Handles on pieces look like beadwork.

Cherokee Rose

	Current Price Range		Prior Year Average
Bud Vase, 6″			
☐ crystal	8.50	11.50	9.00
Bud Vase, 8″			
☐ crystal	11.00	14.00	12.00
Cake Plate, handle, 12½″			
☐ crystal	18.00	22.00	19.00
Candleholder, double branch			
☐ crystal	29.00	35.00	31.00
Cocktail, stemmed, 2 oz.			
☐ crystal	11.00	14.00	12.00
Creamer			
☐ crystal	8.50	11.50	9.00
Finger Bowl, 5″			
☐ crystal	6.50	9.50	7.00
Iced Tea Tumbler, footed, 10½ oz.			
☐ crystal	8.50	11.50	9.00
Luncheon Plate, 8″			
☐ crystal	6.00	9.00	7.00
Pitcher			
☐ crystal	83.00	93.00	85.00
Relish Tray, 3 compartments, 6½″			
☐ crystal	15.00	20.00	16.00
Salad Bowl, 7″			
☐ crystal	8.50	11.50	9.00
Salad Bowl, 10″			
☐ crystal	15.00	20.00	16.00
Sandwich Plate, 14″			
☐ crystal	12.50	15.50	13.00

	Current Price Range		Prior Year Average
Sherbet Plate, 6″			
☐ crystal	2.50	4.50	3.00
Sherbet, stemmed, 5½ oz.			
☐ crystal	10.00	13.00	11.00
Sugar			
☐ crystal	7.50	10.50	8.00
Vase, flared, 12″			
☐ crystal	22.00	29.00	23.00
Water Tumbler, footed, 8 oz.			
☐ crystal	8.00	11.00	9.00
Wine, stemmed, 3½ oz.			
☐ crystal	13.00	17.00	14.00

COLONY
Fostoria Glass Co.

Colony was made from the 1920s to the 1980s. This pattern was mostly made in crystal, though other colors include green, blue and yellow. Some red is being produced now. The pitcher and the vase are the hardest items to find in this pattern.

Colony

Almond Bowl, footed			
☐ crystal	3.00	5.00	3.50
Bowl, low foot, 9″			
☐ crystal	13.00	17.00	14.00

	Current Price Range		Prior Year Average

Candlestick, 9¾″
☐ crystal 11.00 14.00 12.00
Candy Dish, with lid, 6½″
☐ crystal 18.00 22.00 19.00
Celery Bowl, 11½″
☐ crystal 10.50 13.50 11.50
Cocktail Goblet, 3½ oz., 4″
☐ crystal 7.50 10.50 8.50
Creamer
☐ crystal 6.50 9.50 7.50
Finger Bowl, 4¾″
☐ crystal 5.00 8.00 6.00
Goblet, 9 oz., 5¼″
☐ crystal 10.50 13.50 11.50
Oyster Cocktail, 4 oz., 3⅜″
☐ crystal 7.00 10.00 8.00
Pickle Bowl, 9½″
☐ crystal 8.50 11.50 9.50
Plate, 6″
☐ crystal 1.50 3.50 2.00
Plate, 7″
☐ crystal 2.00 4.00 2.50
Plate, 8″
☐ crystal 2.50 4.50 3.00
Plate, 9″
☐ crystal 3.50 5.50 4.00
Plate, 10″
☐ crystal 6.00 9.00 7.00
Sherbet, 5 oz., 3⅜′
☐ crystal 7.50 11.50 8.50
Sugar
☐ crystal 4.00 6.00 4.50
Tumbler, 5 oz.
☐ crystal 6.50 9.50 7.50
Tumbler, 9 oz.
☐ crystal 8.50 11.50 9.50
Tumbler, footed, 5 oz., 4½″
☐ crystal 8.00 11.00 9.00
Tumbler, footed, 12 oz., 5¾″
☐ crystal 10.00 13.00 11.00
Tumbler, 12 oz.
☐ crystal 10.50 13.50 11.50
Vase, 8″
☐ crystal 15.00 20.00 16.50

	Current Price Range		Prior Year Average

Wine Goblet, 3¼ oz., 4¼"
☐ crystal 8.50 11.50 9.50

CRYSTOLITE
A.H. Heisey & Co.

This pattern was produced on blank No. 1503 in crystal. A few pieces are known to exist in other colors, but they are extremely rare.

Crystolite

Ashtray, square, 3½"
☐ crystal 4.00 6.00 5.00
Bon Bon Dish, shell-shaped, 7"
☐ crystal 15.00 19.00 16.00
Candlestick, footed, 1 lite
☐ crystal 15.00 21.00 17.00
Candy Dish, swan shape, 6½"
☐ crystal 31.00 39.00 32.00
Cigarette Box, with cover, 4½"
☐ crystal 15.00 19.00 16.00
☐ sahara 95.00 125.00 110.00
☐ zircon 150.00 180.00 160.00

	Current Price Range		Prior Year Average
Claret Goblet, wide blown, 3½ oz.			
☐ crystal	22.00	28.00	24.00
Cocktail Goblet, wide optic, blown, 3½ oz.			
☐ crystal	18.00	22.00	19.00
Cordial Goblet, wide optic, blown, 1 oz.			
☐ crystal	55.00	65.00	57.00
Creamer			
☐ crystal	12.00	16.00	13.50
Cup			
☐ crystal	10.00	14.00	12.00
Flower Urn, 7″			
☐ crystal	14.00	20.00	16.00
Iced Tea Tumbler, wide optic, blown, 10 oz.			
☐ crystal	18.00	22.00	19.00
Juice Tumbler, footed, wide optic, blown, 5 oz.			
☐ crystal	13.00	17.00	14.00
Mayonnaise Ladle			
☐ crystal	6.00	9.00	6.50
Mustard Dish, with lid			
☐ crystal	26.00	34.00	28.00
Nut Bowl, handle, 3″			
☐ crystal	13.00	17.00	14.00
Pitcher, swan-handled, ice lip, 2 quart			
☐ crystal	400.00	460.00	430.00
Puff Box, with lid, 4¾″			
☐ crystal	42.00	49.00	43.50
Punch Bowl, 7½ quart			
☐ crystal	80.00	95.00	85.00
Punch Cup			
☐ crystal	8.50	11.50	9.50
Relish Tray, 3 sections, 12″			
☐ crystal	20.00	26.00	22.00
Salad Bowl, round, 10″			
☐ crystal	20.00	24.00	21.00
Salad Plate, 7″			
☐ crystal	5.50	8.50	6.50
Salad Plate, 8½″			
☐ crystal	13.00	17.00	14.00
Salt and Pepper			
☐ crystal	21.00	29.00	23.00
Sandwich Plate, 12″			
☐ crystal	18.00	22.00	19.00

	Current Price Range		Prior Year Average
Saucer			
☐ crystal	4.00	6.00	4.50
Sherbet, 6 oz.			
☐ crystal	10.00	14.00	11.00
Sugar			
☐ crystal	11.00	15.00	12.00
Syrup Bottle, drip and metal top			
☐ crystal	45.00	55.00	47.00
Vase, footed, 6″			
☐ crystal	14.00	20.00	16.00

CUPID
Paden City Glass Co.

Manufactured by Paden City in the 1930s, *Cupid* was made in blue, green and pink. Most pieces have delicately scalloped rims, and the repeating etched design features two cupids, in profile, facing an urn. They are surrounded by flowers and scrollwork. Some pieces in black have been reported.

Cupid

Bowl, handled in center, 9¼″			
☐ blue	32.00	38.00	34.00
☐ green	32.00	38.00	34.00
☐ pink	32.00	38.00	34.00

	Current Price Range		Prior Year Average
Cake Plate, 11¾″			
☐ blue	32.00	38.00	34.00
☐ green	32.00	38.00	34.00
☐ pink	32.00	38.00	34.00
Candleholders, pair			
☐ blue	30.00	35.00	31.00
☐ green	30.00	35.00	31.00
☐ pink	30.00	35.00	31.00
Candy Holder, with lid			
☐ blue	42.00	52.00	45.00
☐ green	42.00	52.00	45.00
☐ pink	42.00	52.00	45.00
Creamer, footed, 5″			
☐ blue	30.00	35.00	31.00
☐ green	30.00	35.00	31.00
☐ pink	30.00	35.00	31.00
Dinner Plate, 10½″			
☐ blue	20.00	25.00	21.00
☐ green	20.00	25.00	21.00
☐ pink	20.00	25.00	21.00
Fruit Bowl, footed, 9¼″			
☐ blue	28.00	32.00	29.00
☐ green	28.00	32.00	29.00
☐ pink	28.00	32.00	29.00
Ice Bucket, 6″			
☐ blue	45.00	55.00	47.00
☐ green	45.00	55.00	47.00
☐ pink	45.00	55.00	47.00
Oval Bowl, footed, 8½″			
☐ blue	30.00	35.00	31.00
☐ green	30.00	35.00	31.00
☐ pink	30.00	35.00	31.00
Sugar, footed, 5″			
☐ blue	30.00	35.00	31.00
☐ green	30.00	35.00	31.00
☐ pink	30.00	35.00	31.00
Tray, with handle, 10½″			
☐ blue	25.00	30.00	26.00
☐ green	25.00	30.00	26.00
☐ pink	25.00	30.00	26.00
Vase, 8¼″			
☐ blue	55.00	65.00	57.00
☐ green	55.00	65.00	57.00
☐ pink	55.00	65.00	57.00

DANCING GIRL
Morgantown Glass Co.

Made in pink, green and blue, *Dancing Girl* was introduced in the 1930s.

	Current Price Range		Prior Year Average
Bud Vase, 10"			
☐ blue	31.00	40.00	33.00
☐ green	31.00	40.00	33.00
☐ pink	31.00	40.00	33.00
Cocktail Goblet			
☐ blue	24.00	33.00	25.50
☐ green	24.00	33.00	25.50
☐ pink	24.00	33.00	25.50
Creamer			
☐ blue	24.00	33.00	25.50
☐ green	24.00	33.00	25.50
☐ pink	24.00	33.00	25.50
Pitcher			
☐ blue	140.00	170.00	152.50
☐ green	140.00	170.00	152.50
☐ pink	140.00	170.00	152.50
Plate, 7½"			
☐ blue	11.00	20.00	13.00
☐ green	11.00	20.00	13.00
☐ pink	11.00	20.00	13.00
Sugar Bowl			
☐ blue	21.00	30.00	23.00
☐ green	21.00	30.00	23.00
☐ pink	21.00	30.00	23.00
Tumbler, 9 oz.			
☐ blue	21.00	30.00	23.00
☐ green	21.00	30.00	23.00
☐ pink	21.00	30.00	23.00
Tumbler, 12 oz.			
☐ blue	24.00	33.00	25.50
☐ green	24.00	33.00	25.50
☐ pink	24.00	33.00	25.50

DECAGON
Cambridge Glass Co.

Made in the shape of a decagon, this pattern was made in the 1930s. Pieces were made in green, pink, cobalt blue, amber and red.

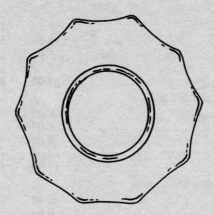

Decagon

	Current Price Range		Prior Year Average
Almond Bowl, 2½″			
☐ green	8.50	11.50	9.50
☐ pink	8.50	11.50	9.50
☐ light blue	8.50	11.50	9.50
☐ red	15.00	20.00	16.50
☐ cobalt	15.00	20.00	16.50
Berry Bowl, 10″			
☐ green	8.50	11.50	9.50
☐ pink	8.50	11.50	9.50
☐ light blue	8.50	11.50	9.50
☐ red	15.00	20.00	16.00
☐ cobalt	15.00	20.00	16.00
Bon Bon Bowl, handles, 5½″			
☐ green	8.50	11.50	9.50
☐ pink	8.50	11.50	9.50
☐ light blue	8.50	11.50	9.50
☐ red	15.00	19.00	16.00
☐ cobalt	15.00	19.00	16.00
Bread and Butter Plate, 6¼″			
☐ pink	2.00	4.00	2.50
☐ green	2.00	4.00	2.50
☐ light blue	2.00	4.00	2.50
☐ red	4.00	6.00	4.50
☐ cobalt	4.00	6.00	4.50

	Current Price Range		Prior Year Average
Celery Tray, 11″			
☐ green	8.50	11.50	9.50
☐ pink	8.50	11.50	9.50
☐ light blue	8.50	11.50	9.50
☐ red	18.00	22.00	19.00
☐ cobalt	18.00	22.00	19.00
Cereal Bowl, bell-shaped, 6″			
☐ green	6.00	8.00	6.50
☐ pink	6.00	8.00	6.50
☐ light blue	6.00	8.00	6.50
☐ red	11.00	14.00	12.00
☐ cobalt	11.00	14.00	12.00
Cereal Bowl, flat rim, 6″			
☐ green	5.00	7.00	5.50
☐ pink	5.00	7.00	5.50
☐ light blue	5.00	7.00	5.50
☐ red	9.50	12.50	10.50
☐ cobalt	9.50	12.50	10.50
Comport, 7″			
☐ green	15.00	20.00	16.00
☐ pink	15.00	20.00	16.00
☐ light blue	15.00	20.00	16.00
☐ red	25.00	30.00	26.00
☐ cobalt	25.00	30.00	26.00
Cream Soup, with liner			
☐ green	8.00	11.00	9.00
☐ pink	8.00	11.00	9.00
☐ light blue	8.00	11.00	9.00
☐ red	13.00	17.00	14.00
☐ cobalt	13.00	17.00	14.00
Creamer, footed			
☐ green	7.50	10.50	8.50
☐ pink	7.50	10.50	8.50
☐ light blue	7.50	10.50	8.50
☐ red	18.00	22.00	19.00
☐ cobalt	18.00	22.00	19.00
Creamer, scalloped edge			
☐ green	6.50	9.50	7.50
☐ pink	6.50	9.50	7.50
☐ light blue	6.50	9.50	7.50
☐ red	16.00	20.00	17.00
☐ cobalt	16.00	20.00	17.00

	Current Price Range		Prior Year Average

Cruet, handle, stopper, 6 oz.

☐ pink	20.00	25.00	21.00
☐ green	20.00	25.00	21.00
☐ light blue	20.00	25.00	21.00
☐ red	35.00	40.00	37.00
☐ cobalt	35.00	40.00	37.00

Cup

☐ green	5.00	7.00	5.50
☐ pink	5.00	7.00	5.50
☐ light blue	5.00	7.00	5.50
☐ red	8.50	11.50	9.50
☐ cobalt	8.50	11.50	9.50

Dinner Plate, 9½″

☐ green	8.50	11.50	9.50
☐ pink	8.50	11.50	9.50
☐ light blue	8.50	11.50	9.50
☐ red	15.00	19.00	16.00
☐ cobalt	15.00	19.00	16.00

Grill Plate, 10″

☐ green	6.50	9.50	7.50
☐ pink	6.50	9.50	7.50
☐ light blue	6.50	9.50	7.50
☐ red	12.00	16.00	13.00
☐ cobalt	12.00	16.00	13.00

Mayonnaise Dish, with liner and ladle

☐ green	16.00	20.00	17.00
☐ pink	16.00	20.00	17.00
☐ light blue	16.00	20.00	17.00
☐ red	26.00	34.00	28.00
☐ cobalt	26.00	34.00	28.00

Pickle Tray, 9″

☐ green	8.50	11.50	9.50
☐ pink	8.50	11.50	9.50
☐ light blue	8.50	11.50	9.50
☐ red	15.00	20.00	16.00
☐ cobalt	15.00	20.00	16.00

Plate, handles, 7″

☐ pink	8.00	11.00	8.50
☐ green	8.00	11.00	8.50
☐ light blue	8.00	11.00	8.50
☐ red	13.00	17.00	14.00
☐ cobalt	13.00	17.00	14.00

	Current Price Range		Prior Year Average
Salad Plate, 8½"			
☐ green	5.00	7.00	5.50
☐ pink	5.00	7.00	5.50
☐ light blue	5.00	7.00	5.50
☐ red	8.50	11.50	9.50
☐ cobalt	8.50	11.50	9.50
Saucer			
☐ green	.75	1.75	1.00
☐ pink	.75	1.75	1.00
☐ light blue	.75	1.75	1.00
☐ red	1.50	3.50	2.00
☐ cobalt	1.50	3.50	2.00
Saucer Boat, with saucer			
☐ green	20.00	24.00	21.00
☐ pink	20.00	24.00	21.00
☐ light blue	20.00	24.00	21.00
☐ red	36.00	44.00	38.00
☐ cobalt	36.00	44.00	38.00
Service Tray, handles, 13"			
☐ green	18.00	22.00	19.00
☐ pink	18.00	22.00	19.00
☐ light blue	18.00	22.00	19.00
☐ red	26.00	34.00	28.00
☐ cobalt	26.00	34.00	28.00
Sugar, footed			
☐ green	6.50	9.50	7.50
☐ pink	6.50	9.50	7.50
☐ light blue	6.50	9.50	7.50
☐ red	16.00	20.00	17.00
☐ cobalt	16.00	20.00	17.00
Sugar, scalloped edge			
☐ green	6.00	9.00	6.50
☐ pink	6.00	9.00	6.50
☐ light blue	6.00	9.00	6.50
☐ red	15.00	20.00	16.00
☐ cobalt	15.00	20.00	16.00
Vegetable Bowl, oval, 9½"			
☐ green	10.50	13.50	11.50
☐ pink	10.50	13.50	11.50
☐ light blue	10.50	13.50	11.50
☐ red	20.00	24.00	21.00
☐ cobalt	20.00	24.00	21.00

DIANE
Cambridge Glass Co.

This pattern was manufactured from 1934 through the early 1950s. It is mainly available in crystal, but pink, yellow and blue are around in small amounts. Add approximately 30% to the crystal value for any one of the colors.

	Current Price Range		Prior Year Average
Basket, two-handled, footed, height 6″			
☐ crystal	15.00	20.00	16.50
Berry Bowl, diameter 5″			
☐ crystal	18.00	23.00	20.00
Bowl, cereal, diameter 6″			
☐ crystal	20.00	26.00	23.00
Bowl, bon-bon, two-handled, footed, diameter 6″			
☐ crystal	18.00	23.00	20.00
Bowl, relish, diameter 7″			
☐ crystal	18.00	24.00	21.00
Bowl, bon-bon, two-handled, footed, diameter 7″			
☐ crystal	20.00	25.00	22.50
Bowl, four-footed, diameter 10″			
☐ crystal	30.00	40.00	34.00
Bowl, baker, diameter 10″			
☐ crystal	32.00	42.00	36.00
Bowl, four-footed, diameter 11″			
☐ crystal	40.00	46.00	43.00
Bowl, footed, tab-handled, diameter 11½″			
☐ crystal	40.00	46.00	43.00
Bowl, four-footed, diameter 12″, several styles			
☐ crystal	39.00	46.00	43.00
Candlesticks, several styles, one, two or three lites			
☐ crystal	20.00	32.00	26.00
Candy Box, with cover			
☐ crystal	60.00	70.00	64.00
Cigarette Urn			
☐ crystal	30.00	40.00	35.00
Cocktail Shaker			
☐ crystal with glass top	80.00	90.00	80.00
☐ crystal with metal top	50.00	70.00	60.00
Comport, diameter 5½″			
☐ crystal	20.00	27.00	23.00

	Current Price Range		Prior Year Average

Creamer, 4 styles

□ crystal 13.00   17.00   15.00

Decanter, 2 styles, footed

□ crystal 110.00   140.00   122.00

Pitcher

□ crystal 120.00   140.00   130.00

Plate, two-handled, diameter 6″

□ crystal 6.00   9.00   8.00

Plate, bread and butter, diameter 6½″

□ crystal 4.00   7.00   5.00

Plate, bon-bon, footed, two-handled, diameter 8″

□ crystal 9.00   12.00   10.00

Plate, salad, diameter 8″

□ crystal 7.00   10.00   8.00

Plate, dinner, diameter 10½″

□ crystal 40.00   50.00   45.00

Plate, two-handled, diameter 13½″

□ crystal 25.00   32.00   28.00

Salt and Pepper Shakers, with glass tops, pair

□ crystal 30.00   36.00   32.00

Tumbler, 2½ oz.

□ crystal 24.00   30.00   27.00

Tumbler, 5 oz., footed, juice

□ crystal 25.00   31.00   28.00

Tumbler, 7 oz., old fashion

□ crystal 26.00   33.00   29.00

Tumbler, 8 oz., footed

□ crystal 20.00   25.00   22.00

Tumbler, 10 oz.

□ crystal 24.00   30.00   27.00

Tumbler, 12 oz.

□ crystal 28.00   34.00   30.00

Tumbler, 13 oz.

□ crystal 28.00   34.00   31.00

Vase, globe, 5″

□ crystal 20.00   26.00   23.00

Vase, flower, height 6″

□ crystal 20.00   24.00   22.00

Vase, flower, height 8″

□ crystal 20.00   24.00   22.00

Vase, height 9″

□ crystal 32.00   38.00   35.00

	Current Price Range		Prior Year Average
Vase, bud, height 10″			
☐ crystal..	17.00	22.00	19.50
Vase, height 12″			
☐ crystal..	40.00	50.00	45.00
Vase, flower, height 13″			
☐ crystal..	45.00	55.00	50.00

EMPRESS
A.H. Heisey & Co.

Colors made in this pattern include crystal, green, yellow, pink, blue, alexandrite and tangerine.

Empress

Ashtray, diamond

☐ crystal..	22.00	28.00	23.00
☐ pink...	100.00	125.00	110.00
☐ yellow..	75.00	90.00	80.00
☐ green...	200.00	225.00	210.00
☐ cobalt..	130.00	160.00	140.00
☐ alexandrite.......................................	175.00	225.00	190.00

	Current Price Range		Prior Year Average
Candlestick, dolphin-footed, 6″			
☐ crystal	26.00	34.00	28.00
☐ pink	90.00	120.00	100.00
☐ yellow	100.00	135.00	110.00
☐ green	150.00	190.00	160.00
☐ alexandrite	150.00	200.00	165.00
Celery Tray, 10″			
☐ crystal	15.00	20.00	17.00
☐ pink	20.00	25.00	22.00
☐ yellow	25.00	30.00	27.00
☐ green	30.00	35.00	32.00
Comport, footed, round, 6″			
☐ crystal	22.00	28.00	23.00
☐ pink	36.00	44.00	38.00
☐ yellow	50.00	60.00	53.00
☐ green	60.00	70.00	63.00
Comport, square, 6″			
☐ crystal	31.00	39.00	33.00
☐ pink	60.00	70.00	63.00
☐ yellow	63.00	77.00	67.00
☐ green	69.00	82.00	63.00
Cream Soup			
☐ crystal	8.00	12.00	9.00
☐ pink	15.00	22.00	17.00
☐ yellow	20.00	27.00	22.00
☐ green	24.00	32.00	26.00
☐ alexandrite	200.00	235.00	210.00
Creamer, dolphin-footed			
☐ crystal	15.00	20.00	16.00
☐ pink	30.00	37.00	34.00
☐ yellow	35.00	43.00	38.00
☐ green	40.00	48.00	42.00
☐ alexandrite	200.00	235.00	210.00
Cup			
☐ crystal	10.00	15.00	12.00
☐ pink	22.00	28.00	23.00
☐ yellow	26.00	34.00	28.00
☐ green	31.00	39.00	33.00
☐ alexandrite	85.00	100.00	90.00
☐ tangerine	500.00	600.00	540.00
Floral Bowl, rolled edge, 9″			
☐ crystal	20.00	24.00	21.00
☐ pink	26.00	34.00	28.00
☐ yellow	31.00	39.00	33.00
☐ green	34.00	41.00	36.00

	Current Price Range		Prior Year Average
Ice Bucket, metal handles			
☐ crystal	40.00	50.00	42.00
☐ pink	100.00	125.00	110.00
☐ yellow	115.00	135.00	125.00
☐ green	100.00	125.00	110.00
☐ alexandrite	350.00	450.00	390.00
Iced Tea, flat bottom, 12 oz.			
☐ crystal	13.00	17.00	14.00
☐ pink	18.00	22.00	19.00
☐ yellow	23.00	30.00	25.00
☐ green	26.00	34.00	28.00
Marmalade Dish, with lid, dolphin-footed			
☐ crystal	40.00	50.00	45.00
☐ pink	60.00	75.00	65.00
☐ yellow	75.00	95.00	80.00
☐ green	100.00	125.00	110.00
Mayonnaise Dish, footed, 5½"			
☐ crystal	20.00	27.00	24.00
☐ pink	30.00	37.00	33.00
☐ yellow	30.00	37.00	33.00
☐ green	45.00	55.00	47.00
☐ alexandrite	130.00	170.00	140.00
Mint Bowl, dolphin-footed, 6"			
☐ crystal	15.00	22.00	16.00
☐ pink	30.00	37.00	33.00
☐ yellow	30.00	37.00	33.00
☐ green	38.00	48.00	42.00
☐ alexandrite	120.00	150.00	130.00
Mustard Dish, with lid			
☐ crystal	22.00	32.00	24.00
☐ pink	45.00	55.00	48.00
☐ yellow	65.00	75.00	68.00
☐ green	75.00	85.00	78.00
Nappy, 4½"			
☐ crystal	5.00	8.00	6.00
☐ pink	9.00	12.00	10.00
☐ yellow	12.00	15.00	11.00
☐ green	15.00	21.00	17.00
Nappy, 8"			
☐ crystal	20.00	24.00	21.00
☐ pink	26.00	34.00	28.00
☐ yellow	31.00	39.00	33.00
☐ green	34.00	42.00	36.00

	Current Price Range		Prior Year Average

Oyster Cocktail

☐ crystal	13.00	17.00	14.00
☐ pink	18.00	22.00	19.00
☐ yellow	22.00	28.00	23.00
☐ green	26.00	34.00	28.00

Pickle / Olive Bowl, 2 sections, 13″

☐ crystal	18.00	22.00	19.00
☐ pink	30.00	36.00	31.00
☐ yellow	38.00	51.00	41.00
☐ green	33.00	41.00	36.00

Plate, 4½″

☐ crystal	4.00	5.00	4.50
☐ pink	8.00	10.00	8.50
☐ yellow	10.00	12.00	10.50
☐ green	12.00	15.00	12.50

Plate, round or square, 6″

☐ crystal	6.00	8.00	4.50
☐ pink	9.00	12.00	9.50
☐ yellow	10.00	12.00	12.00
☐ green	12.00	15.00	14.00
☐ alexandrite	35.00	45.00	33.00
☐ tangerine	100.00	135.00	115.00

Plate, round or square, 7″

☐ crystal	7.00	10.00	6.50
☐ pink	9.00	15.00	11.50
☐ yellow	13.00	17.00	14.00
☐ green	15.00	19.00	16.00
☐ alexandrite	40.00	50.00	42.00
☐ cobalt	350.00	45.00	40.00

Plate, 8″

☐ crystal	9.00	13.00	8.50
☐ pink	18.00	24.00	15.00
☐ yellow	18.00	22.00	19.00
☐ green	22.00	26.00	23.00
☐ tangerine	140.00	180.00	155.00
☐ alexandrite	45.00	55.00	50.00
☐ cobalt	45.00	55.00	50.00

Plate, round, 9″

☐ crystal	10.50	13.50	11.50
☐ pink	22.00	28.00	23.00
☐ yellow	32.00	38.00	33.00
☐ green	36.00	44.00	37.00

	Current Price Range		Prior Year Average

Plate, round or square, 10½″
☐ crystal	24.00	30.00	26.00
☐ pink	47.00	60.00	52.00
☐ yellow	57.00	70.00	61.00
☐ green	70.00	80.00	73.00

Plate, round, 12″
☐ crystal	22.00	27.00	23.00
☐ pink	60.00	70.00	64.00
☐ yellow	60.00	70.00	64.00
☐ green	70.00	80.00	74.00

Platter, oval, 14″
☐ crystal	25.00	30.00	27.00
☐ pink	30.00	35.00	32.00
☐ yellow	35.00	40.00	37.00
☐ green	40.00	45.00	42.00

Punch Cup, 4 oz.
☐ crystal	8.50	11.50	9.50
☐ pink	22.00	28.00	23.00
☐ yellow	25.00	31.00	26.00
☐ green	26.00	34.00	28.00

Relish Bowl, 3 sections, triplex, 7″
☐ crystal	20.00	25.00	22.00
☐ pink	30.00	35.00	32.00
☐ yellow	40.00	47.00	44.00
☐ green	50.00	60.00	53.00
☐ alexandrite	175.00	225.00	195.00

Relish Tray, 3 sections, 10″
☐ crystal	20.00	30.00	23.00
☐ pink	40.00	50.00	43.00
☐ yellow	50.00	60.00	53.00
☐ green	60.00	70.00	63.00

Salad Bowl, square, handles, 10″
☐ crystal	30.00	40.00	34.00
☐ pink	40.00	50.00	43.00
☐ yellow	50.00	60.00	53.00
☐ green	60.00	70.00	63.00
☐ tangerine (only one known to exist)	1,100.00	1,500.00	—

Salt and Pepper
☐ crystal	36.00	44.00	38.00
☐ pink	60.00	70.00	62.00
☐ yellow	80.00	90.00	83.00
☐ green	88.00	100.00	92.00
☐ alexandrite	250.00	350.00	300.00
☐ tangerine	700.00	800.00	750.00

	Current Price Range		Prior Year Average

Sandwich Tray, handle, 12"
☐ crystal	26.00	34.00	28.00
☐ pink	45.00	55.00	50.00
☐ yellow	55.00	65.00	58.00
☐ green	75.00	85.00	78.00
☐ alexandrite	160.00	200.00	175.00

Saucer
☐ crystal	6.00	10.00	7.00
☐ pink	10.00	15.00	12.00
☐ yellow	10.00	15.00	12.00
☐ green	10.00	15.00	12.00
☐ alexandrite	23.00	32.00	26.00
☐ tangerine	90.00	130.00	100.00

Sherbet, 4 oz.
☐ crystal	13.00	17.00	14.00
☐ pink	18.00	22.00	19.00
☐ yellow	22.00	28.00	23.00
☐ green	26.00	34.00	27.00

Sugar, dolphin-footed
☐ crystal	15.00	20.00	17.00
☐ pink	30.00	35.00	32.00
☐ yellow	35.00	40.00	37.00
☐ green	40.00	45.00	42.00
☐ alexandrite	190.00	230.00	205.00

Tumbler, dolphin-footed, 8 oz.
☐ crystal	55.00	65.00	57.00
☐ pink	80.00	90.00	82.00
☐ yellow	108.00	133.00	115.00
☐ green	105.00	140.00	117.00

Tumbler, flat bottom, 8 oz.
☐ crystal	15.00	20.00	17.00
☐ pink	30.00	35.00	32.00
☐ yellow	35.00	40.00	37.00
☐ green	40.00	45.00	42.00

Vase, flared, three-handled, 8"
☐ crystal	41.00	49.00	43.00
☐ pink	60.00	70.00	62.00
☐ yellow	69.00	82.00	63.00
☐ green	78.00	93.00	82.00

Vase, dolphin-footed, 9"
☐ crystal	45.00	55.00	47.00
☐ pink	110.00	130.00	115.00
☐ yellow	110.00	130.00	115.00
☐ green	110.00	145.00	117.00
☐ alexandrite	375.00	475.00	425.00

	Current Price Range		Prior Year Average

Vegetable Bowl, oval, 10″
☐ crystal	25.00	30.00	26.00
☐ pink	31.00	39.00	33.00
☐ yellow	40.00	50.00	42.00
☐ green	50.00	60.00	52.00

FAIRFAX
Fostoria Glass Co.

This pattern was made from 1924 through 1945. It was made in green, yellow, pink, blue, amber, black, crystal and orchid. Blue and orchid are the most popular colors, followed by pink and green. The hardest to find items are the pitcher, the shakers, butter dish and the dressing bottles. *Fairfax* is actually just a blank pattern. Fostoria took the *Fairfax* molds, added designs and turned out several other patterns, such as *June* and *Trojan*.

Fairfax

Ashtray
☐ blue	18.00	22.00	19.00
☐ orchid	18.00	22.00	19.00
☐ pink	16.00	20.00	17.00
☐ green	16.00	20.00	17.00
☐ amber	11.00	15.00	12.00

	Current Price Range		Prior Year Average
Bon Bon Dish			
☐ blue	15.00	20.00	16.00
☐ orchid	15.00	20.00	16.00
☐ pink	13.00	17.00	14.00
☐ green	13.00	17.00	14.00
☐ amber	10.00	14.00	11.00
Bowl, footed, 11¾″			
☐ blue	21.00	25.00	22.00
☐ orchid	21.00	25.00	22.00
☐ pink	17.00	21.00	18.00
☐ green	17.00	21.00	18.00
☐ amber	13.00	17.00	14.00
Bowl, oval, 10½″			
☐ blue	25.00	30.00	26.00
☐ orchid	25.00	30.00	26.00
☐ pink	22.00	28.00	23.00
☐ green	22.00	28.00	23.00
☐ amber	15.00	20.00	16.00
Bread and Butter Plate, 6″			
☐ blue	3.50	5.50	4.00
☐ orchid	3.50	5.50	4.00
☐ pink	3.00	5.00	3.50
☐ green	3.00	5.00	3.50
☐ amber	2.00	4.00	2.50
Cake Plate, handles, 10″			
☐ blue	15.00	20.00	16.00
☐ orchid	15.00	20.00	16.00
☐ pink	13.00	17.00	14.00
☐ green	13.00	17.00	14.00
☐ amber	11.00	14.00	12.00
Candy Dish, with lid, 3 sections			
☐ blue	42.00	52.00	44.00
☐ orchid	42.00	52.00	44.00
☐ pink	33.00	41.00	34.00
☐ green	33.00	41.00	34.00
☐ amber	29.00	35.00	31.00
Cereal Bowl, 6″			
☐ blue	13.00	17.00	14.00
☐ orchid	13.00	17.00	14.00
☐ pink	11.00	14.00	12.00
☐ green	11.00	14.00	12.00
☐ amber	8.50	11.50	9.50

	Current Price Range		Prior Year Average

Cigarette Box

☐ blue	31.00	39.00	33.00
☐ orchid	31.00	39.00	33.00
☐ pink	23.00	33.00	25.00
☐ green	23.00	33.00	25.00
☐ amber	20.00	25.00	21.00

Claret Goblet, 4 oz.

☐ blue	23.00	28.00	24.00
☐ orchid	23.00	28.00	24.00
☐ pink	20.00	25.00	21.00
☐ green	20.00	25.00	21.00
☐ amber	17.00	21.00	18.00

Coaster, 3½″

☐ blue	5.00	7.00	5.50
☐ orchid	5.00	7.00	5.50
☐ pink	3.00	5.00	3.50
☐ green	3.00	5.00	3.50
☐ amber	2.00	4.00	2.50

Cocktail Goblet, 3 oz.

☐ blue	20.00	25.00	21.00
☐ orchid	20.00	25.00	21.00
☐ pink	18.00	22.00	19.00
☐ green	18.00	22.00	19.00
☐ amber	15.00	20.00	16.00

Compote, 7″

☐ blue	20.00	25.00	21.00
☐ orchid	20.00	25.00	21.00
☐ pink	18.00	22.00	19.00
☐ green	18.00	22.00	19.00
☐ amber	14.00	18.00	15.00

Cordial Goblet, ¾ oz.

☐ blue	26.00	34.00	28.00
☐ orchid	26.00	34.00	28.00
☐ pink	25.00	30.00	26.00
☐ green	25.00	30.00	26.00
☐ amber	21.00	26.00	23.00

Cream Soup

☐ blue	12.00	15.00	13.00
☐ orchid	12.00	15.00	13.00
☐ pink	10.50	13.50	11.50
☐ green	10.50	13.50	11.50
☐ amber	8.50	11.50	9.50

	Current Price Range		Prior Year Average

Creamer, footed

☐ blue	8.50	11.50	9.50
☐ orchid	8.50	11.50	9.50
☐ pink	6.50	9.50	7.50
☐ green	6.50	9.50	7.50
☐ amber	5.00	7.00	5.50

Cruet, footed, with handle

☐ blue	112.00	140.00	117.00
☐ orchid	112.00	140.00	117.00
☐ pink	98.00	122.00	104.00
☐ green	98.00	122.00	104.00
☐ amber	82.00	98.00	85.00

Cup, footed

☐ blue	7.00	10.00	8.00
☐ orchid	7.00	10.00	8.00
☐ pink	4.50	7.50	5.50
☐ green	4.50	7.50	5.50
☐ amber	4.00	6.00	4.50

Dinner Plate, 10¼″

☐ blue	25.00	30.00	26.00
☐ orchid	25.00	30.00	26.00
☐ pink	22.00	28.00	23.00
☐ green	22.00	28.00	23.00
☐ amber	18.00	22.00	19.00

Finger Bowl, 4⅝″ × 2″

☐ blue	13.00	17.00	14.00
☐ orchid	13.00	17.00	14.00
☐ pink	11.00	15.00	12.00
☐ green	11.00	15.00	12.00
☐ amber	8.50	11.50	9.50

Fruit Bowl, 5″

☐ blue	7.50	11.50	8.50
☐ orchid	7.50	11.50	8.50
☐ pink	5.00	8.00	6.00
☐ green	5.00	8.00	6.00
☐ amber	5.00	7.00	5.50

Grill Plate, 10¼″

☐ blue	15.00	20.00	16.00
☐ orchid	15.00	20.00	16.00
☐ pink	11.00	14.00	12.00
☐ green	11.00	14.00	12.00
☐ amber	8.50	11.50	9.50

	Current Price Range		Prior Year Average

Ice Bucket, with metal handle

☐ blue	36.00	44.00	38.00
☐ orchid	36.00	44.00	38.00
☐ pink	31.00	39.00	33.00
☐ green	31.00	39.00	33.00
☐ amber	25.00	30.00	26.00

Luncheon Plate, 9½"

☐ blue	7.50	10.50	8.50
☐ orchid	7.50	10.50	8.50
☐ pink	6.50	9.50	7.50
☐ green	6.50	9.50	7.50
☐ amber	6.00	8.00	6.50

Mayonnaise Dish

☐ blue	13.00	17.00	14.00
☐ orchid	13.00	17.00	14.00
☐ pink	9.50	12.50	10.50
☐ green	9.50	12.50	10.50
☐ amber	7.50	10.50	8.50

Mayonnaise Ladle

☐ blue	18.00	22.00	19.00
☐ orchid	18.00	22.00	19.00
☐ pink	13.00	17.00	14.00
☐ green	13.00	17.00	14.00
☐ amber	13.00	17.00	14.00

Oyster Cocktail, footed, 5½ oz.

☐ blue	14.50	18.50	15.50
☐ orchid	14.50	18.50	15.50
☐ pink	12.00	16.00	13.00
☐ green	12.00	16.00	13.00
☐ amber	8.50	11.50	9.50

Parfait, footed, 6½ oz.

☐ blue	15.00	20.00	16.00
☐ orchid	15.00	20.00	16.00
☐ pink	12.00	16.00	13.00
☐ green	12.00	16.00	13.00
☐ amber	11.00	14.00	12.00

Pitcher, footed, 48 oz.

☐ blue	175.00	220.00	180.00
☐ orchid	175.00	220.00	180.00
☐ pink	150.00	190.00	160.00
☐ green	150.00	190.00	160.00
☐ amber	120.00	150.00	127.00

	Current Price Range		Prior Year Average

Platter, oval, 15″

☐ blue	42.00	52.00	45.00
☐ orchid	42.00	52.00	45.00
☐ pink	38.00	46.00	40.00
☐ green	38.00	46.00	40.00
☐ amber	32.00	39.00	33.00

Relish Tray, 2 sections, 8½″

☐ blue	13.00	16.00	14.00
☐ orchid	13.00	16.00	14.00
☐ pink	11.00	14.00	12.00
☐ green	11.00	14.00	12.00
☐ amber	8.50	11.50	9.00

Relish Tray, 3 sections, 11½″

☐ blue	20.00	25.00	21.00
☐ orchid	20.00	25.00	21.00
☐ pink	15.00	20.00	16.00
☐ green	15.00	20.00	16.00
☐ amber	11.00	14.00	12.00

Relish Tray, 3 sections, round

☐ blue	15.00	20.00	16.00
☐ orchid	15.00	20.00	16.00
☐ pink	12.00	15.00	13.00
☐ green	12.00	15.00	13.00
☐ amber	8.50	11.50	9.50

Sauce Boat

☐ blue	31.00	39.00	33.00
☐ orchid	31.00	39.00	33.00
☐ pink	26.00	34.00	28.00
☐ green	26.00	34.00	28.00
☐ amber	23.00	28.00	24.00

Saucer

☐ blue	2.50	4.50	3.00
☐ orchid	2.50	4.50	3.00
☐ pink	1.50	3.50	2.00
☐ green	1.50	3.50	2.00
☐ amber	1.50	3.50	2.00

Sherbet, low, 6 oz.

☐ blue	14.00	17.00	15.00
☐ orchid	14.00	17.00	15.00
☐ pink	12.00	15.00	13.00
☐ green	12.00	15.00	13.00
☐ amber	11.00	14.00	12.00

	Current Price Range		Prior Year Average
Sherbet, tall, 6 oz.			
☐ blue	15.00	20.00	16.00
☐ orchid	15.00	20.00	16.00
☐ pink	12.00	16.00	13.00
☐ green	12.00	16.00	13.00
☐ amber	12.00	16.00	13.00
Soup Bowl			
☐ blue	15.00	20.00	16.00
☐ orchid	15.00	20.00	16.00
☐ pink	13.00	17.00	14.00
☐ green	13.00	17.00	14.00
☐ amber	11.00	14.00	12.00
Sugar, footed			
☐ blue	7.50	10.50	8.50
☐ orchid	7.50	10.50	8.50
☐ pink	6.00	8.00	6.50
☐ green	6.00	8.00	6.50
☐ amber	4.00	6.00	4.50
Tray, handle, 11″			
☐ blue	25.00	30.00	26.00
☐ orchid	25.00	30.00	26.00
☐ pink	20.00	25.00	21.00
☐ green	20.00	25.00	21.00
☐ amber	15.00	20.00	16.00
Tumbler, footed, 12 oz.			
☐ blue	18.00	22.00	19.00
☐ orchid	18.00	22.00	19.00
☐ pink	16.00	20.00	17.00
☐ green	16.00	20.00	17.00
☐ amber	14.00	18.00	15.00
Tumbler, footed, 9 oz.			
☐ blue	15.00	20.00	16.00
☐ orchid	15.00	20.00	16.00
☐ pink	12.00	16.00	13.00
☐ green	12.00	16.00	13.00
☐ amber	10.50	13.50	12.50
Tumbler, footed, 5 oz.			
☐ blue	12.00	16.00	13.00
☐ orchid	12.00	16.00	13.00
☐ pink	9.50	12.50	10.50
☐ green	9.50	12.50	10.50
☐ amber	7.50	10.50	8.50

	Current Price Range		Prior Year Average
Tumbler, footed, 2½ oz.			
☐ blue	12.50	15.50	13.50
☐ orchid...	12.50	15.50	13.50
☐ pink	9.50	12.50	10.50
☐ green	9.50	12.50	10.50
☐ amber	7.50	10.50	8.50
Water Goblet, 10 oz.			
☐ blue	20.00	25.00	21.00
☐ orchid...	20.00	25.00	21.00
☐ pink	16.00	20.00	17.00
☐ green	16.00	20.00	17.00
☐ amber	15.00	18.00	16.00
Wine Goblet, 3 oz.			
☐ blue	25.00	30.00	26.00
☐ orchid...	25.00	30.00	26.00
☐ pink	21.00	25.00	22.00
☐ green	21.00	25.00	22.00
☐ amber	18.00	22.00	19.00

FLANDERS

Tiffin Glass Co.

This pattern was made from the 1920s through to the middle 1930s. Crystal, yellow and pink were the colors made. They are in about equal supply on the market, but pink and yellow are worth about 30% more than the crystal.

	Current Price Range		Prior Year Average
Bon Bon Bowl, two-handled			
☐ crystal	13.00	16.00	14.00
Bowl, console, diameter 12″			
☐ crystal	16.00	20.00	18.00
Candlestick			
☐ crystal	13.00	17.00	15.00
Comport, diameter 3½″			
☐ crystal	12.00	15.00	13.00
Comport, diameter 6″			
☐ crystal	17.00	21.00	19.00
Creamer, footed			
☐ crystal	12.00	16.00	14.00
Oil Bottle and Stopper			
☐ crystal	85.00	100.00	90.00
Plate, diameter 6″			
☐ crystal	4.00	5.25	4.50

	Current Price Range		Prior Year Average

Plate, diameter 7½"
☐ crystal 6.00 8.25 7.00
Plate, dinner, diameter 9½"
☐ crystal 24.00 29.00 26.00
Saucer
☐ crystal 4.00 6.00 5.00
Tumbler, 9 oz., water, footed
☐ crystal 8.00 11.00 9.00
Tumbler, 12 oz., ice tea, footed
☐ crystal 12.00 17.00 13.00

GLORIA
Cambridge Glass Co.

This pattern was manufactured in the 1930s. The colors are crystal, pink, green, amber and heatherbloom (violet). Yellow and crystal are the most common colors.

Basket, two-handled, height 6"
☐ crystal 12.00 16.00 14.00
☐ all colors 16.00 20.00 18.00
Bowl, nut, four-footed, diameter 3"
☐ crystal 17.00 22.00 18.00
☐ all colors 26.00 33.00 30.00
Bowl, bon bon, footed, height 5"
☐ crystal 13.00 17.00 15.00
☐ all colors 22.00 26.00 24.00
Bowl, fruit, square, diameter 5"
☐ crystal 7.00 10.00 8.00
☐ all colors 11.00 16.00 14.00
Bowl, cereal, two styles, diameter 6"
☐ crystal 8.00 13.00 10.00
☐ all colors 12.00 17.00 14.00
Bowl, relish, either two- or three-handled, diameter 8"
☐ crystal 16.00 20.00 18.00
☐ all colors 24.00 30.00 27.00
Bowl, diameter 10"
☐ crystal 23.00 28.00 26.00
☐ all colors 35.00 45.00 40.00
Bowl, fruit, diameter 12"
☐ crystal 25.00 30.00 27.00
☐ all colors 35.00 42.00 37.00

	Current Price Range		Prior Year Average
Bowl, four-footed, console, diameter 12″			
☐ crystal...	20.00	25.00	22.00
☐ all colors...	34.00	42.00	36.00
Bowl, oval, four-footed, diameter 12″			
☐ crystal...	30.00	36.00	34.00
☐ all colors...	45.00	55.00	50.00
Bowl, flared rim, diameter 13″			
☐ crystal...	25.00	30.00	27.00
☐ all colors...	40.00	50.00	45.00
Candlestick, height 6″, pair			
☐ crystal...	30.00	40.00	35.00
☐ all colors...	50.00	65.00	55.00
Candy Box, with cover, four-footed, tab-handled			
☐ crystal...	35.00	42.00	38.00
☐ all colors...	60.00	70.00	65.00
Comport, cocktail, diameter 4″			
☐ crystal...	8.00	12.00	9.00
☐ all colors...	13.00	18.00	15.00
Comport, four-footed, diameter 5″			
☐ crystal...	12.00	16.00	13.50
☐ all colors...	25.00	32.00	28.00
Comport, diameter 7″			
☐ crystal...	25.00	32.00	28.00
☐ all colors...	45.00	60.00	53.00
Creamer, footed			
☐ crystal...	9.00	12.00	10.00
☐ all colors...	14.00	19.00	16.00
Cup, three styles			
☐ crystal...	13.00	17.00	15.00
☐ all colors...	20.00	26.00	24.00
Fruit Cocktail, footed, three styles, 6 oz.			
☐ crystal...	10.00	15.00	12.00
☐ all colors...	14.00	18.00	16.00
Plate, two-handled, diameter 6″			
☐ crystal...	6.00	10.00	8.00
☐ all colors...	12.00	15.00	13.00
Plate, bread and butter, diameter 6″			
☐ crystal...	6.00	9.00	7.00
☐ all colors...	9.00	12.00	10.00
Plate, diameter 7″			
☐ crystal...	7.00	10.00	8.00
☐ all colors...	10.00	13.00	11.00

	Current Price Range		Prior Year Average
Plate, diameter 8½"			
☐ crystal	7.00	10.00	8.00
☐ all colors	10.00	13.00	11.00
Plate, dinner, diameter 9½"			
☐ crystal	26.00	34.00	30.00
☐ all colors	40.00	50.00	45.00
Plate, salad, tab-handled, diameter 10"			
☐ crystal	15.00	20.00	17.00
☐ all colors	20.00	26.00	23.00
Plate, two-handled, diameter 11"			
☐ crystal	15.00	17.00	19.00
☐ all colors	21.00	26.00	23.00
Plate, sandwich, diameter 11¼"			
☐ crystal	15.00	20.00	17.50
☐ all colors	26.00	31.00	28.00
Plate, chop, diameter 14"			
☐ crystal	30.00	40.00	35.00
☐ all colors	45.00	55.00	45.00
Plate, square, dinner			
☐ crystal	26.00	34.00	29.00
☐ all colors	40.00	45.00	43.00
Salt and Pepper Shakers, pair			
☐ crystal	24.00	30.00	27.00
☐ all colors	30.00	40.00	35.00
Saucer, two styles			
☐ crystal	4.00	6.00	5.00
☐ all colors	5.00	7.00	6.00
Sugar, footed			
☐ crystal	7.00	10.00	8.00
☐ all colors	9.00	14.00	11.50
Tray, either two or four partitions, relish			
☐ crystal	24.00	28.00	26.00
☐ all colors	35.00	44.00	39.00
Tumbler, 2½", footed			
☐ crystal	11.00	17.00	14.00
☐ all colors	14.00	20.00	17.00
Tumbler, 5 oz., footed			
☐ crystal	9.00	14.00	11.00
☐ all colors	14.00	20.00	17.00
Tumbler, 5 oz., juice, footed			
☐ crystal	10.00	15.00	12.00
☐ all colors	15.00	20.00	17.50
Tumbler, 8 oz., footed			
☐ crystal	10.00	15.00	12.00
☐ all colors	15.00	20.00	17.50

	Current Price Range		Prior Year Average
Tumbler, 10 oz., footed, three styles			
□ crystal	10.00	15.00	12.00
□ all colors..	15.00	20.00	17.50
Tumbler, 10 oz., water			
□ crystal	10.00	15.00	12.00
□ all colors..	15.00	20.00	17.50
Tumbler, 12 oz., footed, three styles			
□ crystal	12.00	17.00	14.50
□ all colors..	18.00	23.00	20.50
Vase, oval, four indentations, height 9″			
□ crystal	34.00	42.00	38.00
□ all colors..	70.00	80.00	75.00
Vase, height 10″			
□ crystal	32.00	40.00	36.00
□ all colors..	60.00	70.00	65.00
Vase, height 11″			
□ crystal	30.00	37.00	34.00
□ all colors..	55.00	65.00	60.00
Vase, height 12″, two styles			
□ crystal	36.00	44.00	40.00
□ all colors..	62.00	70.00	66.00
Vase, height 14″			
□ crystal	40.00	50.00	44.00
□ all colors..	80.00	87.00	84.00

GREEK KEY
A.H. Heisey & Co.

Greek Key was mostly made in crystal, though some pink punch bowls were also made.

Greek Key

	Current Price Range		Prior Year Average
Almond Bowl, footed, 5″			
☐ crystal	26.00	34.00	28.00
Banana Split Dish, flat, 9″			
☐ crystal	15.00	19.00	16.00
Bowl, low-footed, shallow, 10″			
☐ crystal	39.00	46.00	41.00
Bowl, low-footed, straight sides, 7″			
☐ crystal	26.00	34.00	28.00
Bowl, low-footed, straight sides, 9″			
☐ crystal	36.00	44.00	38.00
Burgundy Goblet, 3½ oz.			
☐ crystal	78.00	93.00	80.00
Candy Jar, with lid, ½ lb.			
☐ crystal	88.00	103.00	92.00
Celery Tray, oval, 9″			
☐ crystal	13.00	17.00	14.00
Cheese and Cracker Set, 10″			
☐ crystal	45.00	55.00	47.00
Claret Goblet, 4½ oz.			
☐ crystal	73.00	87.00	75.00
Cocktail, 3 oz.			
☐ crystal	15.00	19.00	16.00
Compote, 5″			
☐ crystal	45.00	55.00	47.00
Cordial Goblet, ¾ oz.			
☐ crystal	120.00	150.00	130.00

	Current Price Range		Prior Year Average
Creamer			
☐ crystal	22.00	28.00	23.00
Egg Cup, 5 oz.			
☐ crystal	41.00	49.00	43.00
Finger Bowl			
☐ crystal	12.00	16.00	13.00
Goblet, 7 oz.			
☐ crystal	45.00	55.00	47.00
Goblet, 9 oz.			
☐ crystal	53.00	67.00	56.00
Hair Receiver			
☐ crystal	47.00	56.00	49.00
Horseradish Jar, with lid, large			
☐ crystal	60.00	70.00	62.00
Ice Bucket, tab handles, large			
☐ crystal	55.00	65.00	58.00
Jelly Bowl, handle, 5″			
☐ crystal	26.00	34.00	28.00
Nappy, 4″			
☐ crystal	6.50	9.50	7.50
Nappy, scalloped, 8″			
☐ crystal	34.00	43.00	36.00
Nappy, shallow, 6″			
☐ crystal	20.00	25.00	21.00
Nappy, shallow, 11″			
☐ crystal	39.00	46.00	41.00
Pickle Jar, with lid			
☐ crystal	72.00	87.00	75.00
Pitcher, 1 pint			
☐ crystal	45.00	55.00	47.00
Pitcher, 3 pints			
☐ crystal	62.00	77.00	65.00
Plate, 4½″			
☐ crystal	8.50	11.50	9.50
Plate, 5½″			
☐ crystal	9.50	12.50	10.50
Plate, 6½″			
☐ crystal	10.00	14.00	11.00
Plate, 7″			
☐ crystal	11.00	15.00	12.00
Plate, 8″			
☐ crystal	13.00	17.00	14.00
Plate, 9″			
☐ crystal	18.00	22.00	19.00

	Current Price Range		Prior Year Average
Plate, 10″			
☐ crystal...	40.00	50.00	42.00
Punch Bowl, footed, 12″			
☐ crystal...	130.00	170.00	140.00
☐ pink..	620.00	680.00	635.00
Punch Bowl, footed, 15″			
☐ crystal...	90.00	125.00	97.00
Punch Cup, 4½ oz.			
☐ crystal...	16.00	20.00	17.00
☐ pink..	26.00	34.00	28.00
Salt and Pepper			
☐ crystal...	45.00	55.00	47.00
Sherbet, footed, flared rim, 4½ oz.			
☐ crystal...	8.50	11.50	9.50
Sherbet, footed, straight rim, 4½ oz.			
☐ crystal...	8.50	11.50	9.50
Sherbet, low-footed, 6 oz.			
☐ crystal...	9.50	12.50	10.50
Sherry Goblet			
☐ crystal...	100.00	130.00	110.00
Sugar			
☐ crystal...	22.00	28.00	23.00
Tankard, 1 pint			
☐ crystal...	45.00	55.00	47.00
Tumbler, flared or straight side, 5 oz.			
☐ crystal...	13.00	17.00	14.00
Tumbler, flared or straight side, 7 oz.			
☐ crystal...	19.00	23.00	20.00
Tumbler, flared or straight side, 10 oz.			
☐ crystal...	25.00	30.00	26.00
Tumbler, flared or straight side, 12 oz.			
☐ crystal...	26.00	31.00	27.00
Tumbler, flared or straight side, 13 oz.			
☐ crystal...	26.00	34.00	28.00
Water Tumbler, 5½ oz.			
☐ crystal...	14.00	18.00	15.00
Wine Goblet, 2 oz.			
☐ crystal...	105.00	140.00	110.00

IPSWICH
A.H. Heisey & Co.

This distinctive pattern was produced on blank No. 1405 in crystal, green (moongleam), pink (flamingo), yellow (sahara), cobalt and alexandrite.

Ipswich

	Current Price Range		Prior Year Average
Bowl, footed, floral, diameter 11″			
☐ crystal	35.00	42.00	37.00
☐ cobalt	325.00	400.00	350.00
☐ sahara	160.00	210.00	175.00
Candlestick, height 6″			
☐ crystal	150.00	175.00	160.00
☐ green	175.00	215.00	190.00
☐ pink	175.00	215.00	190.00
☐ yellow	175.00	215.00	190.00
Candy Jar, with lid			
☐ crystal	40.00	50.00	43.00
☐ green	240.00	260.00	245.00
☐ pink	220.00	260.00	240.00
☐ yellow	190.00	210.00	195.00
Champagne Goblet, 5 oz.			
☐ crystal	9.00	11.00	9.50
Cocktail Goblet, 4 oz.			
☐ crystal	9.00	11.00	9.50
Cocktail Shaker, with strainer and stopper			
☐ crystal	140.00	160.00	145.00
☐ green	440.00	460.00	445.00
☐ pink	240.00	260.00	245.00
☐ yellow	340.00	360.00	345.00

	Current Price Range		Prior Year Average

Creamer
☐ crystal	15.00	20.00	17.00
☐ green	30.00	40.00	32.50
☐ pink	30.00	40.00	33.00
☐ yellow	30.00	40.00	33.00

Cruet, with stopper, footed, 2 oz.
☐ crystal	55.00	65.00	58.00
☐ green	110.00	140.00	120.00
☐ pink	110.00	140.00	120.00
☐ yellow	110.00	140.00	120.00

Finger Bowl, with underplate
☐ crystal	14.00	16.00	14.50
☐ green	40.00	45.00	42.00
☐ pink	40.00	45.00	42.00
☐ yellow	35.00	42.00	37.00

Goblet, 10 oz.
☐ crystal	14.00	16.00	14.50

Iced Tea, footed, 12 oz.
☐ crystal	24.00	26.00	24.50

Pitcher, 64 oz.
☐ crystal	90.00	110.00	95.00
☐ green	400.00	450.00	415.00
☐ pink	240.00	280.00	250.00
☐ yellow	240.00	280.00	250.00

Plate, square, diameter 7″
☐ crystal	13.00	16.00	13.50
☐ green	24.00	30.00	25.00
☐ pink	18.00	25.00	19.50
☐ yellow	20.00	28.00	21.50

Plate, square, diameter 8″
☐ crystal	15.00	20.00	17.50
☐ green	30.00	35.00	32.00
☐ pink	30.00	35.00	32.00
☐ yellow	30.00	35.00	32.00

Sherbet, 4 oz.
☐ crystal	8.00	10.00	7.50
☐ green	18.00	25.00	19.50
☐ pink	18.00	25.00	16.00
☐ yellow	18.00	25.00	19.50

Sugar Bowl
☐ crystal	15.00	20.00	16.50
☐ green	28.00	35.00	29.50
☐ pink	25.00	30.00	25.00
☐ yellow	34.00	40.00	35.00

	Current Price Range		Prior Year Average
Tumbler, curved rim, 10 oz.			
☐ crystal	8.00	12.00	9.50
☐ green	28.00	35.00	30.00
☐ pink	24.00	30.00	25.00
☐ yellow	27.00	35.00	28.00
Tumbler, footed, 5 oz.			
☐ crystal	8.00	10.00	8.00
☐ green	24.00	30.00	25.00
☐ pink	14.00	20.00	15.00
☐ yellow	19.00	25.00	20.00
Tumbler, footed, 8 oz.			
☐ crystal	8.00	12.00	9.00
☐ green	20.00	26.00	21.50
☐ pink	15.00	20.00	16.00
☐ yellow	20.00	26.00	22.00
Tumbler, footed, 12 oz.			
☐ crystal	10.00	15.00	11.00
☐ green	38.00	45.00	40.00
☐ pink	28.00	35.00	30.00
☐ yellow	35.00	40.00	36.00

JUNE
Fostoria Glass Co.

This pattern was manufactured from 1928 through 1944. The colors that were released were blue, yellow, pink and crystal. Blue is the most popular color, with pink second. The most popular pieces to own are the dinner plates, pitcher, cordials, 7″ soup bowl, and footed oils. This is probably the most popular of all Fostoria's patterns. Such collector interest often breeds reproductions and *June* is no exception. Stemware in all colors have been reported but they are not difficult to spot. The most obvious difference is that the new pieces have a lot more glass in the bottom of the bowl. There is also a second, less obvious difference and that is that the old pieces have three-piece stems (foot, stem and bowl) while the new pieces have two-piece stems (foot and stem together, then the bowl).

Ashtray

☐ yellow	27.00	34.00	32.00
☐ pink	27.00	34.00	32.00
☐ blue	27.00	34.00	32.00
☐ crystal	20.00	25.00	22.00

	Current Price Range		Prior Year Average

Baking Dish, egg shape, length 9″

☐ yellow	70.00	80.00	72.50
☐ pink	40.00	45.00	42.00
☐ blue	50.00	60.00	55.00
☐ crystal	30.00	35.00	32.00

Bon Bon, stemmed

☐ yellow	20.00	25.00	22.00
☐ pink	15.00	20.00	17.00
☐ blue	18.00	22.00	19.00
☐ crystal	10.00	14.00	11.00

Bouillon Bowl, pedestal foot with underplate

☐ pink	20.00	25.00	22.00
☐ yellow	20.00	25.00	22.00
☐ crystal	10.00	14.00	11.00
☐ blue	33.00	36.00	34.00

Bowl, diameter 10″

☐ yellow	33.00	38.00	34.00
☐ pink	38.00	43.00	39.00
☐ blue	48.00	53.00	49.00
☐ crystal	22.00	28.00	24.00

Bread and Butter Plate, diameter 6″

☐ yellow	5.00	7.00	6.00
☐ pink	5.00	7.00	6.00
☐ blue	6.00	8.00	7.00
☐ crystal	4.00	6.00	5.00

Cake Plate, handled, diameter 10″

☐ yellow	33.00	38.00	34.00
☐ pink	35.00	40.00	37.00
☐ blue	43.00	48.00	46.00
☐ crystal	23.00	28.00	24.00

Canape Plate

☐ yellow	12.00	15.00	13.00
☐ pink	12.00	15.00	13.00
☐ blue	14.00	16.00	15.00
☐ crystal	8.00	10.00	9.00

Candlesticks, pair, height 2″

☐ yellow	33.00	38.00	34.00
☐ pink	35.00	40.00	37.00
☐ blue	40.00	45.00	42.00
☐ crystal	28.00	33.00	29.00

	Current Price Range		Prior Year Average

Candlesticks, pair, height 3″

☐ yellow...	35.00	40.00	37.00
☐ pink	38.00	43.00	39.00
☐ blue	45.00	50.00	46.00
☐ crystal	30.00	35.00	32.00

Candlesticks, pair, height 5″

☐ yellow...	40.00	45.00	42.00
☐ pink	45.00	50.00	47.00
☐ blue	55.00	60.00	56.50

Candy Jar, with lid, capacity two cups

☐ yellow...	95.00	110.00	97.50
☐ pink	105.00	115.00	107.50
☐ blue	145.00	155.00	147.50
☐ crystal	63.00	68.00	64.50

Candy Jar, with lid, capacity six cups

☐ yellow...	70.00	90.00	75.00
☐ pink	145.00	155.00	147.50
☐ blue	145.00	155.00	147.50
☐ crystal	40.00	50.00	45.00

Celery Dish, length 11″

☐ yellow...	33.00	37.00	34.00
☐ pink	33.00	38.00	34.00
☐ blue	38.00	43.00	40.00
☐ crystal	20.00	25.00	22.00

Centerpiece Bowl, oval, length 11″

☐ yellow...	30.00	50.00	32.00
☐ pink	40.00	50.00	42.00
☐ blue	40.00	50.00	42.00
☐ crystal	20.00	25.00	22.00

Cereal Bowl, diameter 6″

☐ yellow...	25.00	30.00	27.00
☐ pink	20.00	25.00	22.00
☐ blue	23.00	27.00	24.50
☐ crystal	14.00	16.00	15.00

Cheese and Cracker Set

☐ yellow...	30.00	35.00	32.00
☐ pink	40.00	44.00	42.00
☐ blue	40.00	44.00	42.00
☐ crystal	20.00	25.00	22.00

Chop Plate, diameter 12″

☐ yellow...	35.00	40.00	37.00
☐ pink	35.00	40.00	37.00
☐ blue	40.00	45.00	42.00
☐ crystal	20.00	25.00	22.00

	Current Price Range		Prior Year Average
Comport, diameter 5″			
☐ yellow	22.00	38.00	23.00
☐ pink	30.00	34.00	30.00
☐ blue	30.00	34.00	30.00
☐ crystal	30.00	34.00	29.50
Comport, diameter 6″			
☐ yellow	50.00	60.00	53.00
☐ pink	55.00	65.00	58.00
☐ blue	65.00	75.00	68.00
☐ crystal	38.00	43.00	39.50
Comport, diameter 7″			
☐ yellow	55.00	65.00	58.00
☐ pink	60.00	70.00	63.00
☐ blue	80.00	90.00	83.50
☐ crystal	43.00	48.00	44.00
Comport, diameter 8″			
☐ yellow	65.00	75.00	67.50
☐ pink	70.00	80.00	73.50
☐ blue	90.00	100.00	94.50
☐ crystal	57.00	63.00	58.50
Condiment Bottle, footed, with stopper			
☐ yellow	240.00	260.00	245.00
☐ pink	290.00	310.00	295.00
☐ blue	370.00	380.00	372.00
☐ crystal	145.00	155.00	148.00
Cordial Cup			
☐ yellow	30.00	35.00	32.00
☐ pink	38.00	43.00	39.50
☐ blue	45.00	55.00	48.50
☐ crystal	20.00	25.00	22.00
Cordial Cup Saucer			
☐ yellow	8.00	10.00	8.50
☐ pink	9.00	11.00	9.50
☐ blue	11.00	14.00	12.00
☐ crystal	6.00	8.00	7.00
Cordial Glass, stemmed			
☐ yellow	62.00	68.00	63.00
☐ pink	55.00	65.00	58.00
☐ blue	68.00	73.00	69.00
☐ crystal	30.00	40.00	35.00
Creamer, collar base			
☐ yellow	23.00	28.00	24.00
☐ pink	28.00	33.00	29.50
☐ blue	33.00	38.00	34.00
☐ crystal	20.00	25.00	22.00

	Current Price Range		Prior Year Average
Creamer, pedestal foot			
☐ yellow..	16.00	18.00	17.00
☐ pink	16.00	18.00	17.00
☐ blue	20.00	22.00	21.00
☐ crystal	16.00	18.00	16.50
Cup, pedestal foot			
☐ yellow..	20.00	22.00	21.00
☐ pink	20.00	25.00	22.00
☐ blue	25.00	30.00	26.00
☐ crystal	14.00	16.00	14.50
Decanter, with glass stopper			
☐ yellow..	390.00	410.00	395.00
☐ pink	440.00	460.00	445.00
☐ blue	490.00	510.00	495.00
☐ crystal	290.00	310.00	295.00
Dessert Bowl, handled, diameter 8″			
☐ yellow..	45.00	55.00	48.00
☐ pink	55.00	65.00	59.00
☐ blue	60.00	70.00	64.00
☐ crystal	38.00	43.00	39.00
Dinner Plate, diameter 9″			
☐ yellow..	20.00	25.00	22.00
☐ pink	14.00	16.00	15.00
☐ blue	16.00	18.00	17.00
☐ crystal	11.00	14.00	11.50
Dinner Plate, diameter 10¼″			
☐ yellow..	33.00	38.00	34.00
☐ pink	35.00	40.00	37.00
☐ blue	40.00	50.00	43.00
☐ crystal	23.00	28.00	24.00
Fan Vase, pedestal foot			
☐ yellow..	90.00	100.00	94.00
☐ pink	95.00	105.00	98.00
☐ blue	120.00	130.00	124.00
☐ crystal	70.00	80.00	74.00
Fruit Bowl			
☐ yellow..	23.00	28.00	24.00
☐ pink	23.00	28.00	24.00
☐ blue	30.00	38.00	32.50
☐ crystal	15.00	20.00	17.00
Fruit Bowl, diameter 5″			
☐ yellow..	17.00	20.00	18.00
☐ pink	15.00	20.00	16.00
☐ blue	20.00	25.00	22.00
☐ crystal	11.00	13.00	11.50

	Current Price Range		Prior Year Average

Grapefruit Bowl, footed, with liner

☐ yellow	65.00	75.00	68.00
☐ pink	75.00	85.00	78.00
☐ blue	70.00	75.00	71.50
☐ crystal	45.00	55.00	46.00

Gravy Boat

☐ yellow	95.00	105.00	98.00
☐ pink	95.00	105.00	98.00
☐ blue	140.00	160.00	145.00
☐ crystal	70.00	80.00	72.50

Gravy Boat Platter

☐ yellow	23.00	28.00	24.00
☐ pink	23.00	28.00	24.00
☐ blue	45.00	55.00	48.00
☐ crystal	15.00	20.00	17.00

Grecian Bowl, diameter 10″

☐ yellow	43.00	48.00	44.00
☐ pink	45.00	55.00	48.00
☐ blue	55.00	65.00	58.00

Grecian Candlesticks, pair, height 3″

☐ yellow	38.00	43.00	39.50
☐ pink	40.00	45.00	42.00
☐ blue	45.00	55.00	48.00

Grill Plate, diameter 10″

☐ yellow	25.00	30.00	27.00
☐ pink	25.00	30.00	27.00
☐ blue	30.00	40.00	32.00
☐ crystal	16.00	18.00	17.00

Ice Bowl

☐ yellow	30.00	40.00	32.00
☐ pink	30.00	40.00	32.00
☐ blue	40.00	45.00	42.00
☐ crystal	20.00	25.00	22.00

Ice Bucket, with metal handle

☐ yellow	70.00	80.00	75.00
☐ pink	80.00	90.00	84.00
☐ blue	90.00	100.00	94.00
☐ crystal	60.00	70.00	63.00

Iced Tea Glass, height 8″

☐ yellow	23.00	26.00	23.50
☐ pink	20.00	25.00	22.00
☐ blue	27.00	31.00	28.00
☐ crystal	13.00	15.00	13.50

	Current Price Range		Prior Year Average

Lemon Dish

☐ yellow	18.00	22.00	19.00
☐ pink	18.00	22.00	19.00
☐ blue	20.00	24.00	21.00
☐ crystal	14.00	16.00	15.00

Lunch Plate, diameter 8¾"

☐ yellow	11.00	14.00	11.50
☐ pink	15.00	20.00	16.50
☐ blue	18.00	23.00	19.00
☐ crystal	9.00	11.00	9.50

Mayonnaise Compote

☐ yellow	30.00	35.00	32.50
☐ pink	35.00	40.00	37.00
☐ blue	45.00	50.00	47.00
☐ crystal	25.00	35.00	28.00

Mint Dish

☐ yellow	20.00	25.00	22.00
☐ pink	23.00	28.00	24.00
☐ blue	27.00	33.00	28.00
☐ crystal	14.00	18.00	15.00

Nappy, flat, diameter 7"

☐ yellow	15.00	20.00	16.00
☐ pink	15.00	20.00	16.00
☐ blue	18.00	20.00	19.00
☐ crystal	10.00	14.00	11.00

Nappy, pedestal foot, diameter 6¼"

☐ yellow	15.00	20.00	16.00
☐ pink	15.00	20.00	16.00
☐ blue	18.00	20.00	19.00
☐ crystal	10.00	14.00	11.00

Oil Cruet, pedestal foot

☐ yellow	280.00	320.00	290.00
☐ pink	340.00	360.00	345.00
☐ blue	420.00	430.00	425.00
☐ crystal	140.00	160.00	150.00

Oyster Plate

☐ yellow	20.00	24.00	22.00
☐ pink	20.00	24.00	22.00
☐ blue	28.00	32.00	30.00
☐ crystal	20.00	26.00	22.50

Parfait Glass

☐ yellow	40.00	45.00	42.00
☐ pink	24.00	28.00	25.00
☐ blue	30.00	35.00	32.00
☐ crystal	18.00	20.00	19.00

	Current Price Range		Prior Year Average

Pitcher
☐ yellow..	340.00	360.00	345.00
☐ pink...	340.00	360.00	345.00
☐ blue	465.00	485.00	470.00

Platter, diameter 11″
☐ yellow..	40.00	45.00	42.00
☐ pink	43.00	48.00	44.00
☐ blue	45.00	55.00	48.00
☐ crystal	30.00	40.00	34.00

Platter, diameter 15″
☐ yellow..	85.00	95.00	87.00
☐ pink	95.00	105.00	97.00
☐ blue	115.00	135.00	120.00
☐ crystal	55.00	65.00	58.00

Relish Dish, two compartments, length 8¼″
☐ yellow..	20.00	24.00	21.50
☐ pink	25.00	30.00	26.00
☐ blue	25.00	30.00	26.00
☐ crystal	14.00	16.00	15.00

Salad Plate, diameter 7½″
☐ yellow..	8.00	10.00	8.50
☐ pink	8.00	12.00	9.00
☐ blue	10.00	14.00	11.00
☐ crystal	5.00	7.00	6.00

Salt and Pepper Shakers, pair
☐ yellow..	115.00	125.00	117.50
☐ pink	120.00	130.00	125.00
☐ blue	130.00	140.00	132.00
☐ crystal	85.00	95.00	87.50

Saucer
☐ yellow..	5.00	6.00	5.50
☐ pink	5.00	6.00	5.50
☐ blue	7.00	9.00	7.50
☐ crystal	3.00	5.00	3.50

Sherbet Dish, collar base
☐ yellow..	19.00	23.00	20.00
☐ pink	14.00	16.00	15.00
☐ blue	22.00	26.00	23.00
☐ crystal	11.00	13.00	11.50

Sherbet Dish, long stem
☐ yellow..	14.00	16.00	14.50
☐ pink	25.00	30.00	27.00
☐ blue	30.00	34.00	31.50
☐ crystal	28.00	32.00	29.50

	Current Price Range		Prior Year Average

Sherry Glass

☐ yellow...	20.00	24.00	21.50
☐ pink	30.00	35.00	32.00
☐ blue	60.00	68.00	63.00
☐ crystal	25.00	30.00	36.00

Soup Bowl, diameter 7″

☐ yellow...	33.00	38.00	34.00
☐ pink	35.00	40.00	37.00
☐ blue	42.00	48.00	43.00
☐ crystal	28.00	33.00	29.00

Soup Bowl, pedestal foot

☐ yellow...	16.00	18.00	17.00
☐ pink	16.00	18.00	17.00
☐ blue	18.00	20.00	19.00
☐ crystal	12.00	14.00	13.00

Soup Plate, diameter 7″

☐ yellow...	20.00	25.00	22.00
☐ pink	20.00	25.00	22.00
☐ blue	25.00	30.00	26.00
☐ crystal	14.00	16.00	15.00

Sugar Bowl, large, with lid

☐ yellow...	110.00	120.00	112.00
☐ pink	120.00	130.00	122.00
☐ blue	140.00	160.00	145.00
☐ crystal	65.00	85.00	70.00

Sugar Bowl, small, with lid

☐ yellow...	20.00	25.00	22.00
☐ pink	25.00	30.00	27.00
☐ blue	33.00	38.00	34.00
☐ crystal	20.00	25.00	22.00

Tray, loop handle, diameter 11″

☐ yellow...	33.00	38.00	34.00
☐ pink	38.00	43.00	39.50
☐ blue	45.00	55.00	49.50
☐ crystal	25.00	30.00	27.50

Tumbler, height 3½″

☐ yellow...	30.00	35.00	32.00
☐ pink	30.00	35.00	32.00
☐ blue	35.00	40.00	36.00
☐ crystal	20.00	30.00	22.00

Tumbler, height 5″

☐ yellow...	20.00	30.00	22.00
☐ pink	20.00	30.00	22.00
☐ blue	25.00	30.00	26.00
☐ crystal	14.00	16.00	15.00

	Current Price Range		Prior Year Average
Vase, height 7½"			
☐ yellow..	95.00	100.00	97.50
☐ pink...	95.00	100.00	97.50
☐ blue...	185.00	205.00	187.50
☐ crystal...	30.00	40.00	35.00
Water Glass, stemmed			
☐ yellow..	20.00	30.00	22.50
☐ pink...	30.00	35.00	32.00
☐ blue...	28.00	33.00	29.50
☐ crystal...	18.00	22.00	19.50
Whipped Cream Bowl, large			
☐ yellow..	110.00	120.00	112.00
☐ pink...	123.00	128.00	124.00
☐ blue...	140.00	160.00	145.00
☐ crystal...	65.00	85.00	70.00
Whipped Cream Bowl, small			
☐ yellow..	18.00	22.00	19.00
☐ pink...	20.00	25.00	22.00
☐ blue...	23.00	28.00	24.00
☐ crystal...	15.00	20.00	17.00
Whiskey Tumbler, shot, 2½ oz.			
☐ yellow..	30.00	35.00	32.00
☐ blue...	30.00	35.00	32.00
☐ pink...	40.00	45.00	41.50
☐ crystal...	20.00	25.00	22.00
Wine Glass, stemmed			
☐ yellow..	40.00	45.00	42.00
☐ pink...	35.00	40.00	37.00
☐ blue...	45.00	50.00	47.00
☐ crystal...	19.00	23.00	20.00

LARIAT
A.H. Heisey & Co.

This pattern was produced on blank No. 31540 and was made in crystal. Six black 8" plates are known to exist, but they were experimental.

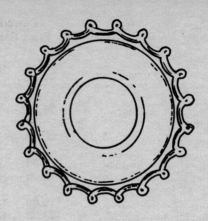

Lariat

	Current Price Range		Prior Year Average
Ashtray, 4″			
☐ crystal	5.00	10.00	6.00
Basket, 7½″			
☐ crystal	58.00	65.00	60.00
Basket, footed, 8½″			
☐ crystal	95.00	120.00	100.00
Basket, footed, 10″			
☐ crystal	125.00	135.00	125.00
Bowl, 4″			
☐ crystal	13.00	20.00	14.00
Bowl, flat, 8″			
☐ crystal	12.00	16.00	12.50
Buffet Plate, 21″			
☐ crystal	33.00	43.00	34.00
Cake Plate, rolled edge, 12″			
☐ crystal	18.00	25.00	19.50
Camellia Bowl, 9½″			
☐ crystal	14.00	20.00	15.00
Candlestick, one candle			
☐ crystal	10.00	12.00	10.00
Candlestick, two candles			
☐ crystal	18.00	26.00	20.00
Candlestick, three candles			
☐ crystal	60.00	70.00	64.00
Candy Box, covered			
☐ crystal	28.00	35.00	29.00

	Current Price Range		Prior Year Average

Candy Dish, covered, 7″
☐ crystal 28.00 40.00 30.00
Celery Bowl, handled, 10″
☐ crystal 24.00 30.00 25.00
Celery Bowl, 13″
☐ crystal 18.00 25.00 19.00
Champagne, blown, 5½ oz.
☐ crystal 8.00 12.00 8.50
Cheese Dish, covered and footed, 5″
☐ crystal 23.00 32.00 24.00
Cheese Dish, covered and footed, 8″
☐ crystal 33.00 42.00 34.00
Cigarette Box
☐ crystal 18.00 25.00 19.50
Claret Goblet, blown, 4 oz.
☐ crystal 9.00 14.00 9.50
Coaster, 4″
☐ crystal 6.00 11.00 7.00
Cocktail Goblet, blown, 3½ oz.
☐ crystal 8.00 11.00 7.50
Cocktail Goblet, 3½ oz.
☐ crystal 8.00 11.00 7.75
Compote, covered, 10″
☐ crystal 45.00 60.00 48.00
Cookie Plate, 11″
☐ crystal 20.00 27.00 21.00
Cordial, 1 oz., 2 loops
☐ crystal 125.00 135.00 128.00
Cordial, blown, 1 oz., 1 loop
☐ crystal 88.00 100.00 90.00
Creamer
☐ crystal 9.00 13.00 10.00
Creamer and Sugar Set, with tray
☐ crystal 40.00 50.00 42.00
Cruet, with handle and stopper, 4 oz.
☐ crystal 70.00 82.00 73.00
Cup
☐ crystal 9.00 12.00 9.50
Deviled Egg Plate, 13″
☐ crystal 110.00 125.00 112.00
Flower Bowl, oval, 13″
☐ crystal 23.00 30.00 24.00
Fruit Bowl, 12″
☐ crystal 15.00 20.00 15.00

	Current Price Range		Prior Year Average

Gardenia Bowl, 13″
☐ crystal .... 18.00 | 25.00 | 19.00

Goblet, 9 oz.
☐ crystal .... 10.00 | 14.00 | 11.00

Goblet, blown, 10 oz.
☐ crystal .... 12.00 | 16.00 | 12.50

Ice Tub
☐ crystal .... 48.00 | 58.00 | 50.00

Iced Tea Tumbler, footed, 12 oz.
☐ crystal .... 11.00 | 18.00 | 12.00

Iced Tea Tumbler, footed, blown, 12 oz.
☐ crystal .... 12.00 | 19.00 | 13.00

Jar, with lid, 12″
☐ crystal .... 90.00 | 105.00 | 95.00

Juice Tumbler, footed, 5 oz.
☐ crystal .... 8.00 | 11.00 | 8.00

Juice Tumbler, footed, blown, 5 oz.
☐ crystal .... 8.00 | 11.00 | 8.00

Mayonnaise Bowl, with underplate
☐ crystal .... 28.00 | 38.00 | 30.00

Nappy, 7″
☐ crystal .... 12.00 | 16.00 | 12.50

Oyster Cocktail, 4¼ oz.
☐ crystal .... 8.00 | 10.00 | 7.50

Oyster Cocktail, blown, 4½ oz.
☐ crystal .... 8.00 | 10.00 | 7.50

Platter, oval, 15″
☐ crystal .... 20.00 | 30.00 | 25.00

Punch Bowl
☐ crystal .... 58.00 | 70.00 | 60.00

Punch Cup
☐ crystal .... 3.00 | 6.00 | 4.00

Relish Bowl, divided, 7″
☐ crystal .... 18.00 | 24.00 | 20.00

Relish Bowl, two handles, 11″
☐ crystal .... 15.00 | 23.00 | 16.00

Salad Bowl, 10½″
☐ crystal .... 25.00 | 30.00 | 25.00

Salad Bowl, two handles, 10½″
☐ crystal .... 23.00 | 33.00 | 25.00

Salad Plate, 7″
☐ crystal .... 5.00 | 12.00 | 6.00

Salad Plate, 8″
☐ crystal .... 8.00 | 12.00 | 9.00
☐ black (six known) .... 750.00 | 1000.00 | 800.00

	Current Price Range		Prior Year Average
Salt and Pepper Shakers, pair			
☐ crystal	140.00	160.00	145.00
Sandwich Plate, two handles, 14″			
☐ crystal	28.00	38.00	30.00
Saucer			
☐ crystal	4.00	7.00	5.00
Sherbet, low, 6 oz.			
☐ crystal	7.00	10.00	7.00
Sherbet/Champagne Goblet, 6 oz.			
☐ crystal	6.00	11.00	6.50
Sugar Bowl			
☐ crystal	9.00	14.00	10.00
Tray, for sugar and creamer			
☐ crystal	11.00	16.00	12.00
Vase, fan-shaped, footed, 7″			
☐ crystal	23.00	33.00	25.00
Wine Goblet, blown, 2½ oz.			
☐ crystal	15.00	23.00	16.00
Wine Goblet, 3½ oz.			
☐ crystal	6.00	10.00	6.50

MOONDROPS
New Martinsville Glass Co.

This pattern was made from 1932 to 1940. The colors made were blue, red, green, pink, amber, crystal and amethyst. The blue and the red are the most popular. The *Moondrop* pattern is not found on the flatware, just a design of four rings. The rare items in this pattern are the pitchers, the covered candy dish, the covered butter dish and the flat bowls. Goblets, tumblers, and most of the bowls are not difficult to find.

Ashtray			
☐ blue	24.00	30.00	25.00
☐ red	24.00	30.00	25.00
☐ crystal	6.00	9.00	7.00
☐ other colors	8.50	11.50	9.00
Berry Bowl, 5¼″			
☐ blue	5.00	7.00	5.50
☐ red	5.00	7.00	5.50
☐ crystal	2.50	4.50	3.00
☐ other colors	3.00	5.00	3.50

	Current Price Range		Prior Year Average
Bread and Butter Plate			
☐ blue	2.50	4.50	3.00
☐ red	2.50	4.50	3.00
☐ crystal	.50	2.00	1.00
☐ other colors	2.00	4.00	2.50
Butter Dish, with cover			
☐ blue	330.00	370.00	340.00
☐ red	330.00	370.00	340.00
☐ crystal	130.00	160.00	140.00
☐ other colors	205.00	245.00	212.00
Candleholders, ruffle design, 2″			
☐ blue	20.00	25.00	21.00
☐ red	20.00	25.00	21.00
☐ crystal	10.00	13.00	11.00
☐ other colors	15.00	20.00	16.00
Candy Dish, ruffle design, 8″			
☐ blue	13.00	17.00	14.00
☐ red	13.00	17.00	14.00
☐ crystal	8.00	11.00	9.00
☐ other colors	11.00	14.00	12.00
Comport, small			
☐ blue	11.00	14.00	12.00
☐ red	11.00	14.00	12.00
☐ crystal	5.00	7.00	5.50
☐ other colors	6.00	9.00	7.00
Comport, large			
☐ blue	25.00	30.00	26.00
☐ red	25.00	30.00	26.00
☐ crystal	11.00	14.00	12.00
☐ other colors	15.00	20.00	16.00
Covered Casserole, 9¾″			
☐ blue	64.00	74.00	66.00
☐ red	64.00	74.00	66.00
☐ crystal	30.00	36.00	32.00
☐ other colors	41.00	49.00	42.50
Creamer, 3¾″			
☐ blue	10.50	13.50	11.25
☐ red	10.50	13.50	11.25
☐ crystal	3.50	5.50	4.00
☐ other colors	6.00	9.00	7.00
Decanter, small			
☐ blue	46.00	54.00	48.00
☐ red	46.00	54.00	48.00
☐ crystal	18.00	22.00	19.00
☐ other colors	30.00	35.00	32.00

	Current Price Range		Prior Year Average
Decanter, medium			
☐ blue	54.00	64.00	55.00
☐ red	54.00	64.00	55.00
☐ crystal	18.00	22.00	19.00
☐ other colors	30.00	35.00	31.00
Decanter, large			
☐ blue	62.00	75.00	64.00
☐ red	62.00	75.00	64.00
☐ crystal	22.00	26.00	23.00
☐ other colors	33.00	42.00	35.00
Dinner Plate, 9½″			
☐ blue	11.00	14.00	12.00
☐ red	11.00	14.00	12.00
☐ crystal	6.00	9.00	7.00
☐ other colors	7.00	10.00	8.00
Juice Tumbler, footed, 3⅛″, 3 oz.			
☐ blue	10.00	13.00	11.00
☐ red	10.00	13.00	11.00
☐ crystal	4.50	7.00	5.50
☐ other colors	6.00	9.00	7.00
Luncheon Plate, 8½″			
☐ blue	7.50	11.50	8.50
☐ red	7.50	11.50	8.50
☐ crystal	2.00	4.00	2.50
☐ other colors	4.00	6.00	4.50
Pitcher, 8¼″, 32 oz.			
☐ blue	125.00	150.00	130.00
☐ red	125.00	150.00	130.00
☐ crystal	65.00	75.00	68.00
☐ other colors	93.00	105.00	95.00
Pitcher, with lip, 8″, 50 oz.			
☐ blue	138.00	160.00	142.00
☐ red	138.00	160.00	142.00
☐ crystal	160.00	170.00	162.00
☐ other colors	98.00	112.00	102.00
Pitcher, 8″, 52 oz.			
☐ blue	130.00	160.00	135.00
☐ red	130.00	160.00	135.00
☐ crystal	65.00	75.00	68.00
☐ other colors	102.00	120.00	105.00
Platter, oval, 12″			
☐ blue	15.00	20.00	16.00
☐ red	15.00	20.00	16.00
☐ crystal	8.00	10.00	8.50
☐ other colors	11.00	14.00	12.00

	Current Price Range		Prior Year Average
Powder Jar, footed			
☐ blue	31.00	39.00	32.00
☐ red..	31.00	39.00	32.00
☐ crystal	15.00	19.00	16.00
☐ other colors...................................	22.00	28.00	23.00
Relish Bowl, divided, footed, 8½"			
☐ blue	11.00	14.00	12.00
☐ red..	11.00	14.00	12.00
☐ crystal	7.50	9.50	8.00
☐ other colors...................................	8.00	11.00	9.00
Salad Plate			
☐ blue	5.00	7.00	5.50
☐ red..	5.00	7.00	5.50
☐ crystal	2.00	4.00	2.50
☐ other colors...................................	3.00	5.00	3.50
Saucer			
☐ blue	2.50	4.50	3.00
☐ red..	2.50	4.50	3.00
☐ crystal	1.00	2.00	1.25
☐ other colors...................................	2.00	4.00	2.50
Sherbet, small			
☐ blue	8.50	11.50	9.00
☐ red..	8.50	11.50	9.00
☐ crystal	3.00	5.00	3.50
☐ other colors...................................	5.00	8.00	5.50
Sherbet Plate, 6⅛"			
☐ blue	3.00	5.00	3.50
☐ red..	3.00	5.00	3.50
☐ crystal	1.00	3.00	1.50
☐ other colors...................................	1.50	3.50	2.00
Soup Bowl, 6¾"			
☐ blue	8.50	11.50	9.00
☐ red..	8.50	11.50	9.00
☐ crystal	5.00	8.00	6.00
☐ other colors...................................	6.50	9.50	7.00
Sugar, 4"			
☐ blue	10.00	13.00	11.00
☐ red..	10.00	13.00	11.00
☐ crystal	4.00	6.00	4.50
☐ other colors...................................	5.00	8.00	6.00
Tumbler, 8 oz.			
☐ blue	10.50	13.50	11.50
☐ red..	10.50	13.50	11.50
☐ crystal	6.00	9.00	7.00
☐ other colors...................................	7.00	10.00	8.00

	Current Price Range		Prior Year Average
Tumbler, 9 oz.			
☐ blue	12.00	15.00	13.00
☐ red..	12.00	15.00	13.00
☐ crystal	6.00	9.00	7.00
☐ other colors.................................	8.50	11.50	9.00
Vase, ruffle design, 7¾"			
☐ blue	38.00	45.00	40.00
☐ red..	38.00	45.00	40.00
☐ crystal	20.00	25.00	21.00
☐ other colors.................................	28.00	34.00	29.00
Vase, rocket design, 7¾"			
☐ blue	70.00	85.00	73.00
☐ red..	70.00	85.00	73.00
☐ crystal	36.00	44.00	38.00
☐ other colors.................................	50.00	60.00	53.00
Vegetable Bowl, oval, 9¾"			
☐ blue	20.00	25.00	21.00
☐ red..	20.00	25.00	21.00
☐ crystal	13.00	17.00	14.00
☐ other colors.................................	15.00	20.00	16.00
Water Goblet, 6¼"			
☐ blue	15.00	20.00	16.00
☐ red..	15.00	20.00	16.00
☐ crystal	9.00	12.00	10.00
☐ other colors.................................	12.00	15.00	13.00
Wine Goblet, 4"			
☐ blue	13.00	17.00	14.00
☐ red..	13.00	17.00	14.00
☐ crystal	6.00	9.00	7.00
☐ other colors.................................	8.00	11.00	9.00
Wine Goblet, metal stem, 5½"			
☐ blue	12.00	15.00	13.00
☐ red..	12.00	15.00	13.00
☐ crystal	5.00	8.00	6.00
☐ other colors.................................	7.00	10.00	8.00

OCTAGON
A.H. Heisey & Co.

This pattern was produced on blanks No. 500, No. 1229 and No. 1231. The colors were crystal, flamingo (pink), sahara (yellow), moongleam (green), hawthorne (light purple), and marigold (deep brassy yellow).

Octagon

	Current Price Range		Prior Year Average
Basket, #500, 5″			
☐ crystal	60.00	80.00	70.00
☐ pink	95.00	115.00	100.00
☐ yellow	240.00	300.00	260.00
☐ green	100.00	130.00	110.00
Bon Bon Dish, upturned sides, #1229, 6″			
☐ crystal	7.00	10.00	8.00
☐ pink	10.00	15.00	11.00
☐ yellow	30.00	35.00	32.00
☐ green	15.00	20.00	17.00
☐ hawthorne	25.00	30.00	27.00
☐ marigold	15.00	21.00	17.00
Bowl, #500, 6″			
☐ crystal	12.00	17.00	14.00
☐ pink	40.00	50.00	42.00
☐ marigold	40.00	50.00	42.00
☐ green	20.00	30.00	23.00
Bowl, footed, #1229, 8″			
☐ crystal	17.00	22.00	18.00
☐ pink	25.00	30.00	27.00
☐ marigold	50.00	60.00	52.00
☐ green	30.00	35.00	32.00
Bread Plate, #1231, 7″			
☐ crystal	5.00	8.00	6.00
☐ pink	9.00	13.00	10.00
☐ marigold	10.00	14.00	11.00
☐ green	12.00	17.00	14.00

	Current Price Range		Prior Year Average
Candlestick, one lite, 3″, pair			
☐ crystal	25.00	30.00	27.00
☐ pink	30.00	40.00	32.00
☐ marigold	19.00	29.00	20.00
☐ green	35.00	45.00	38.00
Celery Tray, #1231, 9″			
☐ crystal	10.00	15.00	11.00
☐ pink	15.00	21.00	16.00
☐ marigold	17.00	27.00	18.00
☐ green	20.00	27.00	22.00
Celery Tray, #1231, 12″			
☐ crystal	16.00	20.00	17.00
☐ pink	20.00	27.00	22.00
☐ green	30.00	37.00	32.00
Cheese Dish, two handles, #1229, 6″			
☐ crystal	5.00	10.00	7.00
☐ pink	10.00	16.00	11.00
☐ green	15.00	22.00	17.00
☐ marigold	30.00	37.00	32.00
☐ hawthorne	25.00	32.00	27.00
Cream Soup Bowl, two handles, and underplate			
☐ crystal	10.00	15.00	10.00
☐ pink	15.00	20.00	15.00
☐ green	25.00	30.00	25.00
Creamer, #500			
☐ crystal	4.00	12.00	5.50
☐ pink	15.00	20.00	17.00
☐ yellow	25.00	30.00	27.00
☐ green	20.00	25.00	22.00
☐ orchid	21.00	30.00	22.50
Demitasse Cup and Saucer, #1231			
☐ crystal	5.00	20.00	5.00
☐ pink	20.00	25.00	10.00
☐ green	25.00	30.00	20.00
Frozen Dessert, #500			
☐ crystal	8.00	12.00	9.00
☐ pink	12.00	16.00	14.00
☐ marigold	30.00	37.00	32.00
☐ green	15.00	22.00	17.00
Grapefruit Bowl, #1231, 6½″			
☐ crystal	5.00	10.00	7.00
☐ pink	10.00	15.00	11.00
☐ green	10.00	15.00	11.00

	Current Price Range		Prior Year Average

Hors d'oeuvre Plate, #1229, 13″

☐ crystal	14.00	24.00	15.00
☐ pink	25.00	30.00	27.00
☐ yellow	30.00	37.00	32.00
☐ green	30.00	37.00	32.00
☐ marigold	50.00	60.00	54.00

Ice Tub, #500

☐ crystal	25.00	35.00	30.00
☐ pink	45.00	60.00	50.00
☐ yellow	80.00	90.00	83.00
☐ green	45.00	60.00	50.00
☐ marigold	150.00	200.00	170.00

Jelly, #1229, 5½″

☐ crystal	5.00	10.00	7.00
☐ pink	10.00	15.00	12.00
☐ yellow	15.00	20.00	17.00
☐ green	15.00	20.00	17.00
☐ marigold	30.00	35.00	32.00
☐ hawthorne	24.00	31.00	26.00

Luncheon Plate, 8″

☐ crystal	10.00	14.00	11.00
☐ pink	10.00	15.00	12.00
☐ yellow	20.00	25.00	22.00
☐ green	10.00	15.00	12.00

Mayonnaise, footed, #1229, 5½″

☐ crystal	7.00	12.00	9.00
☐ pink	15.00	20.00	17.00
☐ yellow	20.00	25.00	22.00
☐ green	20.00	25.00	22.00
☐ hawthorne	30.00	35.00	32.00
☐ marigold	34.00	40.00	36.00

Mint, #1229, 6″

☐ crystal	5.00	10.00	7.00
☐ pink	10.00	15.00	12.00
☐ yellow	15.00	20.00	17.00
☐ green	15.00	20.00	17.00
☐ hawthorne	25.00	30.00	27.00
☐ marigold	30.00	37.00	32.00

Muffin Plate, #1229, 10″ and 12″

☐ crystal	15.00	20.00	17.00
☐ pink	25.00	30.00	27.00
☐ yellow	30.00	35.00	32.00
☐ green	30.00	35.00	32.00
☐ hawthorne	45.00	55.00	32.00
☐ marigold	50.00	60.00	54.00

	Current Price Range		Prior Year Average
Plate, #1231, 14″			
☐ crystal	20.00	26.00	17.00
☐ pink	25.00	35.00	30.00
☐ yellow	35.00	40.00	37.00
☐ green	35.00	40.00	37.00
Platter, #1231, 12¾″			
☐ crystal	15.00	20.00	20.00
☐ pink	20.00	25.00	27.00
☐ green	25.00	30.00	35.00
Salad Bowl, #1231, 12½″			
☐ crystal	20.00	25.00	22.00
☐ pink	25.00	30.00	27.00
☐ green	30.00	35.00	32.00
☐ hawthorne	45.00	60.00	50.00
Sandwich Plate, #1231, 10½″			
☐ crystal	20.00	25.00	22.00
☐ pink	25.00	30.00	27.00
☐ yellow	35.00	40.00	37.00
☐ green	30.00	35.00	32.00
Sandwich Plate, center handle, #1231, 10½″			
☐ crystal	19.00	28.00	20.00
☐ pink	26.00	36.00	27.00
☐ yellow	31.00	40.00	32.00
☐ green	34.00	44.00	35.00
Sandwich Plate, #1229, 10″			
☐ crystal	12.00	20.00	13.00
☐ pink	17.00	27.00	18.00
☐ yellow	21.00	31.00	22.00
☐ green	24.00	34.00	25.00
☐ orchid	29.00	38.00	30.00
Soup Plate, 9″			
☐ crystal	9.00	18.00	10.00
☐ pink	13.00	23.00	14.00
☐ yellow	17.00	28.00	18.00
☐ green	21.00	31.00	22.00
☐ orchid	25.00	35.00	26.00
Sugar Bowl, #500			
☐ crystal	10.00	14.00	12.00
☐ pink	15.00	22.00	17.00
☐ yellow	25.00	31.00	27.00
☐ green	20.00	26.00	22.00

	Current Price Range		Prior Year Average
Tray, #500, 6"			
☐ crystal...............................	8.00	12.00	10.00
☐ pink....................................	15.00	20.00	17.00
☐ green..................................	15.00	20.00	17.00
Tray, four sections, #500, 12"			
☐ crystal...............................	30.00	40.00	33.00
☐ pink....................................	45.00	55.00	48.00
☐ yellow.................................	80.00	92.00	84.00
☐ green..................................	50.00	60.00	54.00
☐ dawn..................................	150.00	200.00	170.00
Vegetable Bowl, #1231, 9"			
☐ crystal...............................	10.00	15.00	10.00
☐ pink....................................	15.00	20.00	15.00
☐ green..................................	20.00	25.00	23.00

OLD SANDWICH

A.H. Heisey & Co.

Produced on blank No. 1404, this pattern is found in crystal, pink (flamingo), yellow (sahara), green (moongleam) and cobalt. A few pieces were also made in tangerine.

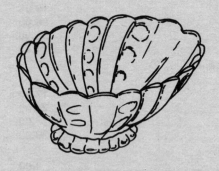

Old Sandwich

Ashtray			
☐ crystal...............................	7.00	10.00	5.00
☐ pink....................................	35.00	40.00	37.00
☐ yellow.................................	30.00	35.00	32.00
☐ green..................................	40.00	45.00	42.00
☐ cobalt.................................	35.00	40.00	37.00

	Current Price Range		Prior Year Average

Bar, 1½ oz.

☐ crystal	9.00	18.00	11.00
☐ pink	24.00	33.00	25.50
☐ yellow	29.00	38.00	29.50
☐ green	34.00	43.00	35.00

Beer Mug, 12 oz.

☐ crystal	28.00	35.00	30.00
☐ pink	275.00	325.00	300.00
☐ yellow	195.00	220.00	200.00
☐ green	240.00	260.00	250.00
☐ cobalt	270.00	285.00	275.00
☐ amber	240.00	300.00	260.00

Beer Mug, 14 oz.

☐ crystal	45.00	55.00	48.00
☐ pink (rare)	350.00	400.00	360.00
☐ yellow	220.00	240.00	225.00
☐ green	270.00	285.00	275.00
☐ cobalt	300.00	350.00	320.00
☐ amber	300.00	350.00	315.00

Beer Mug, 18 oz.

☐ crystal	60.00	80.00	68.00
☐ pink	400.00	500.00	440.00
☐ yellow	245.00	265.00	248.00
☐ green	290.00	320.00	295.00
☐ cobalt	320.00	340.00	324.00
☐ amber	300.00	400.00	340.00

Bowl, curved and footed

☐ crystal	30.00	40.00	33.00
☐ pink	80.00	90.00	84.00
☐ yellow	55.00	75.00	60.00
☐ green	80.00	90.00	84.00

Candleholder, 6″, each

☐ crystal	30.00	40.00	33.00
☐ pink	175.00	200.00	180.00
☐ yellow	165.00	190.00	170.00
☐ green	195.00	220.00	200.00
☐ cobalt	325.00	450.00	350.00

Catsup Bottle, with stopper

☐ crystal	28.00	38.00	31.00
☐ pink	75.00	100.00	85.00
☐ yellow	65.00	85.00	75.00
☐ green	75.00	100.00	85.00

	Current Price Range		Prior Year Average
Champagne, 5 oz.			
☐ crystal	12.00	18.00	14.00
☐ pink	21.00	30.00	21.50
☐ yellow	24.00	33.00	24.50
☐ green	27.00	35.00	28.50
Cigarette Container			
☐ crystal	60.00	70.00	63.00
☐ yellow	60.00	70.00	63.00
☐ cobalt	100.00	150.00	120.00
Claret Goblet, 4 oz.			
☐ crystal	15.00	20.00	17.00
☐ pink	20.00	25.00	22.00
☐ yellow	20.00	25.00	22.00
☐ green	25.00	30.00	27.00
☐ cobalt	88.00	100.00	91.50
Cocktail Goblet, 3 oz.			
☐ crystal	10.00	15.00	17.00
☐ pink	20.00	25.00	22.00
☐ yellow	25.00	30.00	27.00
☐ green	25.00	30.00	27.00
Compote, 6″			
☐ crystal	25.00	35.00	29.00
☐ pink	68.00	78.00	69.00
☐ yellow	74.00	84.00	74.50
☐ green	78.00	88.00	79.00
Creamer, small			
☐ crystal	12.00	18.00	15.00
☐ pink	25.00	30.00	27.00
☐ yellow	25.00	30.00	27.00
☐ green	25.00	30.00	27.00
Creamer, 12 oz.			
☐ crystal	28.00	38.00	29.50
☐ pink	150.00	180.00	155.00
☐ green	165.00	195.00	167.50
Cruet, with stopper			
☐ crystal	55.00	80.00	57.50
☐ pink	65.00	90.00	67.50
☐ yellow	70.00	95.00	72.50
☐ green	75.00	100.00	78.50
Cup			
☐ crystal	18.00	22.00	19.00
☐ pink	24.00	30.00	26.00
☐ yellow	24.00	30.00	26.00
☐ green	24.00	30.00	26.00

	Current Price Range		Prior Year Average
Decanter, with stopper			
☐ crystal	60.00	80.00	65.00
☐ pink	155.00	175.00	158.50
☐ yellow	175.00	195.00	180.00
☐ green	175.00	195.00	178.50
☐ cobalt	320.00	350.00	325.00
Finger Bowl			
☐ crystal	8.00	16.00	9.00
☐ pink	11.00	20.00	11.50
☐ yellow	14.00	24.00	14.50
☐ green	17.00	27.00	17.50
Flower Bowl, oval, footed, 12″			
☐ crystal	25.00	35.00	26.50
☐ pink	75.00	90.00	80.00
☐ yellow	58.00	68.00	59.00
☐ green	75.00	90.00	80.00
Flower Bowl, round, footed, 11″			
☐ crystal	24.00	34.00	26.00
☐ pink	75.00	85.00	77.00
☐ yellow	55.00	75.00	58.00
☐ green	75.00	85.00	77.00
Iced Tea Tumbler, 12 oz.			
☐ crystal	9.00	18.00	10.50
☐ pink	16.00	25.00	17.00
☐ yellow	21.00	30.00	21.50
☐ green	26.00	35.00	27.50
Iced Tea Tumbler, footed, 12 oz.			
☐ crystal	9.00	18.00	10.50
☐ pink	16.00	25.00	17.00
☐ yellow	21.00	30.00	22.50
☐ green	26.00	35.00	27.50
Juice Tumbler, 5 oz.			
☐ crystal	3.00	12.00	4.50
☐ pink	11.00	20.00	12.50
☐ yellow	14.00	23.00	15.50
☐ green	19.00	28.00	21.00
Oyster Cocktail Goblet, 4 oz.			
☐ crystal	3.00	12.00	4.50
☐ pink	8.00	17.00	9.50
☐ yellow	9.00	18.00	10.00
☐ green	11.00	20.00	12.50

	Current Price Range		Prior Year Average
Parfait			
☐ crystal	8.00	16.00	9.50
☐ pink	13.00	21.00	14.50
☐ yellow	18.00	28.00	19.50
☐ green	23.00	33.00	24.50
Pilsner Glass, 8 oz.			
☐ crystal	10.00	20.00	11.50
☐ pink	23.00	33.00	24.50
☐ yellow	28.00	38.00	29.50
☐ green	33.00	43.00	34.50
Pilsner Glass, 10 oz.			
☐ crystal	13.00	23.00	14.50
☐ pink	26.00	36.00	27.50
☐ yellow	30.00	40.00	31.50
☐ green	36.00	46.00	37.50
Pitcher, 64 oz.			
☐ crystal	60.00	85.00	60.00
☐ pink	125.00	165.00	135.00
☐ yellow	120.00	150.00	125.00
☐ green	125.00	155.00	130.00
Pitcher, ice lip, 64 oz.			
☐ crystal	63.00	73.00	64.50
☐ pink	120.00	150.00	124.00
☐ yellow	125.00	155.00	130.00
☐ green	130.00	160.00	135.00
Plate, square, 6″			
☐ crystal	3.00	10.00	4.00
☐ pink	7.00	15.00	7.50
☐ yellow	9.00	17.00	9.50
☐ green	12.00	20.00	12.50
Plate, square, 7″			
☐ crystal	4.00	11.00	4.50
☐ pink	9.00	17.00	9.50
☐ yellow	12.00	20.00	12.50
☐ green	14.00	22.00	14.50
Plate, square, 8″			
☐ crystal	6.00	13.00	7.00
☐ pink	20.00	25.00	22.00
☐ yellow	20.00	25.00	22.00
☐ green	20.00	25.00	22.00
Salt and Pepper Shakers, pair			
☐ crystal	28.00	38.00	29.50
☐ pink	38.00	48.00	39.50
☐ yellow	60.00	70.00	62.00
☐ green	60.00	70.00	62.00

	Current Price Range		Prior Year Average
Sherbet, footed, 4 oz.			
☐ crystal	4.00	13.00	4.50
☐ pink	15.00	22.00	17.00
☐ yellow	15.00	22.00	17.00
☐ green	15.00	22.00	17.00
Sugar Bowl, oval			
☐ crystal	6.00	15.00	7.50
☐ pink	19.00	28.00	20.50
☐ yellow	21.00	30.00	22.00
☐ green	24.00	33.00	24.50
Toddy Tumbler, 6½ oz.			
☐ crystal	6.00	15.00	7.50
☐ pink	13.00	22.00	14.50
☐ yellow	15.00	24.00	15.50
☐ green	20.00	30.00	21.00
Tumbler, 8 oz.			
☐ crystal	6.00	15.00	7.50
☐ pink	14.00	23.00	15.50
☐ yellow	19.00	28.00	20.50
☐ green	24.00	33.00	25.50
Tumbler, 10 oz.			
☐ crystal	8.00	17.00	9.50
☐ pink	14.00	23.00	15.50
☐ yellow	19.00	28.00	20.50
☐ green	24.00	33.00	25.50
Tumbler, footed, 10 oz.			
☐ crystal	8.00	17.00	9.50
☐ pink	14.00	23.00	15.50
☐ yellow	19.00	28.00	19.50
☐ green	24.00	33.00	25.50
Water Goblet, 10 oz.			
☐ crystal	8.00	17.00	9.50
☐ pink	21.00	30.00	22.50
☐ yellow	25.00	34.00	26.50
☐ green	29.00	38.00	31.00
Wine, 2½ oz.			
☐ crystal	10.00	20.00	11.50
☐ pink	30.00	40.00	32.00
☐ yellow	30.00	40.00	32.00
☐ green	30.00	40.00	32.00

ORCHID
Paden City Glass Co.

Another pattern of arranged sprays of blossoms, *Orchid* has two wide drapes of the pretty bloom and foliage alternating with thinner bouquets of the same flower. They are divided by a twisted spear of teardrops.

	Current Price Range		Prior Year Average
Bowl, square, length 5″			
☐ cobalt...............................	15.50	19.50	16.50
☐ pink	7.50	11.50	8.25
☐ green	7.50	11.50	8.25
☐ yellow...............................	7.50	11.50	8.25
Bowl, square, length 9″			
☐ cobalt...............................	27.00	33.00	29.00
☐ pink	11.00	14.00	12.00
☐ green	11.00	14.00	12.00
☐ yellow...............................	11.00	14.00	12.00
Candlesticks, pair			
☐ cobalt...............................	33.00	42.00	35.00
☐ pink	20.00	25.00	21.00
☐ green	20.00	25.00	21.00
☐ yellow...............................	20.00	25.00	21.00
Comport			
☐ cobalt...............................	20.00	25.00	21.00
☐ pink	12.00	15.00	13.00
☐ green	12.00	15.00	13.00
☐ yellow...............................	12.00	15.00	13.00
Creamer			
☐ cobalt...............................	24.00	31.00	26.00
☐ pink	11.00	14.00	12.00
☐ green	11.00	14.00	12.00
☐ yellow...............................	11.00	14.00	12.00
Ice Bucket, height 6″			
☐ cobalt...............................	47.00	53.00	48.00
☐ pink	24.00	31.00	26.00
☐ green	24.00	31.00	26.00
☐ yellow...............................	24.00	31.00	26.00
Mayonnaise Set			
☐ cobalt...............................	30.00	35.00	31.00
☐ pink	15.50	19.50	16.25
☐ green	15.50	19.50	16.25
☐ yellow...............................	15.50	19.50	16.25

	Current Price Range		Prior Year Average
Sugar Bowl			
☐ cobalt	23.00	33.00	25.00
☐ pink	11.00	14.00	12.00
☐ green	11.00	14.00	12.00
☐ yellow	11.00	14.00	12.00
Vase, height 10″			
☐ cobalt	63.00	73.00	65.00
☐ pink	33.00	43.00	35.00
☐ green	33.00	43.00	35.00
☐ yellow	33.00	43.00	35.00

PEACOCK AND WILD ROSE
Unknown Manufacturer

	Current Price Range		Prior Year Average
Bowl, diameter 8½″			
☐ pink	20.00	25.00	21.50
☐ green	20.00	25.00	21.50
Bowl, oval, footed, length 8½″			
☐ pink	30.00	35.00	31.50
☐ green	30.00	35.00	31.50
Bowl, footed, diameter 8¾″			
☐ pink	21.00	26.00	22.00
☐ green	21.00	26.00	22.00
Bowl, footed, diameter 9¼″			
☐ pink	24.00	31.00	25.50
☐ green	24.00	31.00	25.50
Bowl, handle in the center, diameter 9¼″			
☐ pink	28.00	33.00	29.00
☐ green	28.00	33.00	29.00
Bowl, console type, diameter 11″			
☐ pink	28.00	33.00	29.00
☐ green	28.00	33.00	29.00
Bowl, console type, diameter 14″			
☐ pink	33.00	40.00	35.00
☐ green	33.00	40.00	35.00
Cake Plate			
☐ pink	23.00	30.00	25.00
☐ green	23.00	30.00	25.00
Candlesticks, pair			
☐ pink	16.00	20.00	19.00
☐ green	16.00	20.00	19.00

	Current Price Range		Prior Year Average

Candy Dish, with cover, diameter 7"
☐ pink 53.00 63.00 55.00
☐ green 53.00 63.00 55.00
Comport, diameter 6¼"
☐ pink 18.00 22.00 19.00
☐ green 18.00 22.00 19.00
Ice Bucket, height 6"
☐ pink 41.00 49.00 43.00
☐ green 41.00 49.00 43.00
Relish Tray, three compartments
☐ pink 18.00 22.00 19.00
☐ green 18.00 22.00 19.00

PEACOCK REVERSE
Unknown Manufacturer

The motif is the elegant peacock, that regal bird nesting among the most delicate feathery flowers and foliage, glancing back over his shoulders. This scene repeats four times around the body, separated by an urn-like divider. The glass is heavily colored, almost opaque.

Bowl, square, length 4⅞"
☐ red 18.00 22.00 19.00
☐ blue 18.00 22.00 19.00
Bowl, square, length 8¾"
☐ red 43.00 51.00 45.00
☐ blue 43.00 51.00 45.00
Bowl, square, handles, length 8¾"
☐ red 48.00 56.00 50.00
☐ blue 48.00 56.00 50.00
Candlesticks, pair, height 5¾"
☐ red 67.00 77.00 69.00
☐ blue 67.00 77.00 69.00
Candy Dish, square, length 6½"
☐ red 45.00 54.00 47.00
☐ blue 45.00 54.00 47.00
Creamer, height 2¾"
☐ red 43.00 52.00 45.00
☐ blue 43.00 52.00 45.00
Sherbet Dish, diameter 3⅝"
☐ red 28.00 34.00 30.00
☐ blue 28.00 34.00 30.00

	Current Price Range		Prior Year Average
Sherbet Plate, diameter 5¾"			
☐ red	14.50	18.50	15.50
☐ blue	14.50	18.50	15.50
Sugar Bowl, height 2¾"			
☐ red	43.00	53.00	45.00
☐ blue	43.00	53.00	45.00
Tumbler, 10 oz., height 4"			
☐ red	37.00	45.00	39.00
☐ blue	37.00	45.00	39.00

PLANTATION
A.H. Heisey & Co.

This pattern was produced on blank No. 1567. It was made only in crystal. Imperial Glass Co., after they had acquired the Heisey molds, made a similar stemware to *Plantation* with an amber stem, but the bowl was not really very close to the *Plantation* bowl.

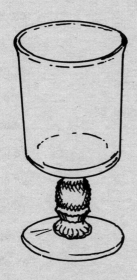

Plantation

Ashtray, 3½"			
☐ crystal	14.00	23.00	15.50

	Current Price Range		Prior Year Average
Buffet Plate, 18″			
☐ crystal	35.00	40.00	37.00
Butter Dish, covered, ¼ lb.			
☐ crystal	50.00	60.00	52.00
Butter Dish, covered, round			
☐ crystal	55.00	65.00	60.00
Cake Plate, footed, 13″			
☐ crystal	64.00	74.00	65.00
Candelabra, three lite			
☐ crystal	75.00	80.00	77.00
Candlestick, one candle			
☐ crystal	30.00	40.00	33.00
Candlestick, two candles			
☐ crystal	50.00	60.00	52.00
Candlestick, three candles			
☐ crystal	60.00	75.00	64.00
Candy Box, covered, 7″			
☐ crystal	74.00	83.00	75.50
Candy Jar, covered, footed, 5″			
☐ crystal	105.00	135.00	112.50
Celery Dish, two sections, 13″			
☐ crystal	30.00	35.00	32.00
Celery Dish, 13″			
☐ crystal	20.00	25.00	22.00
Champagne Goblet, blown, 6½ oz.			
☐ crystal	17.00	22.00	18.00
Cheese Dish, covered, footed, 5″			
☐ crystal	29.00	38.00	29.50
Claret, blown, 4½ oz.			
☐ crystal	20.00	26.00	22.00
Claret, pressed, 4½ oz.			
☐ crystal	20.00	26.00	22.00
Coaster, 4″			
☐ crystal	15.00	20.00	16.00
Cocktail, pressed, 3½ oz.			
☐ crystal	17.00	26.00	18.50
Compote, covered, 5″			
☐ crystal	39.00	48.00	40.50
Compote, 5″			
☐ crystal	17.00	26.00	18.50
Cordial, 1 oz.			
☐ crystal	75.00	90.00	80.00
Creamer, footed			
☐ crystal	18.00	24.00	20.00

	Current Price Range		Prior Year Average

Cruet, with stopper, 3 oz.
☐ crystal .... 70.00 | 80.00 | 72.00

Cup, with saucer
☐ crystal .... 15.00 | 22.00 | 17.00

Epergne, footed, with candleholder, 5″
☐ crystal .... 60.00 | 75.00 | 64.00

Fruit Bowl, fluted edge, 9½″
☐ crystal .... 40.00 | 47.00 | 43.00

Fruit Bowl, fluted edge, 12″
☐ crystal .... 55.00 | 60.00 | 57.00

Fruit Cocktail, 4 oz.
☐ crystal .... 17.00 | 22.00 | 19.00

Gardenia Bowl, 9½″
☐ crystal .... 22.00 | 28.00 | 23.00

Gardenia Bowl, footed, 11½″
☐ crystal .... 25.00 | 35.00 | 28.00

Gardenia Bowl, 13″
☐ crystal .... 27.00 | 36.00 | 28.50

Honey Bowl, footed, 6½″
☐ crystal .... 21.00 | 30.00 | 22.50

Hurricane Candleholder
☐ crystal .... 120.00 | 175.00 | 140.00

Iced Tea Tumbler, footed, blown, 12 oz.
☐ crystal .... 26.00 | 35.00 | 27.50

Iced Tea Tumbler, footed, pressed, 12 oz.
☐ crystal .... 24.00 | 33.00 | 24.50

Jelly Bowl, flared rim, 6½″
☐ crystal .... 17.00 | 26.00 | 18.50

Jelly Bowl, two handles, 6½″
☐ crystal .... 15.00 | 24.00 | 16.50

Juice Tumbler, footed, blown, 5 oz.
☐ crystal .... 23.00 | 32.00 | 24.50

Juice Tumbler, footed, pressed, 5 oz.
☐ crystal .... 19.00 | 28.00 | 21.00

Marmalade Jar, covered
☐ crystal .... 29.00 | 38.00 | 29.50

Mayonnaise Bowl, footed, 4½″
☐ crystal .... 17.00 | 26.00 | 18.50

Mayonnaise Bowl, includes liner, 5¼″
☐ crystal .... 19.00 | 28.00 | 20.00

Nappy, 5″
☐ crystal .... 11.00 | 20.00 | 12.50

Nappy, 5½″
☐ crystal .... 12.00 | 21.00 | 13.50

Oyster Cocktail Goblet, blown, 4½ oz.
☐ crystal .... 16.00 | 24.00 | 17.50

	Current Price Range		Prior Year Average
Pitcher, ice lip, blown, 64 oz.			
☐ crystal...............................	84.00	130.00	90.00
Plate, 10½"			
☐ crystal...............................	17.00	26.00	18.50
Punch Bowl, 2½ gal.			
☐ crystal...............................	85.00	135.00	95.00
Punch Bowl Underplate, 18"			
☐ crystal...............................	23.00	32.00	24.50
Punch Cup			
☐ crystal...............................	11.00	20.00	12.50
Relish Dish, divided, three sections, 11"			
☐ crystal...............................	18.00	27.00	19.50
Relish Dish, oval, divided, five sections, 13"			
☐ crystal...............................	29.00	38.00	31.00
Relish Dish, round, divided, four sections, 8"			
☐ crystal...............................	22.00	31.00	23.50
Salad Bowl, 9"			
☐ crystal...............................	21.00	30.00	22.50
Salad Plate, 7"			
☐ crystal...............................	8.00	17.00	9.50
Salad Plate, 8"			
☐ crystal...............................	10.00	20.00	11.50
Salt and Pepper Shakers, pair			
☐ crystal...............................	23.00	32.00	24.50
Sandwich Plate, 14"			
☐ crystal...............................	21.00	30.00	22.50
Saucer			
☐ crystal...............................	2.00	9.00	3.00
Serving Bowl, divided, two sections, 8½"			
☐ crystal...............................	15.00	24.00	16.50
Sugar Bowl, footed			
☐ crystal...............................	13.00	22.00	14.50
Tray, holds sugar bowl and creamer, 8½"			
☐ crystal...............................	17.00	26.00	18.50
Vase, footed, 5"			
☐ crystal...............................	23.00	32.00	24.50
Vase, footed, 9"			
☐ crystal...............................	27.00	36.00	28.00
Water Goblet, blown, 10 oz.			
☐ crystal...............................	15.00	24.00	15.50
Water Goblet, pressed, 10 oz.			
☐ crystal...............................	14.00	23.00	15.50

	Current Price Range		Prior Year Average
Water Tumbler, 10 oz.			
☐ crystal	25.00	34.00	26.50
Wine Goblet, blown, 3 oz.			
☐ crystal	23.00	32.00	24.50

PLEAT AND PANEL
A.H. Heisey & Co.

Produced on blank No. 1170, this very simple pattern is found in crystal, pink (flamingo) and green (moongleam).

Pleat and Panel

	Current Price Range		Prior Year Average
Bouillon Bowl, two handles, 5″			
☐ crystal	5.00	14.00	6.50
☐ pink	9.00	18.00	10.50
☐ green	11.00	20.00	12.50
Boullion Underplate, 6¾″			
☐ crystal	2.00	9.00	3.50
☐ pink	5.00	12.00	6.50
☐ green	7.00	14.00	8.50
Bowl, 4″			
☐ crystal	4.00	13.00	5.50
☐ pink	7.00	16.00	8.50
☐ green	9.00	18.00	10.50
Bread Plate, 7″			
☐ crystal	3.00	10.00	4.50
☐ pink	6.00	13.00	7.50
☐ green	8.00	15.00	9.50

	Current Price Range		Prior Year Average
Cereal Bowl, 6½″			
☐ crystal	8.00	13.00	5.50
☐ pink	15.00	20.00	17.00
☐ green	15.00	20.00	17.00
Champagne Goblet, 5 oz.			
☐ crystal	4.00	13.00	5.50
☐ pink	12.00	20.00	14.00
☐ green	24.00	35.00	27.00
Cheese and Cracker Set, 10½″			
☐ crystal	19.00	28.00	20.50
☐ pink	25.00	35.00	28.00
☐ green	34.00	40.00	36.00
Compote, covered, footed, 5″			
☐ crystal	24.00	33.00	25.50
☐ pink	50.00	65.00	54.00
☐ green	60.00	75.00	65.00
Cruet, with stopper, 3 oz.			
☐ crystal	16.00	25.00	17.50
☐ pink	45.00	55.00	48.00
☐ green	55.00	65.00	58.00
☐ amber	350.00	400.00	370.00
Cup, with saucer			
☐ crystal	18.00	20.00	17.00
☐ pink	25.00	35.00	29.00
☐ green	30.00	40.00	34.00
Dinner Plate, 10¾″			
☐ crystal	14.00	20.00	16.00
☐ pink	19.00	28.00	20.50
☐ green	24.00	33.00	25.50
Goblet, 7½ oz.			
☐ crystal	8.00	17.00	9.50
☐ pink	14.00	23.00	15.50
☐ green	19.00	28.00	20.50
Goblet, 8 oz.			
☐ crystal	11.00	20.00	12.50
☐ pink	19.00	28.00	20.50
☐ green	24.00	33.00	25.50
Hotel Creamer			
☐ crystal	10.00	15.00	12.00
☐ pink	15.00	20.00	17.00
☐ green	25.00	30.00	27.00
Iced Tea Tumbler, 12 oz.			
☐ crystal	10.00	17.00	11.50
☐ pink	13.00	22.00	14.50
☐ green	16.00	25.00	17.50

	Current Price Range		Prior Year Average
Jelly Bowl, two handles, 5″			
☐ crystal	5.00	14.00	6.50
☐ pink	15.00	20.00	17.00
☐ green	15.00	20.00	17.00
Lemon Bowl, covered, 5″			
☐ crystal	15.00	18.00	10.50
☐ pink	25.00	32.00	28.00
☐ green	35.00	45.00	39.00
Luncheon Plate, 8″			
☐ crystal	4.00	13.00	5.50
☐ pink	9.00	18.00	10.50
☐ green	11.00	20.00	12.50
Marmalade Jar, 4¾″			
☐ crystal	6.00	15.00	7.50
☐ pink	11.00	20.00	12.50
☐ green	16.00	25.00	17.50
Nappy, 4½″			
☐ crystal	4.00	13.00	5.50
☐ pink	7.00	16.00	8.50
☐ green	8.00	17.00	9.50
Nappy, 8″			
☐ crystal	9.00	18.00	10.50
☐ pink	14.00	23.00	15.50
☐ green	16.00	25.00	17.50
Pitcher			
☐ crystal	30.00	40.00	32.00
☐ pink	50.00	60.00	52.00
☐ green	65.00	75.00	67.00
☐ sahara	115.00	140.00	125.00
Pitcher, ice lip			
☐ crystal	40.00	50.00	42.50
☐ pink	60.00	70.00	62.50
☐ green	75.00	85.00	72.50
Plate, 6″			
☐ crystal	2.00	9.00	3.50
☐ pink	5.00	12.00	6.50
☐ green	7.00	14.00	8.50
Platter, oval, 12″			
☐ crystal	16.00	25.00	17.50
☐ pink	29.00	38.00	30.50
☐ green	34.00	43.00	35.50
Sandwich Plate, 14″			
☐ crystal	14.00	23.00	15.50
☐ pink	24.00	33.00	25.50
☐ green	29.00	38.00	30.50

	Current Price Range		Prior Year Average
Saucer			
☐ crystal	2.00	9.00	3.50
☐ pink	4.00	11.00	5.50
☐ green	5.00	12.00	6.50
Sherbet, footed, 5 oz.			
☐ crystal	3.00	10.00	4.50
☐ pink	6.00	13.00	7.50
☐ green	7.00	14.00	8.50
Sugar Bowl, covered, institutional			
☐ crystal	6.00	15.00	7.50
☐ pink	16.00	25.00	17.50
☐ green	21.00	30.00	22.50
Tray, compartments, 10″			
☐ crystal	14.00	23.00	15.50
☐ pink	24.00	33.00	25.50
☐ green	29.00	38.00	30.50
Tumbler, 8 oz.			
☐ crystal	7.00	16.00	8.50
☐ pink	11.00	20.00	12.50
☐ green	14.00	23.00	15.50
Vase, 8″			
☐ crystal	24.00	33.00	25.50
☐ pink	39.00	48.00	40.50
☐ green	44.00	53.00	45.50
Vegetable Bowl, oval, 9″			
☐ crystal	10.00	19.00	11.50
☐ pink	16.00	25.00	17.50
☐ green	18.00	27.00	19.50

PROVINCIAL
A.H. Heisey & Co.

Reminiscent of *Early Thumbprint* pattern glass, *Provincial* was produced on blank No. 1506 in crystal and limelight.

Provincial

	Current Price Range		Prior Year Average
Ashtray, square, 3″			
☐ crystal	15.00	20.00	12.50
Bon Bon Dish, two handles, 7″			
☐ crystal	9.00	18.00	10.50
Bread Plate, 7″			
☐ crystal	9.00	18.00	10.50
Buffet Plate, 18″			
☐ crystal	24.00	33.00	25.50
Butter Dish, covered			
☐ crystal	65.00	85.00	72.00
Candleholder, one candle			
☐ crystal	14.00	23.00	15.50
☐ limelight	120.00	150.00	130.00
Candleholder, three candles			
☐ crystal	34.00	43.00	35.50
Candy Box, covered, footed, 5½″			
☐ crystal	80.00	100.00	85.00
☐ limelight	250.00	300.00	260.00
Celery Tray, oval, 13″			
☐ crystal	19.00	28.00	20.50
Champagne, 5 oz.			
☐ crystal	6.00	15.00	7.50
Cigarette Lighter			
☐ crystal	24.00	33.00	25.50
Coaster, 4″			
☐ crystal	8.00	13.00	9.00

	Current Price Range		Prior Year Average
Creamer and Sugar Bowl Set, on tray, individual			
☐ crystal	40.00	50.00	43.00
Creamer and Sugar, footed			
☐ crystal	14.00	23.00	15.50
☐ limelight	175.00	200.00	180.00
Cruet with stopper, 4 oz.			
☐ crystal	35.00	43.00	37.00
Flower Bowl, 12″			
☐ crystal	29.00	38.00	30.50
Gardenia Bowl, 13″			
☐ crystal	29.00	38.00	30.50
Iced Tea Tumbler, footed, 12 oz.			
☐ crystal	14.00	23.00	15.50
☐ limelight	45.00	55.00	48.00
Iced Tea Tumbler, 13″			
☐ crystal	14.00	21.00	15.50
Jelly Bowl, two handles, 5″			
☐ crystal	15.00	20.00	17.00
Juice Tumbler, footed, 5 oz.			
☐ crystal	9.00	18.00	10.50
☐ limelight	45.00	55.00	47.00
Luncheon Plate, 8″			
☐ crystal	14.00	23.00	15.50
☐ limelight	43.00	50.00	45.00
Mayonnaise Set, includes bowl, plate, and ladle, 7″			
☐ crystal	24.00	33.00	25.50
Nappy, 4½″			
☐ crystal	9.00	18.00	10.50
Nappy, 5½″			
☐ crystal	11.00	20.00	12.50
☐ limelight	35.00	42.00	37.00
Nappy, round, handle, 5½″			
☐ crystal	14.00	23.00	15.50
Nappy, triangular, handle, 5½″			
☐ crystal	16.00	25.00	17.50
Nut Bowl, individual			
☐ crystal	19.00	28.00	20.50
Oyster Cocktail, 3½ oz.			
☐ crystal	9.00	15.00	7.50
Plate, footed, 5″			
☐ crystal	9.00	18.00	10.50
Plate, 14″			
☐ crystal	19.00	28.00	20.50

	Current Price Range		Prior Year Average
Plate, 18″			
☐ crystal..	33.00	40.00	35.00
☐ limelight...	100.00	125.00	110.00
Punch Bowl, 5 quart			
☐ crystal..	60.00	80.00	65.00
Punch Cup			
☐ crystal..	9.00	18.00	10.50
Relish Bowl, divided, four sections, 10″			
☐ crystal..	29.00	38.00	30.50
☐ limelight...	150.00	180.00	160.00
Salt and Pepper Shakers, pair			
☐ crystal..	14.00	23.00	15.50
Snack Plate, two handles, 7″			
☐ crystal..	11.00	20.00	12.50
Tumbler, 8 oz.			
☐ crystal..	11.00	20.00	12.50
Tumbler, footed, 9 oz.			
☐ crystal..	13.00	22.00	14.50
☐ limelight...	45.00	55.00	48.00
Water Goblet, 10 oz.			
☐ crystal..	14.00	23.00	15.50
Wine, 3½ oz.			
☐ crystal..	14.00	23.00	15.50

RADIANCE
New Martinsville Glass Co.

This pattern was manufactured from 1937 through the early 1940s. The colors you will find are cobalt blue, light blue, crystal, amber and red. Cobalt is the most popular among the colors. The butter dish and the pitcher are, as usual, the most desirable pieces to own. Also watch out for the glass lids as they are scarce. The common element that all these pieces share is a band that resembles a series of cotter pins. The long tear-drop shapes are arranged with the knob end toward the center. Some pieces are decorated with enamel in a floral design, and most have a ridge band either on the upper rim or at the neck.

Radiance

	Current Price Range		Prior Year Average
Bon Bon, diameter 6″			
☐ amber	4.50	7.50	5.50
☐ blue	4.50	7.50	5.50
☐ red	8.00	12.00	9.00
☐ crystal	2.00	4.00	2.50
Bon Bon, pedestal foot, diameter 6″			
☐ amber	5.00	8.00	6.00
☐ blue	5.00	8.00	6.00
☐ red	8.50	11.50	9.00
☐ crystal	4.00	6.00	4.50
Bon Bon, with cover, diameter 6″			
☐ amber	12.00	16.00	13.00
☐ blue	12.00	16.00	13.00
☐ red	18.00	22.00	19.00
☐ crystal	8.00	12.00	9.00
Bowl, flared rim, diameter 10″			
☐ amber	8.50	11.50	9.00
☐ blue	8.50	11.50	9.00
☐ red	18.00	22.00	19.00
☐ crystal	6.00	9.00	7.00
Bowl, flared edge, diameter 12″			
☐ amber	11.00	14.00	12.00
☐ blue	11.00	14.00	12.00
☐ red	20.00	25.00	21.00
☐ crystal	6.00	9.00	7.00
Bowl, scalloped edge, diameter 10″			
☐ amber	10.00	13.00	11.00
☐ blue	10.00	13.00	11.00
☐ red	15.00	20.00	16.50
☐ crystal	7.00	10.00	8.00

	Current Price Range		Prior Year Average
Bowl, scalloped edge, diameter 12″			
☐ amber	12.00	15.00	13.00
☐ blue	12.00	15.00	13.00
☐ red	21.00	26.00	22.00
☐ crystal	7.00	10.00	8.00
Butter Dish			
☐ amber	135.00	160.00	140.00
☐ blue	135.00	160.00	140.00
☐ crystal	60.00	80.00	67.00
Candlesticks, double branch			
☐ amber	9.50	12.50	10.00
☐ blue	9.50	12.50	10.00
☐ crystal	6.00	9.00	7.00
☐ red	17.00	21.00	18.00
Candlesticks, low, bowl-shaped			
☐ red	47.00	57.00	52.00
Celery Bowl, length 10″			
☐ amber	6.00	9.00	7.00
☐ blue	6.00	9.00	7.00
☐ red	11.00	14.00	12.00
☐ crystal	5.00	8.00	6.00
Cheese and Cracker Set, with plates			
☐ amber	13.00	17.00	14.00
☐ blue	13.00	17.00	14.00
☐ crystal	8.00	11.00	9.00
☐ red	27.00	33.00	28.50
Comport, height 5″			
☐ amber	7.00	10.00	8.00
☐ blue	7.00	10.00	8.00
☐ red	10.50	13.50	11.25
☐ crystal	5.00	8.00	6.00
Comport, height 6″			
☐ amber	6.50	9.50	7.25
☐ blue	6.50	9.50	7.25
☐ red	11.00	15.00	12.00
☐ crystal	4.50	7.50	5.25
Condiment Set, with tray			
☐ amber	83.00	93.00	95.00
☐ blue	83.00	93.00	95.00
☐ red	115.00	135.00	120.00
☐ crystal	40.00	60.00	47.00

	Current Price Range		Prior Year Average
Creamer			
☐ amber	5.50	8.50	6.50
☐ blue	5.50	8.50	6.50
☐ red..	8.50	11.50	9.00
☐ crystal	4.50	7.00	5.25
Cruet, oil and vinegar			
☐ amber	20.00	25.00	21.00
☐ blue	20.00	25.00	21.00
☐ red..	27.00	33.00	28.00
☐ crystal	10.00	13.00	11.50
Cup			
☐ amber	4.00	6.00	4.50
☐ blue	4.00	6.00	4.50
☐ red..	7.00	10.00	8.00
☐ crystal	3.00	5.00	3.50
Decanter, with handle and stopper			
☐ amber	48.00	56.00	50.00
☐ blue	48.00	56.00	50.00
☐ red..	80.00	90.00	83.00
☐ crystal	24.00	30.00	26.00
Lamp, height 12″			
☐ amber	32.00	41.00	35.00
☐ blue	32.00	41.00	35.00
☐ red..	66.00	74.00	68.00
☐ crystal	16.00	20.00	17.00
Lunch Plate, diameter 8″			
☐ amber	4.00	6.00	4.50
☐ blue	4.00	6.00	4.50
☐ red..	5.50	8.50	6.00
☐ crystal	3.00	5.00	3.50
Mayonnaise Set, three pieces			
☐ amber	10.50	14.00	11.00
☐ blue	10.50	14.00	11.00
☐ red..	23.00	27.00	24.00
☐ crystal	6.00	9.00	7.00
Nut Bowl, handled, diameter 5″			
☐ amber	5.00	8.00	6.00
☐ blue	5.00	8.00	6.00
☐ red..	8.50	11.50	9.00
☐ crystal	3.00	5.00	3.50
Pickle Bowl, length 7″			
☐ amber	5.00	8.00	6.00
☐ blue	5.00	8.00	6.00
☐ red..	8.00	11.00	9.00
☐ crystal	3.00	5.00	3.50

	Current Price Range		Prior Year Average
Pitcher, height 8″			
☐ amber	102.00	112.00	105.00
☐ blue	102.00	112.00	105.00
☐ red	147.00	157.00	149.00
☐ crystal	50.00	60.00	52.00
Punch Bowl			
☐ amber	34.00	41.00	35.00
☐ blue	34.00	41.00	35.00
☐ red	92.00	82.00	73.00
☐ crystal	18.00	24.00	20.00
Punch Cup			
☐ amber	3.00	5.00	3.50
☐ blue	3.00	5.00	3.50
☐ red	5.50	8.50	6.50
☐ crystal	2.00	4.00	2.50
Punch Ladle			
☐ amber	36.00	43.00	38.00
☐ blue	36.00	43.00	38.00
☐ red	70.00	80.00	73.00
☐ crystal	20.00	26.00	22.00
Relish Bowl, two compartments, diameter 7″			
☐ amber	6.00	9.00	7.00
☐ blue	6.00	9.00	7.00
☐ red	11.00	14.00	12.00
☐ crystal	4.00	8.00	5.00
Relish Bowl, three compartments, length 8″			
☐ amber	7.50	11.50	8.00
☐ blue	7.50	11.50	8.00
☐ red	13.00	17.00	14.00
☐ crystal	6.00	9.00	7.00
Salt and Pepper Shakers, pair			
☐ amber	20.00	25.00	21.00
☐ blue	20.00	25.00	21.00
☐ red	30.00	35.00	31.00
☐ crystal	12.00	15.00	13.00
Saucer			
☐ amber	1.50	3.50	2.00
☐ blue	1.50	3.50	2.00
☐ red	2.00	4.00	2.50
☐ crystal	1.00	3.00	1.50

	Current Price Range		Prior Year Average
Sugar Bowl			
☐ amber	5.50	8.50	6.00
☐ blue	5.50	8.50	6.00
☐ red..	9.50	13.00	10.00
☐ crystal	3.00	5.00	3.50
Tray, egg shape, length 10″			
☐ amber	13.00	17.00	14.00
☐ blue	13.00	17.00	14.00
☐ red..	18.00	22.00	19.00
☐ crystal	7.00	10.00	8.00
Tumbler, height 8″			
☐ amber	7.50	10.50	8.25
☐ blue	7.50	10.50	8.25
☐ red..	13.00	17.00	14.00
☐ crystal	6.00	9.00	7.00
Vase, flare top, height 10″			
☐ amber	19.00	24.00	20.00
☐ blue	19.00	24.00	20.00
☐ red..	30.00	35.00	31.00
☐ crystal	12.00	15.00	13.00
Vase, rose bowl rim, height 12″			
☐ amber	34.00	41.00	35.00
☐ blue	34.00	41.00	35.00
☐ red..	42.00	51.00	45.00
☐ crystal	20.00	24.00	21.00

RIDGELEIGH
A.H. Heisey & Co.

This prismatic pattern was made on blank No. 1469. The colors were crystal, sahara (yellow) and zircon (blue-green). The crystal is available but the zircon and sahara are scarce.

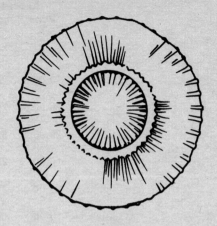

Ridgeleigh

	Current Price Range		Prior Year Average
Ashtray, round			
☐ crystal	5.00	10.00	7.00
Ashtray, round, 4″			
☐ crystal	5.00	10.00	7.00
Ashtray, square			
☐ crystal	4.00	9.00	5.00
☐ sahara	24.00	30.00	26.00
☐ zircon	34.00	40.00	36.00
Ashtray, square, 6″			
☐ crystal	14.00	23.00	15.50
Ashtrays, bridge, set of four			
☐ crystal	45.00	55.00	48.00
Bitters Bottle			
☐ crystal	34.00	40.00	37.00
Bottle, with stopper			
☐ crystal	64.00	75.00	67.00
Box, 8″			
☐ crystal	19.00	28.00	20.50
Candleholder, one candle, footed, 2″			
☐ crystal	17.00	23.00	19.00
☐ zircon	95.00	125.00	105.00
Candleholder, prisms, 7″			
☐ crystal	59.00	80.00	62.50
Candleholder, 2 lite			
☐ crystal	110.00	140.00	120.00

	Current Price Range		Prior Year Average
Candleholder Vase, 6″			
☐ crystal	18.00	23.00	19.50
Celery Tray, 12″			
☐ crystal	19.00	28.00	20.50
Centerpiece Bowl, 8″			
☐ crystal	19.00	28.00	20.50
Centerpiece Bowl, 11″			
☐ crystal	29.00	38.00	30.50
Champagne, blown, 5 oz.			
☐ crystal	16.00	25.00	17.50
Champagne, pressed			
☐ crystal	15.00	20.00	17.00
Cheese Dish, two handles, 6″			
☐ crystal	10.00	15.00	7.50
Cigarette Box, covered, 6″			
☐ crystal	15.00	20.00	17.00
☐ sahara	95.00	115.00	105.00
☐ zircon	150.00	175.00	160.00
Cigarette Box, oval, covered			
☐ crystal	35.00	42.00	37.00
Cigarette Holder, covered			
☐ crystal	30.00	37.00	33.00
Cigarette Holder, round			
☐ crystal	8.00	12.00	9.00
☐ sahara	40.00	50.00	44.00
☐ zircon	75.00	85.00	78.00
Cigarette Holder, square			
☐ crystal	12.00	16.00	13.00
☐ sahara	40.00	50.00	43.00
☐ zircon	75.00	85.00	78.00
Claret, blown, 4 oz.			
☐ crystal	24.00	33.00	25.50
Claret, pressed			
☐ crystal	19.00	28.00	20.50
Coaster			
☐ crystal	5.00	10.00	7.00
☐ sahara	18.00	25.00	21.00
☐ zircon	34.00	40.00	36.00
Cocktail, blown, 3½″ oz.			
☐ crystal	24.00	33.00	25.50
Cocktail, pressed			
☐ crystal	14.00	23.00	15.50
Cocktail Shaker, with strainer and stopper			
☐ crystal	80.00	100.00	82.50

	Current Price Range		Prior Year Average
Cologne Bottle, 4 oz.			
☐ crystal	39.00	48.00	40.50
Compote, footed, 6″			
☐ crystal	19.00	25.00	21.00
Compote, covered, footed, 6″			
☐ crystal	34.00	40.00	36.00
Cordial, blown, 1 oz.			
☐ crystal	90.00	125.00	100.00
Creamer			
☐ crystal	14.00	23.00	15.50
Creamer, small			
☐ crystal	9.00	18.00	10.50
Cruet, with stopper, 3 oz.			
☐ crystal	34.00	43.00	35.50
Cup			
☐ crystal	9.00	18.00	10.50
Decanter, with stopper			
☐ crystal	70.00	80.00	72.00
Flower Bowl, 10″			
☐ crystal	28.00	37.00	29.50
Flower Bowl, 11½″			
☐ crystal	26.00	36.00	28.00
Flower Bowl, oval, 12″			
☐ crystal	31.00	40.00	32.50
☐ sahara...	95.00	125.00	110.00
☐ zircon..	145.00	175.00	155.00
Flower Bowl, 14″			
☐ crystal	39.00	48.00	40.50
Fruit Bowl, 13″			
☐ crystal	31.00	40.00	32.50
Fruit Bowl, flared rim, 10″			
☐ crystal	29.00	38.00	29.50
Fruit Bowl, flared rim, 12″			
☐ crystal	31.00	40.00	32.50
Goblet, tall, 8 oz.			
☐ crystal	14.00	23.00	15.50
☐ blown...	29.00	35.00	31.00
☐ pressed	20.00	27.00	22.00
Hors d'oeuvres Plate, oval			
☐ crystal	19.00	29.00	20.50
Ice Tub			
☐ crystal	50.00	60.00	54.00
Ice Tub Underplate, two handles			
☐ crystal	14.00	23.00	15.50

	Current Price Range		Prior Year Average
Iced Tea Tumbler, blown, 13 oz.			
☐ crystal..	14.00	23.00	15.50
Jelly Bowl, oval, small			
☐ crystal..	11.00	20.00	12.50
Jelly Bowl, two handles, 6″			
☐ crystal..	11.00	20.00	12.50
Jelly Bowl, two handles, divided, 6″			
☐ crystal..	11.00	20.00	12.50
Juice Tumbler, blown, 5 oz.			
☐ crystal..	14.00	23.00	15.50
Lemon Dish, covered, 5″			
☐ crystal..	28.00	35.00	30.00
Luncheon Goblet, low, 8 oz.			
☐ crystal..	15.00	20.00	17.00
Marmalade Bowl, covered			
☐ crystal..	29.00	38.00	31.00
Mayonnaise Bowl			
☐ crystal..	24.00	34.00	25.50
Mustard Jar, covered			
☐ crystal..	30.00	35.00	32.00
Nappy, flared rim, 4½″			
☐ crystal..	8.00	13.00	10.00
Nappy, square, 5″			
☐ crystal..	8.00	14.00	9.50
Nappy, square, 8″			
☐ crystal..	24.00	33.00	25.50
Nappy, square, 9″			
☐ crystal..	24.00	33.00	25.50
Nut Bowl, individual			
☐ crystal..	12.00	16.00	13.50
Nut Bowl, individual, divided into two sections			
☐ crystal..	15.00	19.00	17.00
Old Fashion Tumbler, pressed, 8 oz.			
☐ crystal..	18.00	25.00	20.00
Oyster Cocktail Goblet, pressed			
☐ crystal..	9.00	18.00	10.50
Pitcher, 64 oz.			
☐ crystal..	80.00	92.00	84.00
Pitcher, ice lip, 64 oz.			
☐ crystal..	90.00	100.00	93.00
Plate, footed, 13½″			
☐ crystal..	19.00	28.00	20.50
Plate, round, 6″			
☐ crystal..	5.00	9.00	6.00

	Current Price Range		Prior Year Average

Plate, round, 8″
☐ crystal 7.00 10.00 8.00
Plate, scalloped, 6″
☐ crystal 4.00 11.00 5.50
Plate, square, 6″
☐ crystal 8.00 11.00 9.00
Plate, square, 7″
☐ crystal 10.00 13.00 11.00
Punch Bowl, 11″
☐ crystal 85.00 95.00 88.00
Punch Cup
☐ crystal 10.00 15.00 12.00
Relish Bowl, oval, divided into two sections
☐ crystal 19.00 25.00 21.00
Relish Tray, three sections, 11″
☐ crystal 24.00 33.00 25.50
Relish Tray, two sections, 12″
☐ crystal 24.00 30.00 25.50
Salad Bowl, 9″
☐ crystal 26.00 35.00 27.50
Salt and Pepper Shakers, pair
☐ crystal 19.00 28.00 20.50
Salt Dip
☐ crystal 10.00 16.00 12.00
Salver, 14″
☐ crystal 60.00 70.00 63.00
Sandwich Plate, 13½″
☐ crystal 19.00 28.00 20.50
Saucer
☐ crystal 2.00 9.00 3.50
Sherbet Goblet, blown, 5 oz.
☐ crystal 10.00 15.00 11.50
Sherry Goblet, blown, 2 oz.
☐ crystal 44.00 53.00 45.50
Smoking Set, includes oval holder and two ashtrays
☐ crystal 34.00 43.00 35.50
Soda Tumbler, blown, 8 oz.
☐ crystal 15.00 24.00 15.50
Soda Tumbler, pressed, footed, 5 oz.
☐ crystal 11.00 20.00 12.50
Sugar and Creamer Tray
☐ crystal 9.00 18.00 10.50

	Current Price Range		Prior Year Average
Sugar Bowl, small			
☐ crystal..............................	9.00	18.00	10.50
Sugar Bowl			
☐ crystal..............................	14.00	23.00	15.50
Swan Bowl, 14″			
☐ crystal..............................	49.00	58.00	50.50
Tea Cup			
☐ crystal..............................	11.00	20.00	12.50
Tray, 10½″			
☐ crystal..............................	19.00	28.00	20.50
Tumbler, pressed, 2½ oz.			
☐ crystal..............................	14.00	23.00	15.50
Tumbler, pressed, 10 oz.			
☐ crystal..............................	11.00	20.00	12.50
Vase, small, variety of shapes			
☐ crystal..............................	19.00	28.00	21.00
Vase, 6″			
☐ crystal..............................	14.00	23.00	15.50
Vase, 8″			
☐ crystal..............................	16.00	25.00	17.50
Wine Goblet, blown, 2½ oz.			
☐ crystal..............................	39.00	48.00	40.50
Wine Goblet, pressed			
☐ crystal..............................	19.00	28.00	20.50

SATURN
A.H. Heisey & Co.

This pattern features large concentric rings, and was produced in crystal and a blue-green called either zircon or limelight, depending on when it was issued (see Heisey's production colors).

Saturn

	Current Price Range		Prior Year Average
Ashtray			
☐ crystal	14.00	23.00	15.50
Baked Apple Bowl			
☐ crystal...	4.00	13.00	5.50
☐ zircon...	45.00	55.00	47.00
Bitters Bottle			
☐ crystal	29.00	38.00	31.00
Bread Plate, 7″			
☐ crystal...	4.00	11.00	5.50
☐ zircon...	25.00	32.00	26.00
Cake Plate, 13″			
☐ crystal	14.00	24.00	15.50
Cake Plate, 15″			
☐ crystal	19.00	29.00	20.50
Candleholder, footed, 3″			
☐ crystal...	12.00	21.00	13.00
☐ zircon...	120.00	150.00	130.00
Celery Bowl, 10″			
☐ crystal	12.00	21.00	13.50
Champagne Goblet, 6 oz.			
☐ crystal...	8.00	15.00	9.50
☐ zircon...	50.00	60.00	54.00
Cocktail Goblet, 3 oz.			
☐ crystal...	5.00	14.00	6.50
☐ zircon...	45.00	55.00	48.00
Compote, 7″			
☐ crystal...	29.00	38.00	30.50
☐ zircon...	119.00	128.00	121.00
Creamer and Sugar			
☐ crystal...	25.00	35.00	28.00
☐ zircon...	170.00	200.00	180.00
Cruet, stopper, 2 oz.			
☐ crystal...	39.00	48.00	41.00
☐ zircon...	210.00	240.00	212.00
Cup			
☐ crystal...	8.00	17.00	9.50
☐ zircon...	39.00	48.00	41.00
Finger Bowl			
☐ crystal	7.00	11.00	8.00
Flower Bowl, 13″			
☐ crystal	29.00	38.00	30.50
Fruit Bowl, 12″			
☐ crystal	26.00	35.00	27.50

	Current Price Range		Prior Year Average
Fruit Cocktail, 4 oz.			
☐ crystal	4.00	13.00	5.50
☐ zircon	40.00	50.00	42.00
Hors d'oeuvre Tray, upturned sides			
☐ crystal	24.00	30.00	26.00
☐ zircon	70.00	90.00	75.00
Juice Tumbler, 5 oz.			
☐ crystal	7.00	11.00	8.00
☐ zircon	60.00	72.00	64.00
Luncheon Plate, 8″			
☐ crystal	8.00	13.00	7.50
☐ zircon	35.00	45.00	39.00
Luncheon Tumbler, 9 oz.			
☐ crystal	10.00	16.00	8.50
Marmalade Jar, covered			
☐ crystal	170.00	200.00	180.00
Mustard Jar, covered			
☐ crystal	29.00	38.00	30.50
☐ zircon	218.00	248.00	221.00
Nappy, 4½″			
☐ crystal	7.00	10.00	8.00
Old Fashion Tumbler, 7 oz.			
☐ crystal	8.00	12.00	9.00
Old Fashion Tumbler, 8 oz.			
☐ crystal	8.00	15.00	9.50
Parfait Glass, 5 oz.			
☐ crystal	8.00	17.00	9.50
☐ zircon	41.00	50.00	42.50
Pitcher, ice lip, blown			
☐ crystal	49.00	58.00	51.00
☐ zircon	200.00	250.00	215.00
Plate, 6″			
☐ crystal	2.00	9.00	3.50
☐ zircon	25.00	32.00	27.00
Relish Bowl, three sections, 9″			
☐ crystal	14.00	23.00	15.50
Rose Bowl (pressed)			
☐ crystal	29.00	38.00	32.00
☐ zircon	85.00	95.00	88.00
Salad Bowl, 11″			
☐ crystal	24.00	33.00	25.50
Salt and Pepper Shakers, pair			
☐ crystal	24.00	34.00	25.50
☐ zircon	300.00	350.00	320.00

	Current Price Range		Prior Year Average

`Saucer
| ☐ crystal | 2.00 | 9.00 | 3.50 |
| ☐ zircon | 14.00 | 20.00 | 17.00 |

Sherbet, 4½ oz.
| ☐ crystal | 6.00 | 10.00 | 7.00 |
| ☐ zircon | 35.00 | 45.00 | 38.00 |

Sherbet, 5 oz.
| ☐ crystal | 6.00 | 10.00 | 7.00 |
| ☐ zircon | 40.00 | 50.00 | 44.00 |

Soda Tumbler, 12 oz.
| ☐ crystal | 11.00 | 20.00 | 12.50 |
| ☐ zircon | 40.00 | 50.00 | 43.00 |

Sugar Bowl
| ☐ crystal | 14.00 | 24.00 | 15.50 |
| ☐ zircon | 75.00 | 95.00 | 81.00 |

Sugar Shaker
| ☐ crystal | 29.00 | 39.00 | 30.50 |

Vase (violet)
| ☐ crystal | 19.00 | 28.00 | 21.00 |
| ☐ zircon | 54.00 | 64.00 | 56.00 |

Vase, found in two styles, straight sides or flaring rim, 8½"
| ☐ crystal | 24.00 | 33.00 | 25.50 |
| ☐ zircon | 140.00 | 170.00 | 152.00 |

Water Goblet, 10 oz.
| ☐ crystal | 9.00 | 18.00 | 11.00 |
| ☐ zircon | 64.00 | 74.00 | 65.50 |

Water Tumbler, 10 oz.
| ☐ crystal | 9.00 | 18.00 | 10.50 |

Whipped Cream Bowl, 5"
| ☐ crystal | 9.00 | 18.00 | 10.50 |
| ☐ zircon | 44.00 | 53.00 | 45.50 |

TROJAN
Fostoria Glass Co.

This pattern was manufactured from 1929 through 1944. It is made up of spade shapes created by a framing network with a curly scroll, with a floral design that is somewhat like a fleur-de-lis. These shapes alternate around the rim with draped scrollwork in low relief. The rest of the glass is plain, with no center medallions or base designs. The most desirable pieces in this line are the two-piece items, the pitcher, the vase and the dinner plates. The colors are pink and yellow. Both are equally popular and are similar in value. All pieces are available in both colors.

	Current Price Range		Prior Year Average
Ashtray, large			
☐ pink or yellow	25.00	35.00	25.50
Bon Bon Bowl			
☐ pink or yellow	10.00	20.00	12.00
Bouillon Bowl, footed			
☐ pink or yellow	14.00	25.00	15.00
Cereal Bowl, diameter 6″			
☐ pink or yellow	16.00	26.00	17.50
Bowl, soup, 7″			
☐ pink or yellow	23.00	28.00	25.00
Bowl, oval, 9″			
☐ pink or yellow	32.00	40.00	35.00
Bowl, 10″			
☐ pink or yellow	30.00	35.00	32.00
Bowl, centerpiece, 12″			
☐ pink or yellow	30.00	40.00	34.00
Compote, height 6″			
☐ pink or yellow	20.00	30.00	22.00
Creamer, footed			
☐ pink or yellow	15.00	25.00	16.50
Decanter, with stopper			
☐ pink or yellow	255.00	300.00	275.00
Finger Bowl, with liner			
☐ pink or yellow	20.00	30.00	22.00
Goblet, cordial, 1 oz.			
☐ pink or yellow	60.00	80.00	70.00
Goblet, cocktail, 3 oz.			
☐ pink or yellow	22.00	32.00	27.00
Goblet, wine, 3 oz.			
☐ pink or yellow	40.00	50.00	45.00
Goblet, claret, 4 oz., 6″			
☐ pink or yellow	35.00	45.00	40.00
Goblet, water, 10 oz., 8¼″			
☐ pink or yellow	26.00	31.00	28.00
Grill Plate, diameter 10″			
☐ pink or yellow	30.00	40.00	34.00
Luncheon Plate, diameter 8¾″			
☐ pink or yellow	10.00	20.00	12.00
Mayonnaise Bowl, with liner			
☐ pink or yellow	25.00	35.00	26.50
Parfait			
☐ pink or yellow	24.00	34.00	25.00
Pitcher			
☐ pink or yellow	225.00	300.00	235.00

	Current Price Range		Prior Year Average

Plate, bread and butter, 6″
☐ pink or yellow .... | 4.00 | 7.00 | 5.00 |

Plate, cream soup, 7½″
☐ pink or yellow .... | 8.00 | 11.00 | 9.00 |

Plate, mayonnaise, 7½″
☐ pink or yellow .... | 8.00 | 11.00 | 9.00 |

Plate, salad, 7½″
☐ pink or yellow .... | 6.00 | 9.00 | 7.50 |

Plate, 8½″
☐ pink or yellow .... | 9.00 | 12.00 | 10.00 |

Plate, luncheon, 9½″
☐ pink or yellow .... | 14.00 | 20.00 | 17.00 |

Plate, dinner, 10¼″
☐ pink or yellow .... | 32.00 | 40.00 | 35.00 |

Plate, chop, 13″
☐ pink or yellow .... | 45.00 | 55.00 | 50.00 |

Platter, diameter 12″
☐ pink or yellow .... | 32.00 | 40.00 | 32.00 |

Platter, diameter 15″
☐ pink or yellow .... | 60.00 | 80.00 | 70.00 |

Relish Dish, diameter 8½″
☐ pink or yellow .... | 10.00 | 20.00 | 12.00 |

Relish Dish, three compartments
☐ pink or yellow .... | 20.00 | 30.00 | 22.00 |

Saucer
☐ pink or yellow .... | 4.00 | 10.00 | 6.00 |

Sherbet, height 4¼″
☐ pink or yellow .... | 14.00 | 20.00 | 16.00 |

Sugar, complete
☐ pink or yellow .... | 75.00 | 90.00 | 84.00 |

Sugar Bottom
☐ pink or yellow .... | 15.00 | 20.00 | 16.00 |

Sugar Lid
☐ pink or yellow .... | 65.00 | 80.00 | 70.00 |

Tray, center handle, diameter 11″
☐ pink or yellow .... | 25.00 | 35.00 | 26.50 |

Tumbler, footed, 2½ oz.
☐ pink or yellow .... | 20.00 | 30.00 | 24.00 |

Tumbler, juice, footed, 5 oz.
☐ pink or yellow .... | 14.00 | 20.00 | 17.00 |

Tumbler, parfait, footed, 6 oz.
☐ pink or yellow .... | 35.00 | 45.00 | 40.00 |

Tumbler, water, footed, 9 oz.
☐ pink or yellow .... | 15.00 | 20.00 | 16.00 |

	Current Price Range		Prior Year Average
Tumbler, ice tea, footed, 12 oz.			
☐ pink or yellow	18.00	25.00	21.00
Vase, height 8″			
☐ pink or yellow	75.00	90.00	80.00
Vase, flared top			
☐ pink or yellow	110.00	140.00	120.00
Whipped Cream Tub			
☐ pink or yellow	80.00	100.00	90.00

TWIST
A.H. Heisey & Co.

This pattern was made in several colors, including crystal, pink, green, and yellow. Some alexandrite was also made, but this color is quite rare.

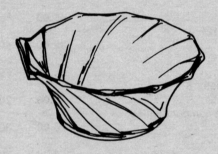

Twist

Almond Bowl, footed			
☐ crystal	8.50	11.50	9.00
☐ pink	18.00	22.00	19.00
☐ green	23.00	27.00	24.00
☐ marigold	50.00	60.00	53.00
☐ yellow...	50.00	60.00	53.00
Baking Dish, oval, 9″			
☐ crystal	8.00	12.00	9.00
☐ pink	30.00	40.00	33.00
☐ green	40.00	45.00	42.00
☐ marigold	60.00	70.00	63.00
Bon Bon Dish			
☐ crystal	8.00	15.00	12.00
☐ pink	10.00	15.00	13.00
☐ green ....,	13.00	17.00	14.00
☐ marigold	18.00	22.00	19.00

	Current Price Range		Prior Year Average
Bowl, handles, 6″			
☐ crystal	5.50	8.50	6.50
☐ pink	13.00	17.00	14.00
☐ green	15.00	19.00	16.00
☐ marigold	18.00	22.00	19.00
Bowl, low-footed, 8″			
☐ crystal	18.00	22.00	19.00
☐ pink	28.00	33.00	29.00
☐ green	32.00	38.00	34.00
☐ marigold	60.00	70.00	63.00
☐ yellow	60.00	70.00	63.00
Candlestick, 1 candle, 2″, each			
☐ crystal	10.00	15.00	12.00
☐ pink	10.00	20.00	14.00
☐ green	17.00	23.00	19.00
☐ marigold	30.00	40.00	37.00
Celery Tray, 10″			
☐ crystal	9.00	16.00	10.50
☐ pink	19.00	27.00	20.50
☐ green	24.00	31.00	25.50
☐ marigold	29.00	37.00	31.00
☐ yellow	25.00	35.00	31.00
Celery Tray, 13″			
☐ crystal	11.00	16.00	12.50
☐ pink	21.00	30.00	22.50
☐ green	26.00	34.00	27.50
☐ marigold	31.00	40.00	32.50
☐ yellow	25.00	32.00	28.00
Champagne, 5 oz.			
☐ crystal	12.00	18.00	14.00
☐ pink	11.00	18.00	12.50
☐ green	25.00	30.00	27.00
☐ marigold	30.00	40.00	33.00
Cheese Dish, handles, 6″			
☐ crystal	8.00	11.00	5.50
☐ pink	10.00	16.00	10.50
☐ green	14.00	22.00	15.50
☐ marigold	19.00	28.00	20.50
Cheese Plate, 8″			
☐ crystal	14.00	23.00	15.50
☐ pink	24.00	33.00	25.50
☐ green	25.00	30.00	27.00
☐ marigold	35.00	40.00	37.00

	Current Price Range		Prior Year Average

Cocktail Goblet, 3 oz.

☐ crystal	10.00	12.00	11.00
☐ pink	12.00	20.00	14.00
☐ green	17.00	24.00	20.00
☐ marigold	25.00	30.00	27.00

Comport, 7″

☐ crystal	25.00	32.00	27.00
☐ pink	44.00	53.00	45.50
☐ green	59.00	68.00	61.00
☐ marigold	115.00	135.00	120.00

Cream Soup Bowl and Plate

☐ crystal	13.00	17.00	14.00
☐ pink	23.00	27.00	24.00
☐ green	26.00	34.00	28.00
☐ marigold	35.00	45.00	39.00

Creamer, angled handles, footed

☐ crystal	19.00	27.00	20.50
☐ pink	24.00	33.00	25.50
☐ green	29.00	37.00	31.00
☐ marigold	58.00	69.00	61.00
☐ yellow	58.00	69.00	61.00

Creamer, individual

☐ crystal	9.00	16.00	10.50
☐ pink	19.00	28.00	21.00
☐ green	24.00	32.00	26.00
☐ marigold	53.00	63.00	55.00
☐ yellow	53.00	63.00	55.00

Cup, angled handles

☐ crystal	20.00	25.00	22.00
☐ pink	12.00	20.00	16.00
☐ green	24.00	33.00	26.00
☐ marigold	29.00	38.00	31.00

Flower Bowl, oval, 8″

☐ crystal	18.00	22.00	19.00
☐ pink	26.00	31.00	27.00
☐ green	32.00	38.00	33.00
☐ marigold	55.00	65.00	57.00
☐ yellow	55.00	65.00	57.00

Flower Bowl, round, 8″

☐ crystal	18.00	22.00	19.00
☐ pink	26.00	30.00	27.00
☐ green	32.00	38.00	33.00
☐ marigold	55.00	65.00	56.00
☐ yellow	55.00	65.00	56.00

	Current Price Range		Prior Year Average

Flower Bowl, 9″

☐ crystal	20.00	24.00	21.00
☐ pink	28.00	33.00	29.00
☐ green	34.00	39.00	35.00
☐ marigold	57.00	67.00	60.00
☐ yellow	57.00	67.00	60.00

Flower Bowl, rolled edge, 9″

☐ crystal	20.00	24.00	21.00
☐ pink	26.00	34.00	28.00
☐ green	34.00	40.00	35.00
☐ marigold	57.00	67.00	60.00
☐ yellow	57.00	67.00	60.00

French Dressing Bottle

☐ crystal	20.00	30.00	23.00
☐ pink	45.00	65.00	50.00
☐ green	60.00	70.00	64.00
☐ marigold	100.00	125.00	110.00
☐ yellow	85.00	95.00	87.00

Ice Tub

☐ crystal	24.00	32.00	26.00
☐ pink	45.00	60.00	50.00
☐ green	55.00	75.00	64.00
☐ marigold	90.00	120.00	105.00
☐ yellow	80.00	100.00	90.00
☐ alexandrite	150.00	200.00	170.00

Iced Tea Tumbler, 12 oz.

☐ crystal	10.00	17.00	11.50
☐ pink	19.00	28.00	20.50
☐ green	24.00	33.00	25.50
☐ marigold	25.00	35.00	29.00

Iced Tea Tumbler, footed, 12 oz.

☐ crystal	11.00	17.00	12.50
☐ pink	21.00	29.00	22.50
☐ green	26.00	34.00	27.50
☐ marigold	35.00	45.00	39.00
☐ yellow	41.00	50.00	43.00

Jelly Bowl, handles, 6″

☐ crystal	10.00	15.00	12.00
☐ pink	13.00	17.00	14.00
☐ green	15.00	19.00	16.00
☐ marigold	18.00	22.00	19.00

	Current Price Range		Prior Year Average

Juice Tumbler, 5 oz.

☐ crystal	3.00	7.00	3.50
☐ pink	11.00	18.00	12.50
☐ green	17.00	25.00	18.50
☐ marigold	23.00	32.00	25.00
☐ yellow	23.00	32.00	25.00

Mayonnaise Bowl

☐ crystal	14.00	21.00	15.50
☐ pink	25.00	32.00	27.00
☐ green	24.00	32.00	25.50
☐ marigold	38.00	47.00	40.00
☐ yellow	32.00	40.00	36.00

Mint Bowl, handles, 6″

☐ crystal	10.00	12.00	10.00
☐ pink	13.00	17.00	14.00
☐ green	15.00	19.00	16.00
☐ marigold	18.00	22.00	19.00
☐ yellow	18.00	22.00	19.00

Muffin Plate, handles, 12″

☐ crystal	19.00	27.00	21.00
☐ pink	34.00	43.00	35.50
☐ green	44.00	54.00	46.00
☐ marigold	32.00	40.00	35.00

Mustard Jar, covered

☐ crystal	19.00	27.00	21.00
☐ pink	45.00	55.00	50.00
☐ green	60.00	70.00	63.00
☐ marigold	74.00	85.00	76.00
☐ yellow	74.00	85.00	76.00

Nappy, 4″

☐ crystal	4.00	6.00	4.50
☐ pink	10.50	13.50	11.50
☐ green	13.00	17.00	14.00
☐ marigold	15.00	19.00	16.00
☐ yellow	15.00	19.00	16.00

Nut Dish, individual

☐ crystal	10.00	15.00	12.00
☐ pink	18.00	22.00	19.00
☐ green	23.00	27.00	24.00
☐ marigold	35.00	42.00	37.00

Oyster Cocktail Goblet, 3 oz.

☐ crystal	10.00	15.00	12.00
☐ pink	15.00	20.00	17.00
☐ green	14.00	23.00	16.00
☐ marigold	25.00	32.00	27.00

	Current Price Range		Prior Year Average
Pickle Tray, 7″			
☐ crystal	6.00	12.00	7.00
☐ pink	12.00	18.00	15.00
☐ green	15.00	20.00	17.00
☐ marigold	24.00	32.00	25.00
Pitcher, 3 pint			
☐ crystal	34.00	43.00	36.00
☐ pink	64.00	75.00	66.00
☐ green	108.00	125.00	112.00
Plate, 8″			
☐ crystal	6.00	12.00	7.50
☐ pink	11.00	17.00	12.50
☐ green	14.00	20.00	16.00
☐ marigold	19.00	26.00	20.50
Platter, 12″			
☐ crystal	18.00	22.00	20.00
☐ pink	25.00	30.00	27.00
☐ green	30.00	35.00	32.00
☐ marigold	59.00	71.00	61.00
Relish Tray, 3 sections, 13″			
☐ crystal	9.00	17.00	10.50
☐ pink	14.00	23.00	15.50
☐ green	25.00	31.00	27.00
☐ marigold	34.00	43.00	35.50
Salt and Pepper			
☐ crystal	19.00	26.00	21.00
☐ pink	29.00	37.00	30.50
☐ green	39.00	48.00	41.00
☐ marigold	49.00	61.00	51.00
Sandwich Plate, handles, 12″			
☐ crystal	15.00	20.00	17.00
☐ pink	20.00	25.00	22.00
☐ green	25.00	30.00	27.00
☐ marigold	30.00	35.00	32.00
Saucer			
☐ crystal	2.00	6.00	3.25
☐ pink	4.00	9.00	5.50
☐ green	6.00	13.00	7.50
☐ marigold	9.00	16.00	10.50
Sherbet, 5 oz.			
☐ crystal	4.00	9.00	5.50
☐ pink	15.00	20.00	17.00
☐ green	20.00	25.00	22.00
☐ marigold	25.00	30.00	27.00

	Current Price Range		Prior Year Average
Soda Tumbler, flared, 8 oz.			
☐ crystal	6.00	14.00	7.50
☐ pink	14.00	23.00	16.00
☐ green	19.00	27.00	20.50
☐ marigold	29.00	38.00	30.50
Soda Tumbler, straight, 8 oz.			
☐ crystal	6.00	13.00	7.50
☐ pink	14.00	23.00	15.50
☐ green	19.00	28.00	21.00
☐ marigold	29.00	38.00	31.00
Soda Tumbler, footed, 9 oz.			
☐ crystal	7.00	13.00	8.50
☐ pink	15.00	24.00	16.50
☐ green	20.00	29.00	22.00
☐ marigold	30.00	39.00	33.00
Sugar, covered, angled handles			
☐ crystal	14.00	23.00	15.50
☐ pink	21.00	29.00	22.50
☐ green	31.00	40.00	32.50
☐ marigold	50.00	61.00	52.00
Sugar, footed			
☐ crystal	19.00	26.00	20.50
☐ pink	24.00	32.00	26.00
☐ green	29.00	37.00	32.00
☐ marigold	49.00	61.00	51.00
Sugar, individual			
☐ crystal	14.00	23.00	15.50
☐ pink	24.00	34.00	25.50
☐ green	29.00	38.00	31.00
☐ marigold	54.00	65.00	56.00
☐ yellow..	54.00	65.00	56.00
Tumbler, footed, 6 oz.			
☐ crystal	4.00	9.00	5.50
☐ pink	12.00	19.00	13.50
☐ green	18.00	27.00	19.50
☐ marigold	24.00	33.00	26.00
☐ yellow..	24.00	33.00	26.00
Tumbler, 8 oz.			
☐ crystal	6.00	12.00	7.50
☐ pink	14.00	22.00	15.50
☐ green	19.00	27.00	20.50
☐ marigold	29.00	38.00	31.00

	Current Price Range		Prior Year Average

Wine Goblet, 2½ oz.

☐ crystal	14.00	20.00	16.00
☐ pink	25.00	30.00	27.00
☐ green	30.00	35.00	32.00
☐ marigold	50.00	60.00	52.00

VERSAILLES
Fostoria Glass Co.

This pattern was made from 1928 through 1942. It was probably Fostoria's top line during the actual production years. It continues to be highly collectible and excites a lot of interest. The colors were blue, pink, green and yellow. The stemware of this pattern was made using two different blanks. The blue, pink and green were made on the same blank as *June*; the yellow on the same blank as *Trojan*. The bowls on the stemware are colored, but the stems are crystal. Blue is the most popular color among collectors. The pitcher is very difficult to find and is very expensive. The vases and shakers are highly sought-after pieces.

Ashtray

☐ blue	28.00	38.00	30.00
☐ green	22.00	32.00	23.00
☐ pink	22.00	32.00	22.00
☐ yellow	25.00	35.00	26.50

Bon Bon Bowl

☐ blue	12.00	22.00	14.00
☐ green	10.00	20.00	12.00
☐ pink	10.00	20.00	12.00
☐ yellow	10.00	20.00	12.00

Bouillon Bowl

☐ blue	20.00	30.00	21.50
☐ green	15.00	25.00	17.00
☐ pink	15.00	25.00	17.00
☐ yellow	16.00	26.00	17.50

Bread and Butter Plate, diameter 6"

☐ blue	4.00	10.00	5.00
☐ green	3.00	9.00	4.00
☐ pink	3.00	9.00	4.00
☐ yellow	3.00	9.00	4.00

	Current Price Range		Prior Year Average
Cereal Bowl, diameter 6″			
☐ blue	25.00	35.00	27.00
☐ green	18.00	28.00	20.00
☐ pink	18.00	28.00	20.00
☐ yellow	20.00	30.00	22.00
Chop Plate, diameter 13″			
☐ blue	33.00	43.00	35.00
☐ green	28.00	38.00	30.00
☐ pink	28.00	38.00	30.00
☐ yellow	30.00	40.00	32.00
Compote, height 6″			
☐ blue	28.00	38.00	30.00
☐ green	20.00	30.00	22.00
☐ pink	20.00	30.00	22.00
☐ yellow	25.00	35.00	26.00
Compote, height 7″			
☐ blue	33.00	43.00	34.00
☐ green	23.00	33.00	24.00
☐ pink	23.00	33.00	24.00
☐ yellow	28.00	38.00	30.00
Creamer, footed			
☐ blue	18.00	28.00	20.00
☐ green	13.00	23.00	15.00
☐ pink	13.00	23.00	15.00
☐ yellow	13.00	23.00	15.00
Demitasse Cup and Saucer			
☐ blue	45.00	55.00	47.00
☐ green	20.00	30.00	22.00
☐ pink	20.00	30.00	22.00
☐ yellow	30.00	40.00	32.00
Decanter			
☐ blue	175.00	250.00	185.00
☐ green	125.00	200.00	135.00
☐ pink	125.00	200.00	135.00
☐ yellow	140.00	180.00	145.00
Finger Bowl, with liner			
☐ blue	25.00	35.00	26.50
☐ green	18.00	28.00	18.50
☐ pink	18.00	28.00	18.50
☐ yellow	23.00	33.00	24.50
Fruit Bowl, diameter 5″			
☐ blue	15.00	25.00	16.50
☐ green	12.00	22.00	14.00
☐ pink	12.00	22.00	14.00
☐ yellow	13.00	23.00	14.00

	Current Price Range		Prior Year Average

Ice Bucket
☐ blue	77.00	87.00	80.00
☐ green	60.00	70.00	62.00
☐ pink	60.00	70.00	62.00
☐ yellow	73.00	84.00	74.50

Lemon Bowl
☐ blue	12.00	22.00	14.00
☐ green	8.00	18.00	10.00
☐ pink	8.00	18.00	10.00
☐ yellow	10.00	20.00	12.00

Luncheon Plate, diameter 8¾″
☐ blue	8.00	18.00	10.00
☐ green	6.00	16.00	7.50
☐ pink	6.00	16.00	7.50
☐ yellow	8.00	18.00	10.00

Mayonnaise Bowl, with liner
☐ blue	45.00	55.00	47.00
☐ green	33.00	43.00	35.00
☐ pink	33.00	43.00	35.00
☐ yellow	38.00	48.00	40.00

Parfait
☐ blue	28.00	38.00	30.00
☐ green	24.00	34.00	25.00
☐ pink	24.00	34.00	25.00
☐ yellow	25.00	35.00	26.50

Pitcher
☐ blue	380.00	440.00	400.00
☐ green	240.00	280.00	245.00
☐ pink	240.00	280.00	245.00
☐ yellow	280.00	330.00	295.00

Platter, diameter 12″
☐ blue	38.00	48.00	40.00
☐ green	28.00	38.00	30.00
☐ pink	28.00	38.00	30.00
☐ yellow	33.00	43.00	34.50

Platter, diameter 15″
☐ blue	58.00	68.00	59.50
☐ green	43.00	53.00	44.00
☐ pink	43.00	53.00	44.00
☐ yellow	45.00	55.00	46.50

Relish, diameter 8½″
☐ blue	38.00	48.00	39.50
☐ green	28.00	38.00	32.00
☐ pink	28.00	38.00	32.00
☐ yellow	33.00	43.00	34.50

	Current Price Range		Prior Year Average
Sauce Boat and Underplate			
☐ blue	57.00	67.00	58.00
☐ green	43.00	53.00	44.00
☐ pink	43.00	53.00	44.00
☐ yellow...	38.00	48.00	40.00
Saucer			
☐ blue	4.00	10.00	5.00
☐ green	3.00	9.00	4.00
☐ pink	3.00	9.00	4.00
☐ yellow...	3.00	8.00	3.50
Soup Bowl, diameter 7″			
☐ blue	28.00	38.00	30.00
☐ green	23.00	33.00	24.50
☐ pink	23.00	33.00	24.50
☐ yellow...	25.00	35.00	26.50
Sugar, footed			
☐ blue	18.00	28.00	20.00
☐ green	13.00	23.00	15.00
☐ pink	13.00	23.00	15.00
☐ yellow...	13.00	23.00	15.00
Tray, diameter 11″, with center handle			
☐ blue	28.00	38.00	30.00
☐ green	18.00	28.00	20.00
☐ pink	18.00	28.00	20.00
☐ yellow...	23.00	33.00	24.50
Tumbler, height 4½″, 5 oz.			
☐ blue	22.00	32.00	23.50
☐ green	18.00	28.00	21.50
☐ pink	18.00	28.00	21.50
☐ yellow...	20.00	30.00	22.50
Tumbler, height 5¼″, 9 oz.			
☐ blue	23.00	33.00	24.50
☐ green	18.00	28.00	19.50
☐ pink	18.00	28.00	19.50
☐ yellow...	19.50	29.50	20.00
Tumbler, height 6″, 12 oz.			
☐ blue	25.00	35.00	26.50
☐ green	20.00	30.00	22.00
☐ pink	20.00	30.00	22.00
☐ yellow...	23.00	33.00	24.50
Vase, height 8″			
☐ blue	120.00	150.00	127.50
☐ green	70.00	90.00	72.50
☐ pink	70.00	90.00	72.50
☐ yellow...	90.00	125.00	97.50

WAVERLY
A.H. Heisey & Co.

This pattern was produced on blank No. 1519 in crystal. At date of publication, five pieces are known to exist in amber.

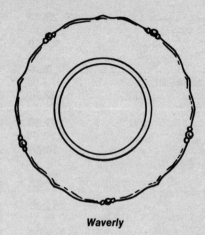

Waverly

	Current Price Range		Prior Year Average
Bowl, 10″			
☐ crystal...	14.00	23.00	15.50
Bowl, 12″			
☐ crystal...	34.00	43.00	35.50
Butter Dish, covered, square, 6″			
☐ crystal...	49.00	58.00	50.50
Cake Plate, footed, 13½″			
☐ crystal...	39.00	48.00	40.50
Candleholder, one candle			
☐ crystal...	79.00	90.00	80.50
Candleholder, two candles			
☐ crystal...	19.00	28.00	20.50
Candleholder, three candles			
☐ crystal...	49.00	60.00	51.00
Candy Box, box tie knob, 6″			
☐ crystal...	24.00	33.00	25.50
Candy Box, covered, 5″			
☐ crystal...	29.00	38.00	30.50
Celery Tray, 12″			
☐ crystal...	12.00	21.00	13.50
Champagne Goblet, 5½ oz.			
☐ crystal...	14.00	23.00	15.50

	Current Price Range		Prior Year Average

Cheese Dish, footed, 5½"
| ☐ crystal | 5.00 | 14.00 | 6.50 |

Cigarette Holder
| ☐ crystal | 29.00 | 38.00 | 31.00 |

Cocktail Goblet, 3½ oz.
| ☐ crystal | 29.00 | 38.00 | 30.50 |

Compote, footed, 6"
| ☐ crystal | 5.00 | 12.00 | 6.50 |

Compote, oval, pedestal, 7"
| ☐ crystal | 27.00 | 36.00 | 28.50 |

Cordial Goblet, 1 oz.
| ☐ crystal | 89.00 | 100.00 | 91.00 |

Creamer, footed
| ☐ crystal | 14.00 | 23.00 | 15.50 |

Creamer and Sugar Set, with tray, small
| ☐ crystal | 24.00 | 33.00 | 25.50 |

Cruet, with stopper, footed, 3 oz.
| ☐ crystal | 39.00 | 48.00 | 40.50 |

Cup
| ☐ crystal | 9.00 | 18.00 | 10.50 |

Flower Bowl, seahorse-footed, 11"
| ☐ crystal | 54.00 | 63.00 | 55.50 |

Fruit Bowl, 9"
| ☐ crystal | 29.00 | 38.00 | 30.50 |

Gardenia Bowl, 10"
| ☐ crystal | 14.00 | 23.00 | 15.50 |

Gardenia Bowl, 13"
| ☐ crystal | 16.00 | 25.00 | 17.50 |

Goblet, blown, 10 oz.
| ☐ crystal | 19.00 | 28.00 | 20.50 |

Honey Dish, footed, 6½"
| ☐ crystal | 5.00 | 14.00 | 6.50 |

Ice Bowl, handles, 6½"
| ☐ crystal | 44.00 | 53.00 | 45.50 |

Iced Tea Tumbler, blown, footed, 13 oz.
| ☐ crystal | 19.00 | 28.00 | 20.50 |

Juice Tumbler, blown, footed, 5 oz.
| ☐ crystal | 14.00 | 23.00 | 15.50 |

Lemon Bowl, covered, oval, 6"
| ☐ crystal | 24.00 | 33.00 | 25.50 |

Luncheon Plate, 8"
| ☐ crystal | 5.00 | 14.00 | 6.50 |

Mayonnaise Bowl, liner and ladle, 5½"
| ☐ crystal | 24.00 | 33.00 | 25.50 |

	Current Price Range		Prior Year Average
Relish Bowl, round, four sections, 9″			
☐ crystal	21.00	30.00	22.50
Relish Bowl, three sections, 7″			
☐ crystal	24.00	32.00	25.50
Salad Bowl, 7″			
☐ crystal	19.00	28.00	20.50
Salad Plate, 7″			
☐ crystal	3.00	10.00	4.50
Salt and Pepper Shakers, pair			
☐ crystal	30.00	35.00	32.00
Sandwich Plate, 11″			
☐ crystal	11.00	20.00	12.50
Sandwich Plate, center handle, 14″			
☐ crystal	35.00	50.00	37.00
Saucer			
☐ crystal	5.00	10.00	6.00
Serving Plate, 10½″			
☐ crystal	15.00	20.00	16.00
Sugar Bowl, footed			
☐ crystal	14.00	23.00	15.50
Vase, 3½″			
☐ crystal	19.00	28.00	20.50
Vase, fan, 7″			
☐ crystal	24.00	33.00	25.50
Vase, footed, 7″			
☐ crystal	21.00	30.00	22.50
Vegetable Bowl, 9″			
☐ crystal	29.00	38.00	30.50
Wine Goblet, blown, 3 oz.			
☐ crystal	20.00	25.00	22.00

CHILDREN'S DISHES

Many manufacturers of Depression glass also produced children's dishes. Such makers often turned to these miniature items in an effort to stimulate a new interest in the glassware.

While many companies produced dishes for children, Akro Agate Co. is among the best known. Established in Akron, Ohio, Akro Agate Co. later moved to West Virginia. Along with small dish sets, the company also made games and marbles. Other makers of children's Depression glass include Jeannette Glass Co., McKee Glass Co., Hazel Atlas Co. and Anchor Hocking.

CHERRY BLOSSOM
Jeannette Glass Co.

Made in pink and delphite, this pattern was called *Jeannette's Junior Dinner Set* in catalogs of the period.

	Current Price Range		Prior Year Average
Creamer, 2¾"			
☐ pink	26.00	28.00	26.50
☐ delphite	23.00	26.00	24.00
Cup, 1½"			
☐ pink	21.00	23.00	21.50
☐ delphite	21.00	23.00	21.50
Plate, 6"			
☐ pink	8.00	10.00	8.50
☐ delphite	5.50	7.00	6.00
Saucer, 4½"			
☐ pink	4.50	6.00	5.00
☐ delphite	4.50	6.00	5.00
Sugar, 2⅝"			
☐ pink	23.00	26.00	24.00
☐ delphite	21.00	24.00	22.00

CHIQUITA
Akro Agate

Green opaque is the most common color found in this pattern made for J. Pressman.

	Current Price Range		Prior Year Average
Complete Set, 16 pieces, in box			
☐ green opaque	48.00	60.00	51.00
☐ cobalt	110.00	125.00	114.00
☐ crystal	150.00	180.00	160.00
☐ baked-on color	57.00	60.00	58.00
Complete Set, 22 pieces, in box			
☐ green opaque	63.00	75.00	65.00
Creamer, 1½"			
☐ green opaque	4.00	5.00	4.25
☐ cobalt	9.00	10.00	9.25
☐ crystal	13.00	15.00	13.50
☐ baked-on color	5.50	6.50	5.75

	Current Price Range		Prior Year Average
Cup, 1½″			
☐ green opaque	3.50	4.50	3.75
☐ cobalt	5.00	6.00	5.25
☐ crystal	10.00	12.00	10.50
☐ baked-on color	4.25	5.00	4.50
Plate, 3¾″			
☐ green opaque	2.00	2.50	2.15
☐ cobalt	5.25	6.00	5.50
☐ crystal	10.00	12.00	10.50
☐ baked-on color	1.75	2.25	1.85
Saucer, 3⅛″			
☐ green opaque	1.75	2.25	1.85
☐ cobalt	2.75	3.25	2.85
☐ crystal	4.75	5.75	5.00
☐ baked-on color	1.25	1.50	1.30
Sugar, 1½″			
☐ green opaque	3.75	4.25	3.85
☐ cobalt	7.00	8.00	7.25
☐ crystal	11.00	13.00	11.50
☐ baked-on color	4.25	4.75	4.35

CONCENTRIC RIB
Akro Agate

	Current Price Range		Prior Year Average
Complete Set, 7 pieces, in box			
☐ green and white	23.00	27.00	24.50
☐ other opaque colors	27.00	32.00	28.00
Creamer, 1¼″			
☐ green and white	3.75	4.75	4.00
☐ other opaque colors	4.50	6.00	5.00
Cup, 1¼″			
☐ green and white	2.25	2.75	2.35
☐ other opaque colors	2.75	3.75	3.00
Plate, 3¼″			
☐ green and white	1.75	2.50	2.00
☐ other opaque colors	2.75	3.50	3.00
Saucer, 2¾″			
☐ green and white	1.75	2.25	1.85
☐ other opaque colors	1.75	2.50	2.00

	Current Price Range		Prior Year Average

Sugar, 1¼″
☐ green and white	4.00	5.00	4.25
☐ other opaque colors	4.50	6.00	5.00

CONCENTRIC RING
Akro Agate

Made in a large and small children's size, this pattern is similar to *Concentric Rib*. However, *Concentric Ring* is of better quality than *Concentric Rib*.

Complete Set, 21 pieces, large size, in box
☐ cobalt	335.00	385.00	345.00
☐ blue marble	430.00	470.00	440.00

Complete Set, 16 pieces, small size, in box
☐ cobalt	240.00	270.00	250.00
☐ blue marble	300.00	335.00	310.00

Cereal Bowl, 3⅜″
☐ cobalt	24.00	26.00	24.50
☐ blue marble	29.00	33.00	30.00
☐ other opaque colors	16.00	19.00	17.00

Creamer, 1⅜″
☐ cobalt	23.00	26.00	24.00
☐ blue marble	32.00	37.00	33.00
☐ other opaque colors	11.00	14.00	12.00

Creamer, 1¼″
☐ cobalt	19.00	22.00	20.00
☐ blue marble	25.00	28.00	26.00
☐ other opaque colors	9.00	11.00	9.50

Cup, 1⅜″
☐ cobalt	23.00	26.00	24.00
☐ blue marble	27.00	31.00	28.00
☐ other opaque colors	13.00	15.00	13.50

Cup, 1¼″
☐ cobalt	25.00	28.00	26.00
☐ blue marble	28.00	31.00	29.00
☐ other opaque colors	9.00	11.00	9.50

Plate, 4¼″
☐ cobalt	11.00	14.00	12.00
☐ blue marble	16.00	19.00	17.00
☐ other opaque colors	6.50	8.00	7.00

	Current Price Range		Prior Year Average

Plate, 3¼"
☐ cobalt..	11.00	13.00	11.50
☐ blue marble......................................	12.00	14.00	12.50
☐ other opaque colors...........................	4.50	6.00	5.00

Saucer, 3⅛"
☐ cobalt..	6.00	8.00	6.50
☐ blue marble......................................	8.50	10.00	9.00
☐ other opaque colors...........................	4.50	5.50	4.75

Saucer, 2¾"
☐ cobalt..	8.00	10.00	8.50
☐ blue marble......................................	9.00	11.00	9.50
☐ other opaque colors...........................	3.00	4.00	3.25

Sugar, 1⅞"
☐ cobalt..	31.00	34.00	32.00
☐ blue marble......................................	37.00	42.00	39.00
☐ other opaque colors...........................	17.00	20.00	18.00

Sugar, 1¼"
☐ cobalt..	19.00	22.00	20.00
☐ blue marble......................................	25.00	27.00	25.50
☐ other opaque colors...........................	9.00	11.00	9.50

DORIC AND PANSY
Jeannette Glass Co.

This pattern was made for only a short period of time. The colors were pink and ultramarine and catalogs called it *Pretty Polly Party Dishes*.

Creamer, 2¾"
☐ pink	26.00	29.00	27.00
☐ ultramarine.......................................	29.00	32.00	30.00

Cup, 1½"
☐ pink	24.00	26.00	24.50
☐ ultramarine.......................................	24.00	26.00	24.50

Plate, 5⅞"
☐ pink	6.50	8.00	7.00
☐ ultramarine.......................................	6.50	8.00	7.00

Saucer, 4½"
☐ pink	4.00	5.50	4.50
☐ ultramarine.......................................	5.00	6.50	5.50

Sugar, 2½"
☐ pink	21.00	24.00	22.00
☐ ultramarine.......................................	23.00	26.00	24.00

FIRE-KING
Anchor Hocking Glass Co.

Period catalogs called this pattern *Sunny Suzy Baking Set, No. 261.*

	Current Price Range		Prior Year Average
Complete Set			
☐ 8 pieces, in box	38.00	44.00	40.00
☐ crystal	3.25	4.00	3.50
Custard Cup, 5 oz.			
☐ crystal	2.00	2.50	2.15
Pastry Board			
☐ crystal	2.75	3.75	3.00
Rolling Pin			
☐ crystal	2.25	3.25	2.50

HOMESPUN
Jeannette Glass Co.

	Current Price Range		Prior Year Average
Complete Set, 14 pieces, in box			
☐ pink	195.00	220.00	200.00
Complete Set, 12 pieces, in box			
☐ crystal	75.00	90.00	80.00
Cup, 1⅝″			
☐ pink	28.00	32.00	29.00
☐ crystal	13.00	15.00	13.50
Plate, 4½″			
☐ pink	5.50	7.00	6.00
☐ crystal	4.00	5.50	4.50

HOUZEX
Houze

This pattern, made only in opaque colors, is very similar to *Miss America* by Akro Agate Co.

	Current Price Range		Prior Year Average
Complete Set, 18 pieces, in box			
☐ green	210.00	240.00	215.00
☐ yellow..	210.00	240.00	215.00
☐ blue	240.00	280.00	247.00
Creamer, 1¾″			
☐ green	19.00	21.00	19.50
☐ yellow..	19.00	21.00	19.50
☐ blue	21.00	23.00	21.50

	Current Price Range		Prior Year Average
Cup, 1¼"			
☐ green	19.00	22.00	20.00
☐ yellow	19.00	22.00	20.00
☐ blue	21.00	23.00	21.50
Plate, 4"			
☐ green	8.50	10.50	9.25
☐ yellow	8.50	10.50	9.25
☐ blue	11.00	13.00	11.50
Saucer, 3¼"			
☐ green	6.50	8.50	7.00
☐ yellow	6.50	8.50	7.00
☐ blue	6.50	8.50	7.00
Sugar, with lid, 2⅞"			
☐ green	26.00	29.00	27.00
☐ yellow	26.00	29.00	27.00
☐ blue	28.00	31.00	29.00

INTERIOR PANEL
Akro Agate

This pattern was made in a large and a small children's size.

Complete Set, 21 pieces, in box, large size			
☐ green	130.00	145.00	135.00
☐ yellow	110.00	130.00	115.00
☐ blue and white	305.00	330.00	310.00
☐ red and white	330.00	360.00	335.00
☐ green and white	245.00	275.00	250.00
☐ lemonade and oxblood	320.00	350.00	330.00
Complete Set, 8 pieces, in box, small size			
☐ pink	38.00	50.00	40.00
☐ green	38.00	50.00	40.00
☐ blue	110.00	115.00	105.00
☐ yellow	110.00	115.00	105.00
☐ green	33.00	45.00	35.00
☐ topaz	33.00	45.00	35.00
☐ blue and white	105.00	120.00	110.00
☐ red and white	90.00	100.00	93.00
☐ green and white	60.00	70.00	63.00
Complete Set, 16 pieces, in box, small size			
☐ pink	110.00	125.00	115.00
☐ green	110.00	125.00	115.00
☐ blue	215.00	240.00	220.00
☐ yellow	215.00	240.00	220.00
☐ green	80.00	95.00	85.00

	Current Price Range		Prior Year Average
☐ topaz...................................	80.00	95.00	85.00
☐ blue and white......................	215.00	230.00	220.00
☐ red and white	200.00	225.00	210.00
☐ green and white.....................	120.00	140.00	125.00
Creamer, 1⅜″			
☐ blue and white......................	21.00	24.00	22.00
☐ red and white	23.00	26.00	24.00
☐ green and white.....................	17.00	19.00	17.50
☐ lemonade and oxblood.............	23.00	27.00	24.00
☐ green	10.00	12.00	10.50
☐ topaz.................................	9.00	11.00	9.50
Creamer, 1¼″			
☐ pink	21.00	23.00	21.50
☐ green	21.00	23.00	21.50
☐ blue	25.00	28.00	26.00
☐ yellow................................	25.00	28.00	26.00
☐ green	9.00	11.00	9.50
☐ topaz.................................	9.00	11.00	9.50
☐ blue and white......................	21.00	24.00	22.00
☐ red and white	23.00	27.00	24.00
☐ green and white.....................	14.00	17.00	15.00
Cup, 1⅜″			
☐ green	5.50	7.00	6.00
☐ topaz.................................	4.50	6.00	5.00
☐ blue and white......................	19.00	21.00	19.50
☐ red and white	20.00	23.00	21.00
☐ green and white.....................	14.00	17.00	15.00
☐ lemonade and oxblood.............	19.00	22.00	20.00
Cup, 1¼″			
☐ pink	7.00	9.00	7.50
☐ green	7.00	9.00	7.50
☐ blue	24.00	27.00	25.00
☐ yellow................................	24.00	27.00	25.00
☐ green	6.00	7.50	6.50
☐ topaz.................................	6.00	7.50	6.50
☐ blue and white......................	19.00	22.00	20.00
☐ red and white	21.00	24.00	22.00
☐ green and white.....................	14.00	17.00	15.00
Plate, 4¼″			
☐ green	4.50	6.00	5.00
☐ topaz.................................	3.50	6.00	4.00
☐ blue and white......................	9.00	11.00	9.50
☐ red and white	9.00	11.00	9.50
☐ green and white.....................	7.50	10.00	8.00
☐ lemonade and oxblood.............	10.00	12.00	10.50

	Current Price Range		Prior Year Average

Plate, 3¾"

☐ pink	4.00	5.00	4.25
☐ green	4.00	5.00	4.25
☐ blue	4.50	6.50	5.00
☐ yellow	4.50	6.50	5.00
☐ green	3.00	4.00	3.25
☐ topaz	3.00	4.00	3.25
☐ blue and white	9.00	10.00	9.25
☐ red and white	6.50	8.00	7.00
☐ green and white	5.50	7.00	6.00

Saucer, 3⅛"

☐ green	3.00	4.00	3.25
☐ topaz	2.50	3.50	3.00
☐ blue and white	6.50	8.00	7.00
☐ red and white	7.50	9.00	8.00
☐ green and white	6.50	8.00	7.00
☐ lemonade and oxblood	6.50	8.00	7.00

Saucer, 2⅜"

☐ pink	3.00	4.00	3.25
☐ green	3.00	4.00	3.25
☐ blue	6.00	8.00	6.50
☐ yellow	6.00	8.00	6.50
☐ green	3.25	4.00	3.50
☐ topaz	3.25	4.00	3.50
☐ blue and white	6.50	8.00	7.00
☐ red and white	6.50	8.00	7.00
☐ green and white	3.25	4.00	3.50

Sugar, 1⅞"

☐ green	14.00	17.00	15.00
☐ topaz	14.00	17.00	15.00
☐ blue and white	29.00	32.00	30.00
☐ red and white	30.00	33.00	31.00
☐ green and white	22.00	25.00	23.00
☐ lemonade and oxblood	30.00	33.00	31.00

Sugar, 1¼"

☐ pink	21.00	24.00	22.00
☐ green	21.00	24.00	22.00
☐ blue	25.00	28.00	26.00
☐ yellow	25.00	28.00	26.00
☐ green	9.00	11.00	9.50
☐ topaz	9.00	11.00	9.50
☐ blue and white	21.00	24.00	22.00
☐ red and white	23.00	26.00	24.00
☐ green and white	15.00	18.00	16.00

J.P.
Akro Agate

This pattern was made for the J. Pressman Company.

	Current Price Range		Prior Year Average
Complete Set, 17 pieces, in box			
☐ blue	163.00	187.00	167.00
☐ brown..	225.00	265.00	235.00
☐ crystal	240.00	270.00	230.00
☐ green	163.00	187.00	167.00
☐ red...	225.00	265.00	235.00
☐ baked-on colors	55.00	70.00	58.00
Complete Set, 21 pieces, in box			
☐ baked-on colors	75.00	92.00	78.00
Cereal Bowl, 3¾″			
☐ baked-on colors	5.50	7.00	6.00
Creamer, 1½″			
☐ green	21.00	24.00	22.00
☐ blue	21.00	24.00	22.00
☐ crystal	26.00	30.00	27.00
☐ red...	26.00	30.00	27.00
☐ brown...	26.00	30.00	27.00
☐ baked-on colors	5.50	7.00	6.00
Cup, 1½″			
☐ blue	12.00	15.00	13.00
☐ brown...	16.00	19.00	17.00
☐ crystal	16.00	20.00	17.00
☐ green	12.00	15.00	13.00
☐ red...	16.00	19.00	17.00
☐ baked-on colors	4.00	5.00	4.25
Plate, 4¼″			
☐ blue	8.00	10.00	8.50
☐ brown...	11.00	13.00	11.50
☐ crystal	11.00	14.00	12.00
☐ green	8.00	10.00	8.50
☐ red...	11.00	14.00	12.00
☐ baked-on colors	2.00	3.50	2.50
Saucer, 3¼″			
☐ blue	4.00	5.00	4.25
☐ brown...	6.50	8.00	7.00
☐ crystal	6.00	9.00	7.00
☐ green	4.00	5.00	4.25
☐ red...	6.50	8.00	7.00
☐ baked-on colors	1.50	2.00	1.65

	Current Price Range		Prior Year Average
Sugar, with lid, 1½″			
☐ blue	23.00	26.00	24.00
☐ brown	31.00	33.00	31.50
☐ crystal	30.00	34.00	32.00
☐ green	23.00	26.00	24.00
☐ red	31.00	33.00	31.50
☐ baked-on colors	6.50	8.00	7.00

LAUREL
McKee Glass Co.

	Current Price Range		Prior Year Average
Creamer, 2⅝″			
☐ ivory	22.00	24.00	22.50
☐ ivory with decorated trim	26.00	30.00	27.00
☐ jade	23.00	26.00	24.00
☐ scottie dog decal	34.00	38.00	35.00
Cup, 1½″			
☐ ivory	22.00	26.00	23.00
☐ ivory with decorated trim	25.00	29.00	26.00
☐ jade	23.00	26.00	24.00
☐ scottie dog decal	30.00	34.00	31.00
Plate, 5⅞″			
☐ ivory	8.00	10.00	8.50
☐ ivory with decal	10.00	13.00	11.00
☐ jade	8.00	10.00	8.50
☐ scottie dog decal	13.00	15.00	13.50
Saucer, 4⅜″			
☐ ivory	5.00	6.50	5.50
☐ ivory with decorated trim	6.25	8.25	7.00
☐ jade	5.50	7.00	6.00
☐ scottie dog decal	5.50	7.00	6.00
Sugar, 2⅜″			
☐ ivory	19.00	23.00	20.00
☐ ivory with decorated trim	24.00	29.00	25.00
☐ jade	21.00	24.00	22.00
☐ scottie dog decal	34.00	37.00	35.00

MISS AMERICA
Akro Agate

	Current Price Range		Prior Year Average
Complete Set, in box			
☐ white	300.00	330.00	307.00
☐ white with decal	450.00	480.00	460.00
☐ orange and white	360.00	385.00	370.00
☐ green	360.00	385.00	370.00
Creamer			
☐ white	26.00	29.00	27.00
☐ white with decal	38.00	44.00	40.00
☐ orange and white	33.00	38.00	35.00
☐ green	33.00	38.00	35.00
Cup			
☐ white	26.00	29.00	27.00
☐ white with decal	38.00	44.00	40.00
☐ orange and white	30.00	34.00	31.00
☐ green	30.00	34.00	31.00
Plate			
☐ white	15.00	17.00	15.50
☐ white with decal	22.00	25.00	23.00
☐ orange and white	16.00	19.00	17.00
☐ green	16.00	19.00	17.00
Saucer			
☐ white	9.00	12.00	10.00
☐ white with decal	12.00	15.00	13.00
☐ orange and white	10.00	13.00	11.00
☐ green	10.00	13.00	11.00
Sugar			
☐ white	33.00	38.00	35.00
☐ white with decal	46.00	52.00	48.00
☐ orange and white	47.00	50.00	48.00
☐ green	47.00	50.00	48.00
Teapot, with lid			
☐ white	52.00	57.00	54.00
☐ white with decal	75.00	82.00	77.00
☐ orange and white	67.00	73.00	69.00
☐ green	67.00	73.00	69.00

MODERNTONE
Hazel Atlas

Catalogs called this pattern *Little Hostess Party Set*. It sold in sets of pastel colors and dark colors. Colors included light green, light yellow, light blue, light pink, orange, gold, gray, turquoise, dark green, maroon and chartreuse.

	Current Price Range		Prior Year Average
Complete Set, in box			
☐ pastel colors....................................	35.00	42.00	37.00
☐ dark colors......................................	58.00	64.00	60.00
Creamer, 1¾″			
☐ pastel colors....................................	3.50	4.50	3.75
☐ dark colors......................................	3.50	4.50	3.75
Cup, 1¾″			
☐ pastel colors....................................	3.00	4.50	3.50
☐ dark colors......................................	3.00	4.50	3.50
Plate, 5¼″			
☐ pastel colors....................................	2.50	3.50	2.75
☐ dark colors......................................	3.00	3.75	3.25
Saucer, 3⅞″			
☐ pastel colors....................................	1.25	2.00	1.75
☐ dark colors......................................	2.50	3.25	2.75
Sugar, 1¾″			
☐ pastel colors....................................	3.50	4.50	3.75
☐ dark colors......................................	3.50	4.75	4.00

OCTAGONAL
Akro Agate

This pattern was made in small and large children's sizes.

	Current Price Range		Prior Year Average
Complete Set, 21 pieces, in box, large size			
☐ green..	46.00	52.00	48.00
☐ white..	46.00	52.00	48.00
☐ dark blue	46.00	52.00	48.00
☐ lemonade and oxblood.......................	280.00	310.00	290.00
☐ pink	75.00	90.00	80.00
☐ yellow..	75.00	90.00	80.00
Complete Set, 16 pieces, in box, small size			
☐ green..	85.00	110.00	92.00
☐ blue...	85.00	110.00	92.00
☐ white..	85.00	110.00	92.00
Cereal Bowl, 3⅜″			
☐ green..	4.00	5.00	4.25
☐ white..	4.00	5.00	4.25
☐ dark blue	4.00	5.00	4.25
☐ lemonade and oxblood.......................	22.00	25.00	23.00
☐ pink	6.00	7.00	6.25
☐ yellow..	6.00	7.00	6.25

	Current Price Range		Prior Year Average

Creamer, closed handle, 1½"

☐ green	3.50	4.50	3.75
☐ white	3.50	4.50	3.75
☐ dark blue	3.50	4.50	3.75
☐ ivory	11.00	14.00	12.00
☐ orange	11.00	14.00	12.00
☐ light blue	11.00	14.00	12.00
☐ lemonade and oxblood	21.00	24.00	22.00
☐ pink	4.50	6.00	5.00
☐ yellow	4.50	6.00	5.00

Creamer, open handle, 1½"

☐ green	4.50	5.50	4.75
☐ white	4.50	5.50	4.75
☐ dark blue	4.50	5.50	4.75
☐ ivory	13.00	15.00	13.50
☐ orange	13.00	15.00	13.50
☐ light blue	13.00	15.00	13.50
☐ lemonade and oxblood	25.00	29.00	26.00
☐ pink	5.00	7.00	5.50
☐ yellow	5.00	7.00	5.50

Creamer, 1¼"

☐ green	11.00	14.00	12.00
☐ blue	11.00	14.00	12.00
☐ white	11.00	14.00	12.00

Cup, closed handle, 1½"

☐ green	1.75	2.50	2.00
☐ white	1.75	2.50	2.00
☐ dark blue	1.75	2.50	2.00
☐ ivory	9.00	12.00	10.00
☐ orange	19.00	24.00	20.00
☐ light blue	9.00	12.00	10.00
☐ lemonade and oxblood	16.00	19.00	17.00
☐ pink	3.25	4.00	3.50
☐ yellow	3.25	4.00	3.50

Cup, open handle, 1½"

☐ green	2.50	3.75	2.75
☐ white	2.50	3.75	2.75
☐ dark blue	2.50	3.75	2.75
☐ ivory	11.00	14.00	12.00
☐ orange	24.00	28.00	25.00
☐ light blue	11.00	14.00	12.00
☐ lemonade and oxblood	19.00	22.00	20.00
☐ pink	4.50	5.50	4.75
☐ yellow	4.50	5.50	4.75

	Current Price Range		Prior Year Average
Cup, closed handle, 1¼"			
☐ green	8.50	10.00	9.00
☐ blue	8.50	10.00	9.00
☐ white	8.50	10.00	9.00
☐ orange	15.00	18.00	16.00
☐ yellow	15.00	18.00	16.00
☐ light green	15.00	18.00	16.00
Cup, open handle, 1¼"			
☐ green	7.00	9.00	7.50
☐ blue	7.00	9.00	7.50
☐ white	7.00	9.00	7.50
☐ orange	12.00	14.00	12.50
☐ yellow	12.00	14.00	12.50
☐ light green	12.00	14.00	12.50
Plate, 4½"			
☐ green	2.00	2.75	2.25
☐ white	2.00	2.75	2.25
☐ dark blue	2.00	2.75	2.25
☐ ivory	6.00	8.00	6.50
☐ orange	6.00	8.00	6.50
☐ light blue	6.00	8.00	6.50
☐ lemonade and oxblood	9.00	11.00	9.50
☐ pink	2.75	3.50	3.00
☐ yellow	2.75	3.50	3.00
Plate, 3⅜"			
☐ green	4.00	4.75	4.25
☐ blue	4.00	4.75	4.25
☐ white	4.00	4.75	4.25
☐ orange	5.00	6.50	5.50
☐ yellow	5.00	6.50	5.50
☐ light green	5.00	6.50	5.50
Saucer, 3⅜"			
☐ green	1.25	1.75	1.35
☐ white	1.25	1.75	1.35
☐ dark blue	1.25	1.75	1.35
☐ lemonade and oxblood	5.50	7.00	6.00
☐ pink	1.75	2.50	2.00
☐ yellow	1.75	2.50	2.00
Saucer, 2¾"			
☐ green	2.50	3.50	2.75
☐ blue	2.50	3.50	2.75
☐ white	2.50	3.50	2.75
☐ orange	3.50	5.50	4.00
☐ yellow	3.50	5.50	4.00
☐ light green	3.50	5.50	4.00

	Current Price Range		Prior Year Average
Sugar, closed handle			
☐ green	5.00	6.00	5.25
☐ white	5.00	6.00	5.25
☐ dark blue	5.00	6.00	5.25
☐ ivory	15.00	18.00	16.00
☐ orange	15.00	18.00	16.00
☐ light blue	15.00	18.00	16.00
☐ lemonade and oxblood	27.00	30.00	28.00
☐ pink	6.50	8.00	7.00
☐ yellow	6.50	8.00	7.00
Sugar, open handle			
☐ green	7.00	9.00	7.50
☐ white	7.00	9.00	7.50
☐ dark blue	7.00	9.00	7.50
☐ ivory	19.00	22.00	20.00
☐ orange	19.00	22.00	20.00
☐ light blue	19.00	22.00	20.00
☐ lemonade and oxblood	31.00	35.00	32.00
☐ pink	8.00	11.00	9.00
☐ yellow	8.00	11.00	9.00
Sugar, 1¼″			
☐ green	11.00	14.00	12.00
☐ blue	11.00	14.00	12.00
☐ white	11.00	14.00	12.00
Tumbler, 2″			
☐ green	4.50	6.00	5.00
☐ blue	4.50	6.00	5.00
☐ white	4.50	6.00	5.00
☐ orange	13.00	16.00	14.00
☐ yellow	13.00	16.00	14.00
☐ light green	13.00	16.00	14.00

RAISED DAISY
Akro Agate

This pattern was made using only opaque colors.

Creamer, 1¾″			
☐ yellow	25.00	28.00	26.00

	Current Price Range		Prior Year Average
Cup, 1¾″			
☐ blue	25.00	28.00	26.00
☐ green	13.00	16.00	13.50
Plate, 3″			
☐ blue	10.00	12.00	10.50
Saucer, 2½″			
☐ yellow	7.00	9.00	7.50
☐ tan	7.00	9.00	7.50
Sugar			
☐ yellow	26.00	28.00	26.50
Tumbler, 2″			
☐ yellow	16.00	19.00	17.00
☐ blue	30.00	33.00	31.00
☐ tan	17.00	19.00	17.50

STACKED DISC
Akro Agate

This pattern is most commonly found in opaque green and white.

	Current Price Range		Prior Year Average
Complete Set, 21 pieces, in box			
☐ green	35.00	40.00	36.00
☐ white	35.00	40.00	36.00
Creamer, 1¼″			
☐ green	3.00	3.50	3.15
☐ white	3.00	3.50	3.15
☐ orange	10.00	12.00	10.50
Cup, 1¼″			
☐ green	1.75	2.25	1.90
☐ white	1.75	2.25	1.90
Plate, 3¼″			
☐ green	1.75	2.00	1.80
☐ white	1.75	2.00	1.80
Saucer, 2¾″			
☐ green	1.75	2.00	1.80
☐ white	1.75	2.00	1.80
Sugar, 1¼″			
☐ green	3.00	3.75	3.25
☐ white	3.00	3.75	3.25
☐ orange	10.00	13.00	11.00
Teapot, with lid, 3⅝″			
☐ green	7.00	8.50	7.25
☐ white	7.00	8.50	7.25
☐ orange	18.00	22.00	19.00

	Current Price Range		Prior Year Average

Tumbler, 2″

☐ green	3.25	4.50	3.50
☐ white	3.25	4.50	3.50
☐ orange	8.00	11.00	9.00

STACKED DISC AND INTERIOR PANEL
Akro Agate

This pattern was made in small and large children's sizes. There are many opaque colors as well as clear blue and green. Blue marble is the most rare.

Complete Set, 21 pieces, large, in box

☐ opaque colors	215.00	245.00	225.00
☐ blue marble	405.00	440.00	415.00
☐ clear green	250.00	280.00	257.00
☐ clear blue	310.00	340.00	320.00

Complete Set, 8 pieces, small, in box

☐ opaque colors	52.00	60.00	54.00
☐ blue marble	142.00	160.00	147.00
☐ clear green	130.00	145.00	132.00
☐ clear blue	180.00	210.00	185.00

Cereal Bowl, 3⅜″

☐ opaque colors	15.00	19.00	16.00
☐ blue marble	28.00	31.00	29.00
☐ clear green	16.00	19.00	17.00
☐ clear blue	19.00	22.00	20.00

Creamer, 1⅜″

☐ opaque colors	11.00	13.00	11.50
☐ blue marble	26.00	29.00	27.00
☐ clear green	15.00	18.00	16.00
☐ clear blue	23.00	26.00	24.00

Creamer, 1¼″

☐ opaque colors	5.50	7.00	6.00
☐ blue marble	26.00	29.00	27.00
☐ clear green	14.00	16.00	14.50
☐ clear blue	19.00	22.00	20.00

Cup, 1⅜″

☐ opaque colors	14.00	16.00	14.50
☐ blue marble	25.00	28.00	26.00
☐ clear green	14.00	17.00	15.00
☐ clear blue	17.00	19.00	17.50

Cup, 1¼″

☐ opaque colors	9.50	11.00	10.00
☐ blue marble	25.00	28.00	26.00
☐ clear green	10.00	11.00	10.25
☐ clear blue	14.50	17.00	15.50

	Current Price Range		Prior Year Average
Pitcher, 2¾"			
☐ clear green	9.50	11.00	10.00
☐ clear blue	16.00	19.00	17.00
Plate, 4¾"			
☐ opaque colors	6.50	8.00	7.00
☐ blue marble	11.00	13.00	11.50
☐ clear green	9.00	11.00	9.50
☐ clear blue	9.50	11.00	10.00
Plate, 3¼"			
☐ opaque colors	4.00	5.00	4.25
☐ blue marble	11.00	13.00	11.50
☐ clear green	6.50	8.00	7.00
☐ clear blue	8.50	11.00	9.00
Saucer, 3⅛"			
☐ opaque colors	4.50	5.50	4.75
☐ blue marble	9.50	11.00	10.00
☐ clear green	6.50	8.00	7.00
☐ clear blue	7.50	9.00	8.00
Saucer, 2¾"			
☐ opaque colors	3.25	3.75	3.40
☐ blue marble	9.50	11.00	10.00
☐ clear green	4.50	5.50	4.75
☐ clear blue	5.50	7.00	6.00
Sugar, with lid, 1⅞"			
☐ opaque colors	17.00	19.00	17.50
☐ blue marble	38.00	41.00	39.00
☐ clear green	24.00	27.00	25.00
☐ clear blue	31.00	34.00	32.00
Sugar, 1¼"			
☐ opaque colors	5.50	7.00	6.00
☐ blue marble	26.00	29.00	27.00
☐ clear green	14.00	17.00	15.00
☐ clear blue	19.00	21.00	19.50
Tumbler, 2"			
☐ opaque colors	19.00	23.00	20.00
☐ clear green	7.50	9.00	8.00
☐ clear blue	9.50	11.00	10.00

STIPPLED BAND
Akro Agate

This pattern was made in small and large children's sizes.

	Current Price Range		Prior Year Average
Complete Set, 17 pieces, in box			
☐ clear amber....................................	130.00	160.00	140.00
☐ clear green	75.00	90.00	78.00
☐ clear blue	220.00	260.00	225.00
Complete Set, 8 pieces, small, in box			
☐ clear amber....................................	37.00	45.00	39.00
☐ clear green	32.00	37.00	34.00
Creamer, 1½″			
☐ clear amber....................................	13.00	15.00	13.50
☐ clear green	5.50	7.00	6.00
☐ clear blue	21.00	23.00	21.50
Creamer, 1¼″			
☐ clear amber....................................	5.50	7.00	6.00
☐ clear green	5.00	6.00	5.25
Cup, 1½″			
☐ clear amber....................................	8.50	10.50	9.00
☐ clear green	4.50	5.50	4.75
☐ clear blue	16.00	19.00	17.00
Cup, 1¼″			
☐ clear amber....................................	4.50	5.50	4.75
☐ clear green	4.25	4.75	4.40
Plate, 4¼″			
☐ clear amber....................................	6.50	7.50	6.75
☐ clear green	4.00	5.00	4.25
☐ clear blue	9.00	11.00	9.50
Plate, 3¼″			
☐ clear amber....................................	3.00	4.00	3.25
☐ clear green	2.75	3.75	3.00
Saucer, 3¼″			
☐ clear amber....................................	4.25	5.50	4.50
☐ clear green	1.75	2.50	2.00
☐ clear blue	8.50	11.50	9.50
Saucer, 2¾″			
☐ clear amber....................................	2.00	2.75	2.25
☐ clear green	1.75	2.50	2.00
Sugar, with lid, 1⅞″			
☐ clear amber....................................	17.00	20.00	18.00
☐ clear green	9.00	11.00	9.50
☐ clear blue	26.00	30.00	27.00
Sugar, 1¼″			
☐ clear amber....................................	5.50	7.00	6.00
☐ clear green	5.00	6.00	5.25

	Current Price Range		Prior Year Average
Tumbler, 1¾"			
☐ clear amber......................................	5.50	7.00	6.00
☐ clear green	5.00	6.00	5.25

TWENTIETH CENTURY
Hazel Atlas Glass Co.

This pattern was made in mixed pastel colors.

	Current Price Range		Prior Year Average
Creamer			
☐ pastel colors......................................	2.75	3.50	3.00
Cup			
☐ pastel colors......................................	2.25	3.00	2.25
Plate			
☐ pastel colors......................................	1.75	2.25	1.90
Saucer			
☐ pastel colors......................................	1.25	1.75	1.35
Sugar			
☐ pastel colors......................................	2.75	3.25	2.90

BIBLIOGRAPHY

Often glass collectors are attracted to more than one type of glass. For this reason, the following bibliography lists a variety of books pertaining to glass.

Addis, Wily P., *What's Behind Old Carnival: A Study of Patterns Seldom Seen*, Lakewood, OH, privately printed, 1971.

Arwas, Victor, *Glass: Art Nouveau to Art Deco*, NY, Rizzoli International, 1977.

Avila, George C., *The Pairpont Glass Story*, Reynolds-DeWalt Printing, Inc., 1968.

Barret, Richard Carter, *A Collector's Handbook of American Art Glass*, Manchester, VT, Forward's Color Productions, Inc., 1971.

Barret, Richard Carter, *A Collector's Handbook of Blown and Pressed American Glass*, Manchester, VT, Forward's Color Productions, Inc., 1967.

Belknap, E.M., *Milk Glass*, NY, Crown Publishers.

Boggess, Bill and Louise, *American Brilliant Cut Glass*, NY, Crown Publishers, 1977.

Bones, Frances, *The Book of Duncan Glass*, Des Moines, IA, Wallace-Homestead Book Co., 1973.

Bount, Henry, and Berniece Blount, *French Cameo Glass*, Des Moines, IA, Wallace-Homestead Book Co., 1968.

Brahmer, Bonnie J., *Custard Glass*, Springfield, MO, privately published, 1966.

Bridgeman, Harriet, and Elizabeth Drury, *The Encyclopedia of Victoriana*, Macmillan, Inc., 1975.

Brown, Clark W., *A Supplement to Salt Dishes*, Des Moines, IA, Wallace-Homestead Book Co., 1970.

Butler, Joseph T., *American Antiques 1800–1900*, Odyssey Press, 1965.

Carved and Decorated European Glass, Charles E. Tuttle Co., Inc., 1970.

Cole, Ann Kilborn, *Golden Guide to American Antiques*, NY, Golden Press, 1967.

Contemporary Art Glass, NY, Crown Publishers, Inc., 1975.

Cooke, Lawrence S., (ed.), *Lighting in America: From Colonial Rushlights to Victorian Chandeliers*, Antiques Magazine Library, NY, Main Street/Universe Books, 1977.

Cosentino, Geraldine, and Regina Stewart, *Carnival Glass, A Guide for the Beginning Collector*, Golden Press, 1976.

Daniel, Dorothy, *Cut and Engraved Glass 1771–1905*, NY, M. Barrows & Company, 1950.

Darr, Patrick, *A Guide to Art and Pattern Glass,* Pilgrim House Publishing Co., 1960.

Davidson, Marshall B., (ed.), *The American Heritage History of Colonial Antiques*, NY, American Heritage Publishing Company, 1967.

Davis, Derek C. and Keith Middlemas, *Colored Glass*, Clarkson N. Potter, Inc., Publisher, NY.

Davis, Frank, *Antique Glass and Glass Collecting*, London, Hamlyn, 1973.

Davis, Frank, *The Country Life Book of Glass*, Glasgow, The University Press, 1966.

DiBartolomeo, Robert E., (ed.), *American Glass From the Pages of Antiques*, Vol. II, Pressed and Cut, Princeton, The Pyne Press, 1974.

Drepperd, Carl W., *ABC's of Old Glass*, NY, Doubleday & Company, 1968.

Drepperd, Carl W., *A Dictionary of American Antiques*, NY, Doubleday & Company, 1968.

Edwards, Bill, *Millersburg, The Queen of Carnival Glass*, Collector Books, 1976.

Elville, E.M., *English and Irish Cut Glass*, Country Life Limited, 1953.

Ericson, Eric E., *A Guide To Colored Steuben Glass* (1903–1933), two vols., CO, The Lithographic Press, 1963–65.

Florence, Gene, *The Collector's Encyclopedia of Akro Agate Glassware*, Paducah, KY, Collector Books, 1982.

Florence, Gene, *The Collector's Encyclopedia of Depression Glass*, seventh edition, Paducah, KY, Collector Books, 1984.

Florence, Gene, *Elegant Glassware of the Depression Era*, Paducah, KY, Collector Books, 1983.

Florence, Gene, *Kitchen Glassware of the Depression Years*, Paducah, KY, Collector Books, 1981.

Florence, Gene, *Pocket Guide to Depression Glass*, revised third edition, Paducah, KY, Collector Books, 1983.

Frazer, Margaret, *Colored Glass, Discovering Antiques*, vol. 8, NY, Greystone Press, 1973.

Gardner, Paul V., *The Glass of Frederick Carder*, NY, Crown Publishers, 1971.

Greguire, Helen, *Carnival in Lights*, 103 Trimmer Road, Hilton, NY 14468, privately published, 1975.

Grover, Ray and Lee Grover, *Art Glass Nouveau*, Rutland, VT, Charles E. Tuttle Co., 1967.

Grover, Ray and Lee Grover, *Carved & Decorated European Art Glass*, Rutland, VT, Charles E. Tuttle Co., 1967.

Hammond, Dorothy, *Confusing Collectibles*, IA, Mid-American Book Company, 1969.

Hammond, Dorothy, *More Confusing Collectibles*, KS, C.B.P. Publishing Company, 1972.

Hand, Sherman, *Colors in Carnival Glass*, Books 1-4, Des Moines, IA, Wallace-Homestead Book Co., 1967–1974.

Hartley, Julia M., and Mary M. Cobb, *The States Series, Early American Pattern Glass*, privately published, 1976.

Hartung, Marion T., *Carnival Glass*, Books 1–10, 718 Constitution Street, Emporia, KS 66801, privately published, 1967–1973.

Hartung, Marion T., *Northwood Pattern Glass In Color*, privately published, 1969.

Haslam, Malcolm, *Marks and Monograms of the Modern Movement*, 1875–1930, NY, Charles Scribner's Sons, 1977.

Heacock, William, *Encyclopedia of Victorian Colored Pattern Glass, Book III*, Antique Publications, 1976.

Hinds, Maxine, *Smashed Glass Reclaimed and Restored*, Route 2, P.O. Box 540, Galt, CA 95632, privately printed, 1972.

Hollister, Paul, Jr., *The Encyclopedia of Glass Paperweights*, NY, Clarkson N. Potter, 1969.

Hotchkiss, John F., *Art Glass Handbook*, NY, Hawthorn Books, 1972.

Hunter, Frederick William, *Stiegel Glass*, NY, Dover Publications, 1950.

Innes, Lowell, *Pittsburgh Glass 1797–1891: A History and Guide for Collectors*, Houghton Mifflin Company, 1976.

Jenkins, Dorothy H., *A Fortune in the Junk Pile*, NY, Crown Publishers, 1963.

Kamm, Minnie Watson, *A Fourth Pitcher Book*, Kamm Publications, 1950.

Kamm, Minnie Watson, *A Second Two Hundred Pattern Glass Pitchers*, Kamm Publications, 1940.

Kamm, Minnie Watson, *Two Hundred Pattern Glass Pitchers*, six volumes, Grosse Pointe Farms, MI, privately published.

Kamm, Minnie W., and Serry Wood, (eds.), *Encyclopedia of Antique Pattern Glass I*, Kamm Publications, 1961.

Kamm, Minnie W., and Serry Wood, (eds.), *Encyclopedia of Antique Pattern Glass II*, Kamm Publications, 1961.

Klamkin, Marion, *The Collector's Guide to Carnival Glass*, NY, Hawthorn Books, 1976.

Klein, William Karl, *Repairing and Restoring China and Glass*, NY, Harper & Row, 1962.

Koch, Robert, *Louis C. Tiffany, Rebel in Glass*, NY, Crown Publishers, 1964.

Koch, Robert, *Louis C. Tiffany's Glass—Bronzes—Lamps*, NY, Crown Publishers.

Lagerberg, Theodore and Viola, *Collectible Glass*, vols. 1, 2, and 4, New Port Richey, FL, privately published, 1963–1968.

Lee, Ruth Webb, *Early American Pressed Glass*, Wellesley Hills, MA, Lee Publications, 1933.

Lee, Ruth Webb, *Nineteenth Century Art Glass*, NY, M. Barrows and Company, 1952.

Lee, Ruth Webb, *Sandwich Glass*, Wellesley Hills, MA, Lee Publications, 1966.

Lee, Ruth Webb, *Victorian Glass Handbook*, Wellesley Hills, MA, Lee Publications, 1946.

Lee, Ruth Webb, and James H. Rose, *American Glass Cup Plates*, Wellesley Hills, MA, Lee Publications, 1948.

Libbey Glass, A Tradition of 150 Years, Toledo Museum of Art, 1968.

Lindsey, Bessie M., *American Historical Glass*, VT, Charles E. Tuttle, 1967.

Malone, Laurence Adams, *How to Mend Your Treasures: Porcelain—China—Pottery—Glass*, NY, Phaedra Publishers, 1972.

McClinton, Katharine M., *Collecting American Victorian Antiques*, NY, Charles Scribner's Sons, 1966.

McKean, Hugh F., *The "Lost" Treasures of Louis Comfort Tiffany*, Garden City, NY, Doubleday, 1980.

McKearin, George and Helen, *American Glass*, NY, Crown Publishers, 1966.

Mebane, John, *Collecting Brides' Baskets and Other Glass Fancies*, Des Moines, IA, Wallace-Homestead Book Co., 1976.

Metz, Alice Hulett, *Early American Pattern Glass*, Chicago, IL, privately published.

Metz, Alice Hulett, *More Early American Pattern Glass*, vol. II, Chicago, privately published, 1965.

Moore, Donald E., *The Shape of Things in Carnival Glass*, 2101 Shoreline Drive, Alameda, CA 94501, privately published, 1975.

New England Glass Co. 1818–1888, Toledo Museum of Art, 1963.

Newman, Harold, *An Illustrated Dictionary of Glass*, London, Thames and Hudson, 1977.

Oliver, Elizabeth, *American Antique Glass*, NY, Golden Press, 1977.

Owens, Richard E., *Carnival Glass Tumblers*, 2611 Brass Lantern Drive, La Habra, CA 90361, privately published, 1975.

Papert, Emma, *The Illustrated Guide to American Glass*, NY, Hawthorn Books, 1972.

Pearson, J. Michael, *Encyclopedia of American Cut and Engraved Glass (1880–1917)*, Vol. I: *Geometric Conceptions*, 402844 Ocean View Station, Miami Beach, FL 33140, privately printed, 1975.

Pearson, J. Michael, *Encyclopedia of American Cut and Engraved Glass (1880–1917)*, Vol. II: *Realistic Patterns*, 402844 Ocean View Station, Miami Beach, FL 33140, privately printed, 1977.

Pearson, J. Michael and Dorothy T., *American Cut Glass for the Discriminating Collector*, Miami, FL, The Franklin Press, 1965.

Pennsylvania Glassware, 1870–1904, American Historical Catalog Collection, Princeton, The Pyne Press, 1972.

Peterson, Arthur G., *400 Trademarks on Glass*, Takoma Park, MD, Washington College Press, 1968.

Peterson, Arthur G., *Glass Salt Shakers: 1,000 Patterns*, Des Moines, IA, Wallace-Homestead Book Co.

Peterson, Arthur G., *Salt and Salt Shakers*, Washington, D.C., Washington College Press.

Peterson, Arthur G., *333 Glass Salt Shakers*, Washington, D.C., Washington College Press.

Polak, Ada, *Glass, Its Tradition and Its Makers*, G.P. Putnam's Sons, 1975.

Presznick, Rose M., *Carnival Glass*, Books 1–6, 7810 Avon Lake Road, Lodi, OH 44254, privately published, 1966.

Presznick, Rose M., *Encyclopedia of New Carnival Glass and Iridescent Glass*, 7810 Avon Lake Road, Lodi, OH 44254, privately published, 1974.

Rainwater, Dorothy T. and H. Ivan, *American Silverplate*, TN, Thomas Nelson, and PA, Everybody's Press.

Rainwater, Dorothy T., and H. Ivan, *Sterling Silver Holloware*, Princeton, NJ, Pyne Press.

Revi, Albert Christian, *American Art Nouveau Glass*, TN, Thomas Nelson, 1968.

Revi, Albert C., *American Cut and Engraved Glass*, Thomas Nelson, 1970.

Revi, Albert C., *American Pressed Glass and Figure Bottles*, Thomas Nelson, 1964.

Revi, Albert Christian, *Nineteenth Century Glass,* NY, Galahad Books, 1967.

Revi, Albert Christian, (ed.), *The Spinning Wheel's Complete Book of Antiques*, NY, Grosset & Dunlap, 1972.

Rose, James H., *The Story of American Pressed Glass of the Lacy Period, 1825–1850*, The Corning Museum of Glass, 1954.

Schrijver, Elka, *Glass and Crystal*, Universe Books, Inc., 1964.

Schwartz, Marvin D., *American Glass: Blown and Molded*, NJ, Pyne Press, 1974.

Schwartz, Marvin D., *Collector's Guide to Antique American Glass*, NY, Doubleday & Company, Inc., 1969.

Shull, Thelma, *Victorian Antiques*, Rutland, VT, Charles E. Tuttle Company.

Springer, L. Elsinore, *The Collector's Book of Bells*, NY, Crown Publishers.

Stout, Sandra McPhee, *Depression Glass in Color*, Ephrata, WA, privately published.

Stout, Sandra M., *Depression Glass III*, Des Moines, IA, Wallace-Homestead Book Co., 1976.

Swan, Frank H., *Portland Glass*, Des Moines, IA, Wallace-Homestead Book Co.

Traub, Jules S., *The Glass of Desire Christian*, Chicago, The Art Glass Exchange, 1978.

Warren, Phelps, *Irish Glass*, NY, Charles Scribner's Sons, 1970.

Watkins, Laura W., *Cambridge Glass*, 1818–1888, Bramhill House, 1930.

Weatherman, Hazel Marie, *Colored Glassware of the Depression Era*, revised and expanded edition, Springfield, MO, privately published.

Weatherman, Hazel Marie, *Colored Glassware of the Depression Era 2*, privately printed, 1970.

Webb, Jack Lawton, *A Guide to New Carnival Glass*, Joplin, MO, Imperial Publishing Company.

Webber, Norman W., *Collecting Glass*, NY, Arco, 1972.

Weiss, Gustav, *Books of Glass*, Praeger Publishers, Inc., 1971.

Whitlow, Harry H., *Art, Colored and Cameo Glass*, Riverview, MI, privately published, 1967.

Whitmyer, Margaret and Kenn, *Children's Dishes*, Paducah, KY, Collector Books, 1984.

Wiener, Herbert, and Freda Lipkowitz, *Rarities in American Cut Glass*, The Collectors House of Books Publishing Co., 1975.

Wilson, Kenneth M., *New England Glass and Glassmaking*, Old Sturbridge, Inc., 1972.

Ziegfeld, Edwin, Ray Faulkner, and Gerald Hill, *Art Today*, NY, Holt, Rinehart and Winston, 1965.

THE OFFICIAL PRICE GUIDES TO:

☐ 199-3 **American Silver & Silver Plate** 5th Ed.	11.95
☐ 513-1 **Antique Clocks** 3rd Ed.	10.95
☐ 283-3 **Antique & Modern Dolls** 3rd Ed.	10.95
☐ 287-6 **Antique & Modern Firearms** 6th Ed.	11.95
☐ 517-4 **Antiques & Collectibles** 7th Ed.	9.95
☐ 289-2 **Antique Jewelry** 5th Ed.	11.95
☐ 270-1 **Beer Cans & Collectibles,** 3rd Ed.	7.95
☐ 262-0 **Bottles Old & New** 9th Ed.	10.95
☐ 255-8 **Carnival Glass** 1st Ed.	10.95
☐ 295-7 **Collectible Cameras** 2nd Ed.	10.95
☐ 277-9 **Collectibles of the Third Reich** 2nd Ed.	10.95
☐ 281-7 **Collectible Toys** 3rd Ed.	10.95
☐ 490-9 **Collector Cars** 6th Ed.	11.95
☐ 267-1 **Collector Handguns** 3rd Ed.	11.95
☐ 290-6 **Collector Knives** 8th Ed.	11.95
☐ 266-3 **Collector Plates** 4th Ed.	11.95
☐ 296-5 **Collector Prints** 7th Ed.	12.95
☐ 489-5 **Comic Books & Collectibles** 8th Ed.	9.95
☐ 433-X **Depression Glass** 1st Ed.	9.95
☐ 472-0 **Glassware** 2nd Ed.	10.95
☐ 243-4 **Hummel Figurines & Plates** 6th Ed.	10.95
☐ 451-8 **Kitchen Collectibles** 2nd Ed.	10.95
☐ 291-4 **Military Collectibles** 5th Ed.	11.95
☐ 268-X **Music Collectibles** 5th Ed.	11.95
☐ 313-9 **Old Books & Autographs** 7th Ed.	11.95
☐ 298-1 **Oriental Collectibles** 3rd Ed.	11.95
☐ 297-3 **Paper Collectibles** 5th Ed.	10.95
☐ 276-0 **Pottery & Porcelain** 5th Ed.	11.95
☐ 263-9 **Radio, T.V. & Movie Memorabilia** 2nd Ed.	11.95
☐ 288-4 **Records** 7th Ed.	10.95
☐ 247-7 **Royal Doulton** 5th Ed.	11.95
☐ 280-9 **Science Fiction & Fantasy Collectibles** 2nd Ed.	10.95
☐ 299-X **Star Trek/Star Wars Collectibles** 2nd Ed.	7.95
☐ 248-5 **Wicker** 3rd Ed.	10.95

THE OFFICIAL:

☐ 445-3 **Collector's Journal** 1st Ed.	4.95
☐ 365-1 **Encyclopedia of Antiques** 1st Ed.	9.95
☐ 369-4 **Guide to Buying & Selling Antiques** 1st Ed.	9.95
☐ 414-3 **Identification Guide to Early American Furniture** 1st Ed.	9.95
☐ 413-5 **Identification Guide to Glassware** 1st Ed.	9.95
☐ 448-8 **Identification Guide to Gunmarks** 2nd Ed.	9.95
☐ 412-7 **Identification Guide to Pottery & Porcelain** 1st Ed.	9.95
☐ 415-1 **Identification Guide to Victorian Furniture** 1st Ed.	9.95

THE OFFICIAL (SMALL SIZE) PRICE GUIDES TO:

☐ 473-9 **Antiques & Flea Markets** 3rd Ed.	3.95
☐ 269-8 **Antique Jewelry** 3rd Ed.	4.95
☐ 509-3 **Baseball Cards** 6th Ed.	4.95
☐ 488-7 **Bottles** 2nd Ed.	4.95
☐ 468-2 **Cars & Trucks** 2nd Ed.	4.95
☐ 260-4 **Collectible Americana** 1st Ed.	4.95
☐ 294-9 **Collectible Records** 3rd Ed.	4.95
☐ 469-0. **Collector Guns** 2nd Ed.	4.95
☐ 474-7 **Comic Books** 3rd Ed.	3.95
☐ 486-0 **Dolls** 3rd Ed.	4.95
☐ 292-2 **Football Cards** 5th Ed.	4.95
☐ 258-2 **Glassware** 2nd Ed.	4.95
☐ 487-9 **Hummels** 3rd Ed.	4.95
☐ 279-5 **Military Collectibles** 3rd Ed.	4.95
☐ 480-1 **Paperbacks & Magazines** 3rd Ed.	4.95
☐ 278-7 **Pocket Knives** 3rd Ed.	4.95
☐ 479-8 **Scouting Collectibles** 3rd Ed.	4.95
☐ 439-1 **Sports Collectibles** 2nd Ed.	3.95
☐ 494-1 **Star Trek/Star Wars Collectibles** 3rd Ed.	3.95
☐ 307-4 **Toys** 4th Ed.	4.95

THE OFFICIAL BLACKBOOK PRICE GUIDES OF:

☐ 510-7 **U.S. Coins** 25th Ed.	3.95
☐ 511-5 **U.S. Paper Money** 19th Ed.	3.95
☐ 512-3 **U.S. Postage Stamps** 9th Ed.	3.95

THE OFFICIAL INVESTORS GUIDE TO BUYING & SELLING:

☐ 496-8 **Gold, Silver and Diamonds** 2nd Ed.	9.95
☐ 497-6 **Gold Coins** 2nd Ed.	9.95
☐ 498-4 **Silver Coins** 2nd Ed.	9.95
☐ 499-2 **Silver Dollars** 2nd Ed.	9.95

THE OFFICIAL NUMISMATIC GUIDE SERIES:

☐ 481-X **Coin Collecting** 3rd Ed.	9.95
☐ 254-X **The Official Guide to Detecting Counterfeit Money** 2nd Ed.	7.95
☐ 257-4 **The Official Guide to Mint Errors** 4th Ed.	7.95
☐ 162-4 **Variety & Oddity Guide of U.S. Coins** 8th Ed.	4.95

SPECIAL INTEREST SERIES:

☐ 506-9 **From Hearth to Cookstove** 3rd Ed.	17.95
☐ 508-5 **Lucky Number Lottery Guide** 1st Ed.	3.50
☐ 504-2 **On Method Acting** 8th Printing	6.95

	TOTAL	

FOR IMMEDIATE DELIVERY

VISA & MASTER CARD CUSTOMERS

ORDER TOLL FREE!
1-800-638-6460

This number is for orders only; it is not tied into the customer service or business office. Customers not using charge cards must use mail for ordering since payment is required with the order — sorry no C.O.D.'s.

OR SEND ORDERS TO ▮ ▮ ▮ ▮ ▮

THE HOUSE OF COLLECTIBLES, *201 East 50th Street New York, New York 10022*

—— POSTAGE & HANDLING RATES ——

First Book $1.00
Each Additional Copy or Title $0.50

Total from columns on reverse side. **Quantity**_____ $ _____

| | Check or money order enclosed $_____ _____ (include postage and handling)

| | Please charge $_____ to my: | | MASTERCARD | | VISA

Charge Card Customers Not Using Our Toll Free Number Please Fill Out The Information Below

Account No. (All Digits) _____ Expiration Date _____

Signature_____

NAME (please print) _____ PHONE _____

ADDRESS _____ APT. # _____ ⑩

CITY _____ STATE _____ ZIP _____